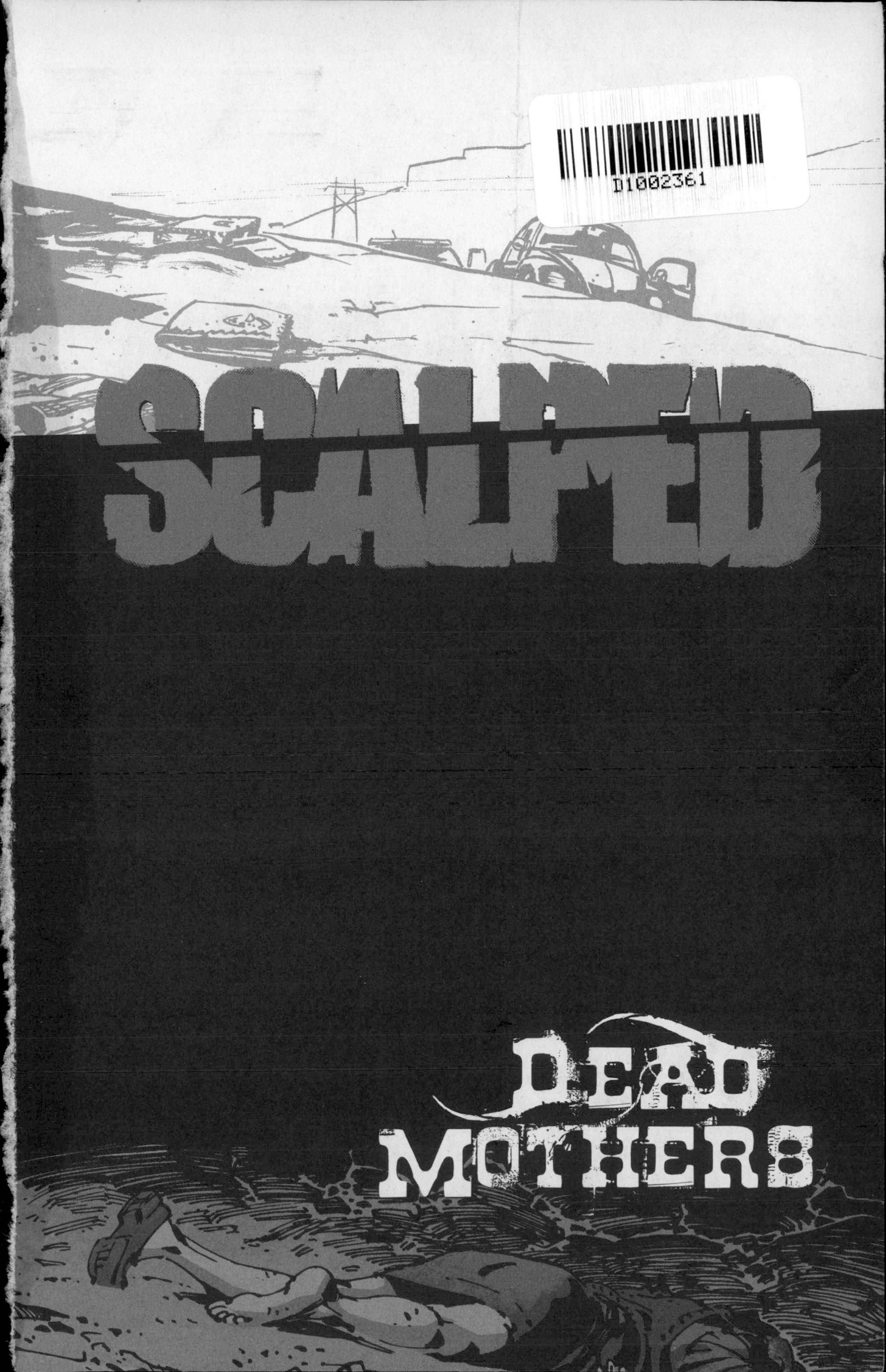
SCALPED
DEAD MOTHERS

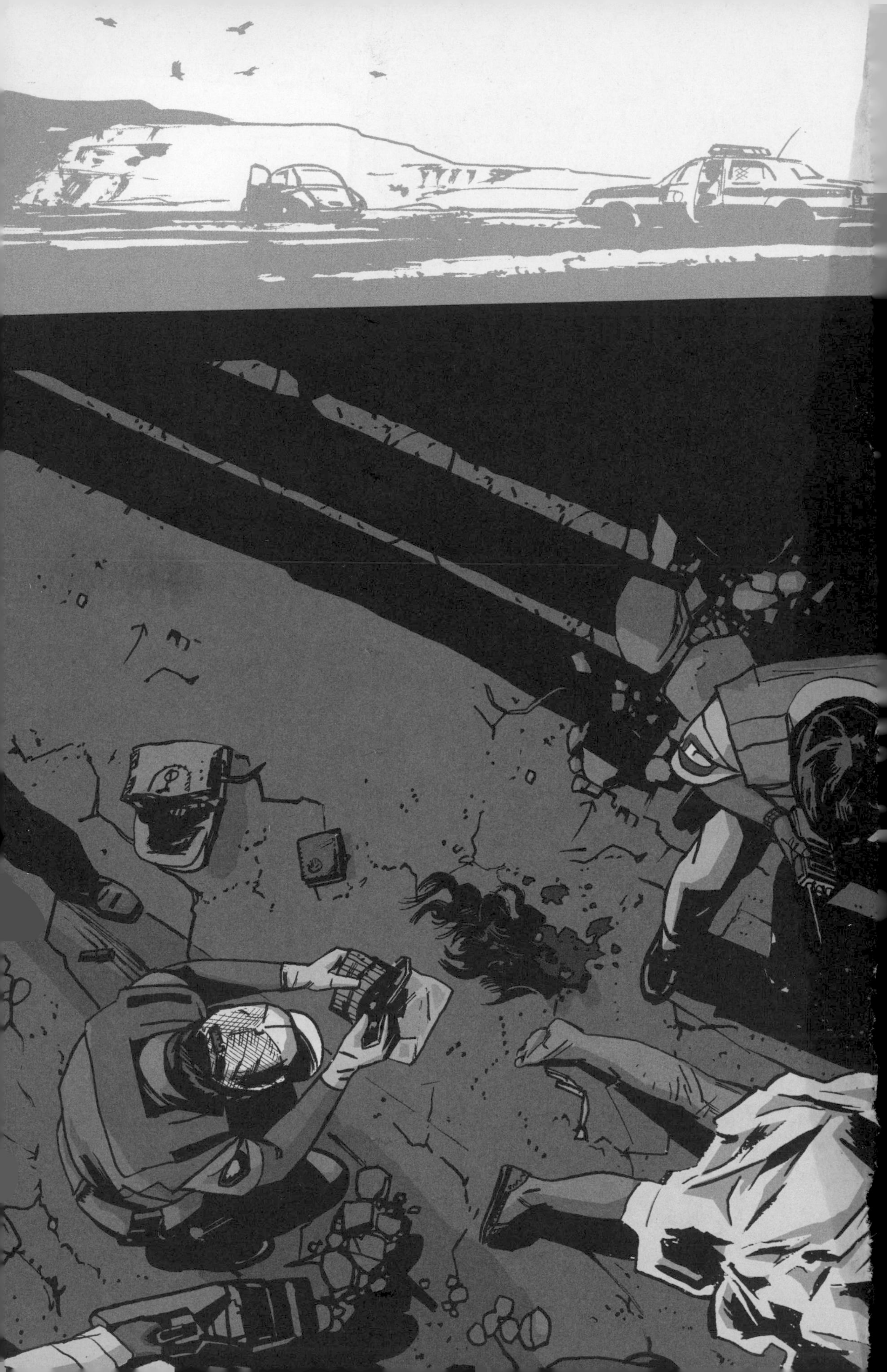

SCALPED

JASON AARON
WRITER

JOHN PAUL LEON
DREAMING HIMSELF INTO THE REAL WORLD
ARTIST

R.M. GUÉRA
DEAD MOTHERS
ARTIST

DAVIDE FURNÒ
FALLS DOWN
ARTIST

GIULIA BRUSCO
COLORIST

STEVE WANDS
LETTERER

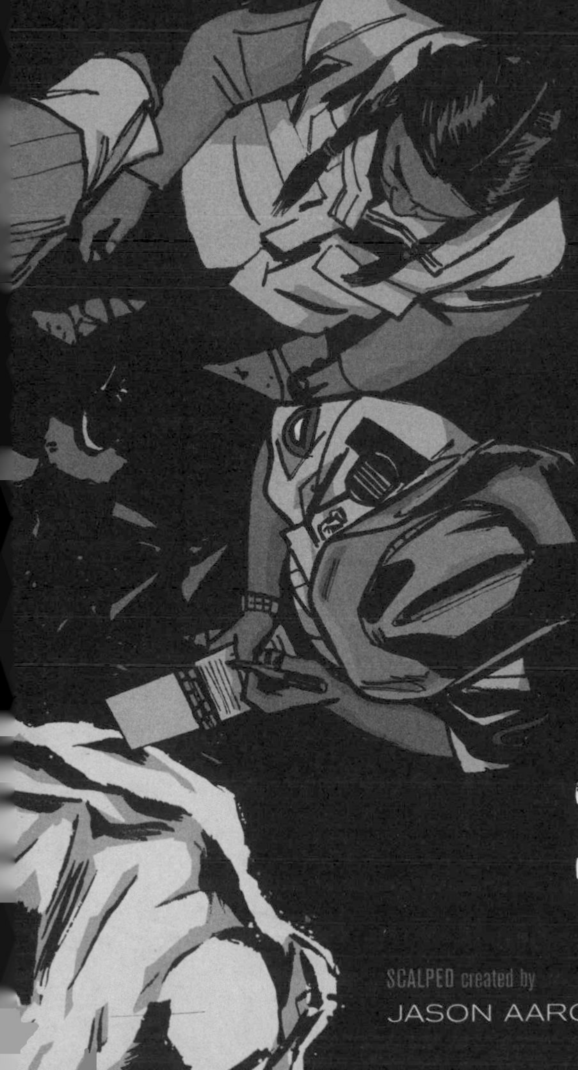

DEAD MOTHERS

SCALPED created by
JASON AARON and R.M. GUÉRA

KAREN BERGER
Senior VP-Executive Editor

WILL DENNIS
Editor-original series

CASEY SEIJAS
Assistant Editor-original series

BOB HARRAS
Editor-collected edition

ROBBIN BROSTERMAN
Senior Art Director

PAUL LEVITZ
President & Publisher

GEORG BREWER
VP-Design & DC Direct Creative

RICHARD BRUNING
Senior VP-Creative Director

PATRICK CALDON
Executive VP-Finance & Operations

CHRIS CARAMALIS
VP-Finance

JOHN CUNNINGHAM
VP-Marketing

TERRI CUNNINGHAM
VP-Managing Editor

ALISON GILL
VP-Manufacturing

DAVID HYDE
VP-Publicity

HANK KANALZ
VP-General Manager, WildStorm

JIM LEE
Editorial Director-WildStorm

PAULA LOWITT
Senior VP-Business & Legal Affairs

MARYELLEN MCLAUGHLIN
VP-Advertising & Custom Publishing

JOHN NEE
Senior VP-Business Development

GREGORY NOVECK
Senior VP-Creative Affairs

SUE POHJA
VP-Book Trade Sales

STEVE ROTTERDAM
Senior VP-Sales & Marketing

CHERYL RUBIN
Senior VP-Brand Management

JEFF TROJAN
VP-Business Development, DC Direct

BOB WAYNE
VP-Sales

Logo and cover illustration by JOCK
Publication design by BRAINCHILD STUDIOS/NYC

SCALPED-DEAD MOTHERS
Published by DC Comics. Cover, text and compilation
Copyright © 2008 DC Comics. All Rights Reserved.

Originally published in single magazine form as SCALPED
12-18. Copyright © 2008 Jason Aaron and Raijko
Milosevic. All Rights Reserved. VERTIGO and all characters,
their distinctive likenesses and related elements featured in
this publication are trademarks of DC Comics. The stories,
characters and incidents featured in this publication are
entirely fictional. DC Comics does not read or accept
unsolicited submissions of ideas, stories or artwork.

DC Comics. 1700 Broadway, New York, NY 10019
A Warner Bros. Entertainment Company.
Printed in Canada. First Printing.
ISBN: 978-1-4012-1919-2

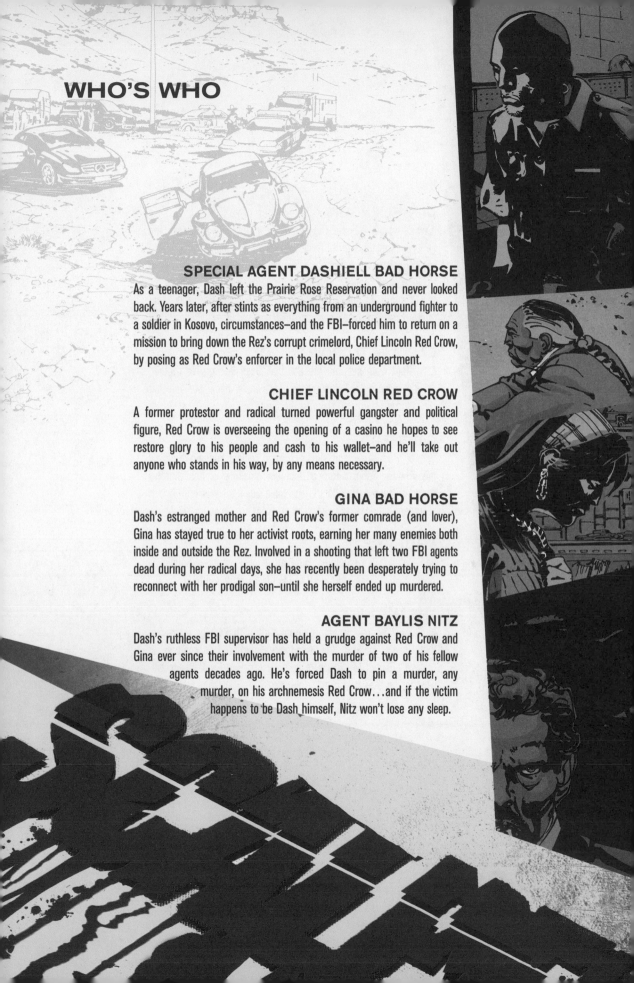

WHO'S WHO

SPECIAL AGENT DASHIELL BAD HORSE

As a teenager, Dash left the Prairie Rose Reservation and never looked back. Years later, after stints as everything from an underground fighter to a soldier in Kosovo, circumstances—and the FBI—forced him to return on a mission to bring down the Rez's corrupt crimelord, Chief Lincoln Red Crow, by posing as Red Crow's enforcer in the local police department.

CHIEF LINCOLN RED CROW

A former protestor and radical turned powerful gangster and political figure, Red Crow is overseeing the opening of a casino he hopes to see restore glory to his people and cash to his wallet—and he'll take out anyone who stands in his way, by any means necessary.

GINA BAD HORSE

Dash's estranged mother and Red Crow's former comrade (and lover), Gina has stayed true to her activist roots, earning her many enemies both inside and outside the Rez. Involved in a shooting that left two FBI agents dead during her radical days, she has recently been desperately trying to reconnect with her prodigal son—until she herself ended up murdered.

AGENT BAYLIS NITZ

Dash's ruthless FBI supervisor has held a grudge against Red Crow and Gina ever since their involvement with the murder of two of his fellow agents decades ago. He's forced Dash to pin a murder, any murder, on his archnemesis Red Crow...and if the victim happens to be Dash himself, Nitz won't lose any sleep.

DIESEL ENGINE
A white wannabe brave, Diesel claims to be 1/16th Kickapoo, and he's psychotic enough to force everyone to go along. His criminal enterprises have put him at murderous odds with Red Crow's drive to clean up whatever crime he himself can't monopolize—while his secret status as Special Agent Brett Fillenworth, the FBI's other man on the Rez, is unknown to Dash.

CAROL RED CROW ELLROY
As distant from her dad the Chief as Dash is from his mother, Carol's sexually self-destructive, and she's been pushing her illicit, torrid affair with Dash to the limit.

CATCHER
One of Red Crow and Gina's former radical running buddies, this Rhodes Scholar turned hopeless alcoholic claims that his people's revered Thunder Beings have been sending him visions of impending doom—all centered on Dash.

SHUNKA
Red Crow's right-hand man and most loyal enforcer, Shunka is suspicious of Dash—and wary of his boss's sentimentality.

THE HMONGS
An Asian-American organized crime outfit with a vested interest in Red Crow's dealings, the Hmongs have offered to send in an "expert" named Mr. Brass to help ensure Red Crow's success—whether he likes it or not.

DREAMING HIMSELF INTO THE REAL WORLD

COVER ART BY DAVE JOHNSON

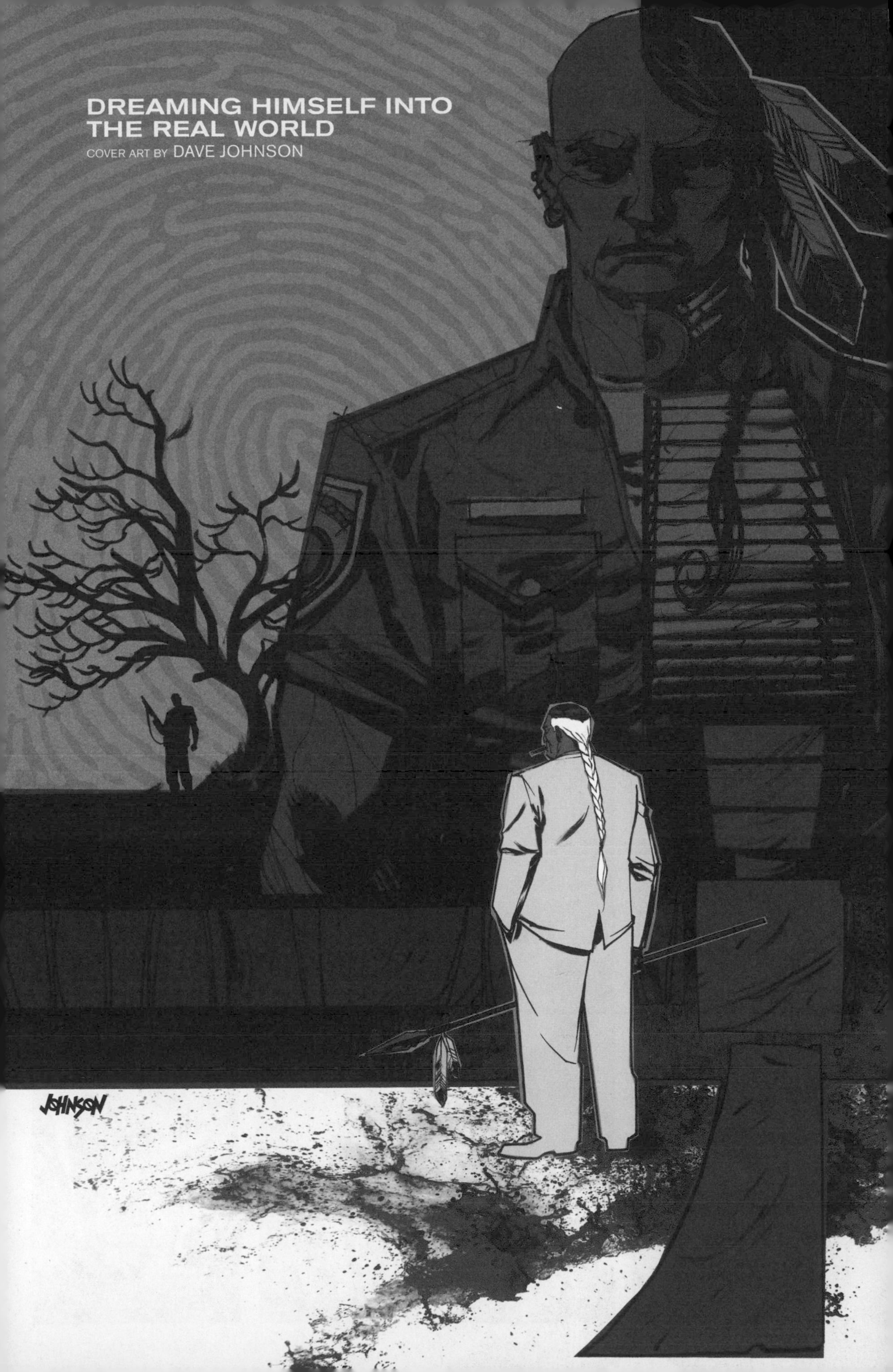
JOHNSON

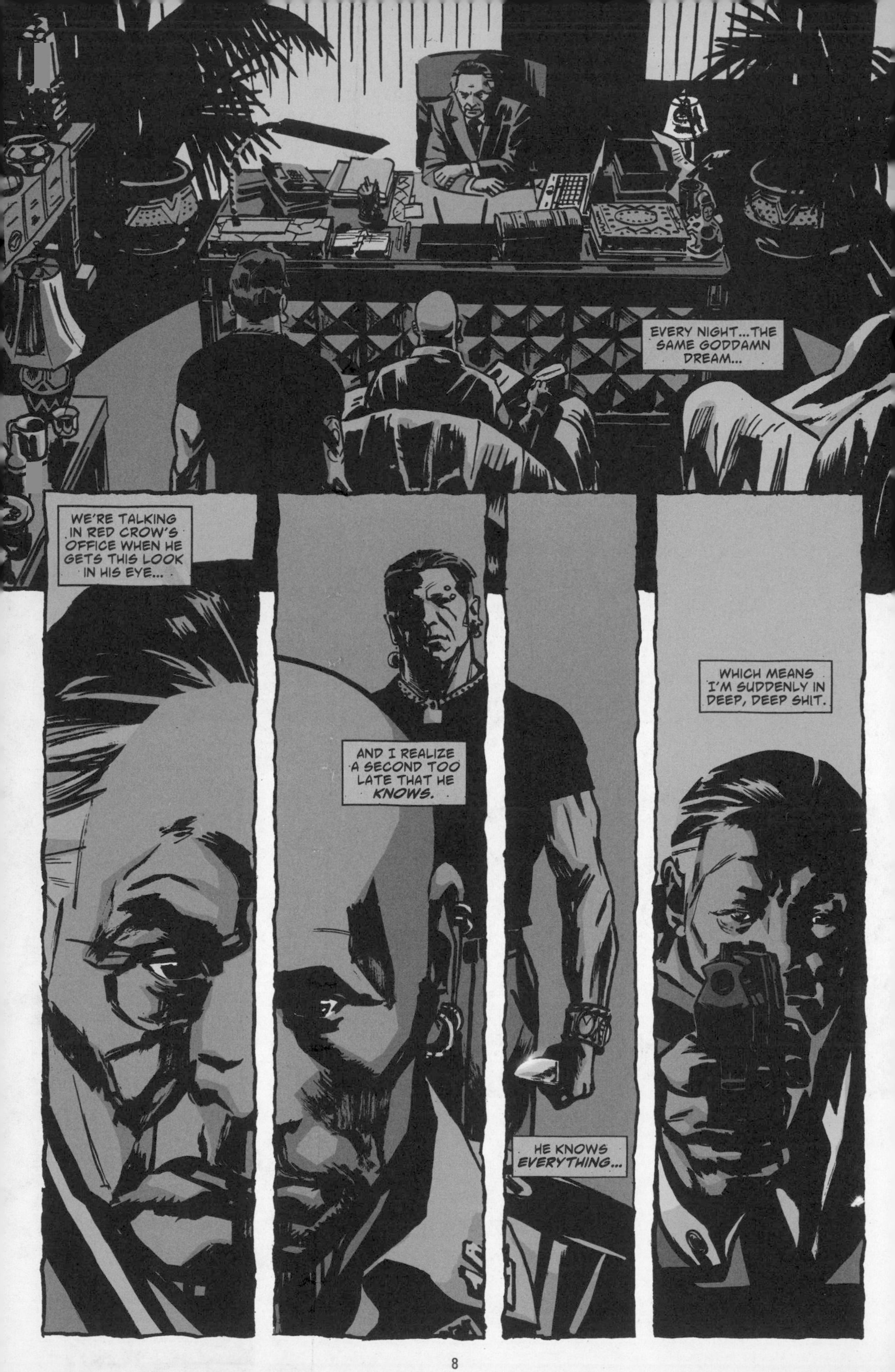
EVERY NIGHT...THE SAME GODDAMN DREAM...
WE'RE TALKING IN RED CROW'S OFFICE WHEN HE GETS THIS LOOK IN HIS EYE...
AND I REALIZE A SECOND TOO LATE THAT HE KNOWS.
HE KNOWS EVERYTHING...
WHICH MEANS I'M SUDDENLY IN DEEP, DEEP SHIT.

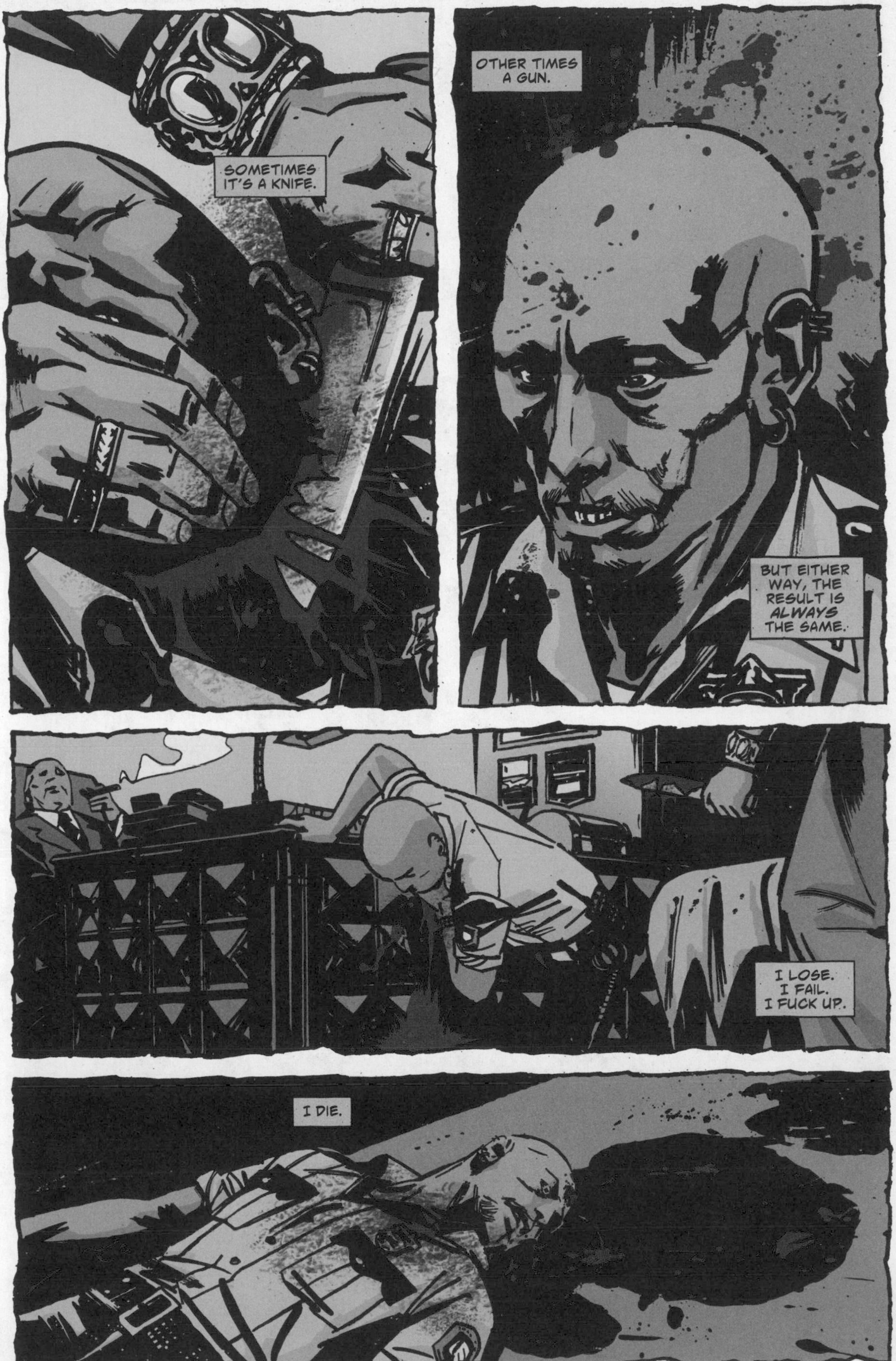
SOMETIMES IT'S A KNIFE.
OTHER TIMES A GUN.
BUT EITHER WAY, THE RESULT IS ALWAYS THE SAME.
I LOSE. I FAIL. I FUCK UP.
I DIE.

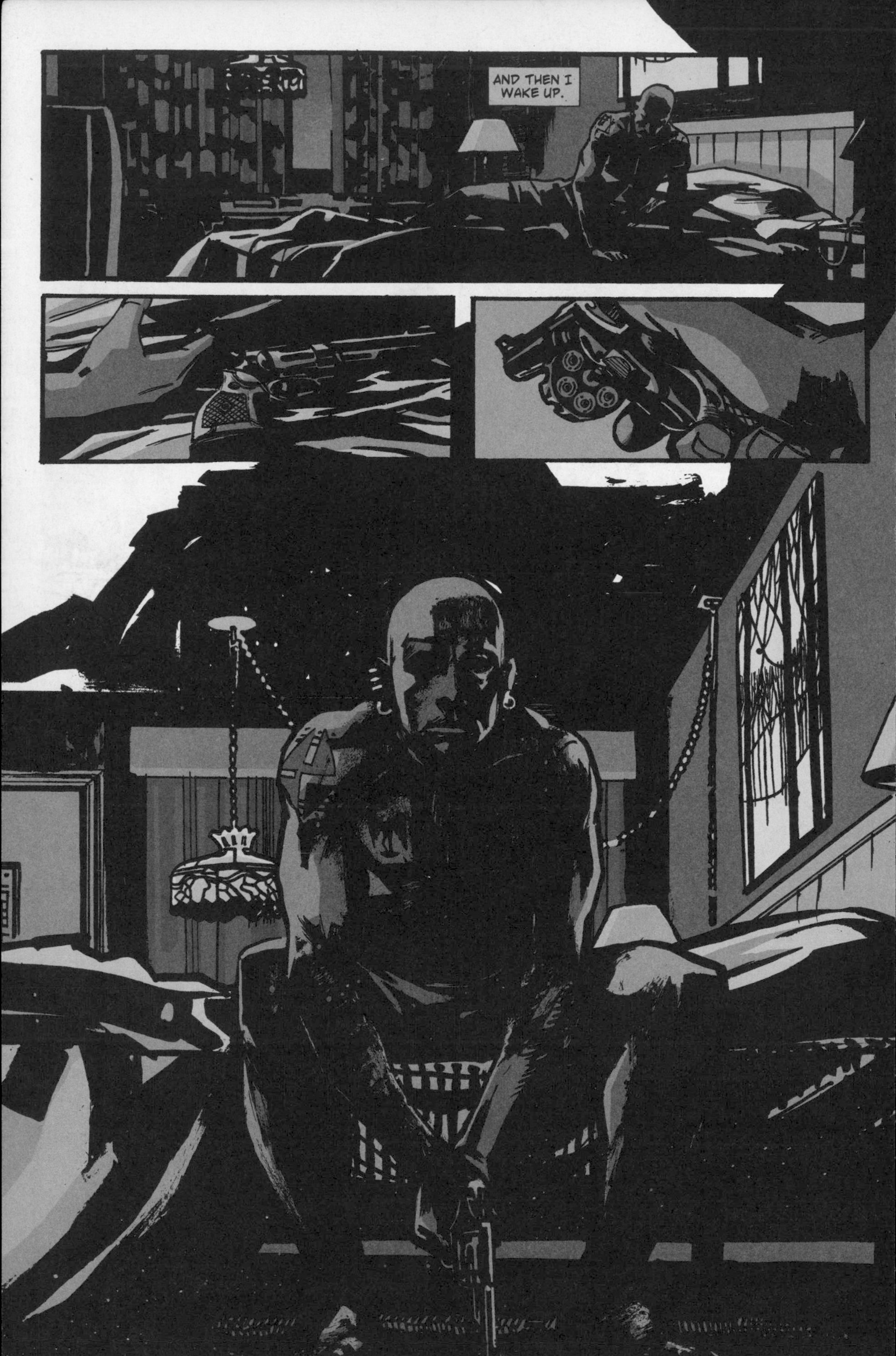
AND THEN I WAKE UP.

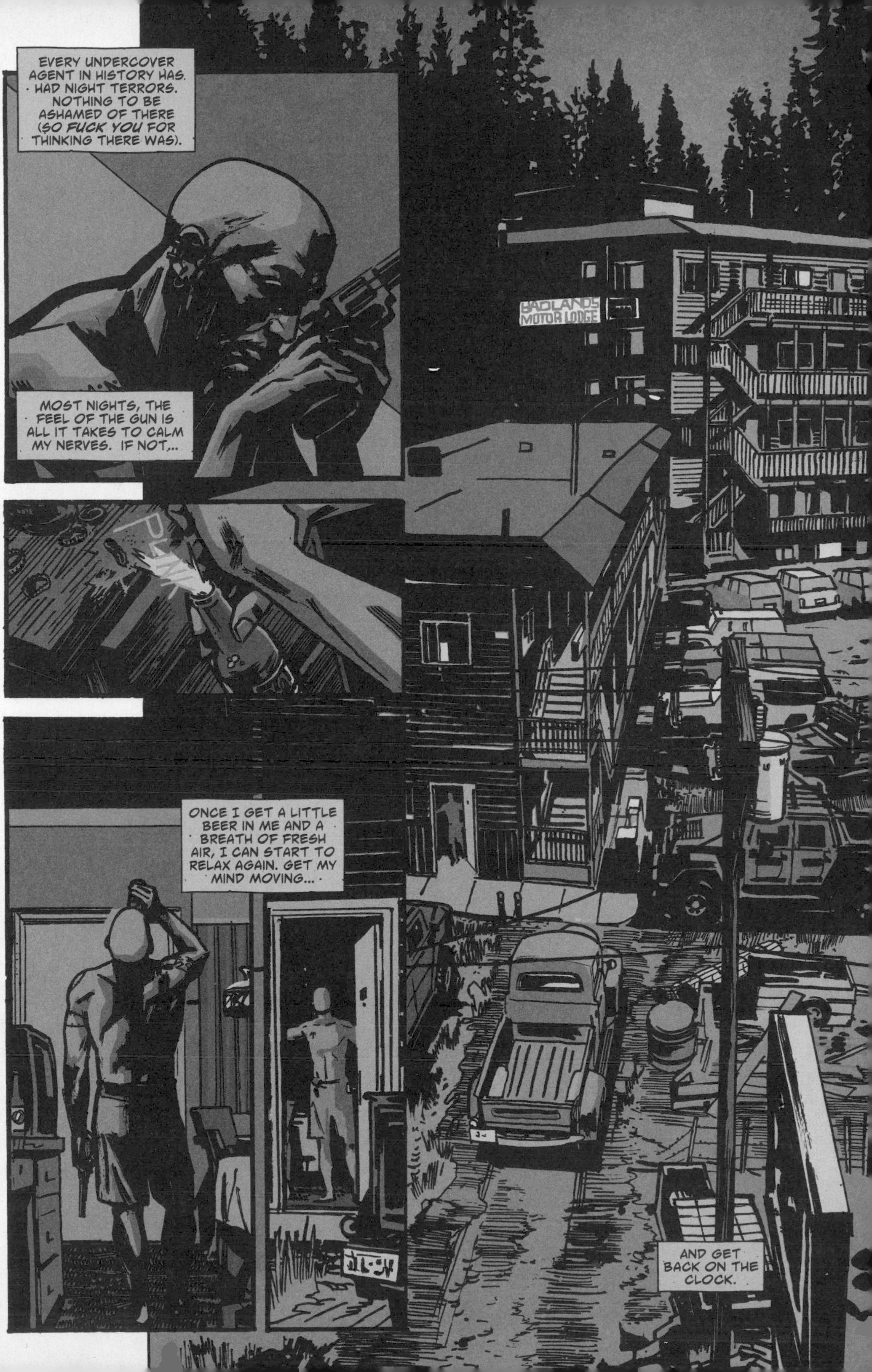
EVERY UNDERCOVER AGENT IN HISTORY HAS HAD NIGHT TERRORS. NOTHING TO BE ASHAMED OF THERE (SO FUCK YOU FOR THINKING THERE WAS).
MOST NIGHTS, THE FEEL OF THE GUN IS ALL IT TAKES TO CALM MY NERVES. IF NOT...
PLINK
ONCE I GET A LITTLE BEER IN ME AND A BREATH OF FRESH AIR, I CAN START TO RELAX AGAIN. GET MY MIND MOVING...
BADLANDS MOTOR LODGE
AND GET BACK ON THE CLOCK.

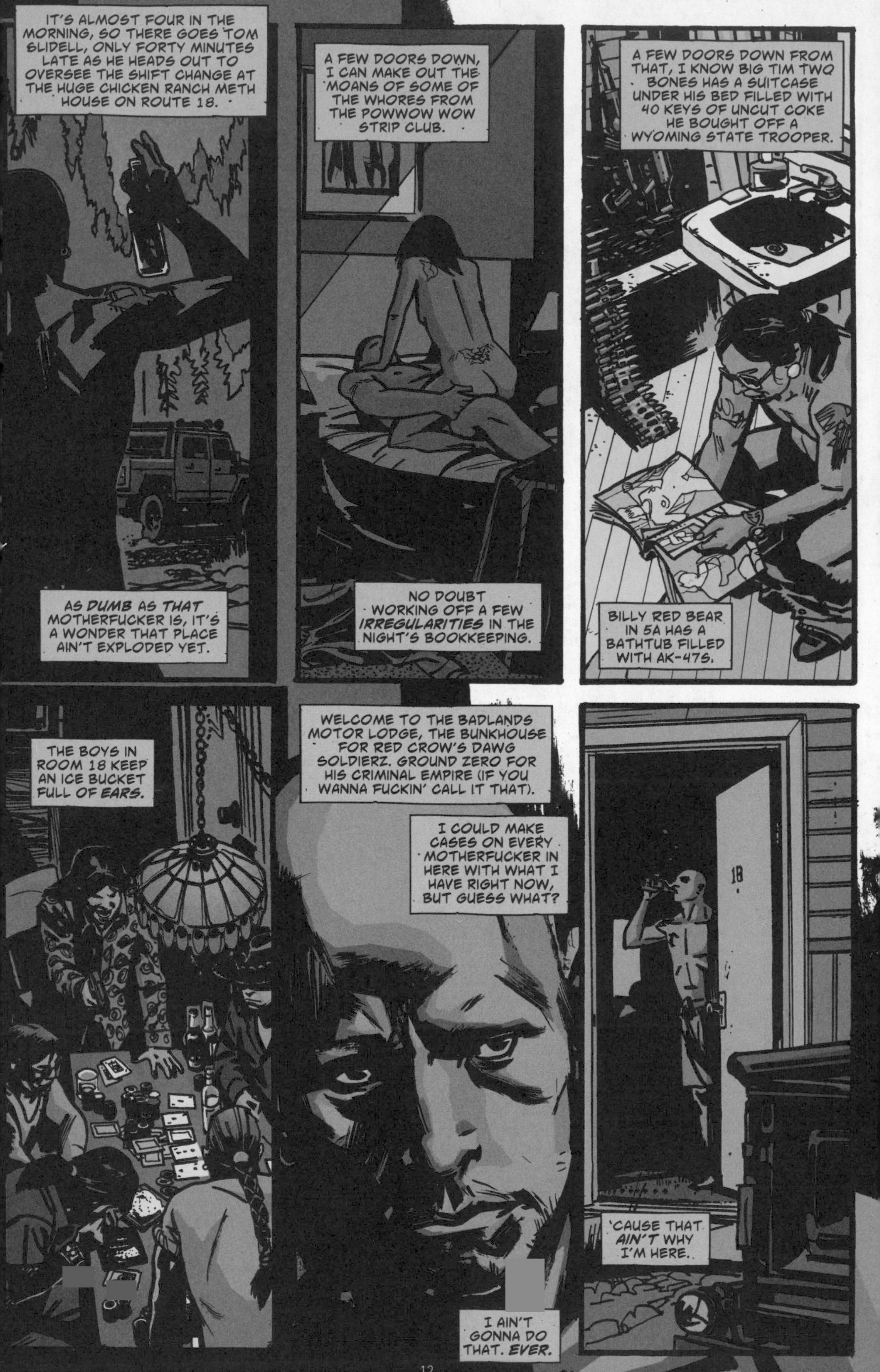
IT'S ALMOST FOUR IN THE MORNING, SO THERE GOES TOM SLIDELL, ONLY FORTY MINUTES LATE AS HE HEADS OUT TO OVERSEE THE SHIFT CHANGE AT THE HUGE CHICKEN RANCH METH HOUSE ON ROUTE 18.
AS *DUMB* AS *THAT* MOTHERFUCKER IS, IT'S A WONDER THAT PLACE AIN'T EXPLODED YET.
A FEW DOORS DOWN, I CAN MAKE OUT THE MOANS OF SOME OF THE WHORES FROM THE POWWOW WOW STRIP CLUB.
NO DOUBT WORKING OFF A FEW *IRREGULARITIES* IN THE NIGHT'S BOOKKEEPING.
A FEW DOORS DOWN FROM THAT, I KNOW BIG TIM TWO BONES HAS A SUITCASE UNDER HIS BED FILLED WITH 40 KEYS OF UNCUT COKE HE BOUGHT OFF A WYOMING STATE TROOPER.
BILLY RED BEAR IN 5A HAS A BATHTUB FILLED WITH AK-47S.
THE BOYS IN ROOM 18 KEEP AN ICE BUCKET FULL OF *EARS*.
WELCOME TO THE BADLANDS MOTOR LODGE, THE BUNKHOUSE FOR RED CROW'S DAWG SOLDIERZ. GROUND ZERO FOR HIS CRIMINAL EMPIRE (IF YOU WANNA FUCKIN' CALL IT THAT).
I COULD MAKE CASES ON EVERY MOTHERFUCKER IN HERE WITH WHAT I HAVE RIGHT NOW, BUT GUESS WHAT?
I AIN'T GONNA DO THAT. *EVER*.
18
'CAUSE THAT *AIN'T* WHY I'M HERE.

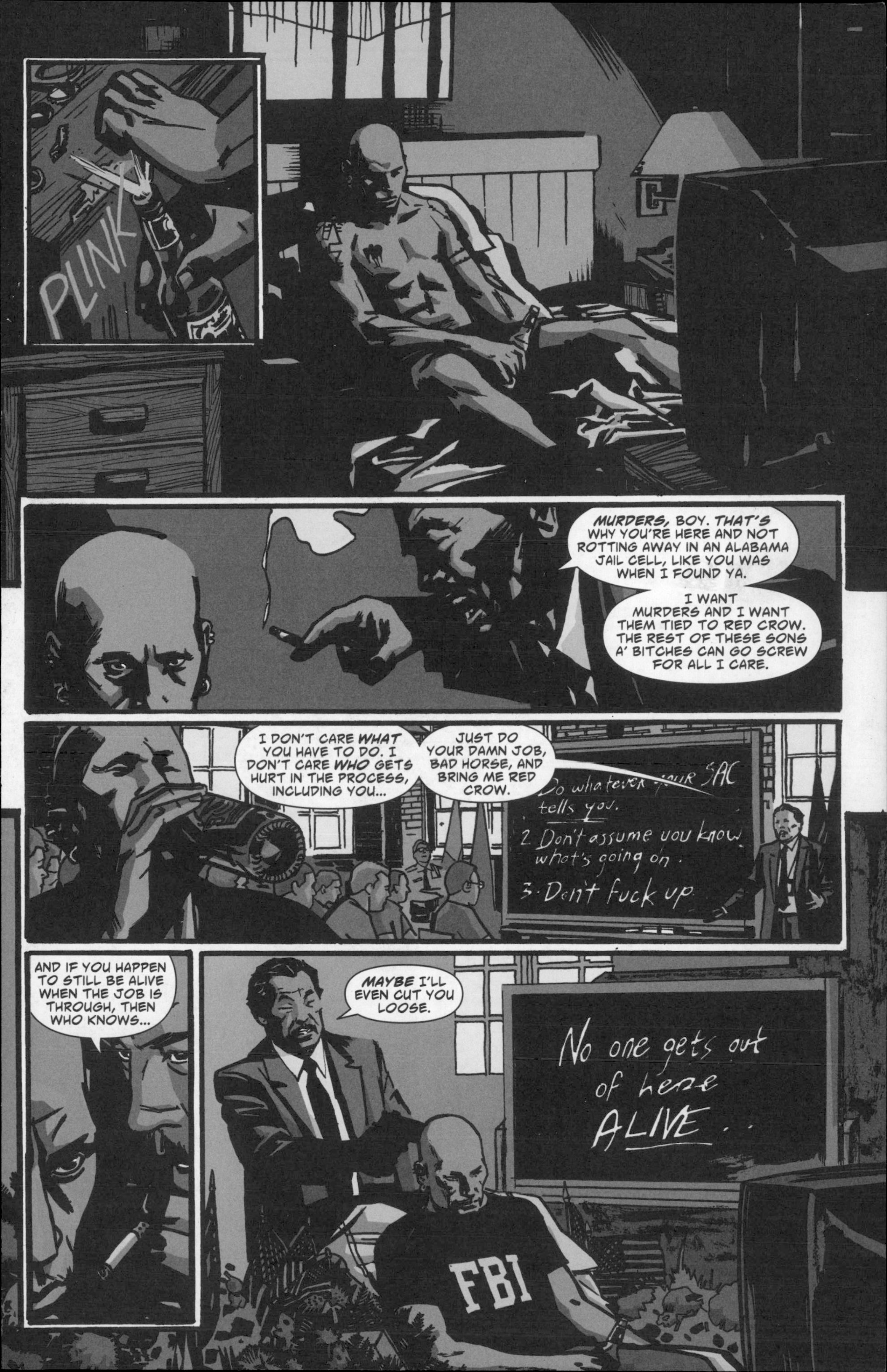
PLINK
MURDERS, BOY. THAT'S WHY YOU'RE HERE AND NOT ROTTING AWAY IN AN ALABAMA JAIL CELL, LIKE YOU WAS WHEN I FOUND YA.
I WANT MURDERS AND I WANT THEM TIED TO RED CROW. THE REST OF THESE SONS A' BITCHES CAN GO SCREW FOR ALL I CARE.
I DON'T CARE WHAT YOU HAVE TO DO. I DON'T CARE WHO GETS HURT IN THE PROCESS, INCLUDING YOU...
JUST DO YOUR DAMN JOB, BAD HORSE, AND BRING ME RED CROW.
tells you.
2. Don't assume you know what's going on.
3. Don't fuck up.
AND IF YOU HAPPEN TO STILL BE ALIVE WHEN THE JOB IS THROUGH, THEN WHO KNOWS...
MAYBE I'LL EVEN CUT YOU LOOSE.
No one gets out of here ALIVE..
FBI

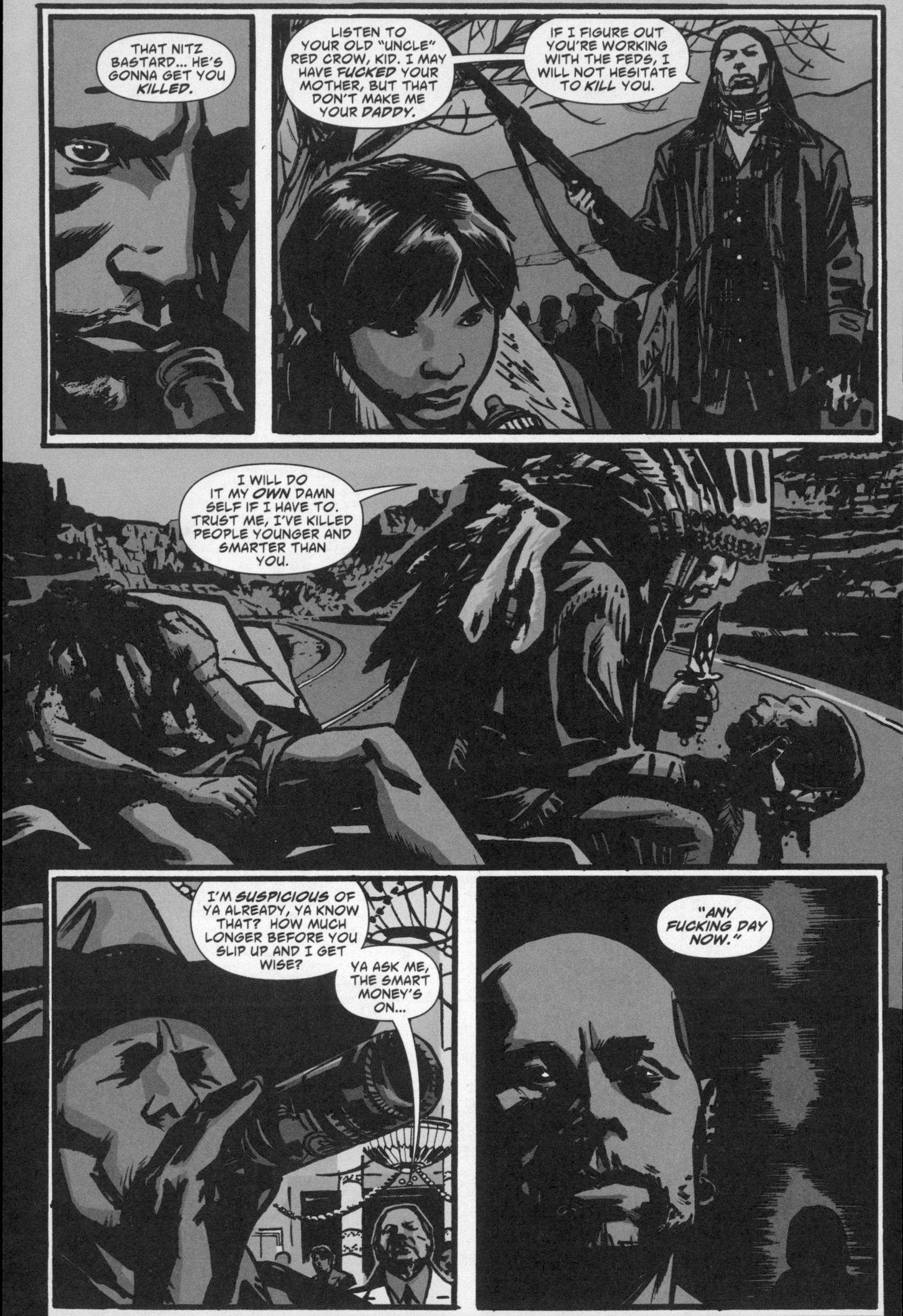
THAT NITZ BASTARD... HE'S GONNA GET YOU KILLED.
LISTEN TO YOUR OLD "UNCLE" RED CROW, KID. I MAY HAVE FUCKED YOUR MOTHER, BUT THAT DON'T MAKE ME YOUR DADDY.
IF I FIGURE OUT YOU'RE WORKING WITH THE FEDS, I WILL NOT HESITATE TO KILL YOU.
I WILL DO IT MY OWN DAMN SELF IF I HAVE TO. TRUST ME, I'VE KILLED PEOPLE YOUNGER AND SMARTER THAN YOU.
I'M SUSPICIOUS OF YA ALREADY, YA KNOW THAT? HOW MUCH LONGER BEFORE YOU SLIP UP AND I GET WISE?
YA ASK ME, THE SMART MONEY'S ON...
"ANY FUCKING DAY NOW."

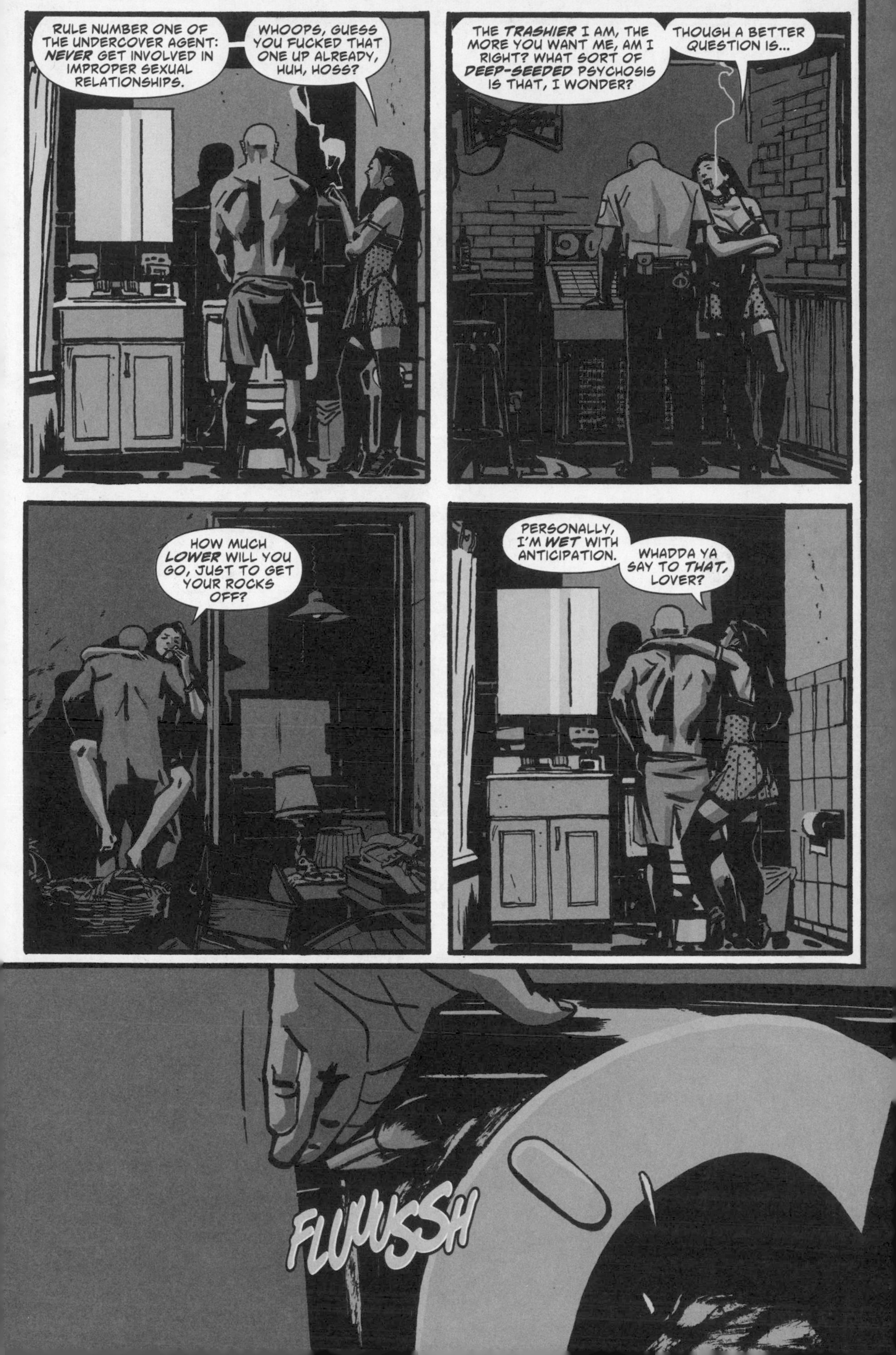

RULE NUMBER ONE OF THE UNDERCOVER AGENT: NEVER GET INVOLVED IN IMPROPER SEXUAL RELATIONSHIPS.
WHOOPS, GUESS YOU FUCKED THAT ONE UP ALREADY, HUH, HOSS?
THE TRASHIER I AM, THE MORE YOU WANT ME, AM I RIGHT? WHAT SORT OF DEEP-SEEDED PSYCHOSIS IS THAT, I WONDER?
THOUGH A BETTER QUESTION IS...
HOW MUCH LOWER WILL YOU GO, JUST TO GET YOUR ROCKS OFF?
PERSONALLY, I'M WET WITH ANTICIPATION.
WHADDA YA SAY TO THAT, LOVER?
FLUUUSSH

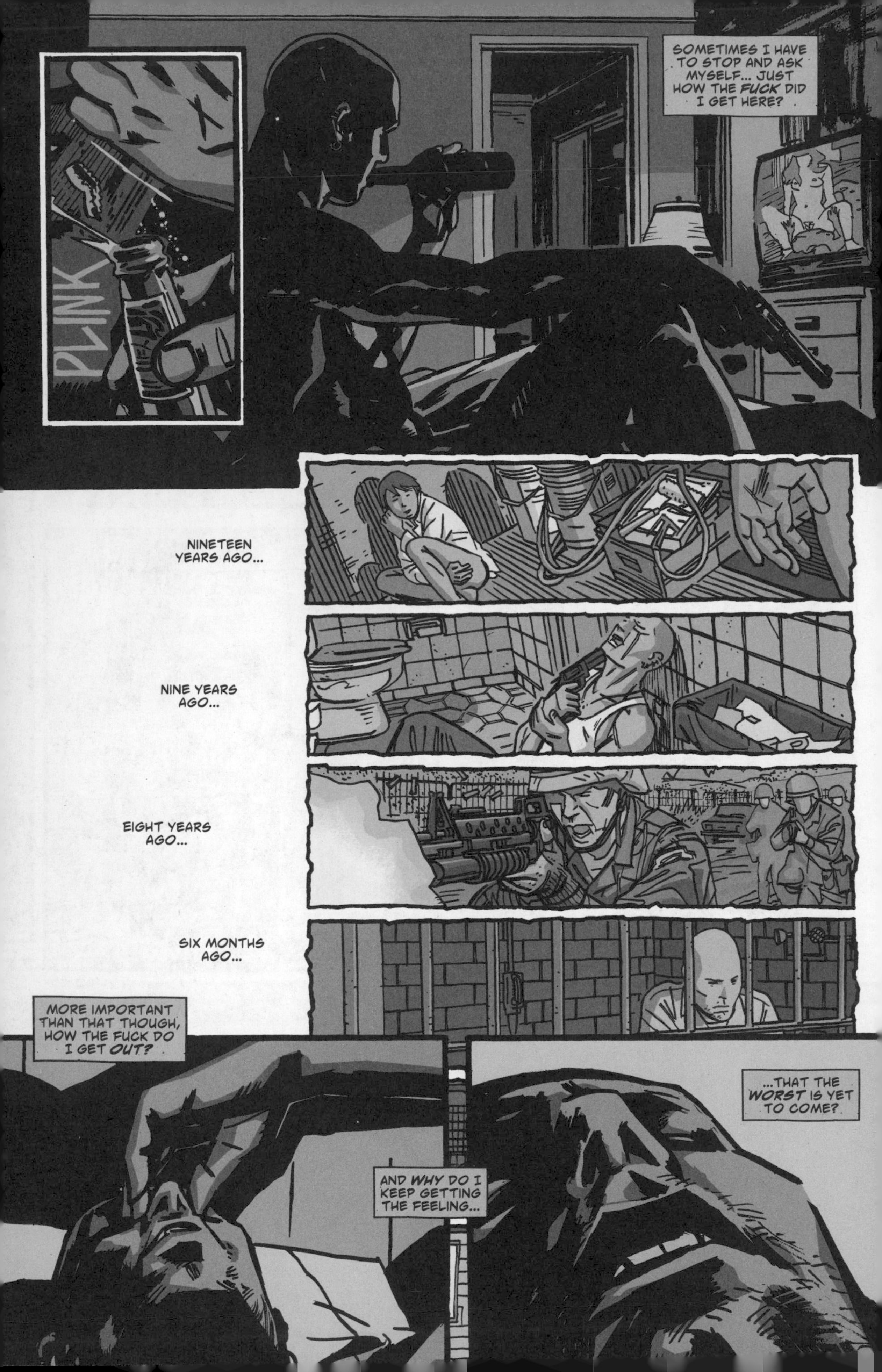
PLINK
SOMETIMES I HAVE TO STOP AND ASK MYSELF... JUST HOW THE FUCK DID I GET HERE?
NINETEEN YEARS AGO...
NINE YEARS AGO...
EIGHT YEARS AGO...
SIX MONTHS AGO...
MORE IMPORTANT THAN THAT THOUGH, HOW THE FUCK DO I GET OUT?
AND WHY DO I KEEP GETTING THE FEELING...
...THAT THE WORST IS YET TO COME?

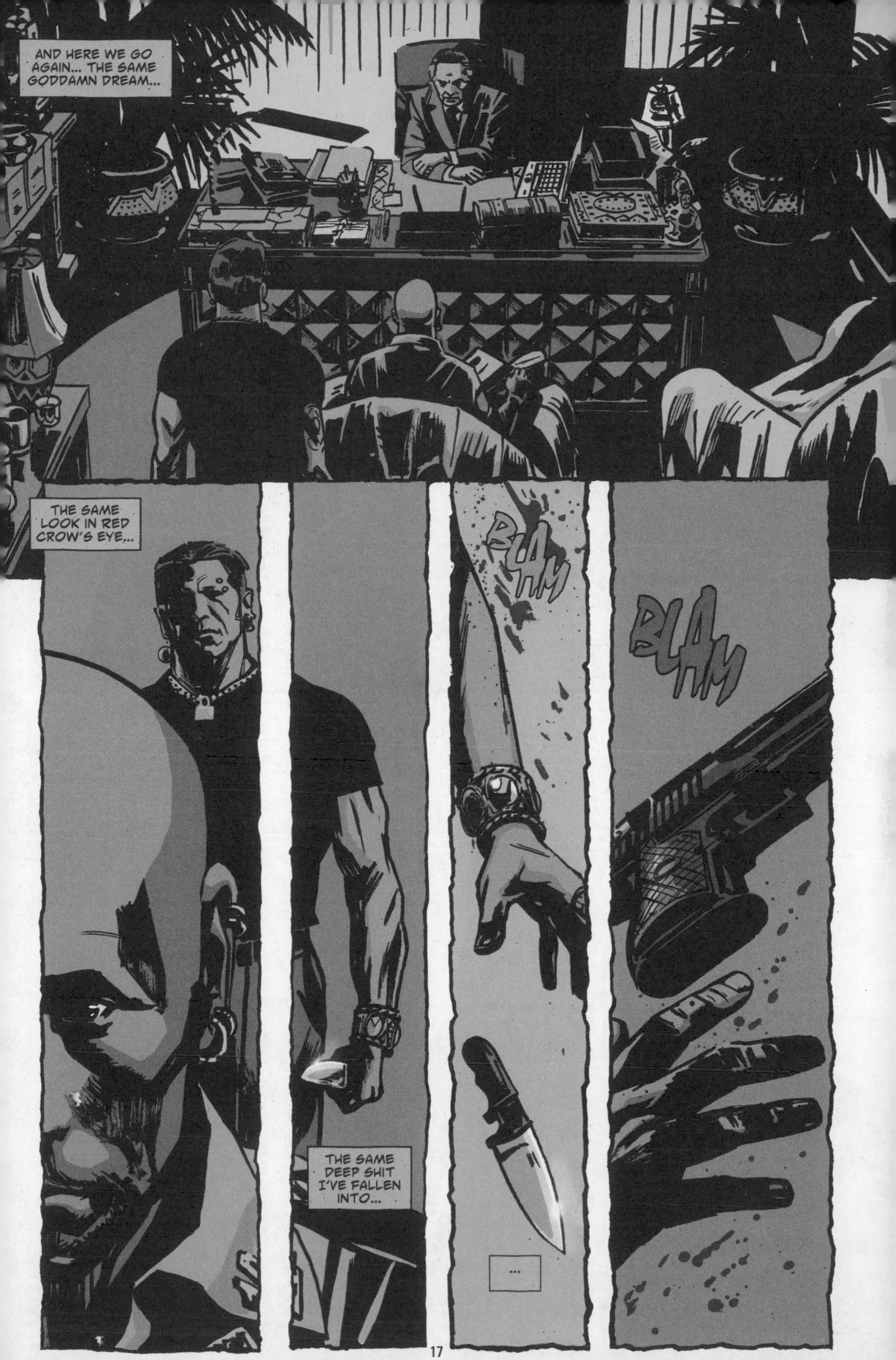
AND HERE WE GO AGAIN... THE SAME GODDAMN DREAM...
THE SAME LOOK IN RED CROW'S EYE...
THE SAME DEEP SHIT I'VE FALLEN INTO...
BLAM
...
BLAM

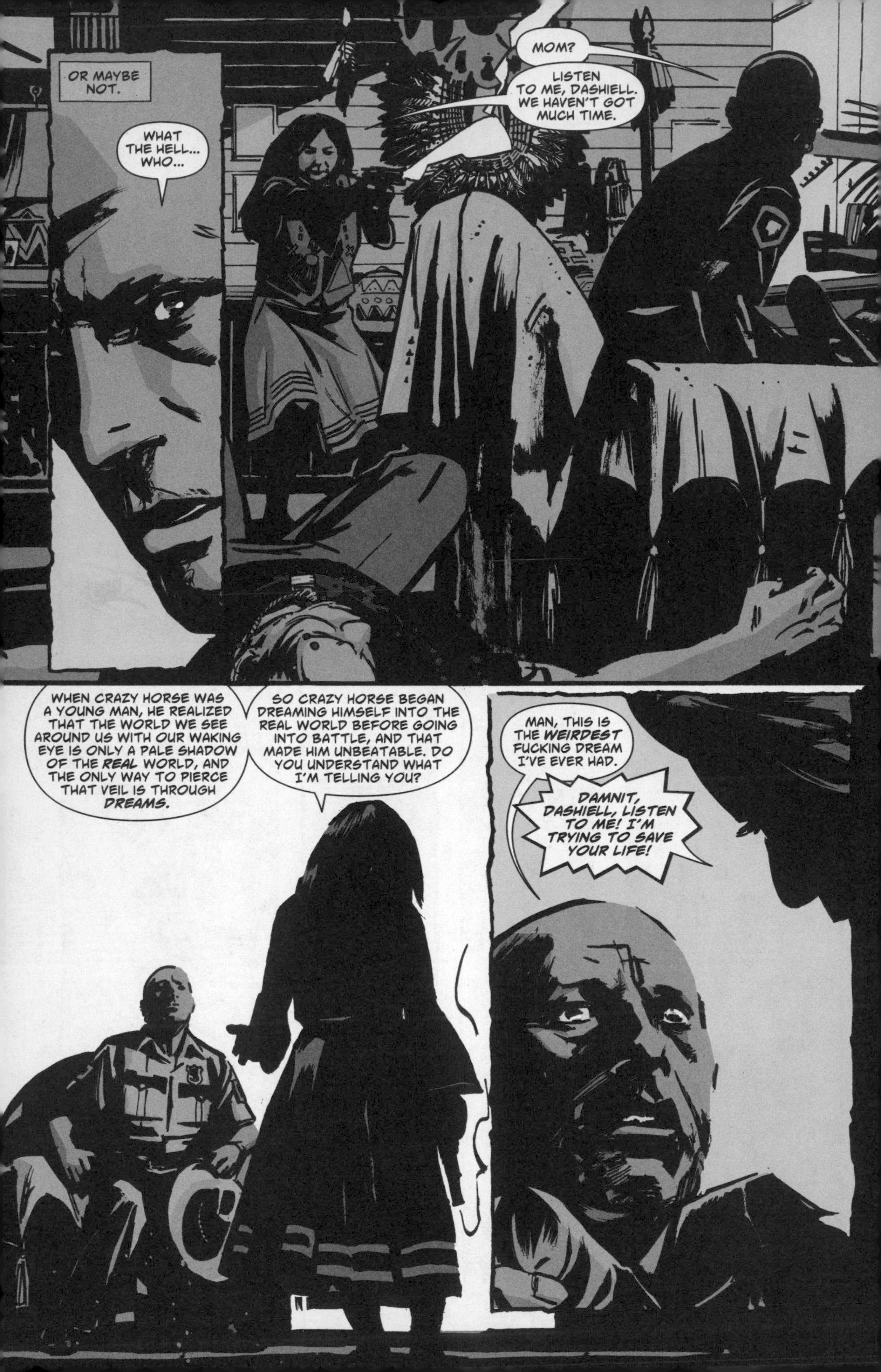
OR MAYBE NOT.
MOM?
LISTEN TO ME, DASHIELL. WE HAVEN'T GOT MUCH TIME.
WHAT THE HELL... WHO...
WHEN CRAZY HORSE WAS A YOUNG MAN, HE REALIZED THAT THE WORLD WE SEE AROUND US WITH OUR WAKING EYE IS ONLY A PALE SHADOW OF THE *REAL* WORLD, AND THE ONLY WAY TO PIERCE THAT VEIL IS THROUGH *DREAMS*.
SO CRAZY HORSE BEGAN DREAMING HIMSELF INTO THE REAL WORLD BEFORE GOING INTO BATTLE, AND THAT MADE HIM UNBEATABLE. DO YOU UNDERSTAND WHAT I'M TELLING YOU?
MAN, THIS IS THE *WEIRDEST* FUCKING DREAM I'VE EVER HAD.
DAMNIT, DASHIELL, LISTEN TO ME! I'M TRYING TO SAVE YOUR LIFE!

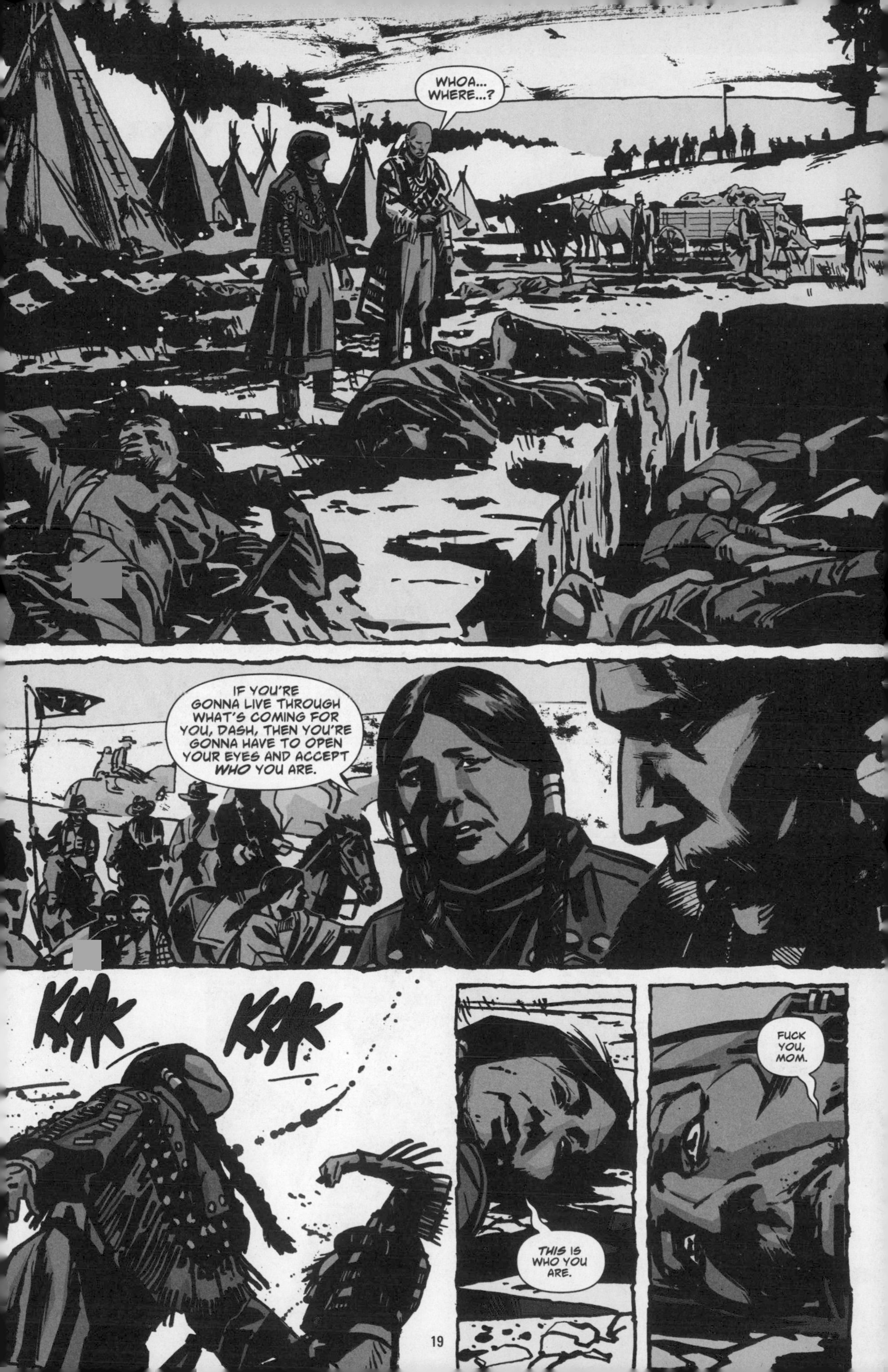
WHOA... WHERE...?
IF YOU'RE GONNA LIVE THROUGH WHAT'S COMING FOR YOU, DASH, THEN YOU'RE GONNA HAVE TO OPEN YOUR EYES AND ACCEPT WHO YOU ARE.
KRAK
KRAK
THIS IS WHO YOU ARE.
FUCK YOU, MOM.

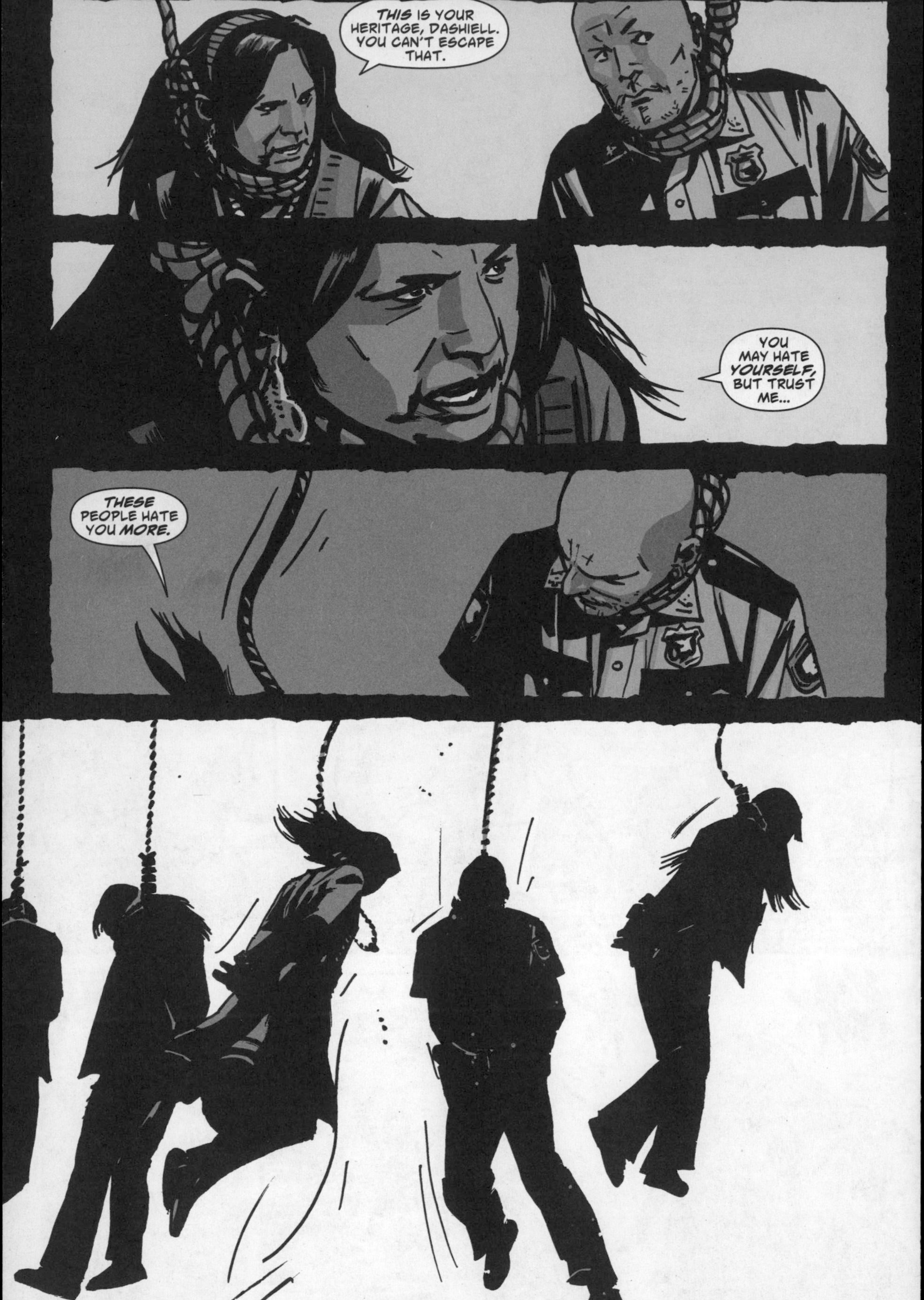
THIS IS YOUR HERITAGE, DASHIELL. YOU CAN'T ESCAPE THAT.
YOU MAY HATE YOURSELF, BUT TRUST ME...
THESE PEOPLE HATE YOU MORE.

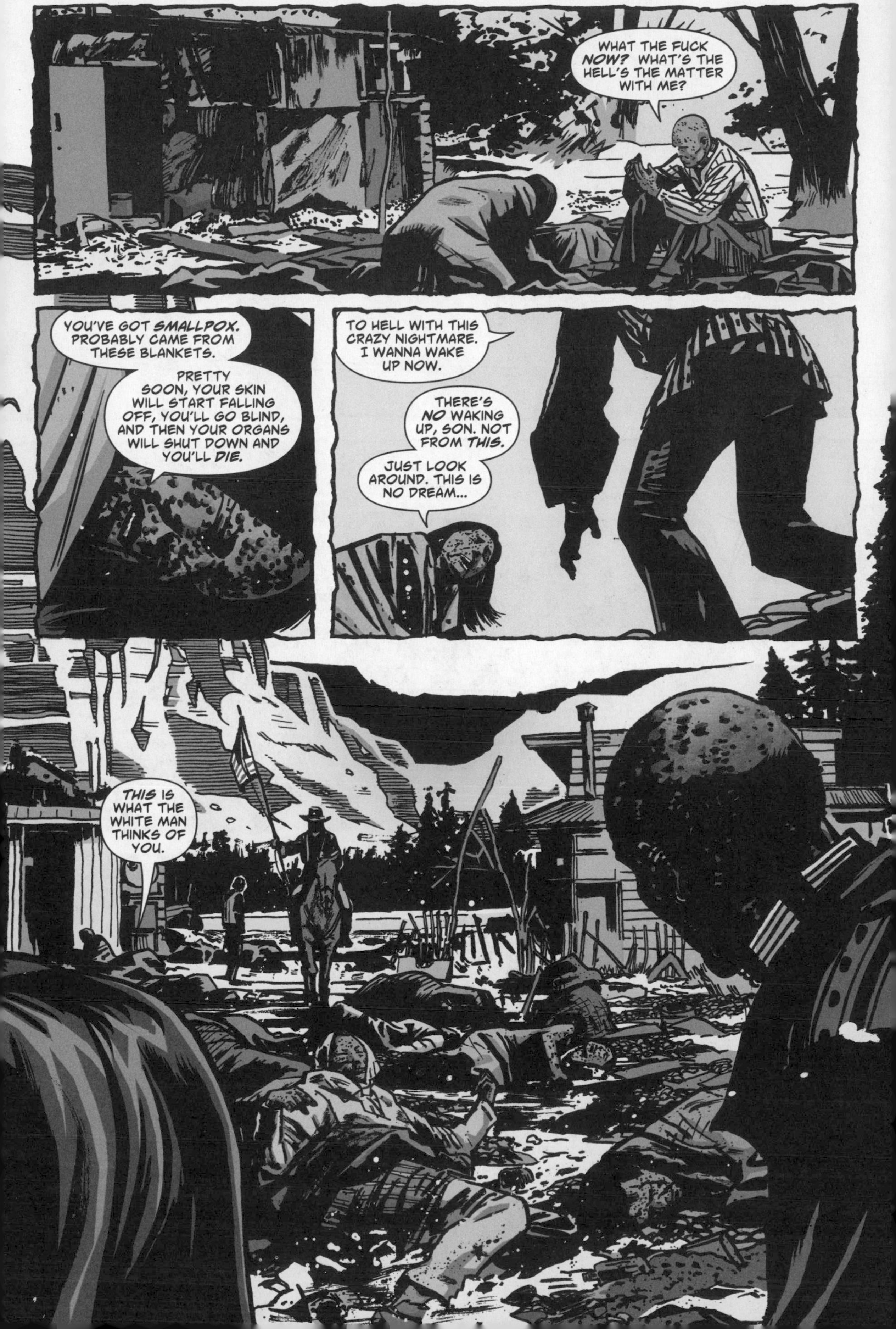
WHAT THE FUCK NOW? WHAT'S THE HELL'S THE MATTER WITH ME?
YOU'VE GOT SMALLPOX. PROBABLY CAME FROM THESE BLANKETS.
PRETTY SOON, YOUR SKIN WILL START FALLING OFF, YOU'LL GO BLIND, AND THEN YOUR ORGANS WILL SHUT DOWN AND YOU'LL DIE.
TO HELL WITH THIS CRAZY NIGHTMARE. I WANNA WAKE UP NOW.
THERE'S NO WAKING UP, SON. NOT FROM THIS.
JUST LOOK AROUND. THIS IS NO DREAM...
THIS IS WHAT THE WHITE MAN THINKS OF YOU.

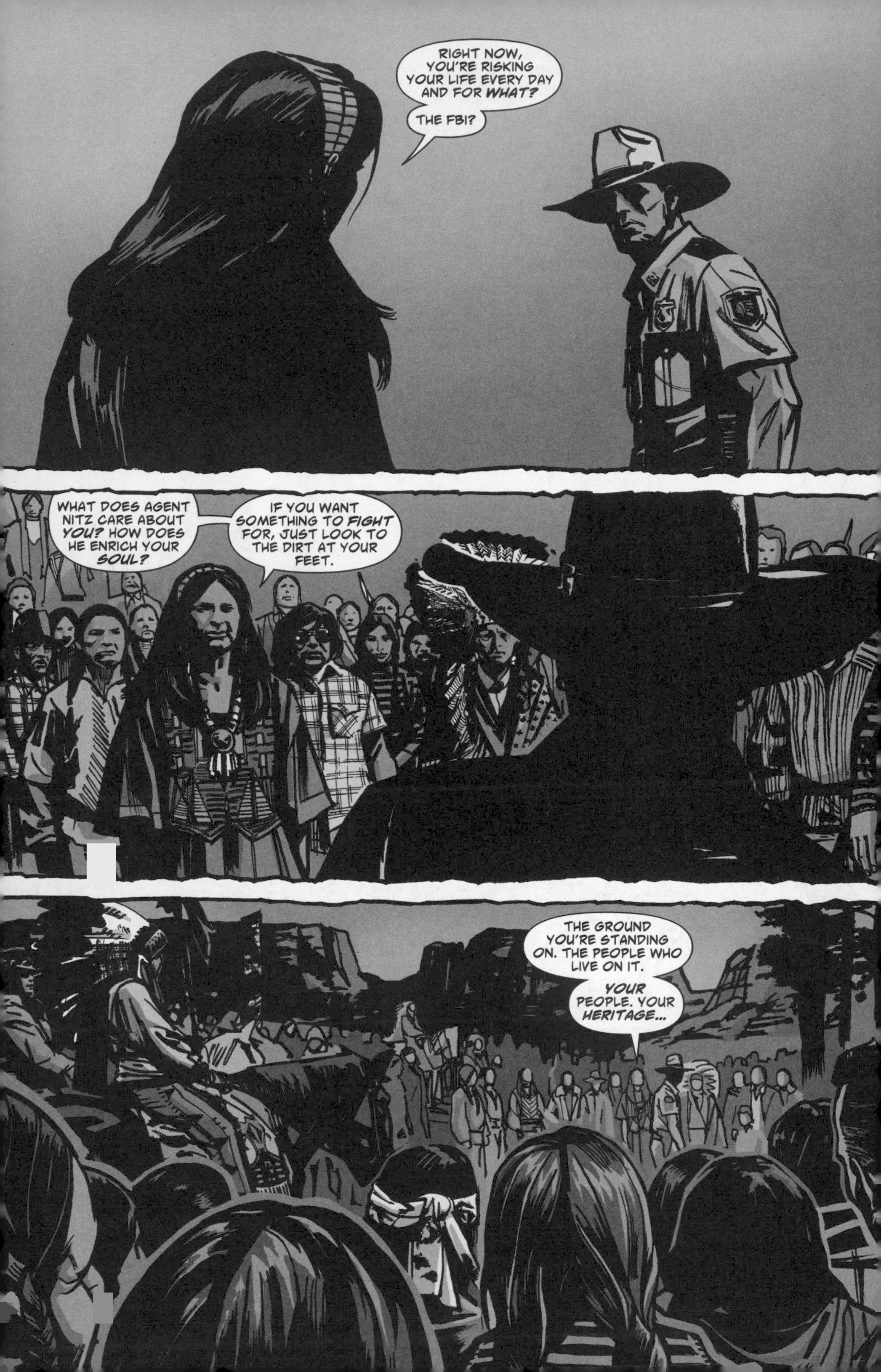
RIGHT NOW, YOU'RE RISKING YOUR LIFE EVERY DAY AND FOR *WHAT?*
THE FBI?
WHAT DOES AGENT NITZ CARE ABOUT *YOU?* HOW DOES HE ENRICH YOUR *SOUL?*
IF YOU WANT SOMETHING TO *FIGHT* FOR, JUST LOOK TO THE DIRT AT YOUR FEET.
THE GROUND YOU'RE STANDING ON. THE PEOPLE WHO LIVE ON IT.
YOUR PEOPLE. YOUR *HERITAGE...*

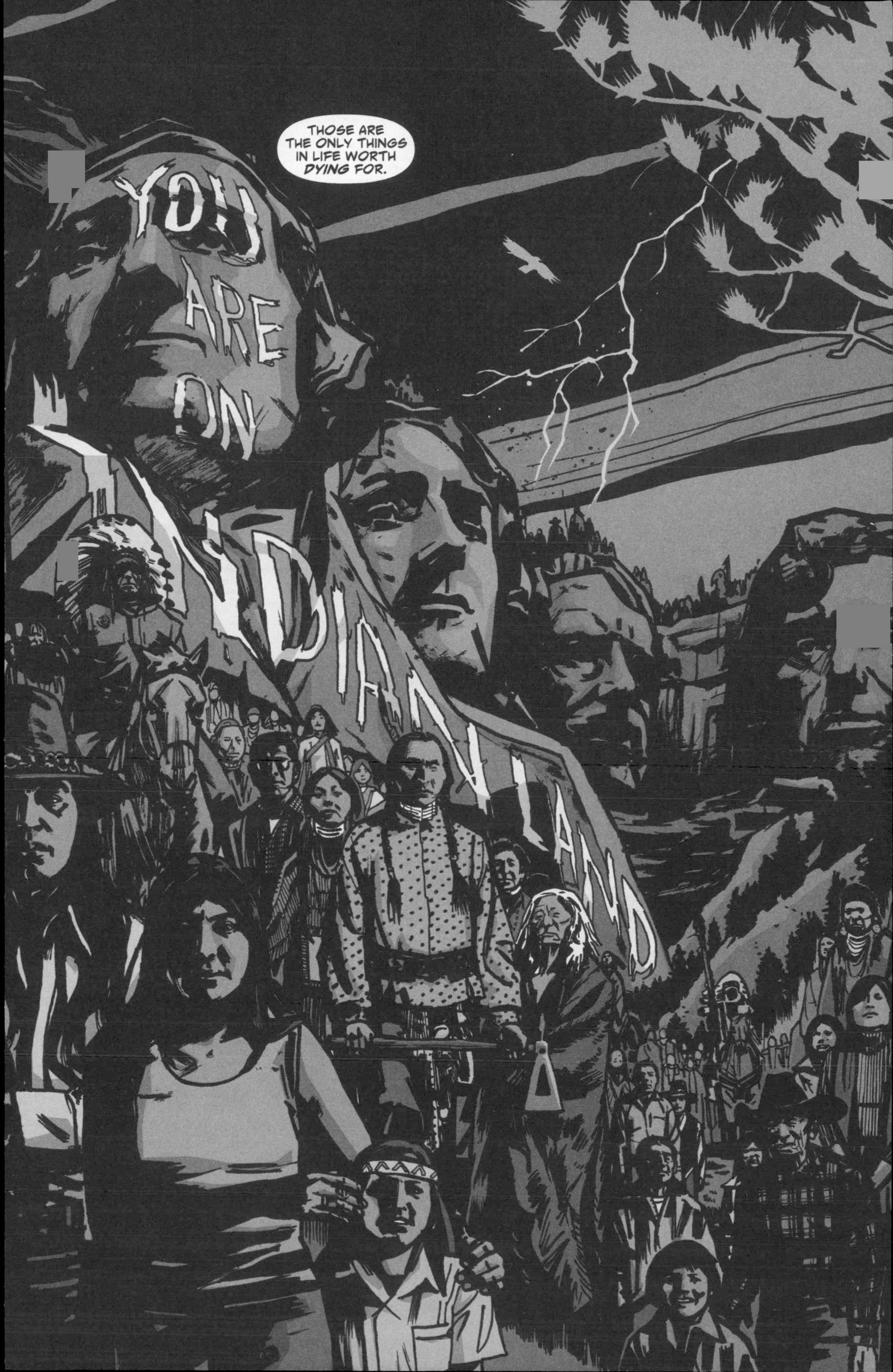

THOSE ARE THE ONLY THINGS IN LIFE WORTH DYING FOR.
YOU ARE ON INDIAN LAND

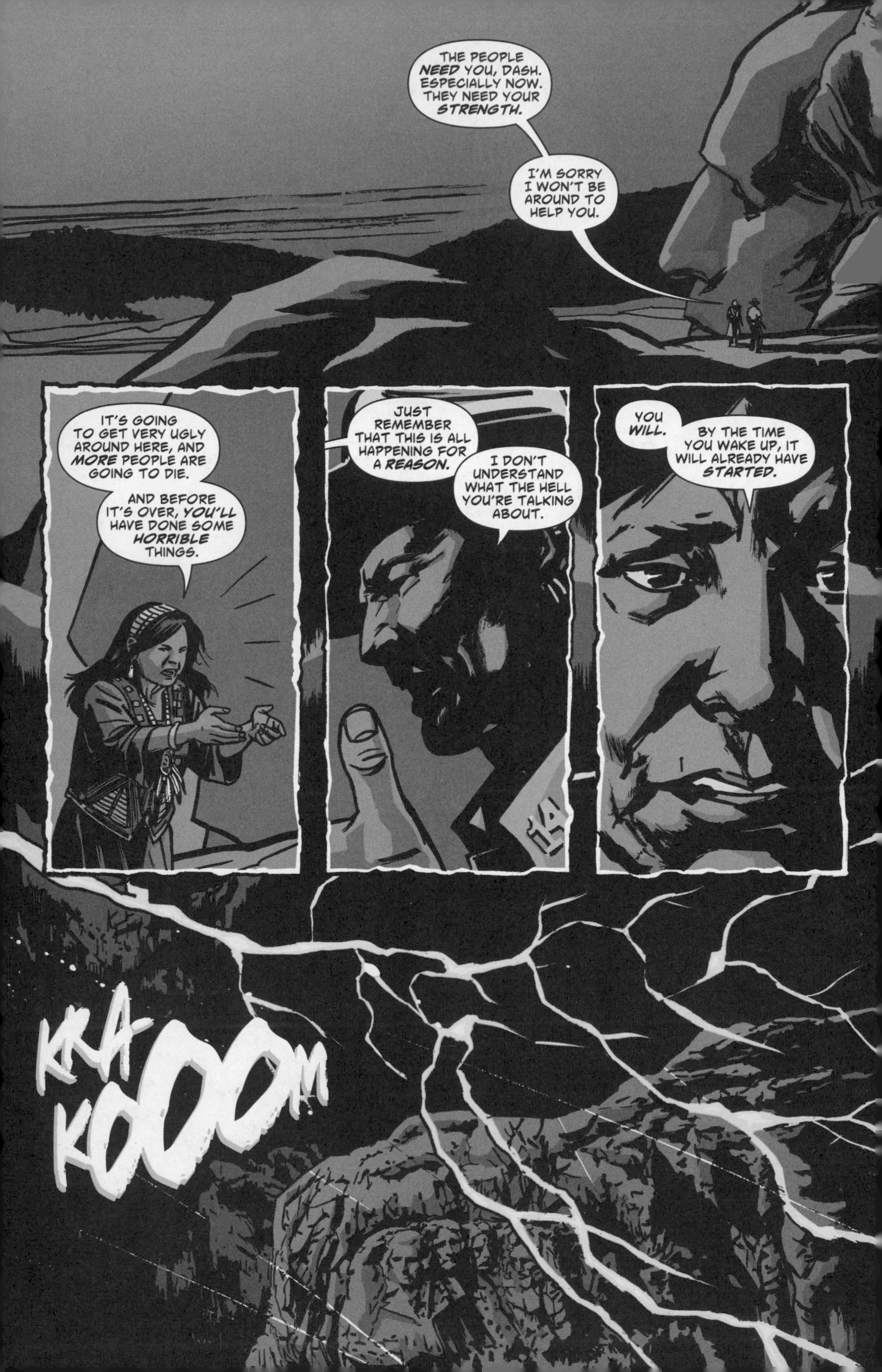
THE PEOPLE NEED YOU, DASH. ESPECIALLY NOW. THEY NEED YOUR STRENGTH.
I'M SORRY I WON'T BE AROUND TO HELP YOU.
IT'S GOING TO GET VERY UGLY AROUND HERE, AND MORE PEOPLE ARE GOING TO DIE.
AND BEFORE IT'S OVER, YOU'LL HAVE DONE SOME HORRIBLE THINGS.
JUST REMEMBER THAT THIS IS ALL HAPPENING FOR A REASON.
I DON'T UNDERSTAND WHAT THE HELL YOU'RE TALKING ABOUT.
YOU WILL.
BY THE TIME YOU WAKE UP, IT WILL ALREADY HAVE STARTED.
KRA-KOOOM

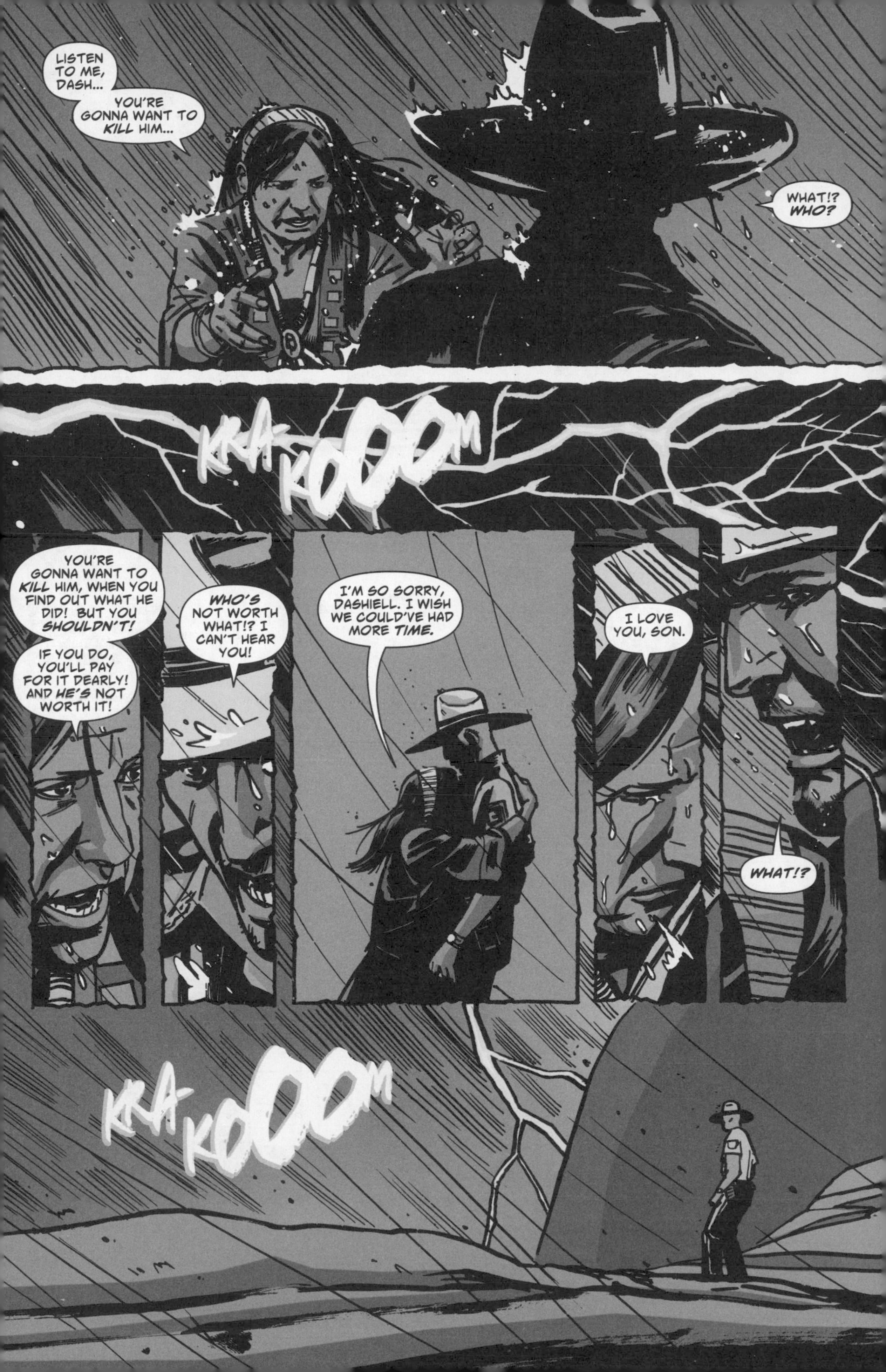
LISTEN TO ME, DASH...
YOU'RE GONNA WANT TO KILL HIM...
WHAT!? WHO?
KRA-KOOOM
YOU'RE GONNA WANT TO KILL HIM, WHEN YOU FIND OUT WHAT HE DID! BUT YOU SHOULDN'T!
IF YOU DO, YOU'LL PAY FOR IT DEARLY! AND HE'S NOT WORTH IT!
WHO'S NOT WORTH WHAT!? I CAN'T HEAR YOU!
I'M SO SORRY, DASHIELL. I WISH WE COULD'VE HAD MORE TIME.
I LOVE YOU, SON.
WHAT!?
KRA-KOOOM

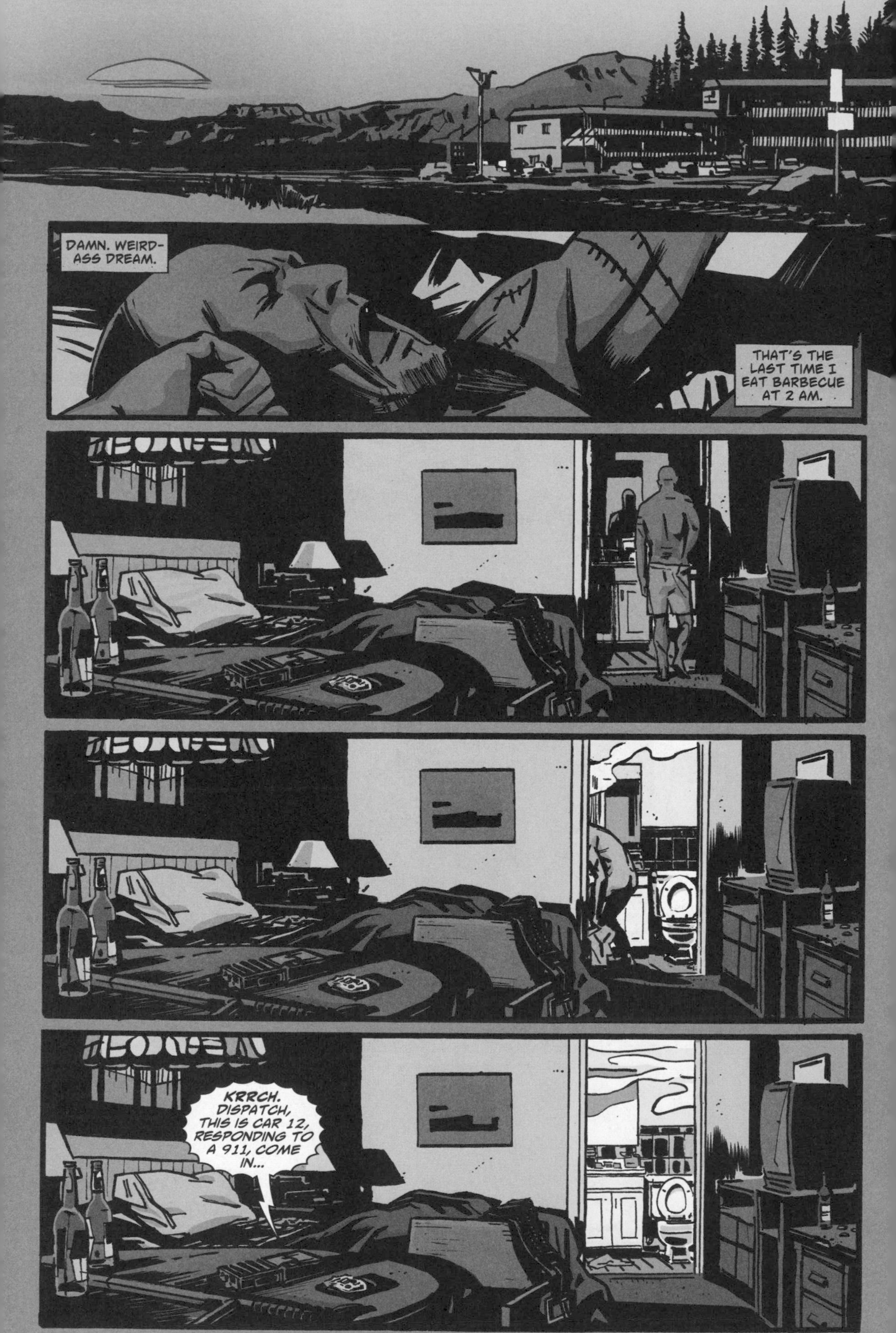
DAMN. WEIRD-ASS DREAM.
THAT'S THE LAST TIME I EAT BARBECUE AT 2 AM.
KRRCH. DISPATCH, THIS IS CAR 12, RESPONDING TO A 911, COME IN...

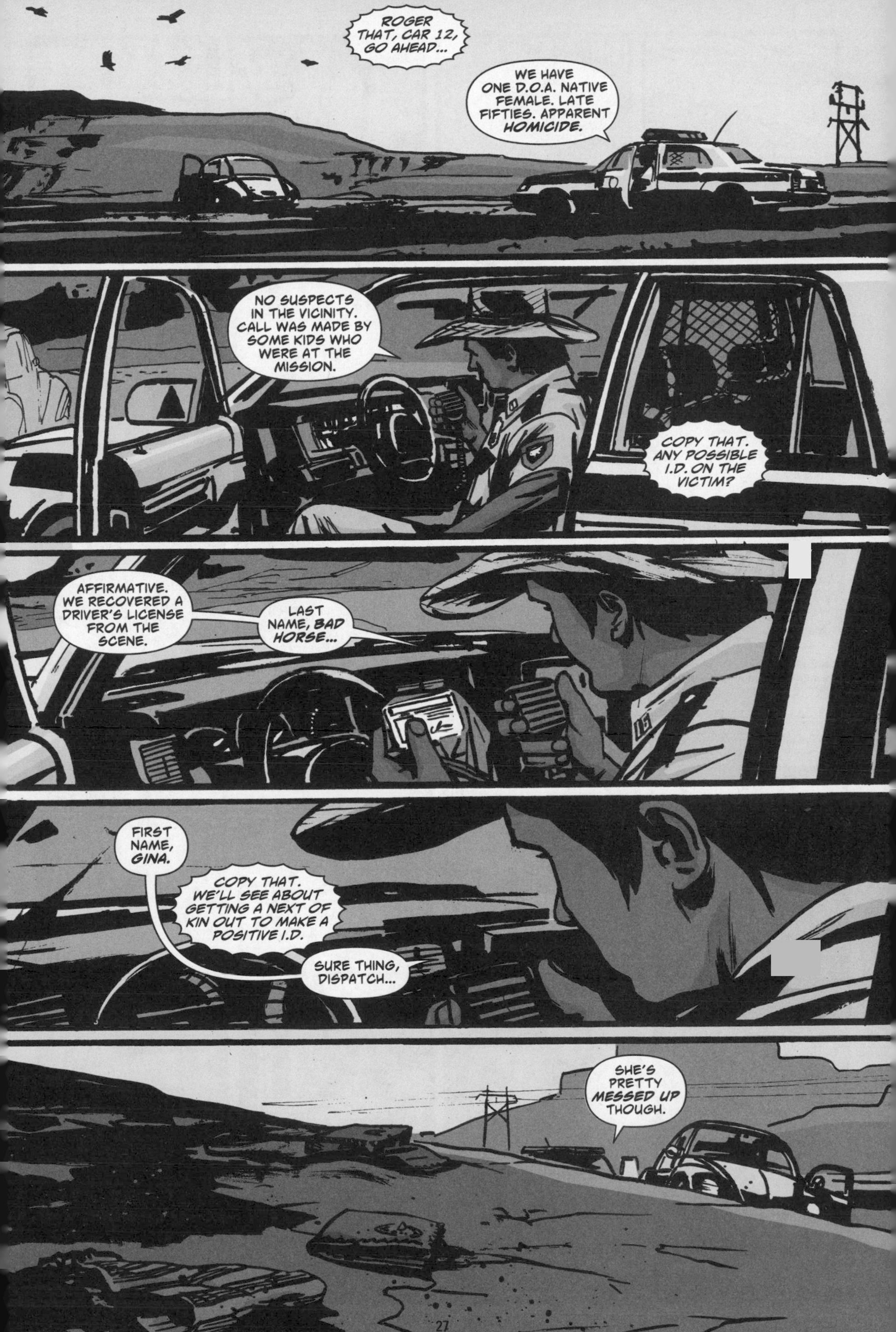
ROGER THAT, CAR 12, GO AHEAD...
WE HAVE ONE D.O.A. NATIVE FEMALE. LATE FIFTIES. APPARENT HOMICIDE.
NO SUSPECTS IN THE VICINITY. CALL WAS MADE BY SOME KIDS WHO WERE AT THE MISSION.
COPY THAT. ANY POSSIBLE I.D. ON THE VICTIM?
AFFIRMATIVE. WE RECOVERED A DRIVER'S LICENSE FROM THE SCENE.
LAST NAME, BAD HORSE...
FIRST NAME, GINA.
COPY THAT. WE'LL SEE ABOUT GETTING A NEXT OF KIN OUT TO MAKE A POSITIVE I.D.
SURE THING, DISPATCH...
SHE'S PRETTY MESSED UP THOUGH.

TIME NOW TO BRUSH ASIDE THE CRAZY DREAMS.

AND FOCUS.

WITHOUT FOCUS, I'M DEAD.

I CAME HERE TO DO A JOB, AND THAT'S WHAT THE HELL I'M DOING.

I AIN'T LOOKING TO MAKE UP WITH DEAR OLD MOMMY OR GET IN TOUCH WITH MY INJUN ROOTS.

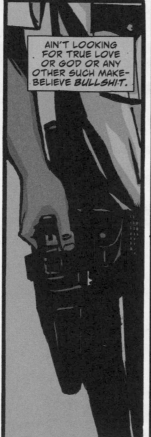

AIN'T LOOKING FOR TRUE LOVE OR GOD OR ANY OTHER SUCH MAKE-BELIEVE BULLSHIT.

YOU CAN BET YOUR ASS, AIN'T NOTHING IN THE WORLD CAN HOLD ME HERE ONCE THIS GODDAMN JOB IS DONE.

AND IT'LL BE DONE MOST DIRECTLY, I ASSURE YOU.

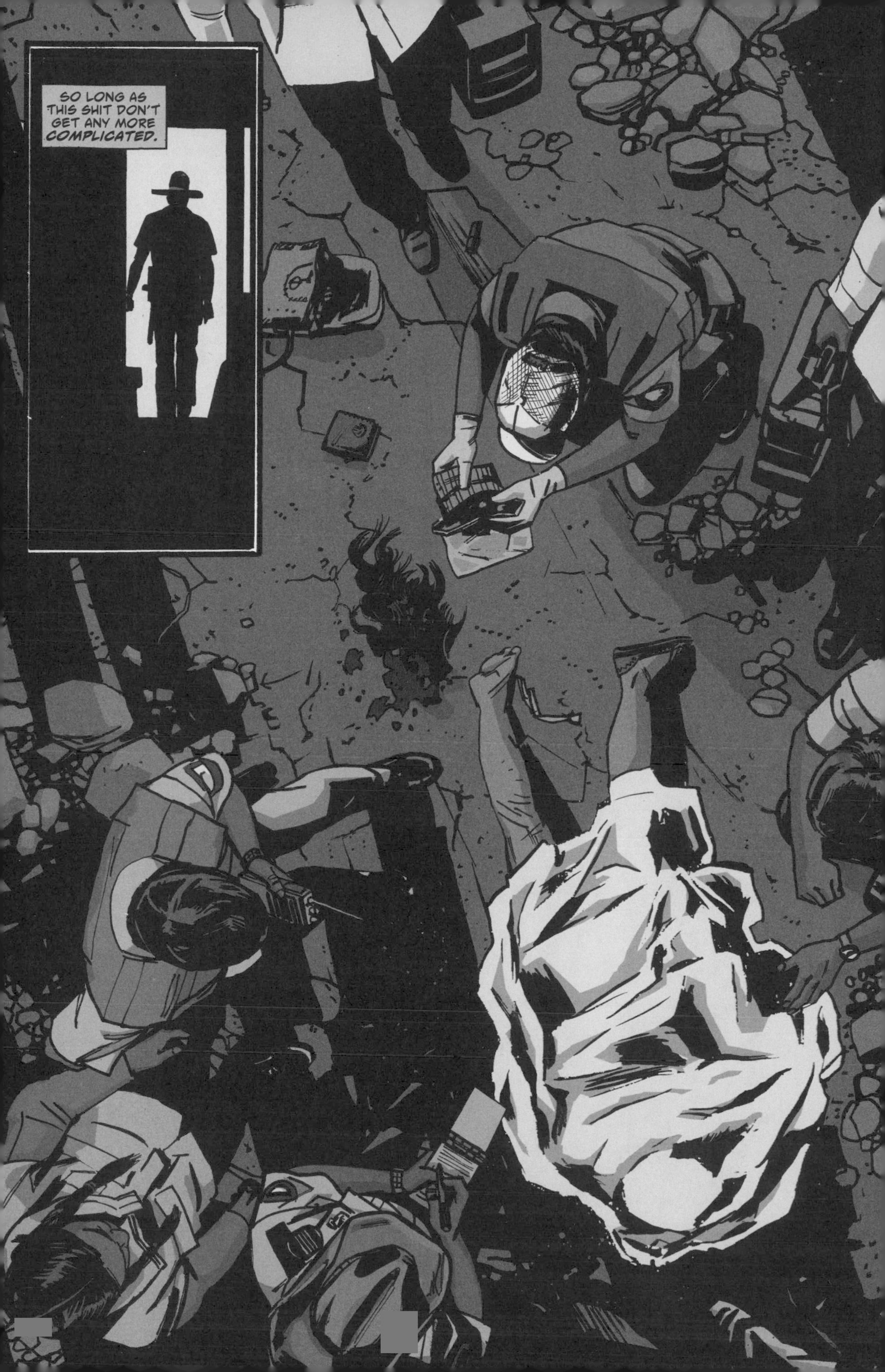
SO LONG AS THIS SHIT DON'T GET ANY MORE *COMPLICATED.*

DEAD MOTHERS PART 1

COVER ART BY JOCK

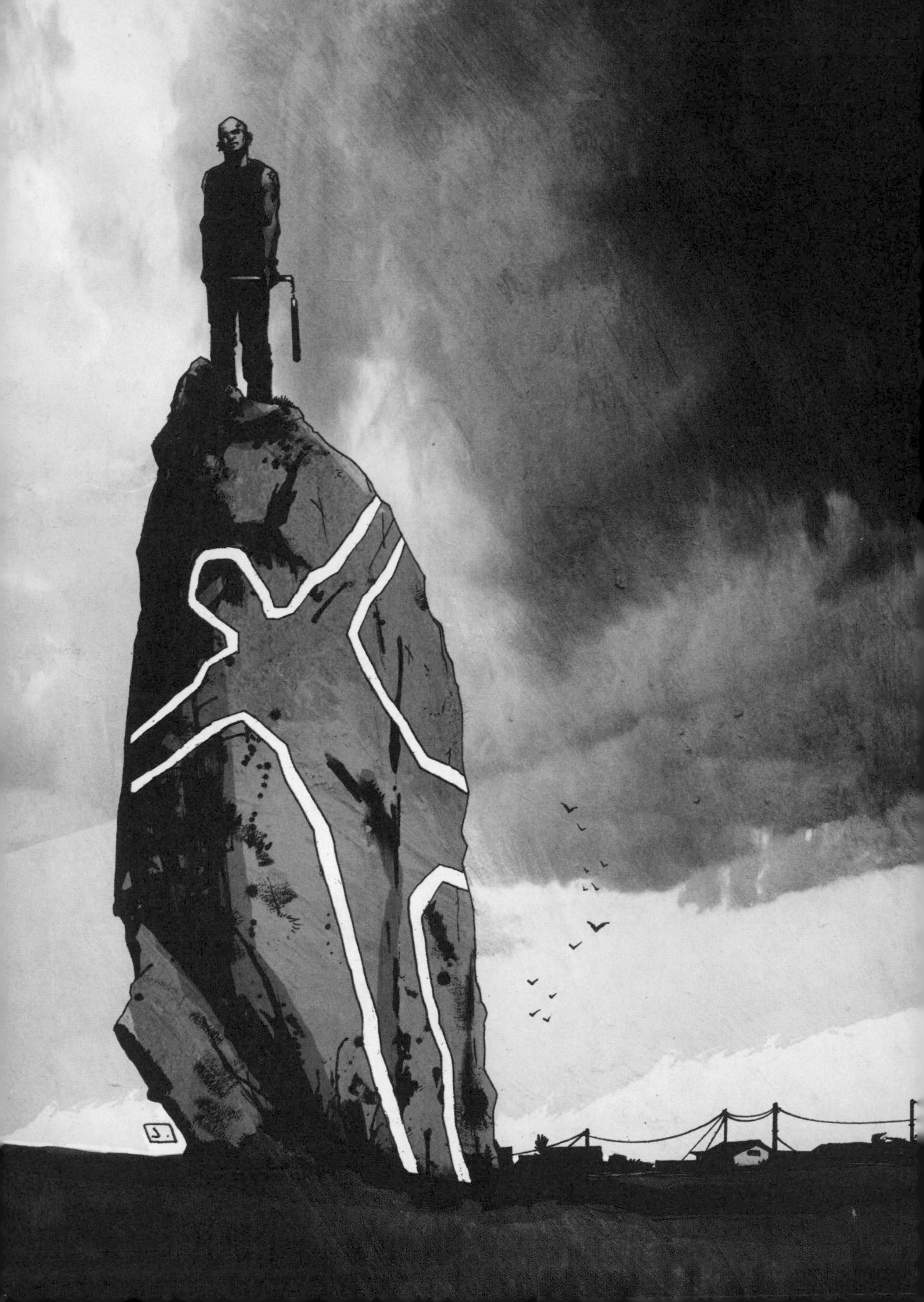

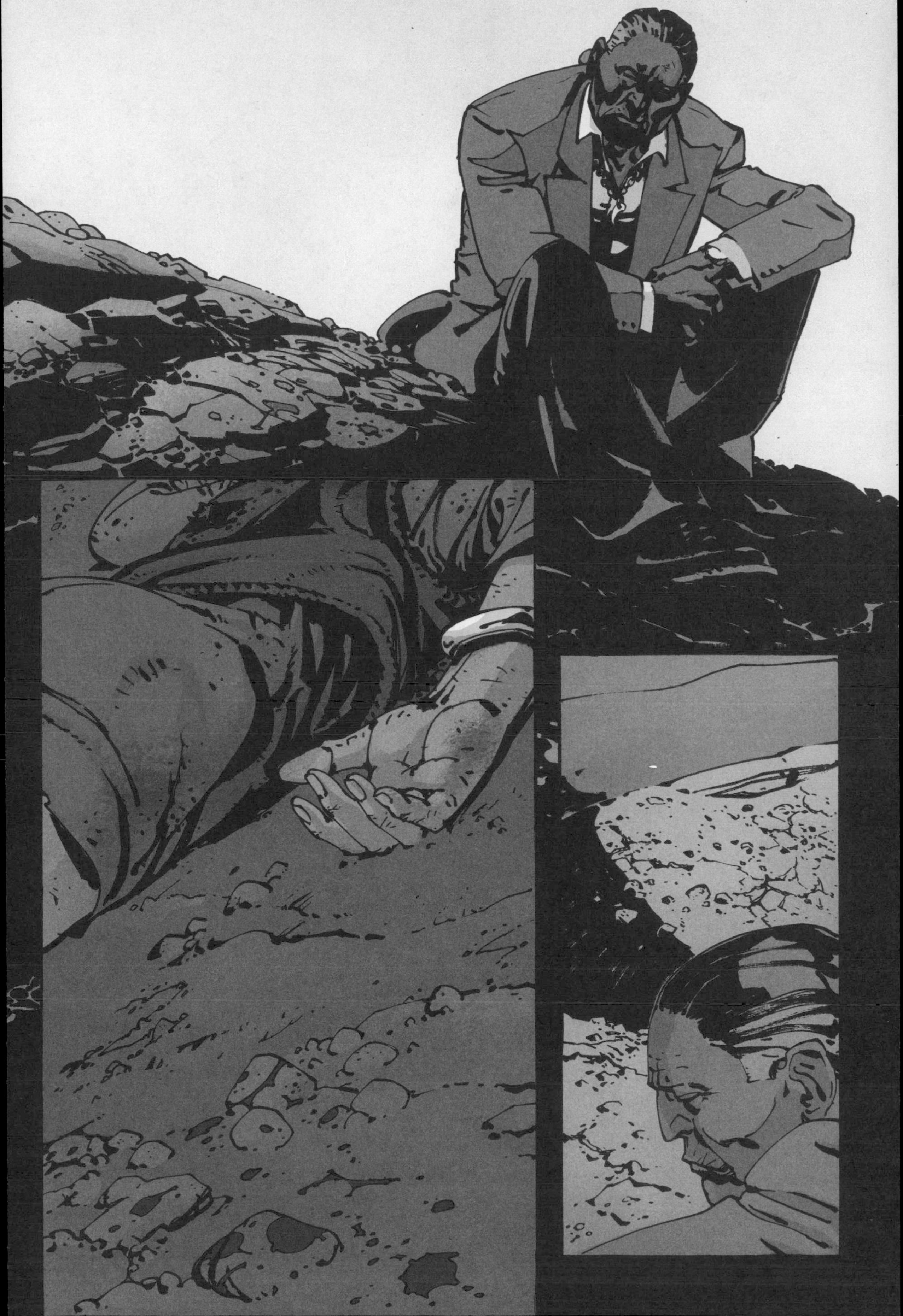

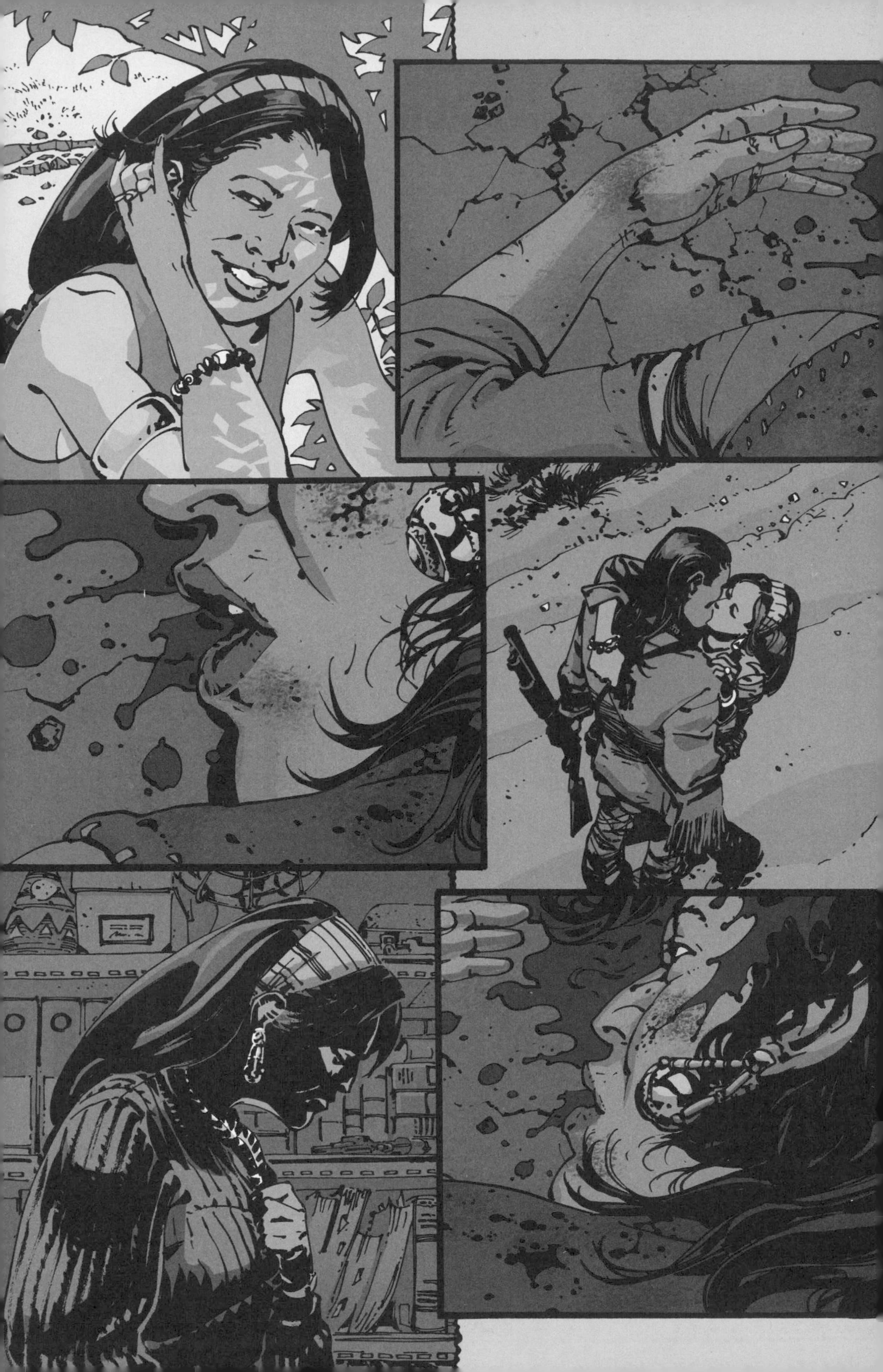

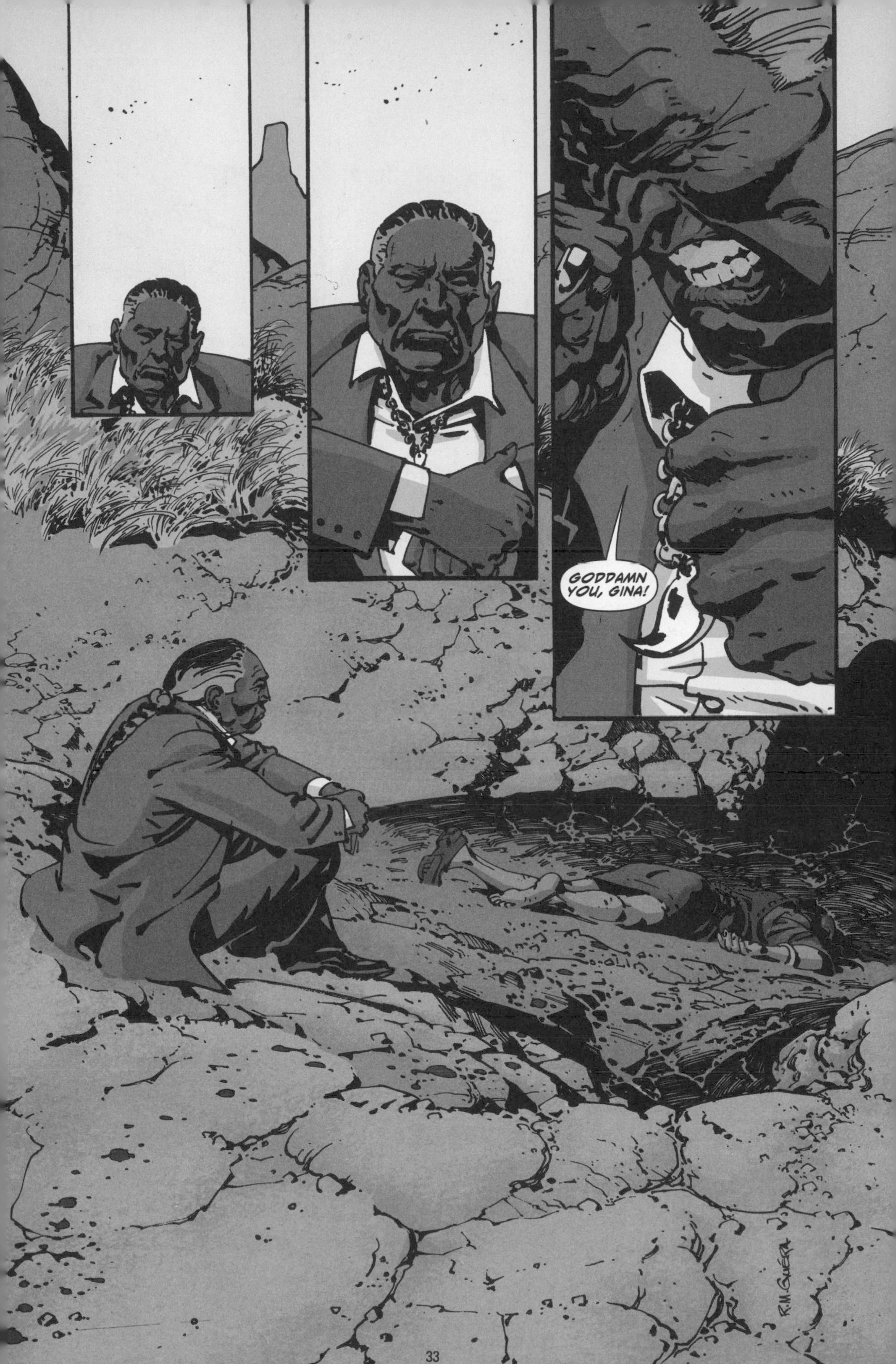
GODDAMN YOU, GINA!
R.M. GUERA

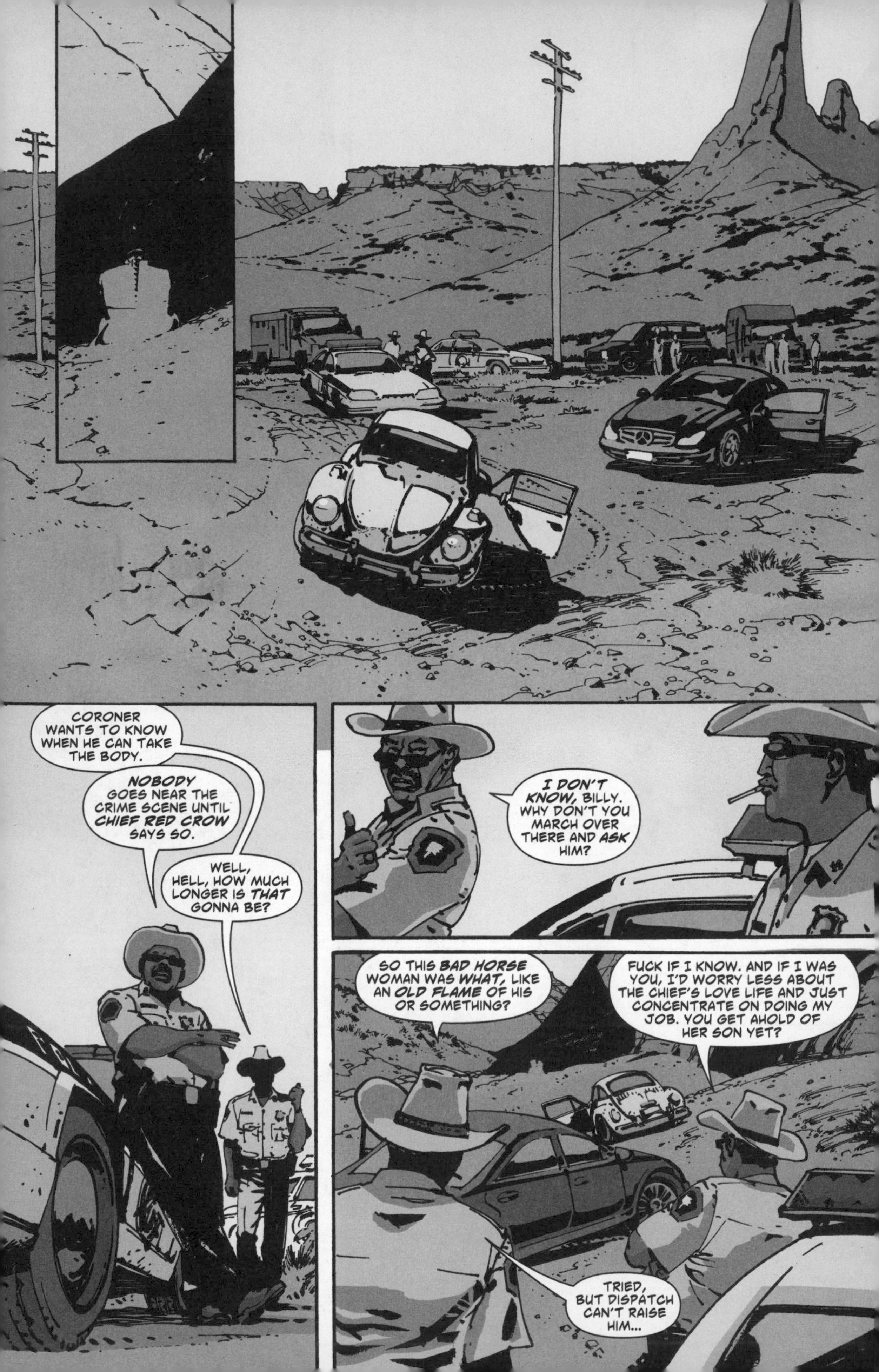
CORONER WANTS TO KNOW WHEN HE CAN TAKE THE BODY.
NOBODY GOES NEAR THE CRIME SCENE UNTIL CHIEF RED CROW SAYS SO.
WELL, HELL, HOW MUCH LONGER IS THAT GONNA BE?
I DON'T KNOW, BILLY. WHY DON'T YOU MARCH OVER THERE AND ASK HIM?
SO THIS BAD HORSE WOMAN WAS WHAT, LIKE AN OLD FLAME OF HIS OR SOMETHING?
FUCK IF I KNOW. AND IF I WAS YOU, I'D WORRY LESS ABOUT THE CHIEF'S LOVE LIFE AND JUST CONCENTRATE ON DOING MY JOB. YOU GET AHOLD OF HER SON YET?
TRIED, BUT DISPATCH CAN'T RAISE HIM...

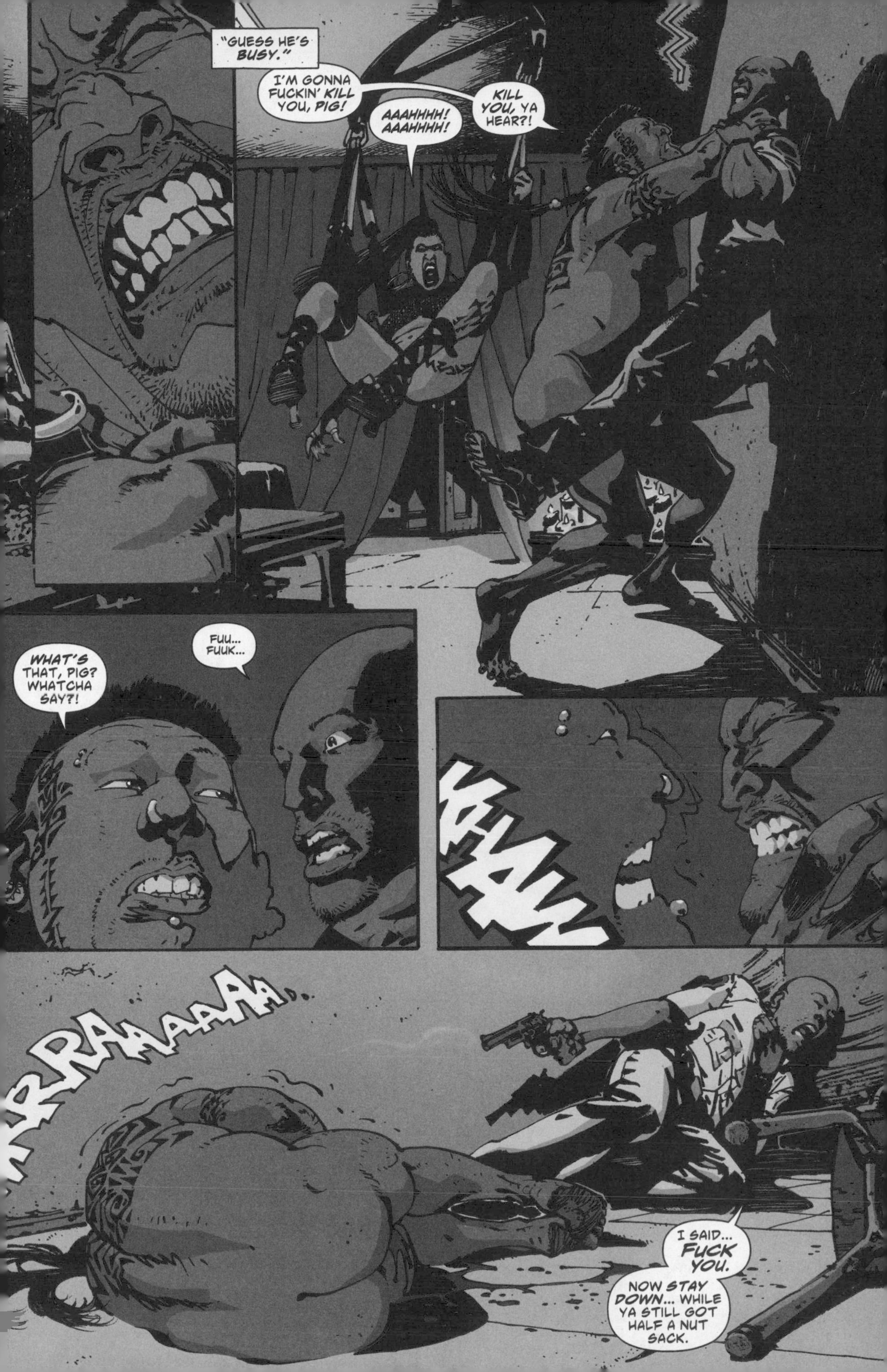
"GUESS HE'S BUSY."
I'M GONNA FUCKIN' KILL YOU, PIG!
KILL YOU, YA HEAR?!
AAAHHHH! AAAHHHH!
WHAT'S THAT, PIG? WHATCHA SAY?!
FUU... FUUK...
RRRAAAAAA..
I SAID... FUCK YOU.
NOW STAY DOWN... WHILE YA STILL GOT HALF A NUT SACK.

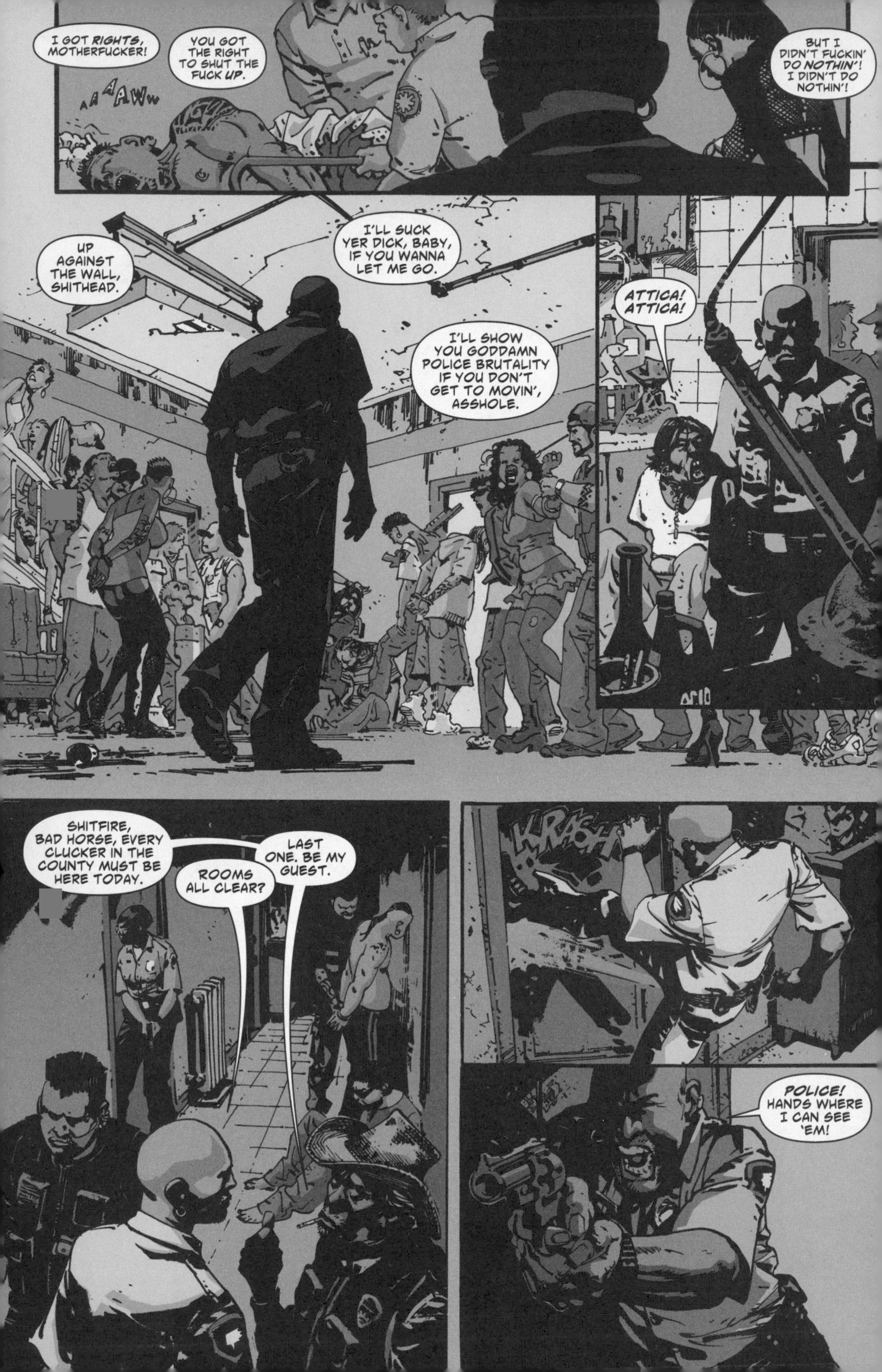
I GOT RIGHTS, MOTHERFUCKER!
YOU GOT THE RIGHT TO SHUT THE FUCK UP.
AAAAWW
BUT I DIDN'T FUCKIN' DO NOTHIN'! I DIDN'T DO NOTHIN'!
UP AGAINST THE WALL, SHITHEAD.
I'LL SUCK YER DICK, BABY, IF YOU WANNA LET ME GO.
I'LL SHOW YOU GODDAMN POLICE BRUTALITY IF YOU DON'T GET TO MOVIN', ASSHOLE.
ATTICA! ATTICA!
SHITFIRE, BAD HORSE, EVERY CLUCKER IN THE COUNTY MUST BE HERE TODAY.
ROOMS ALL CLEAR?
LAST ONE. BE MY GUEST.
KRASH
POLICE! HANDS WHERE I CAN SEE 'EM!

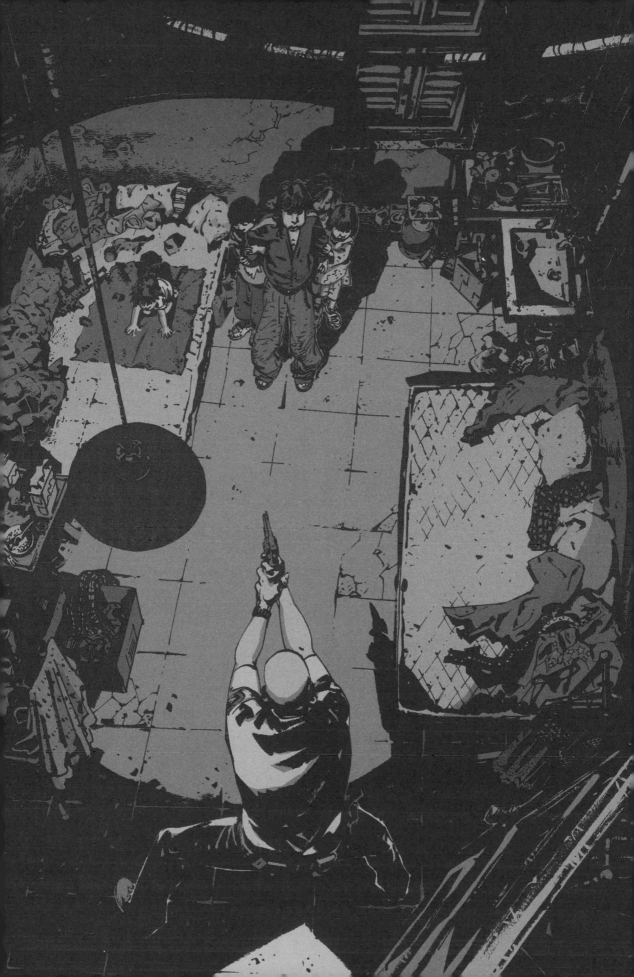

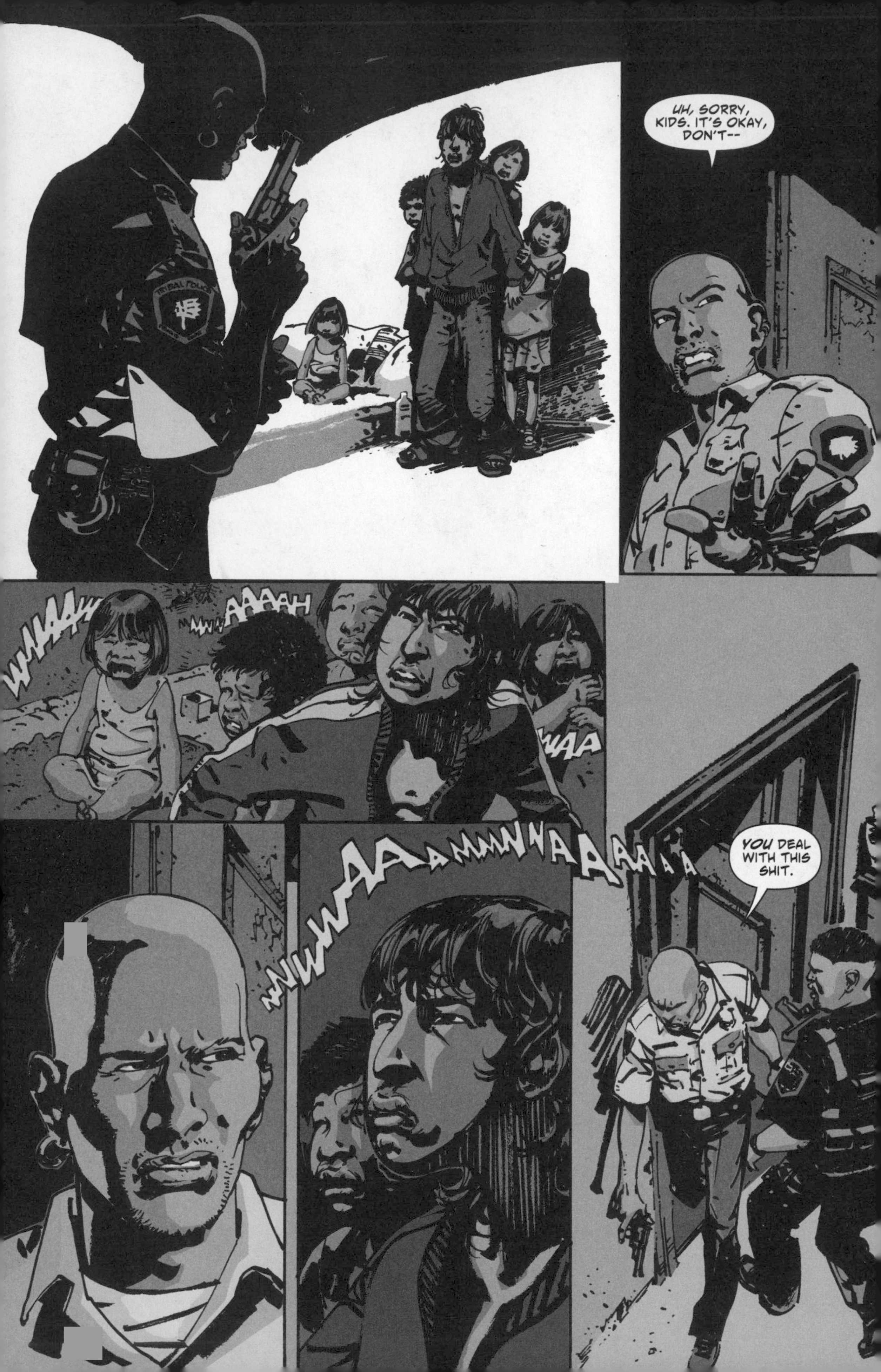
UH, SORRY, KIDS. IT'S OKAY, DON'T--
WAAAW
AAAAH
WAA
WAAAMMMWAAAAAAA
YOU DEAL WITH THIS SHIT.

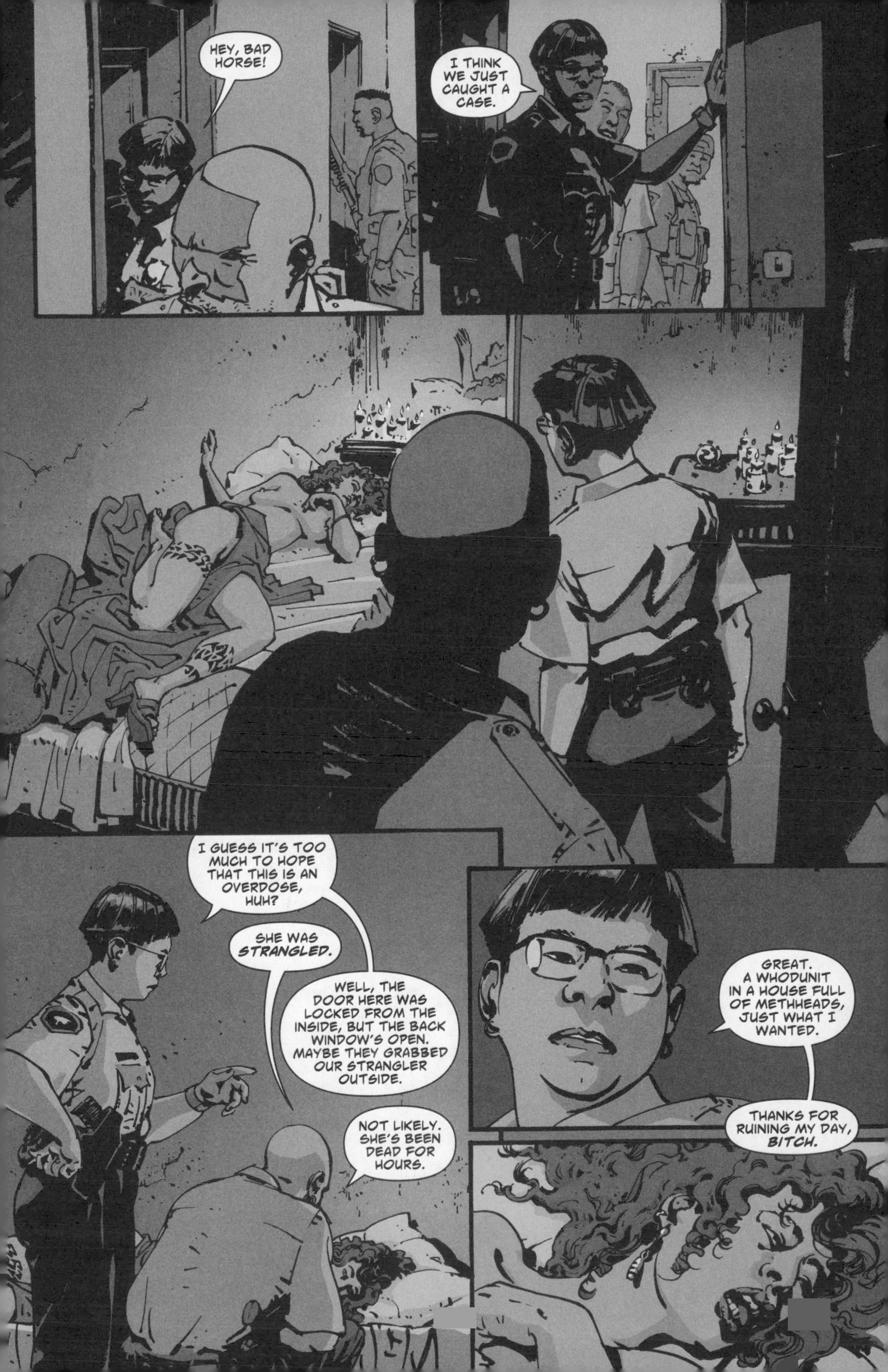

HEY, BAD HORSE!
I THINK WE JUST CAUGHT A CASE.
I GUESS IT'S TOO MUCH TO HOPE THAT THIS IS AN OVERDOSE, HUH?
SHE WAS STRANGLED.
WELL, THE DOOR HERE WAS LOCKED FROM THE INSIDE, BUT THE BACK WINDOW'S OPEN. MAYBE THEY GRABBED OUR STRANGLER OUTSIDE.
NOT LIKELY. SHE'S BEEN DEAD FOR HOURS.
GREAT. A WHODUNIT IN A HOUSE FULL OF METHHEADS, JUST WHAT I WANTED.
THANKS FOR RUINING MY DAY, BITCH.

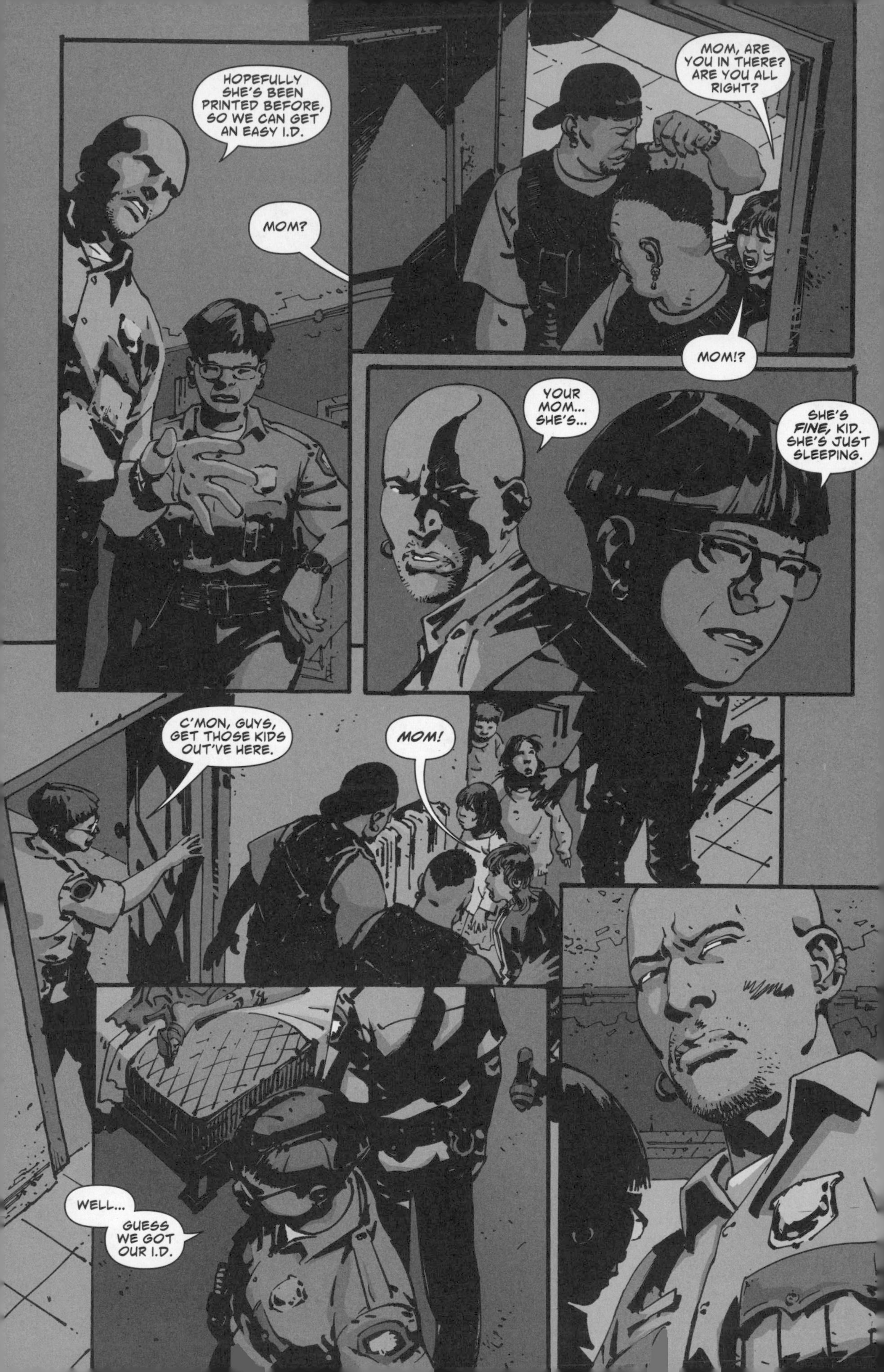
HOPEFULLY SHE'S BEEN PRINTED BEFORE, SO WE CAN GET AN EASY I.D.
MOM?
MOM, ARE YOU IN THERE? ARE YOU ALL RIGHT?
MOM!?
YOUR MOM... SHE'S...
SHE'S FINE, KID. SHE'S JUST SLEEPING.
C'MON, GUYS, GET THOSE KIDS OUT'VE HERE.
MOM!
WELL... GUESS WE GOT OUR I.D.

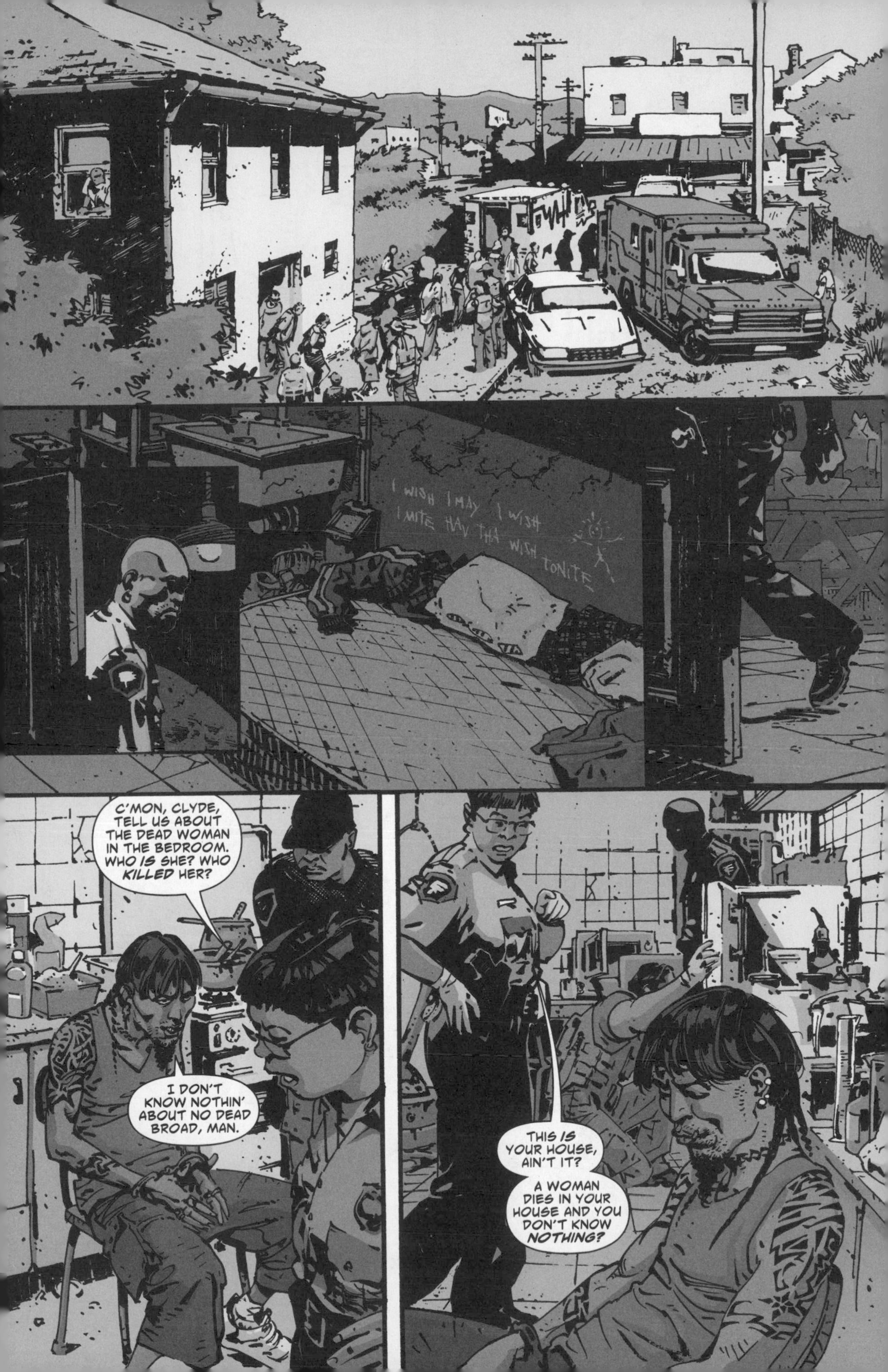

I WISH I MAY I WISH I MITE HAV THA WISH TONITE
C'MON, CLYDE, TELL US ABOUT THE DEAD WOMAN IN THE BEDROOM. WHO *IS* SHE? WHO *KILLED* HER?
I DON'T KNOW NOTHIN' ABOUT NO DEAD BROAD, MAN.
THIS *IS* YOUR HOUSE, AIN'T IT?
A WOMAN DIES IN YOUR HOUSE AND YOU DON'T KNOW *NOTHING*?

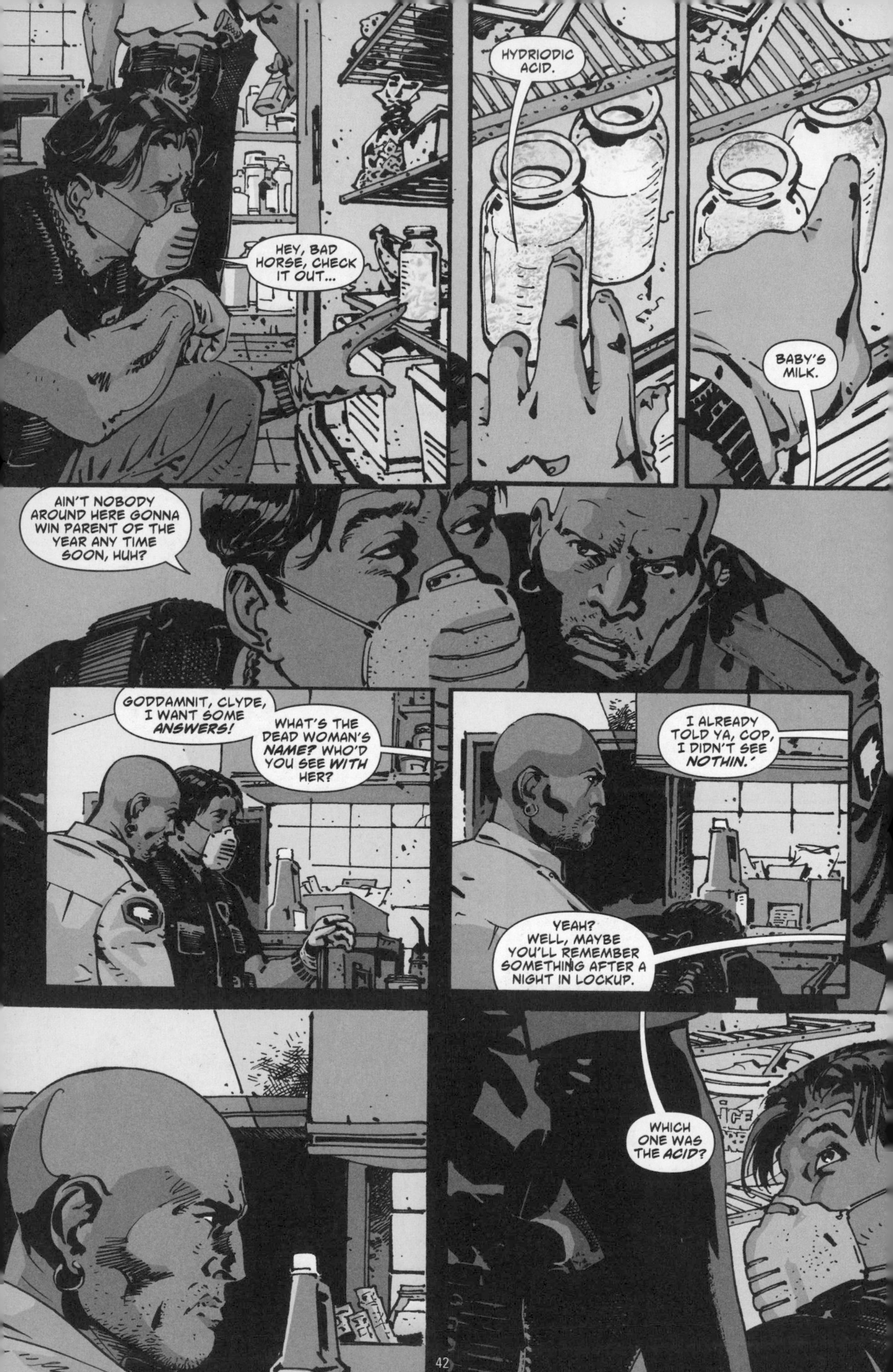
HEY, BAD HORSE, CHECK IT OUT...
HYDRIODIC ACID.
BABY'S MILK.
AIN'T NOBODY AROUND HERE GONNA WIN PARENT OF THE YEAR ANY TIME SOON, HUH?
GODDAMNIT, CLYDE, I WANT SOME ANSWERS!
WHAT'S THE DEAD WOMAN'S NAME? WHO'D YOU SEE WITH HER?
I ALREADY TOLD YA, COP, I DIDN'T SEE NOTHIN.'
YEAH? WELL, MAYBE YOU'LL REMEMBER SOMETHING AFTER A NIGHT IN LOCKUP.
WHICH ONE WAS THE ACID?

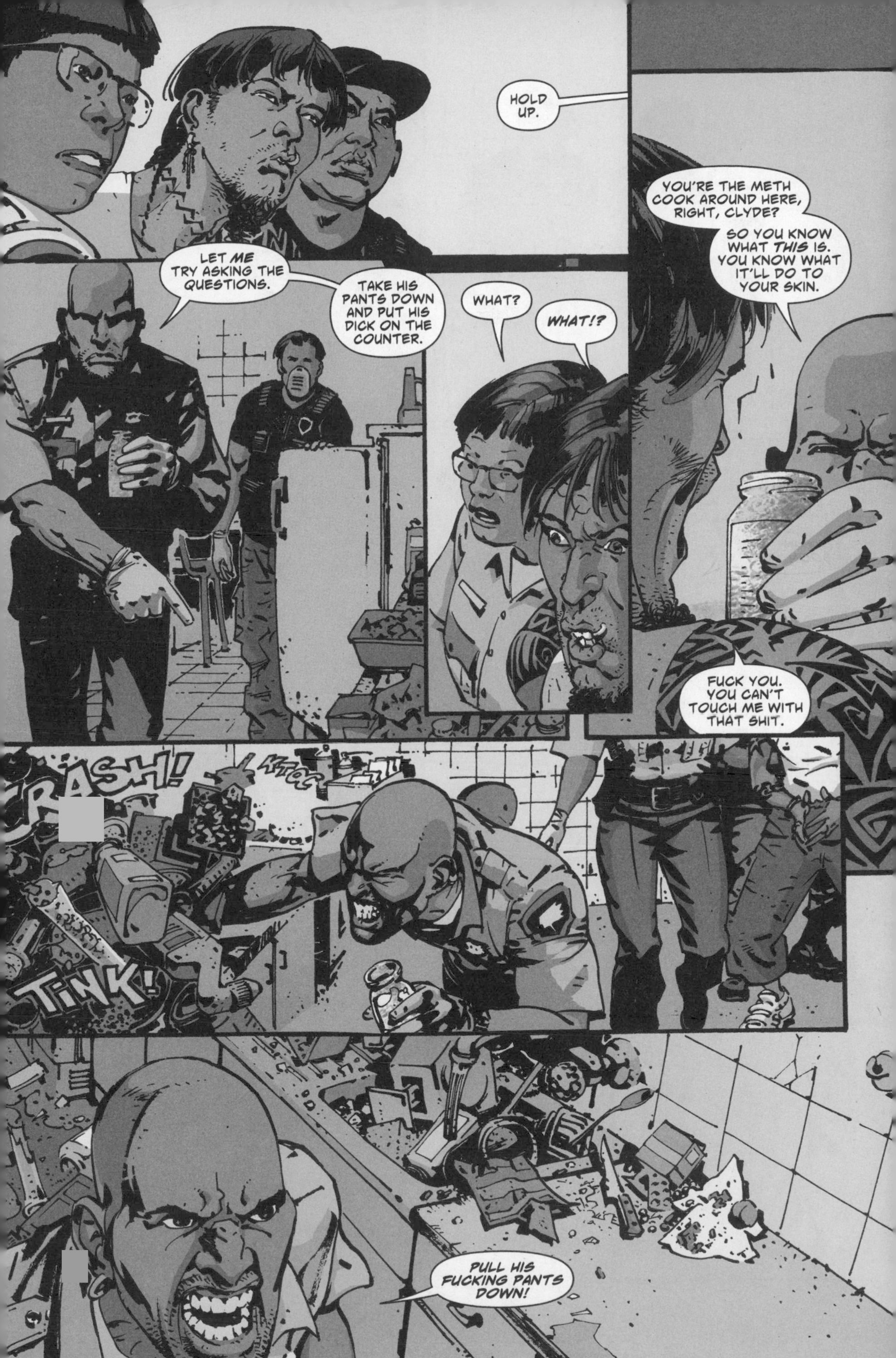
HOLD UP.
YOU'RE THE METH COOK AROUND HERE, RIGHT, CLYDE?
SO YOU KNOW WHAT THIS IS. YOU KNOW WHAT IT'LL DO TO YOUR SKIN.
FUCK YOU. YOU CAN'T TOUCH ME WITH THAT SHIT.
LET ME TRY ASKING THE QUESTIONS.
TAKE HIS PANTS DOWN AND PUT HIS DICK ON THE COUNTER.
WHAT?
WHAT!?
CRASH!
TINK!
PULL HIS FUCKING PANTS DOWN!

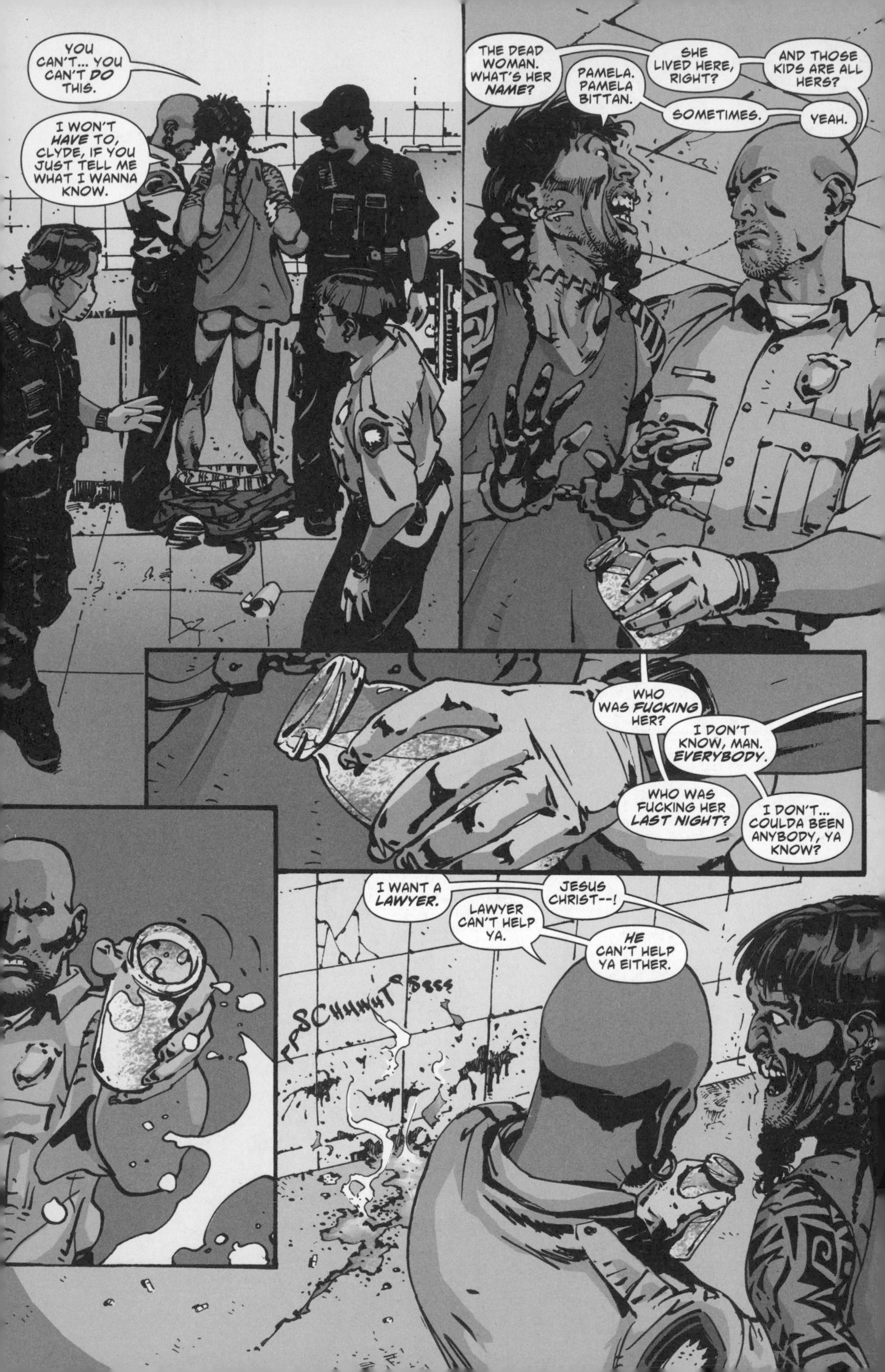
YOU CAN'T... YOU CAN'T DO THIS.
I WON'T HAVE TO, CLYDE, IF YOU JUST TELL ME WHAT I WANNA KNOW.
THE DEAD WOMAN. WHAT'S HER NAME?
PAMELA. PAMELA BITTAN.
SHE LIVED HERE, RIGHT?
SOMETIMES.
AND THOSE KIDS ARE ALL HERS?
YEAH.
WHO WAS FUCKING HER?
I DON'T KNOW, MAN. EVERYBODY.
WHO WAS FUCKING HER LAST NIGHT?
I DON'T... COULDA BEEN ANYBODY, YA KNOW?
I WANT A LAWYER.
JESUS CHRIST--!
LAWYER CAN'T HELP YA.
HE CAN'T HELP YA EITHER.
FFSCHMMMT

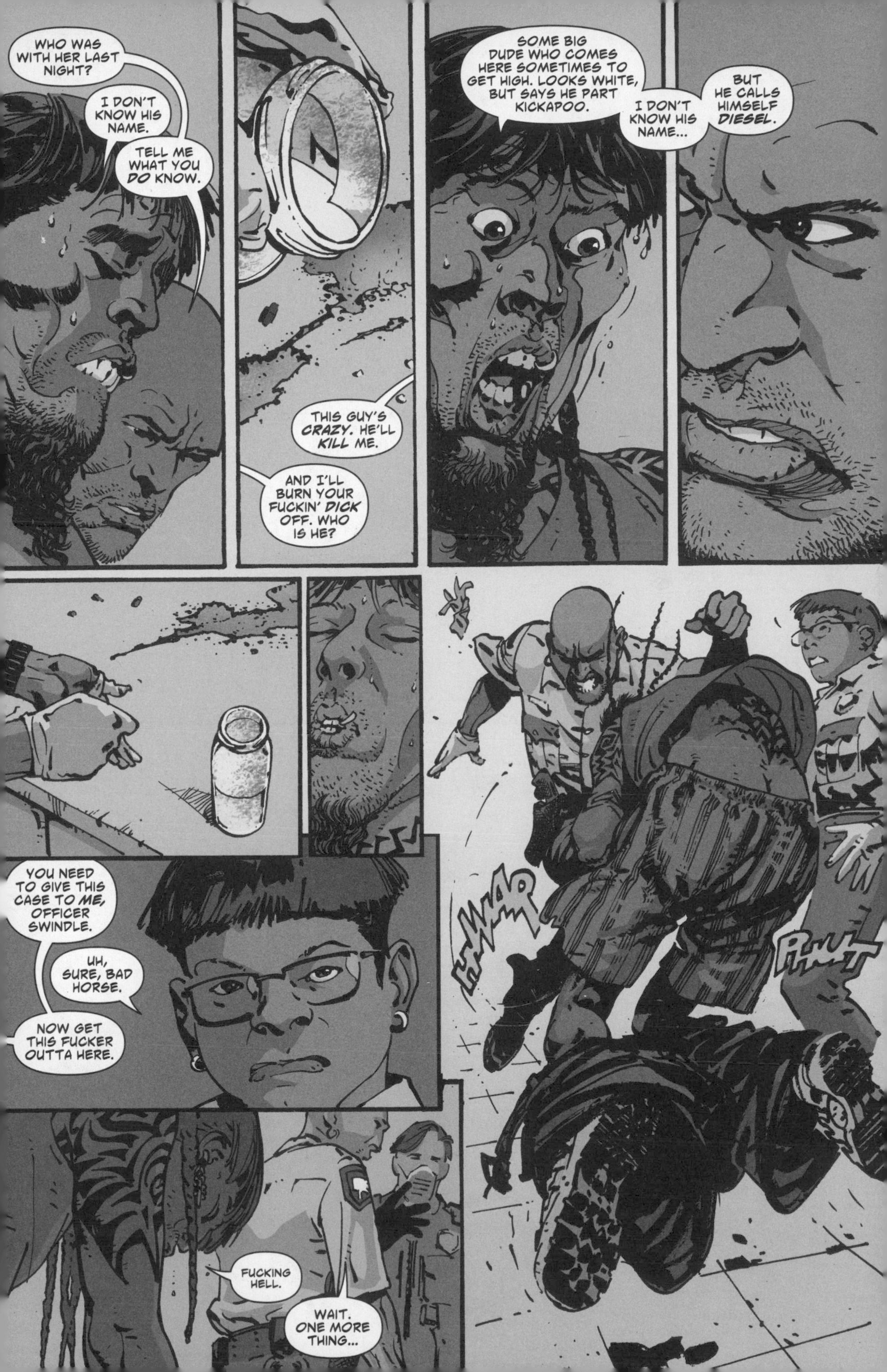

WHO WAS WITH HER LAST NIGHT?
I DON'T KNOW HIS NAME.
TELL ME WHAT YOU *DO* KNOW.
THIS GUY'S *CRAZY*. HE'LL *KILL* ME.
AND I'LL BURN YOUR FUCKIN' *DICK* OFF. WHO IS HE?
SOME BIG DUDE WHO COMES HERE SOMETIMES TO GET HIGH. LOOKS WHITE, BUT SAYS HE PART KICKAPOO.
I DON'T KNOW HIS NAME...
BUT HE CALLS HIMSELF *DIESEL*.
YOU NEED TO GIVE THIS CASE TO *ME*, OFFICER SWINDLE.
UH, SURE, BAD HORSE.
NOW GET THIS FUCKER OUTTA HERE.
FUCKING HELL.
WAIT. ONE MORE THING...

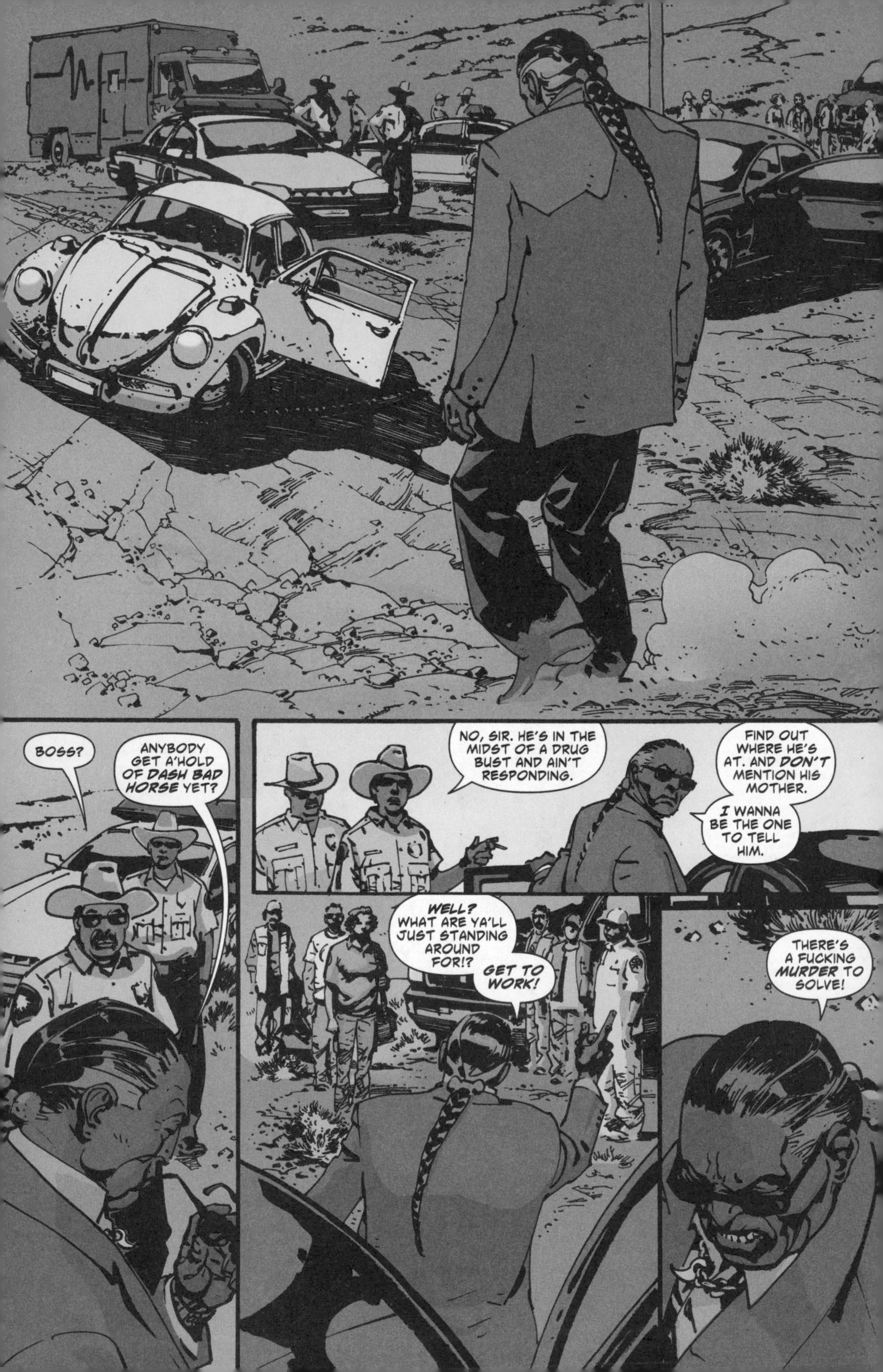
BOSS?
ANYBODY GET A'HOLD OF DASH BAD HORSE YET?
NO, SIR. HE'S IN THE MIDST OF A DRUG BUST AND AIN'T RESPONDING.
FIND OUT WHERE HE'S AT. AND DON'T MENTION HIS MOTHER.
I WANNA BE THE ONE TO TELL HIM.
WELL? WHAT ARE YA'LL JUST STANDING AROUND FOR!?
GET TO WORK!
THERE'S A FUCKING MURDER TO SOLVE!

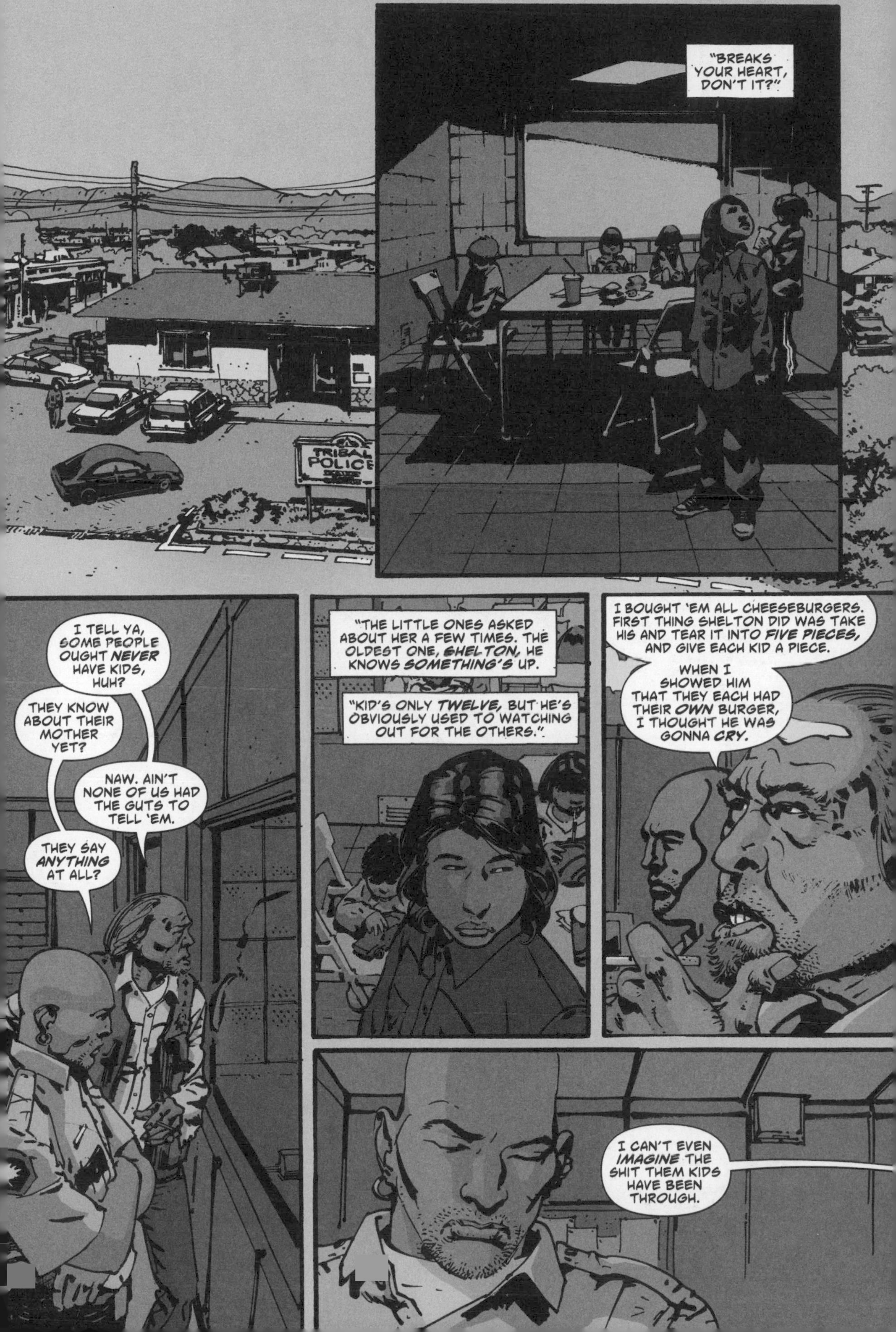
"BREAKS YOUR HEART, DON'T IT?"
TRIBAL POLICE
I TELL YA, SOME PEOPLE OUGHT NEVER HAVE KIDS, HUH?
THEY KNOW ABOUT THEIR MOTHER YET?
NAW. AIN'T NONE OF US HAD THE GUTS TO TELL 'EM.
THEY SAY ANYTHING AT ALL?
"THE LITTLE ONES ASKED ABOUT HER A FEW TIMES. THE OLDEST ONE, SHELTON, HE KNOWS SOMETHING'S UP.
"KID'S ONLY TWELVE, BUT HE'S OBVIOUSLY USED TO WATCHING OUT FOR THE OTHERS."
I BOUGHT 'EM ALL CHEESEBURGERS. FIRST THING SHELTON DID WAS TAKE HIS AND TEAR IT INTO FIVE PIECES, AND GIVE EACH KID A PIECE.
WHEN I SHOWED HIM THAT THEY EACH HAD THEIR OWN BURGER, I THOUGHT HE WAS GONNA CRY.
I CAN'T EVEN IMAGINE THE SHIT THEM KIDS HAVE BEEN THROUGH.

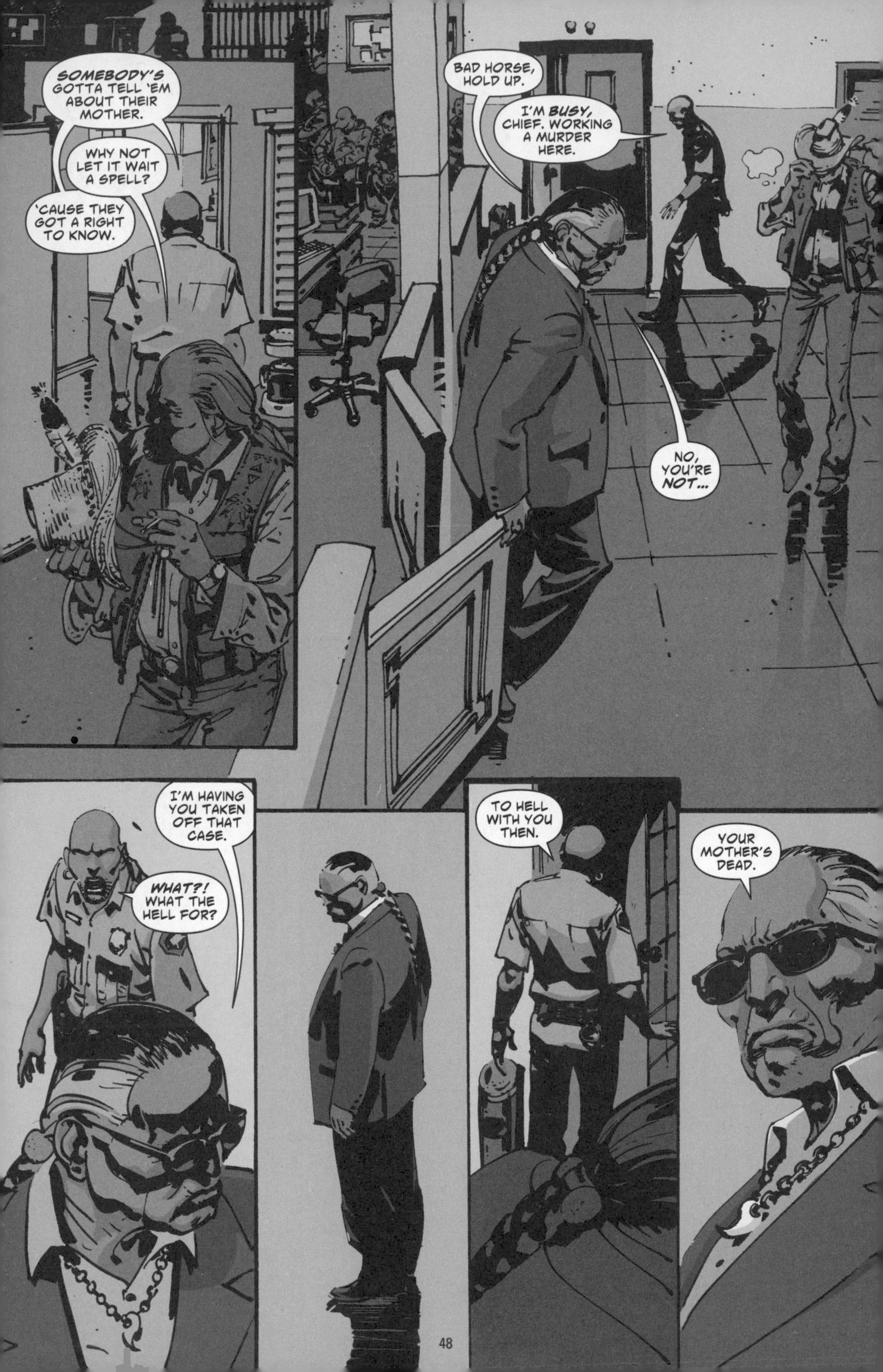
SOMEBODY'S GOTTA TELL 'EM ABOUT THEIR MOTHER.
WHY NOT LET IT WAIT A SPELL?
'CAUSE THEY GOT A RIGHT TO KNOW.
BAD HORSE, HOLD UP.
I'M BUSY, CHIEF. WORKING A MURDER HERE.
NO, YOU'RE NOT...
I'M HAVING YOU TAKEN OFF THAT CASE.
WHAT?! WHAT THE HELL FOR?
TO HELL WITH YOU THEN.
YOUR MOTHER'S DEAD.

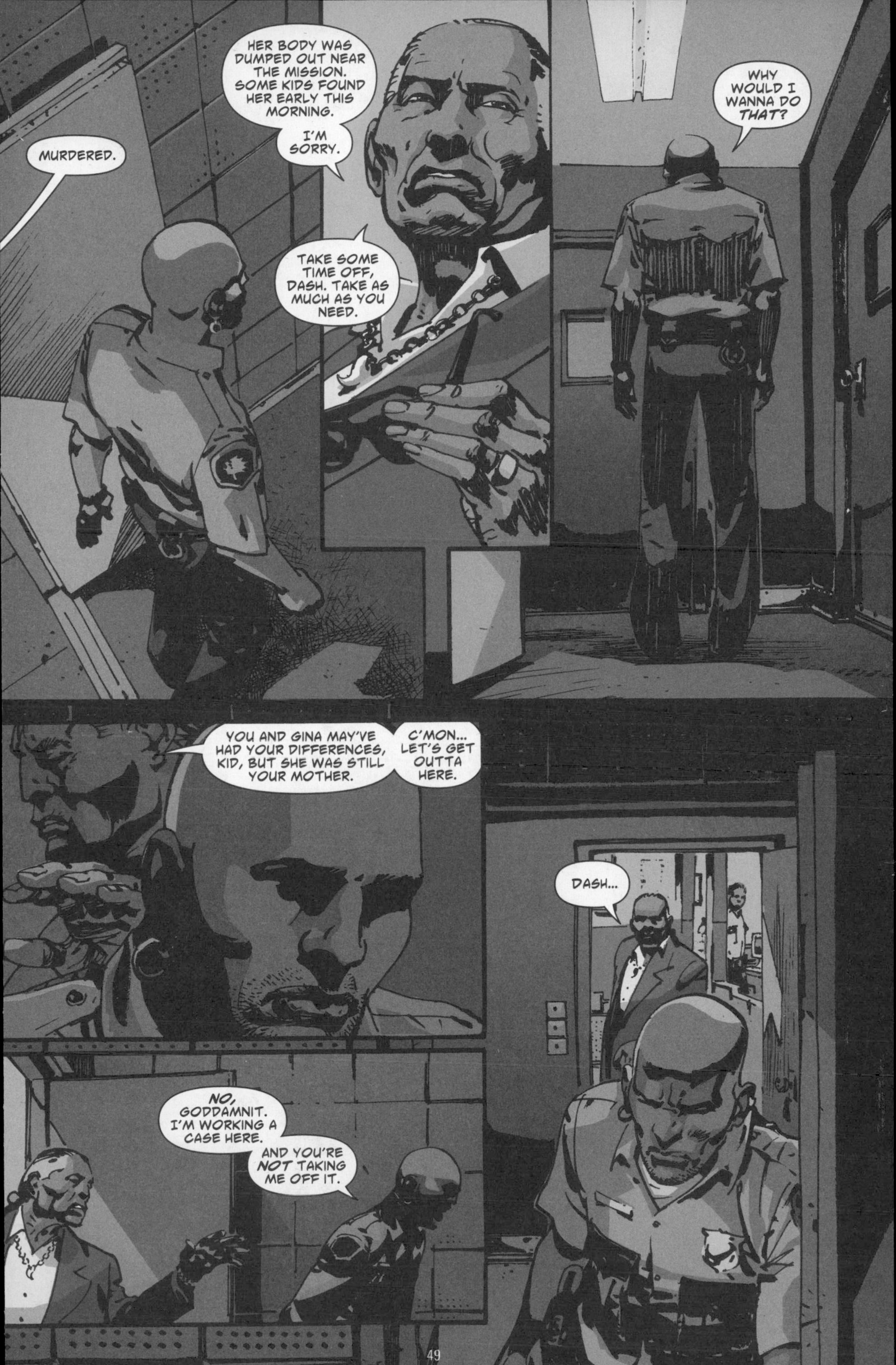
HER BODY WAS DUMPED OUT NEAR THE MISSION. SOME KIDS FOUND HER EARLY THIS MORNING.
I'M SORRY.
MURDERED.
TAKE SOME TIME OFF, DASH. TAKE AS MUCH AS YOU NEED.
WHY WOULD I WANNA DO *THAT*?
YOU AND GINA MAY'VE HAD YOUR DIFFERENCES, KID, BUT SHE WAS STILL YOUR MOTHER.
C'MON... LET'S GET OUTTA HERE.
DASH...
NO, GODDAMNIT. I'M WORKING A CASE HERE.
AND YOU'RE *NOT* TAKING ME OFF IT.

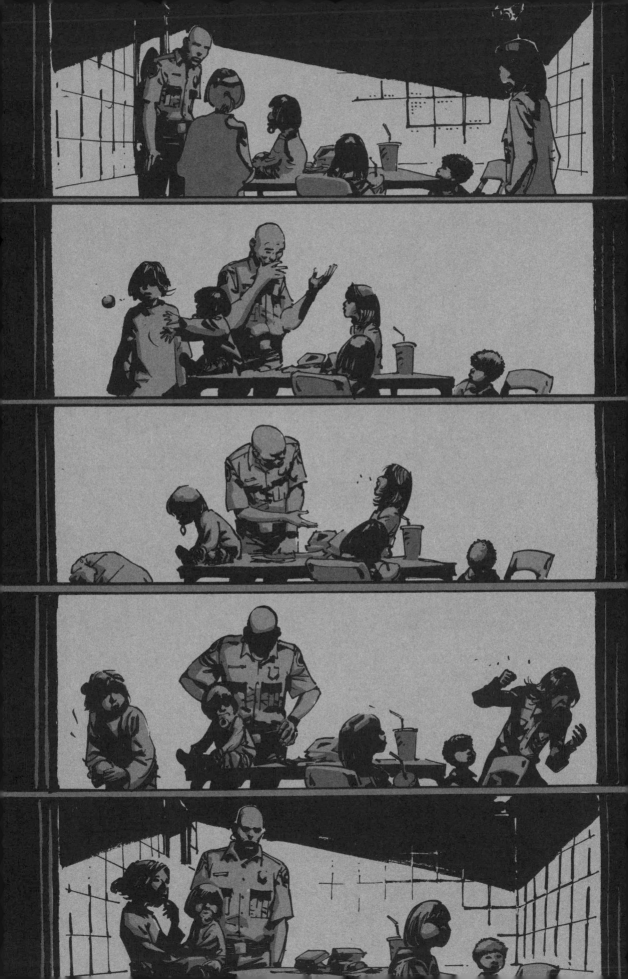

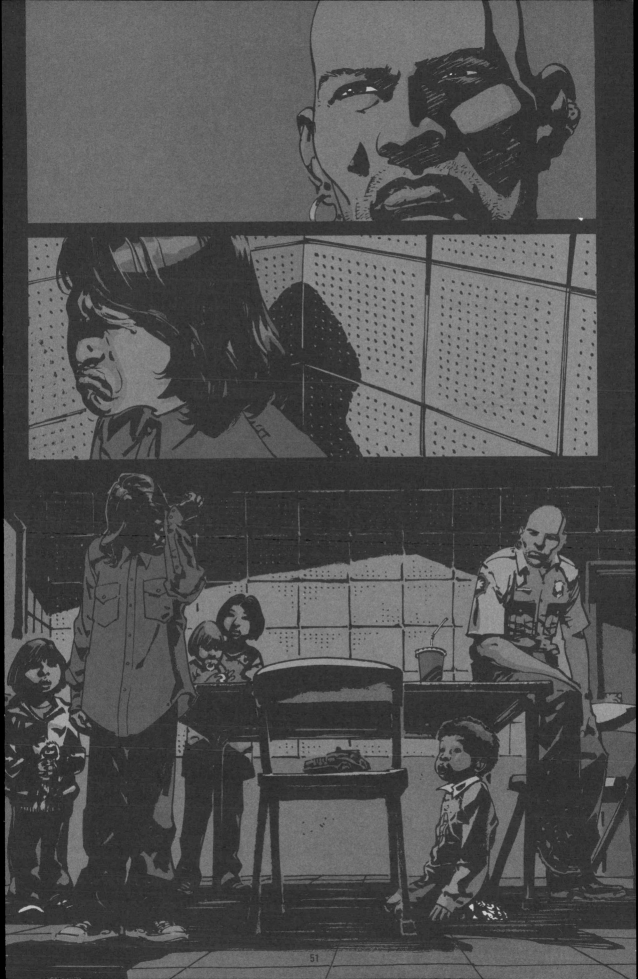

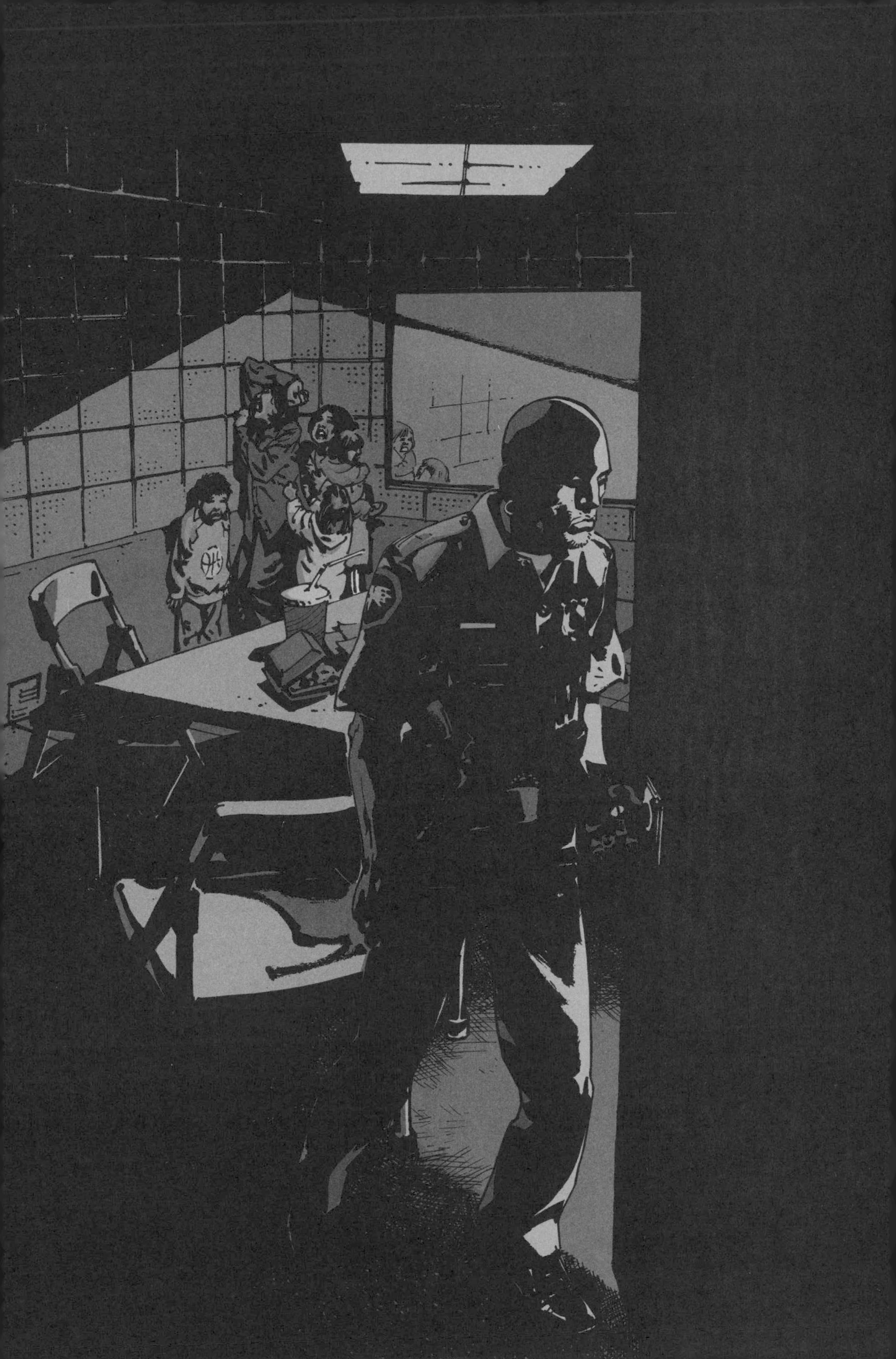

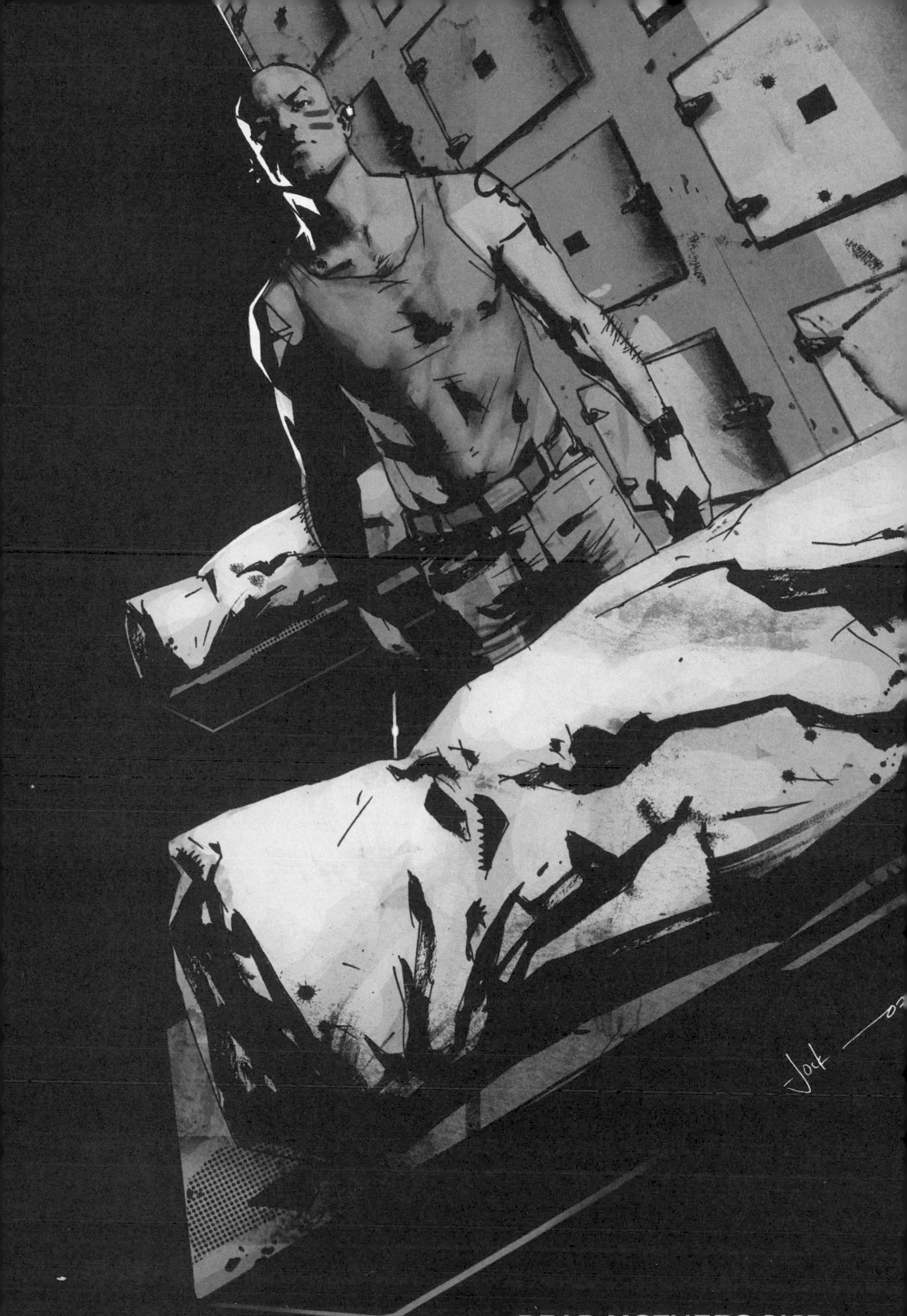

DEAD MOTHERS PART 2
COVER ART BY JOCK

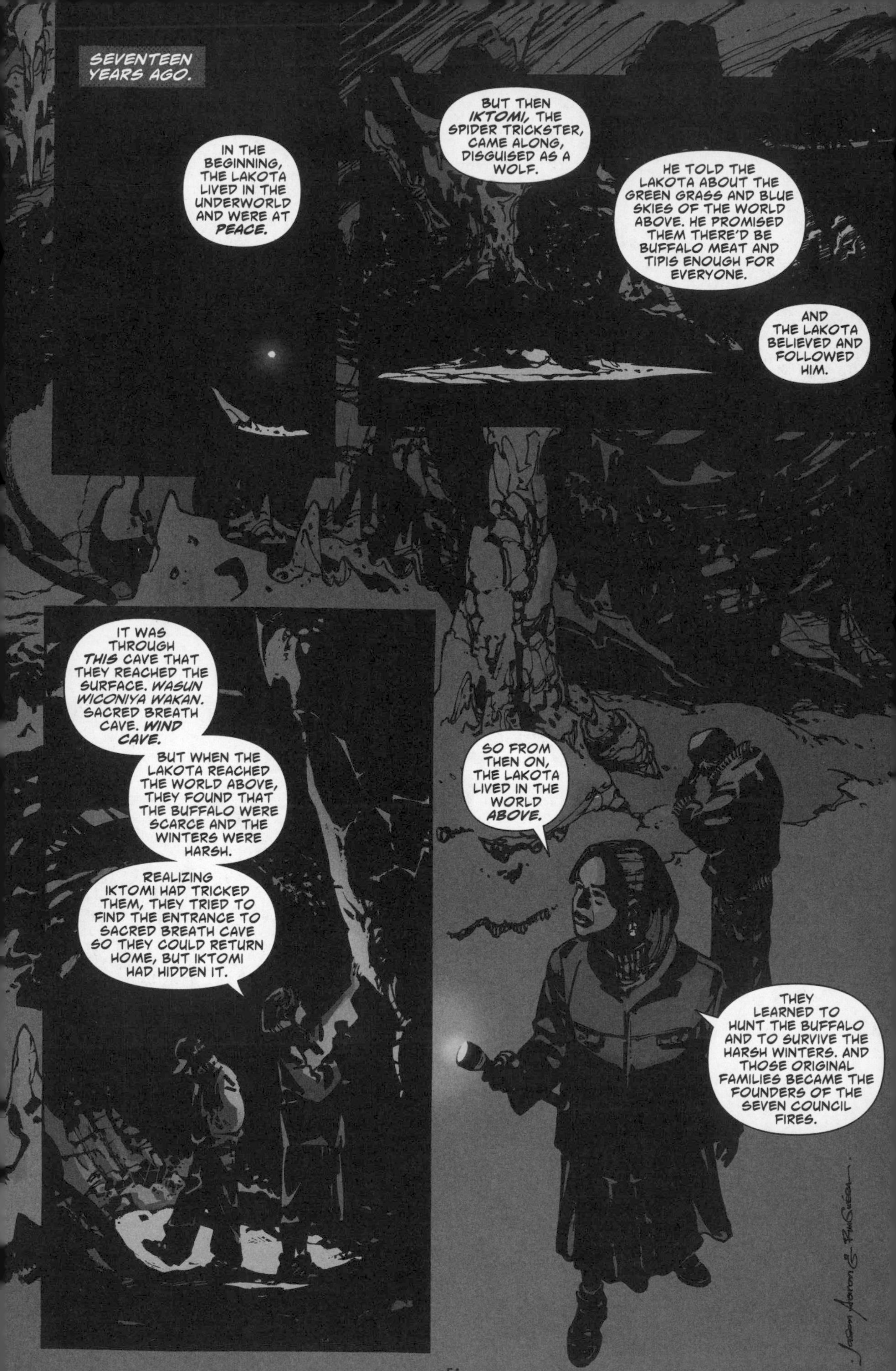
SEVENTEEN YEARS AGO.
IN THE BEGINNING, THE LAKOTA LIVED IN THE UNDERWORLD AND WERE AT PEACE.
BUT THEN IKTOMI, THE SPIDER TRICKSTER, CAME ALONG, DISGUISED AS A WOLF.
HE TOLD THE LAKOTA ABOUT THE GREEN GRASS AND BLUE SKIES OF THE WORLD ABOVE. HE PROMISED THEM THERE'D BE BUFFALO MEAT AND TIPIS ENOUGH FOR EVERYONE.
AND THE LAKOTA BELIEVED AND FOLLOWED HIM.
IT WAS THROUGH THIS CAVE THAT THEY REACHED THE SURFACE. WASUN WICONIYA WAKAN. SACRED BREATH CAVE. WIND CAVE.
BUT WHEN THE LAKOTA REACHED THE WORLD ABOVE, THEY FOUND THAT THE BUFFALO WERE SCARCE AND THE WINTERS WERE HARSH.
REALIZING IKTOMI HAD TRICKED THEM, THEY TRIED TO FIND THE ENTRANCE TO SACRED BREATH CAVE SO THEY COULD RETURN HOME, BUT IKTOMI HAD HIDDEN IT.
SO FROM THEN ON, THE LAKOTA LIVED IN THE WORLD ABOVE.
THEY LEARNED TO HUNT THE BUFFALO AND TO SURVIVE THE HARSH WINTERS. AND THOSE ORIGINAL FAMILIES BECAME THE FOUNDERS OF THE SEVEN COUNCIL FIRES.

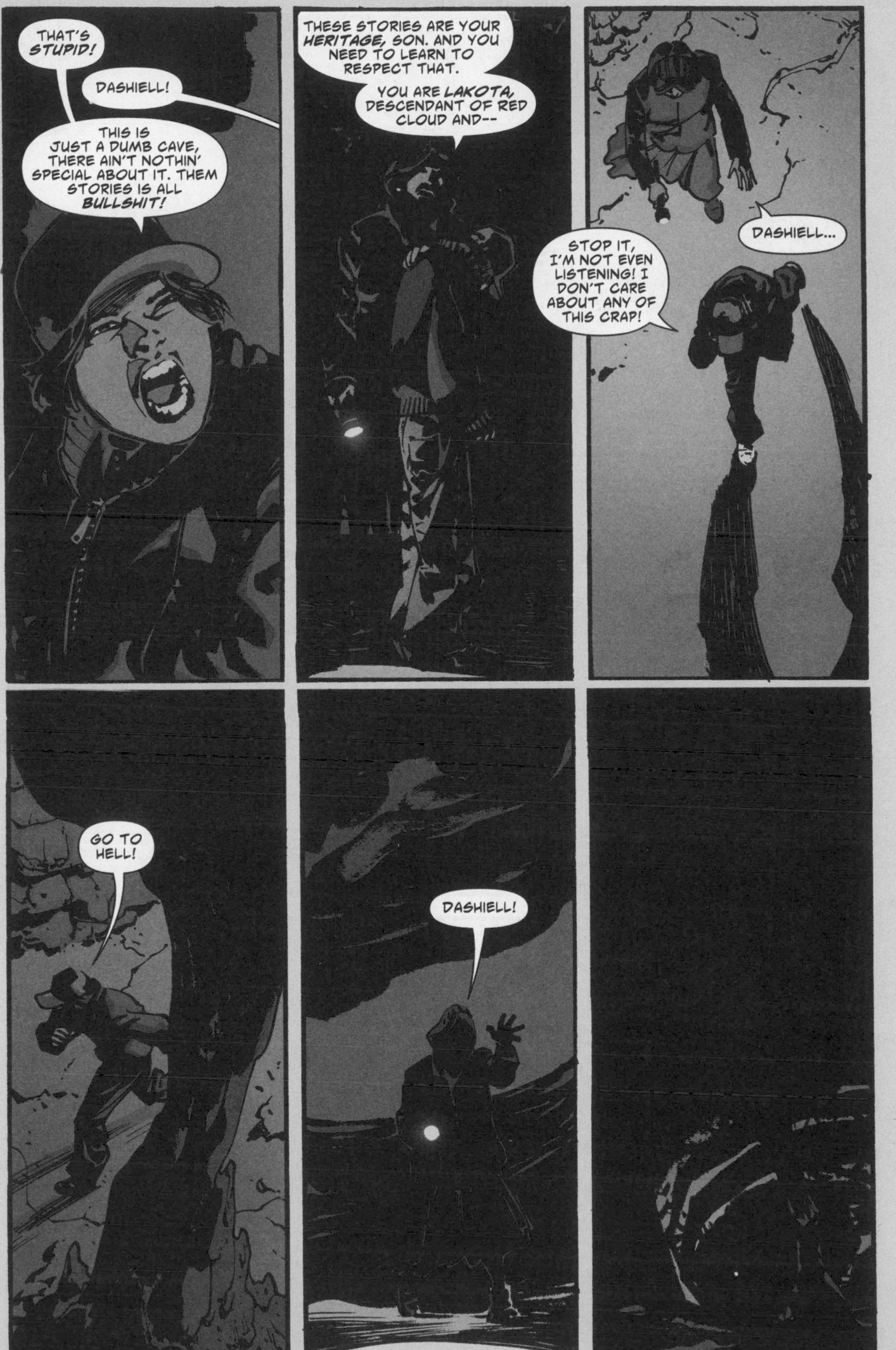
THAT'S STUPID!
DASHIELL!
THIS IS JUST A DUMB CAVE, THERE AIN'T NOTHIN' SPECIAL ABOUT IT. THEM STORIES IS ALL BULLSHIT!
THESE STORIES ARE YOUR HERITAGE, SON. AND YOU NEED TO LEARN TO RESPECT THAT.
YOU ARE LAKOTA, DESCENDANT OF RED CLOUD AND--
DASHIELL...
STOP IT, I'M NOT EVEN LISTENING! I DON'T CARE ABOUT ANY OF THIS CRAP!
GO TO HELL!
DASHIELL!

THE PRESENT.

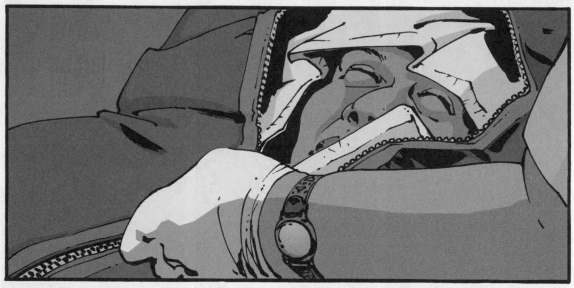

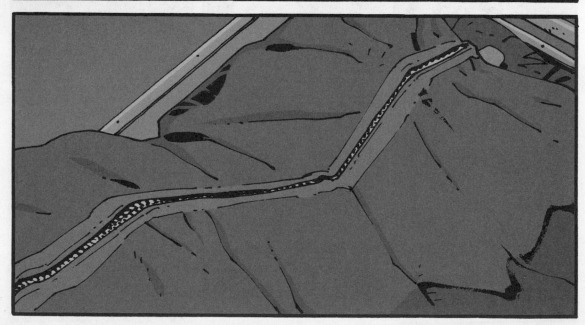

56

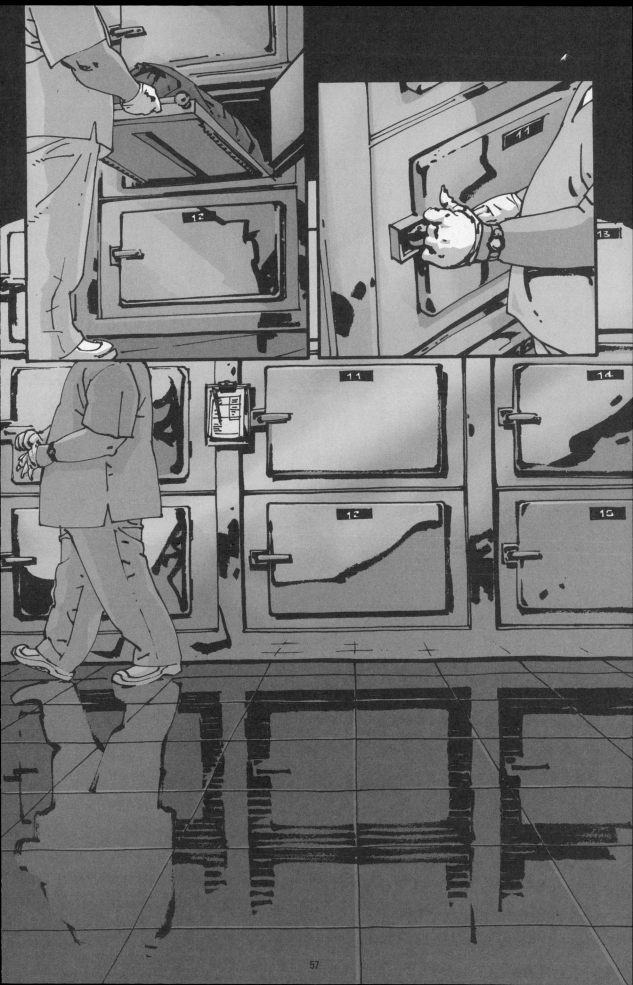

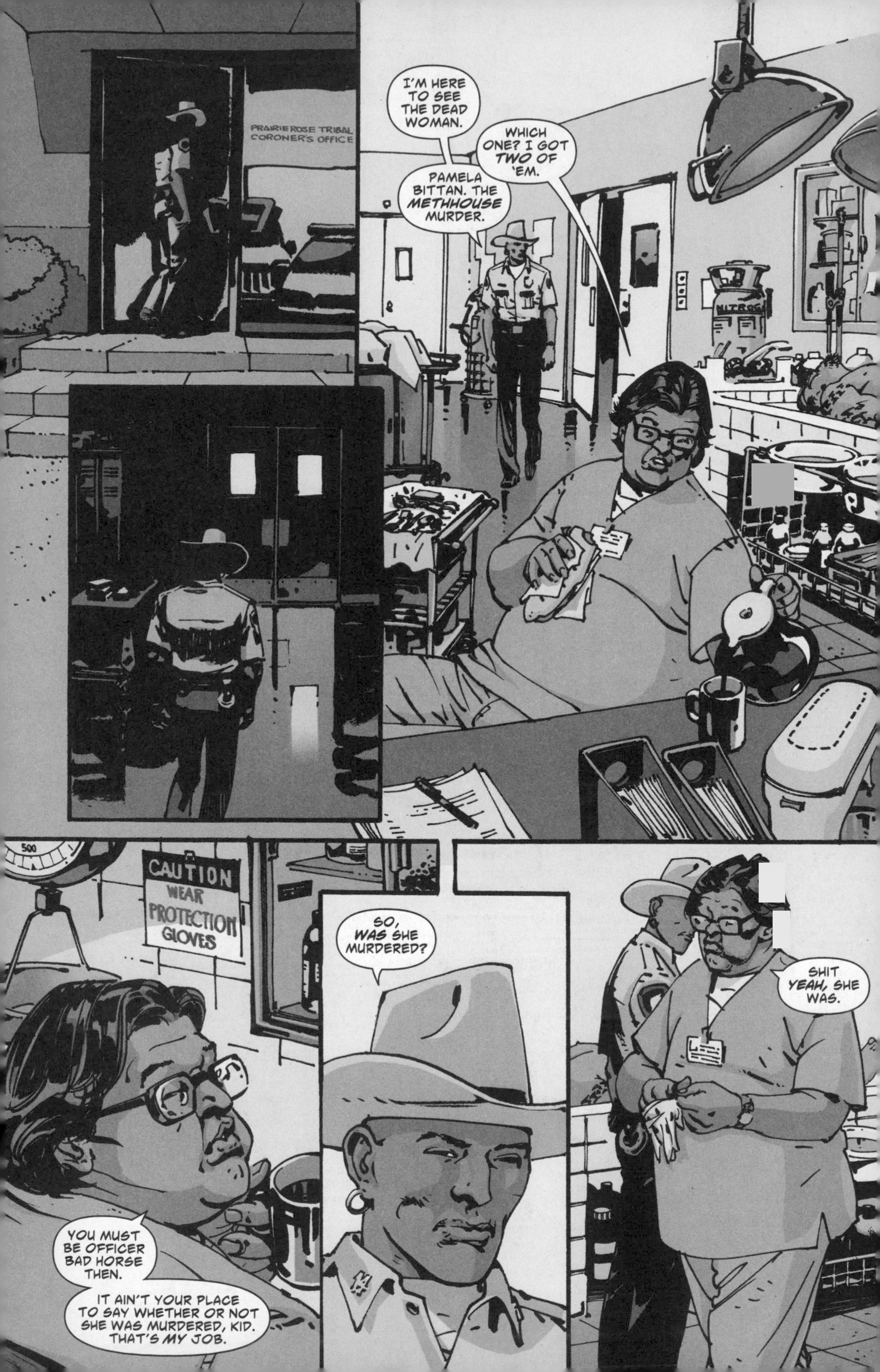
PRAIRIE ROSE TRIBAL CORONER'S OFFICE
I'M HERE TO SEE THE DEAD WOMAN.
WHICH ONE? I GOT TWO OF 'EM.
PAMELA BITTAN. THE METHHOUSE MURDER.
NITROG
500
CAUTION WEAR PROTECTION GLOVES
YOU MUST BE OFFICER BAD HORSE THEN.
IT AIN'T YOUR PLACE TO SAY WHETHER OR NOT SHE WAS MURDERED, KID. THAT'S MY JOB.
SO, WAS SHE MURDERED?
SHIT YEAH, SHE WAS.

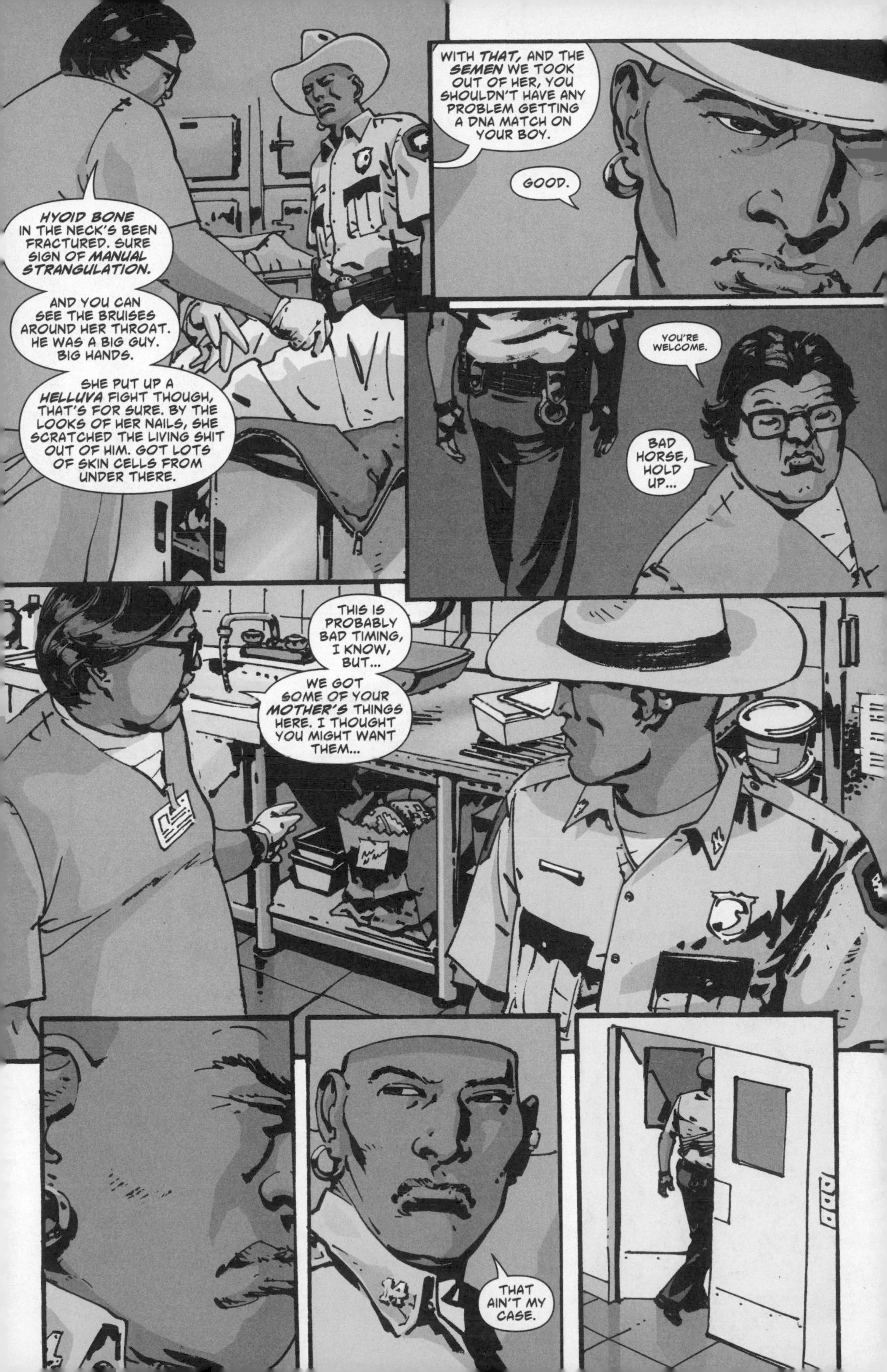
HYOID BONE IN THE NECK'S BEEN FRACTURED. SURE SIGN OF MANUAL STRANGULATION.
AND YOU CAN SEE THE BRUISES AROUND HER THROAT. HE WAS A BIG GUY. BIG HANDS.
SHE PUT UP A HELLUVA FIGHT THOUGH, THAT'S FOR SURE. BY THE LOOKS OF HER NAILS, SHE SCRATCHED THE LIVING SHIT OUT OF HIM. GOT LOTS OF SKIN CELLS FROM UNDER THERE.
WITH THAT, AND THE SEMEN WE TOOK OUT OF HER, YOU SHOULDN'T HAVE ANY PROBLEM GETTING A DNA MATCH ON YOUR BOY.
GOOD.
YOU'RE WELCOME.
BAD HORSE, HOLD UP...
THIS IS PROBABLY BAD TIMING, I KNOW, BUT...
WE GOT SOME OF YOUR MOTHER'S THINGS HERE. I THOUGHT YOU MIGHT WANT THEM...
THAT AIN'T MY CASE.

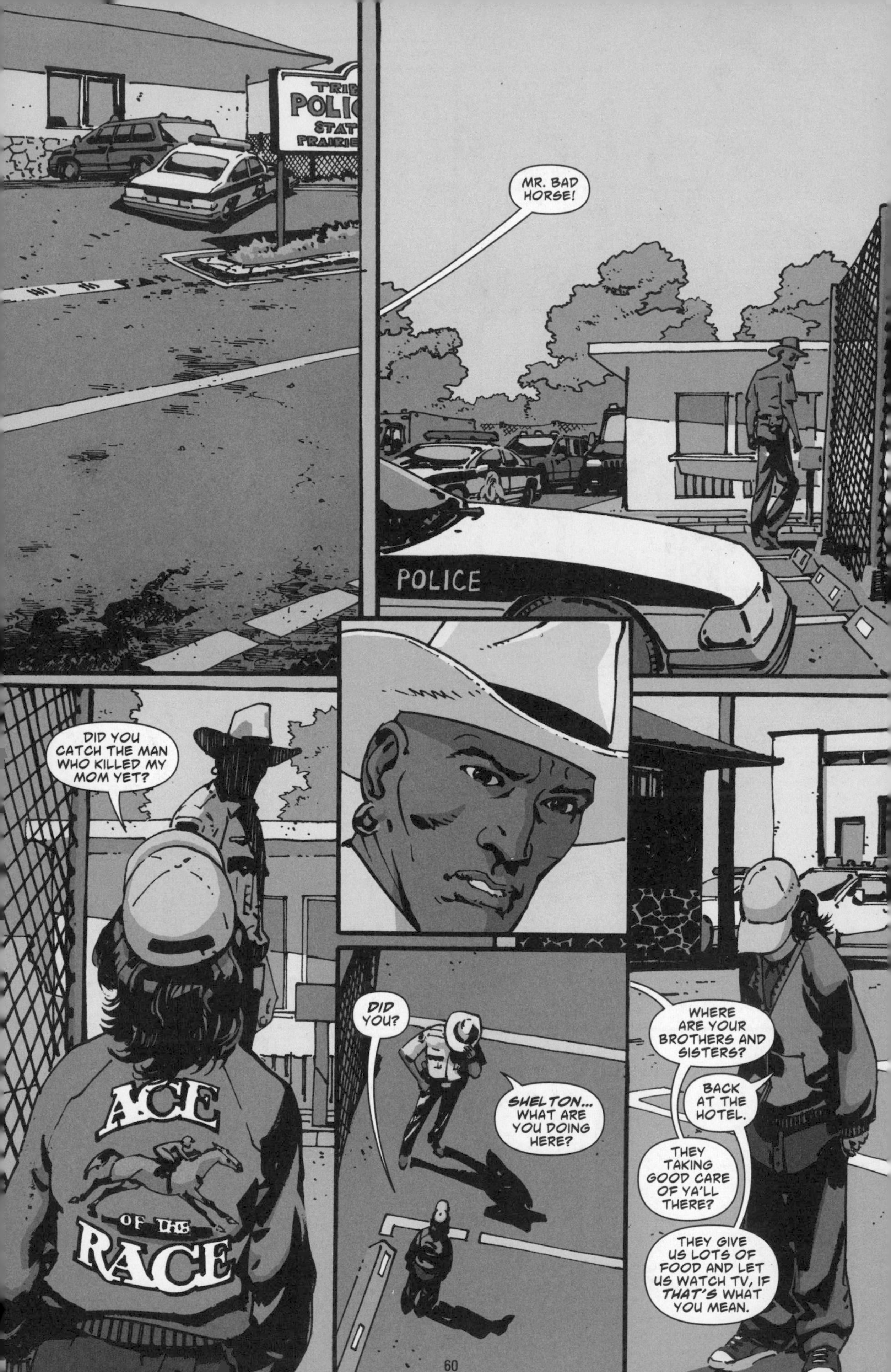
MR. BAD HORSE!
POLICE
DID YOU CATCH THE MAN WHO KILLED MY MOM YET?
ACE OF THE RACE
DID YOU?
SHELTON... WHAT ARE YOU DOING HERE?
WHERE ARE YOUR BROTHERS AND SISTERS?
BACK AT THE HOTEL.
THEY TAKING GOOD CARE OF YA'LL THERE?
THEY GIVE US LOTS OF FOOD AND LET US WATCH TV, IF *THAT'S* WHAT YOU MEAN.

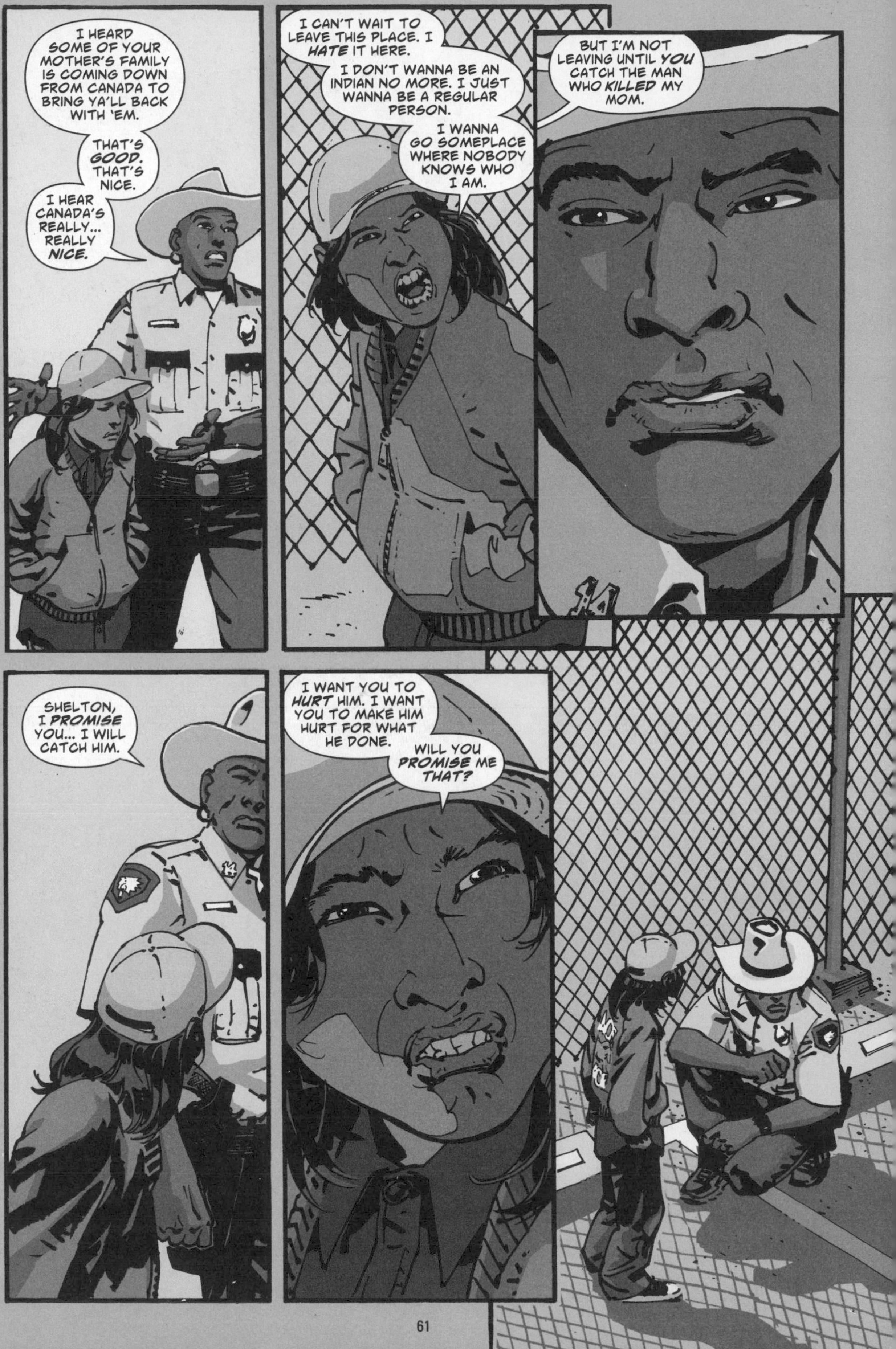
I HEARD SOME OF YOUR MOTHER'S FAMILY IS COMING DOWN FROM CANADA TO BRING YA'LL BACK WITH 'EM.
THAT'S GOOD. THAT'S NICE.
I HEAR CANADA'S REALLY... REALLY NICE.
I CAN'T WAIT TO LEAVE THIS PLACE. I HATE IT HERE.
I DON'T WANNA BE AN INDIAN NO MORE. I JUST WANNA BE A REGULAR PERSON.
I WANNA GO SOMEPLACE WHERE NOBODY KNOWS WHO I AM.
BUT I'M NOT LEAVING UNTIL YOU CATCH THE MAN WHO KILLED MY MOM.
SHELTON, I PROMISE YOU... I WILL CATCH HIM.
I WANT YOU TO HURT HIM. I WANT YOU TO MAKE HIM HURT FOR WHAT HE DONE.
WILL YOU PROMISE ME THAT?

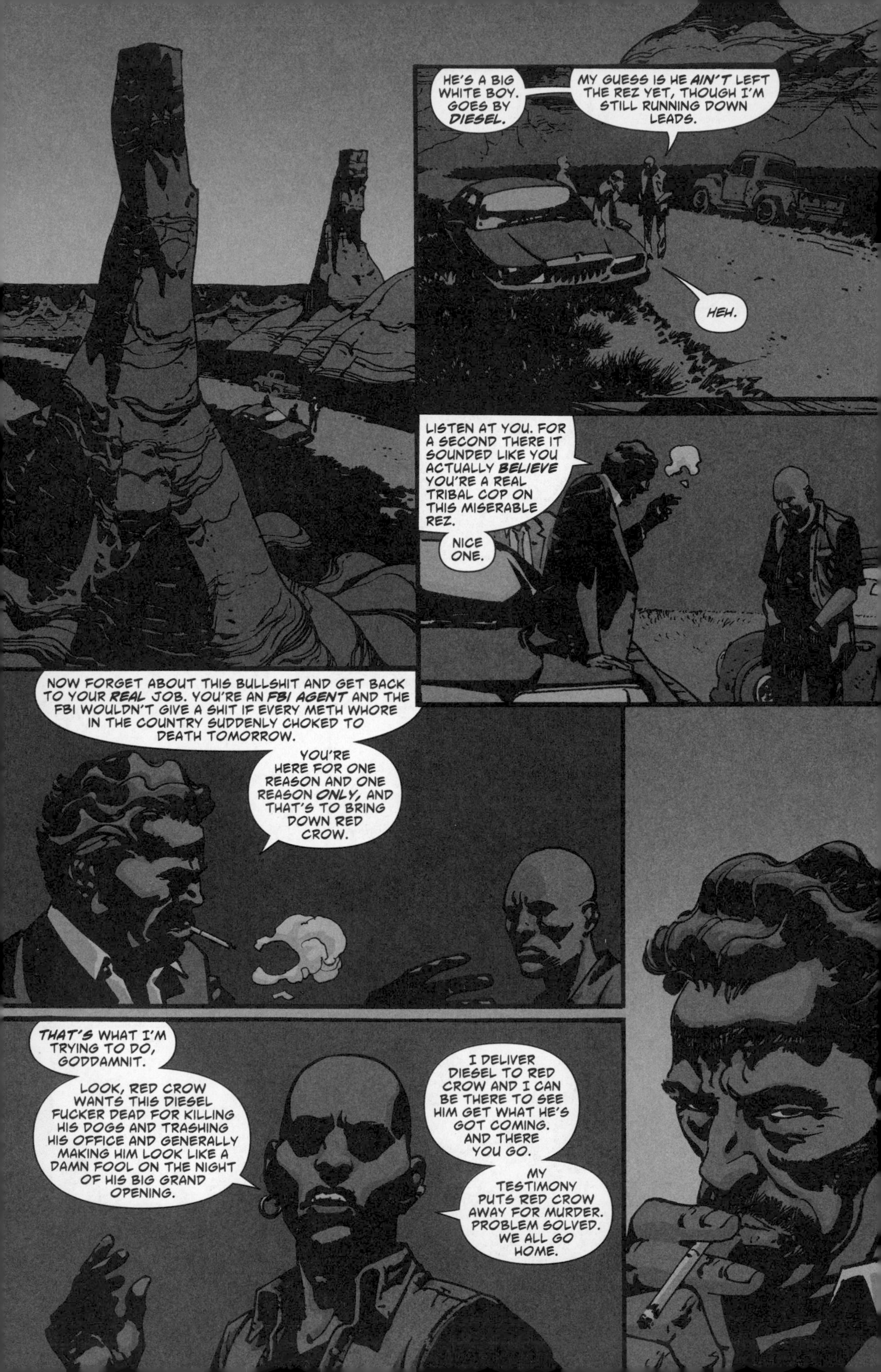
HE'S A BIG WHITE BOY. GOES BY DIESEL.
MY GUESS IS HE AIN'T LEFT THE REZ YET, THOUGH I'M STILL RUNNING DOWN LEADS.
HEH.
LISTEN AT YOU. FOR A SECOND THERE IT SOUNDED LIKE YOU ACTUALLY BELIEVE YOU'RE A REAL TRIBAL COP ON THIS MISERABLE REZ.
NICE ONE.
NOW FORGET ABOUT THIS BULLSHIT AND GET BACK TO YOUR REAL JOB. YOU'RE AN FBI AGENT AND THE FBI WOULDN'T GIVE A SHIT IF EVERY METH WHORE IN THE COUNTRY SUDDENLY CHOKED TO DEATH TOMORROW.
YOU'RE HERE FOR ONE REASON AND ONE REASON ONLY, AND THAT'S TO BRING DOWN RED CROW.
THAT'S WHAT I'M TRYING TO DO, GODDAMNIT.
LOOK, RED CROW WANTS THIS DIESEL FUCKER DEAD FOR KILLING HIS DOGS AND TRASHING HIS OFFICE AND GENERALLY MAKING HIM LOOK LIKE A DAMN FOOL ON THE NIGHT OF HIS BIG GRAND OPENING.
I DELIVER DIESEL TO RED CROW AND I CAN BE THERE TO SEE HIM GET WHAT HE'S GOT COMING. AND THERE YOU GO.
MY TESTIMONY PUTS RED CROW AWAY FOR MURDER. PROBLEM SOLVED. WE ALL GO HOME.

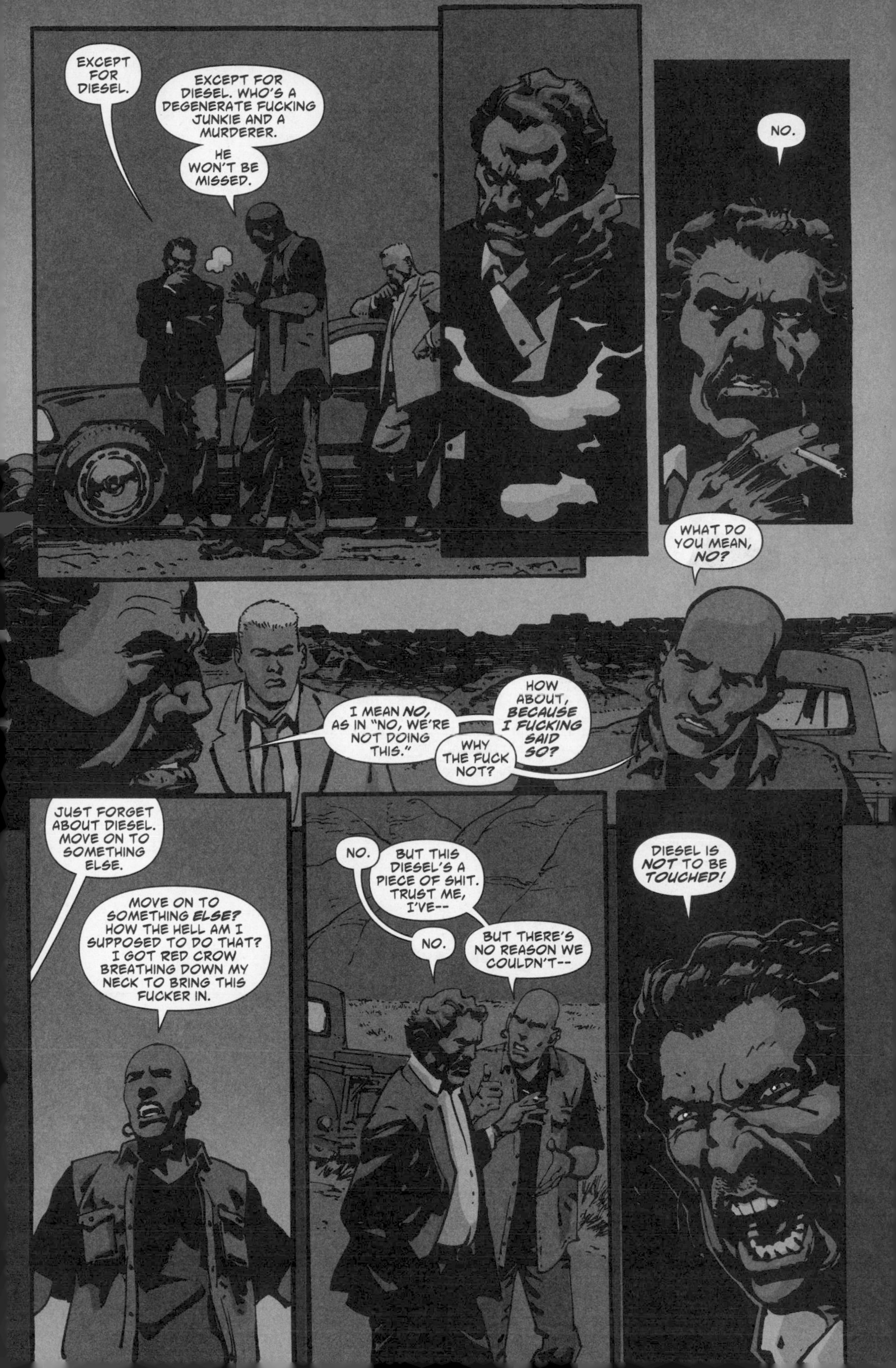
EXCEPT FOR DIESEL.
EXCEPT FOR DIESEL. WHO'S A DEGENERATE FUCKING JUNKIE AND A MURDERER.
HE WON'T BE MISSED.
NO.
WHAT DO YOU MEAN, NO?
I MEAN NO, AS IN "NO, WE'RE NOT DOING THIS."
WHY THE FUCK NOT?
HOW ABOUT, BECAUSE I FUCKING SAID SO?
JUST FORGET ABOUT DIESEL. MOVE ON TO SOMETHING ELSE.
MOVE ON TO SOMETHING ELSE? HOW THE HELL AM I SUPPOSED TO DO THAT? I GOT RED CROW BREATHING DOWN MY NECK TO BRING THIS FUCKER IN.
BUT THIS DIESEL'S A PIECE OF SHIT. TRUST ME, I'VE--
NO.
BUT THERE'S NO REASON WE COULDN'T--
NO.
DIESEL IS NOT TO BE TOUCHED!

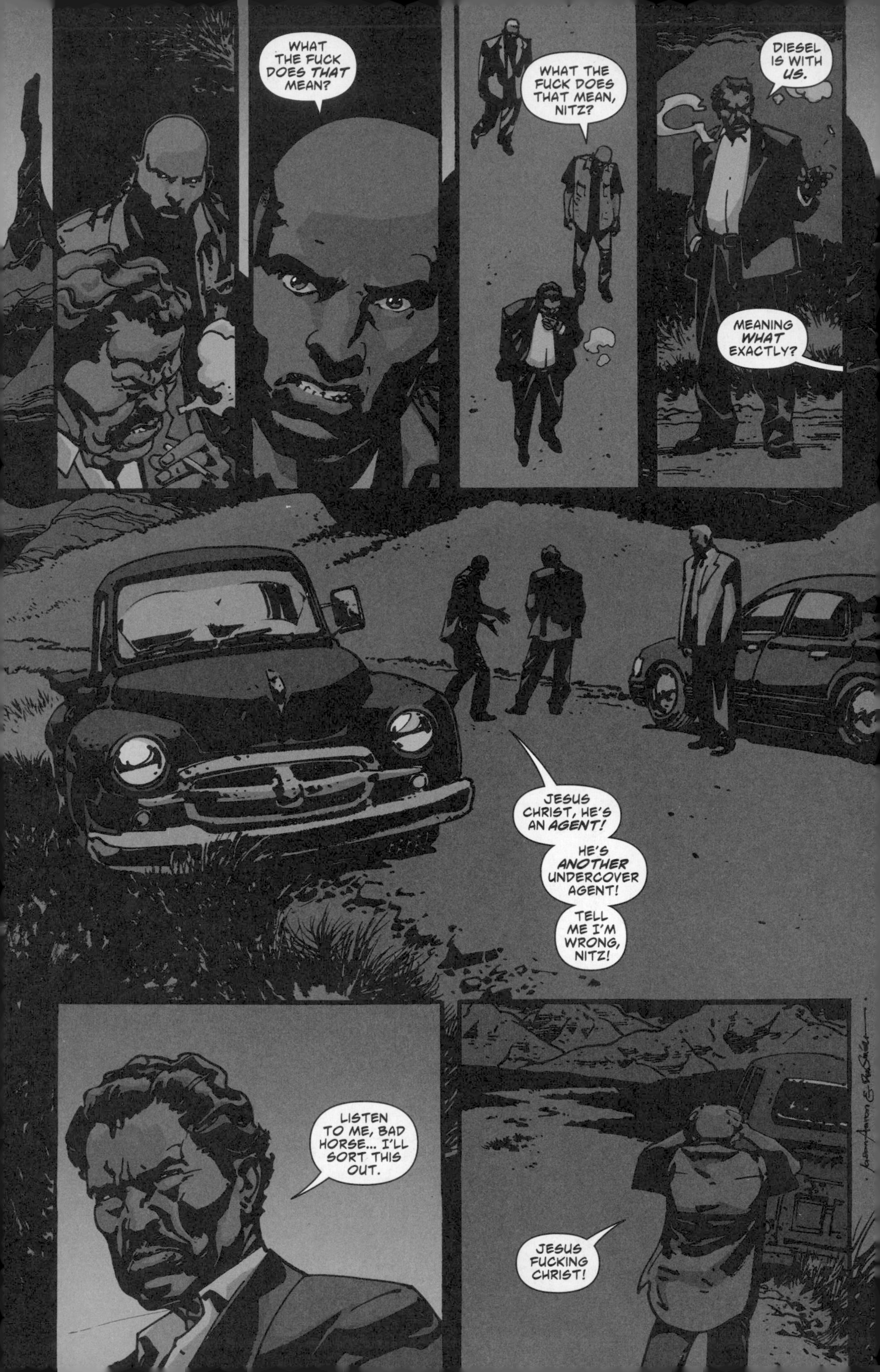
WHAT THE FUCK DOES THAT MEAN?
WHAT THE FUCK DOES THAT MEAN, NITZ?
DIESEL IS WITH US.
MEANING WHAT EXACTLY?
JESUS CHRIST, HE'S AN AGENT!
HE'S ANOTHER UNDERCOVER AGENT!
TELL ME I'M WRONG, NITZ!
LISTEN TO ME, BAD HORSE... I'LL SORT THIS OUT.
JESUS FUCKING CHRIST!

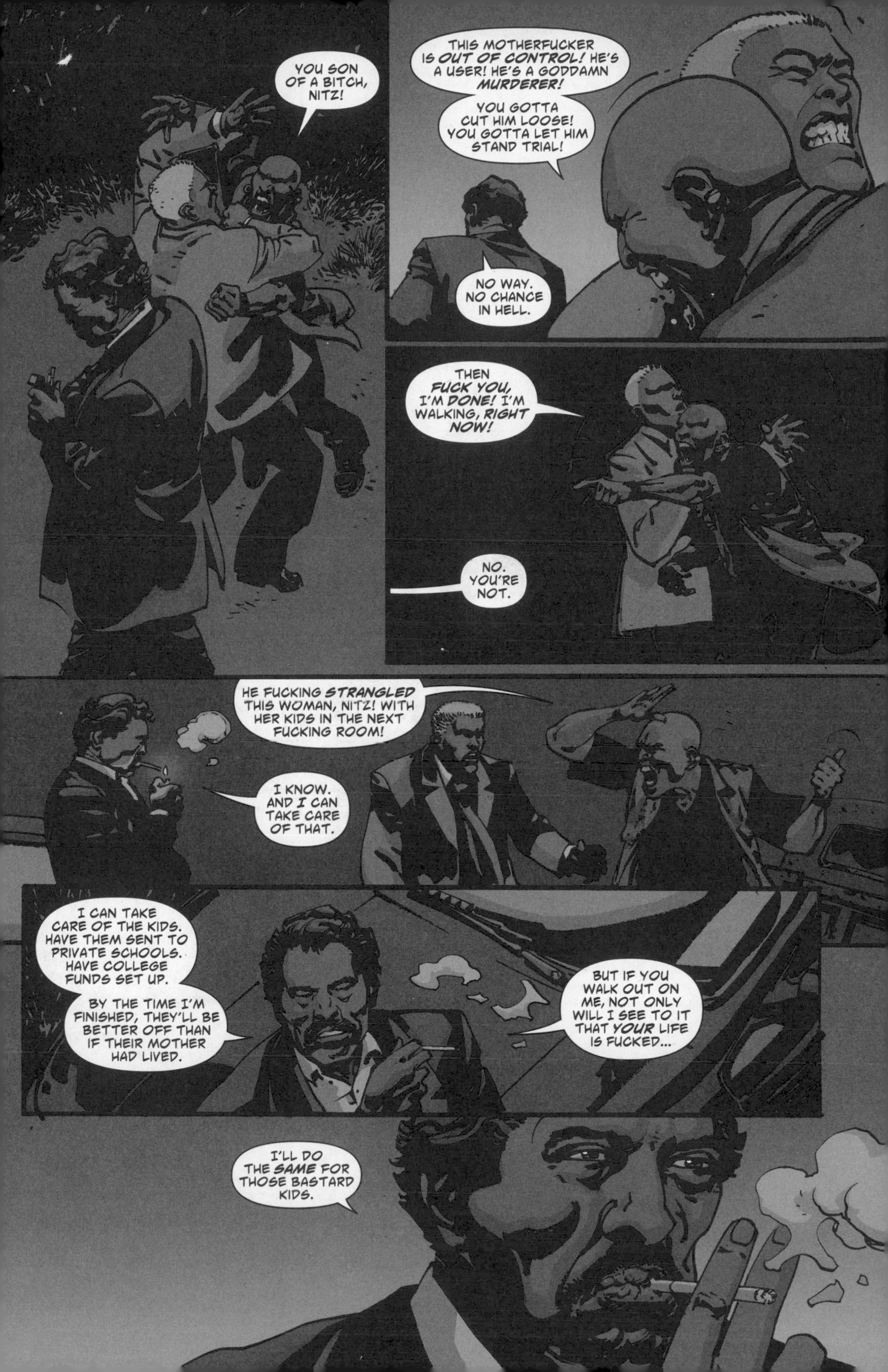
YOU SON OF A BITCH, NITZ!
THIS MOTHERFUCKER IS OUT OF CONTROL! HE'S A USER! HE'S A GODDAMN MURDERER!
YOU GOTTA CUT HIM LOOSE! YOU GOTTA LET HIM STAND TRIAL!
NO WAY. NO CHANCE IN HELL.
THEN FUCK YOU, I'M DONE! I'M WALKING, RIGHT NOW!
NO. YOU'RE NOT.
HE FUCKING STRANGLED THIS WOMAN, NITZ! WITH HER KIDS IN THE NEXT FUCKING ROOM!
I KNOW. AND I CAN TAKE CARE OF THAT.
I CAN TAKE CARE OF THE KIDS. HAVE THEM SENT TO PRIVATE SCHOOLS. HAVE COLLEGE FUNDS SET UP.
BY THE TIME I'M FINISHED, THEY'LL BE BETTER OFF THAN IF THEIR MOTHER HAD LIVED.
BUT IF YOU WALK OUT ON ME, NOT ONLY WILL I SEE TO IT THAT YOUR LIFE IS FUCKED...
I'LL DO THE SAME FOR THOSE BASTARD KIDS.

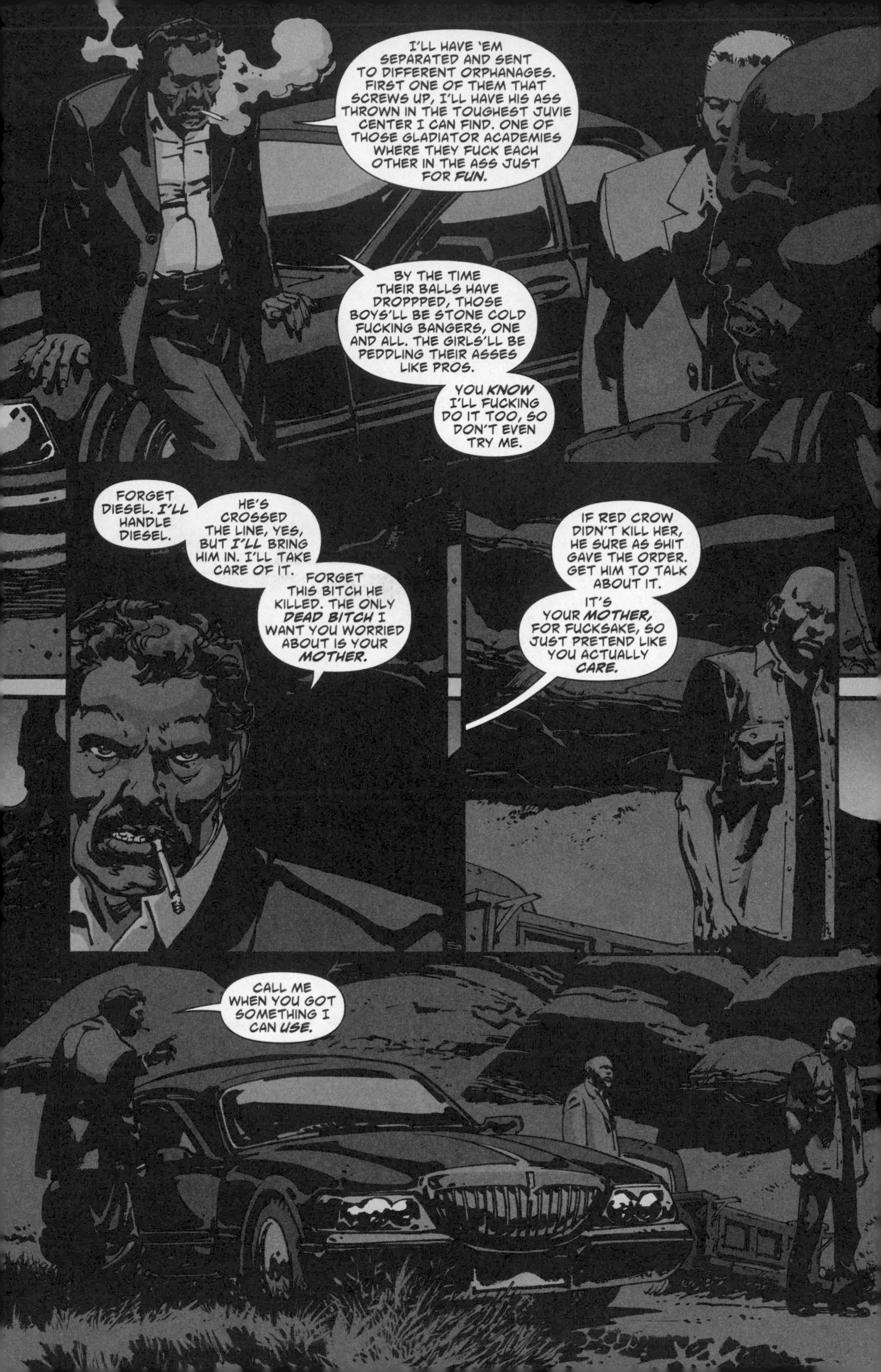
I'LL HAVE 'EM SEPARATED AND SENT TO DIFFERENT ORPHANAGES. FIRST ONE OF THEM THAT SCREWS UP, I'LL HAVE HIS ASS THROWN IN THE TOUGHEST JUVIE CENTER I CAN FIND. ONE OF THOSE GLADIATOR ACADEMIES WHERE THEY FUCK EACH OTHER IN THE ASS JUST FOR FUN.
BY THE TIME THEIR BALLS HAVE DROPPPED, THOSE BOYS'LL BE STONE COLD FUCKING BANGERS, ONE AND ALL. THE GIRLS'LL BE PEDDLING THEIR ASSES LIKE PROS.
YOU KNOW I'LL FUCKING DO IT TOO, SO DON'T EVEN TRY ME.
FORGET DIESEL. I'LL HANDLE DIESEL.
HE'S CROSSED THE LINE, YES, BUT I'LL BRING HIM IN. I'LL TAKE CARE OF IT.
FORGET THIS BITCH HE KILLED. THE ONLY DEAD BITCH I WANT YOU WORRIED ABOUT IS YOUR MOTHER.
IF RED CROW DIDN'T KILL HER, HE SURE AS SHIT GAVE THE ORDER. GET HIM TO TALK ABOUT IT.
IT'S YOUR MOTHER, FOR FUCKSAKE, SO JUST PRETEND LIKE YOU ACTUALLY CARE.
CALL ME WHEN YOU GOT SOMETHING I CAN USE.

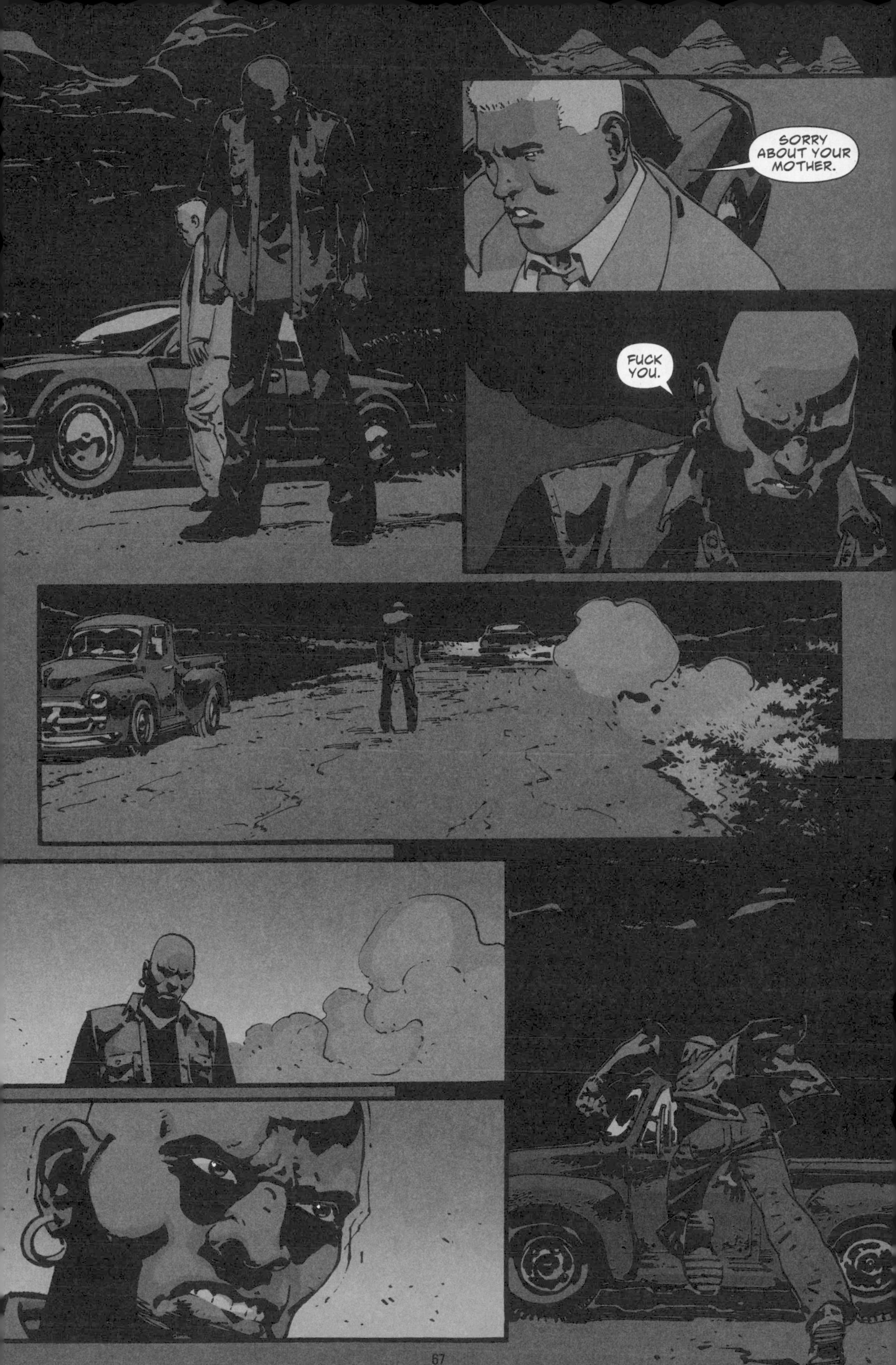
SORRY ABOUT YOUR MOTHER.
FUCK YOU.

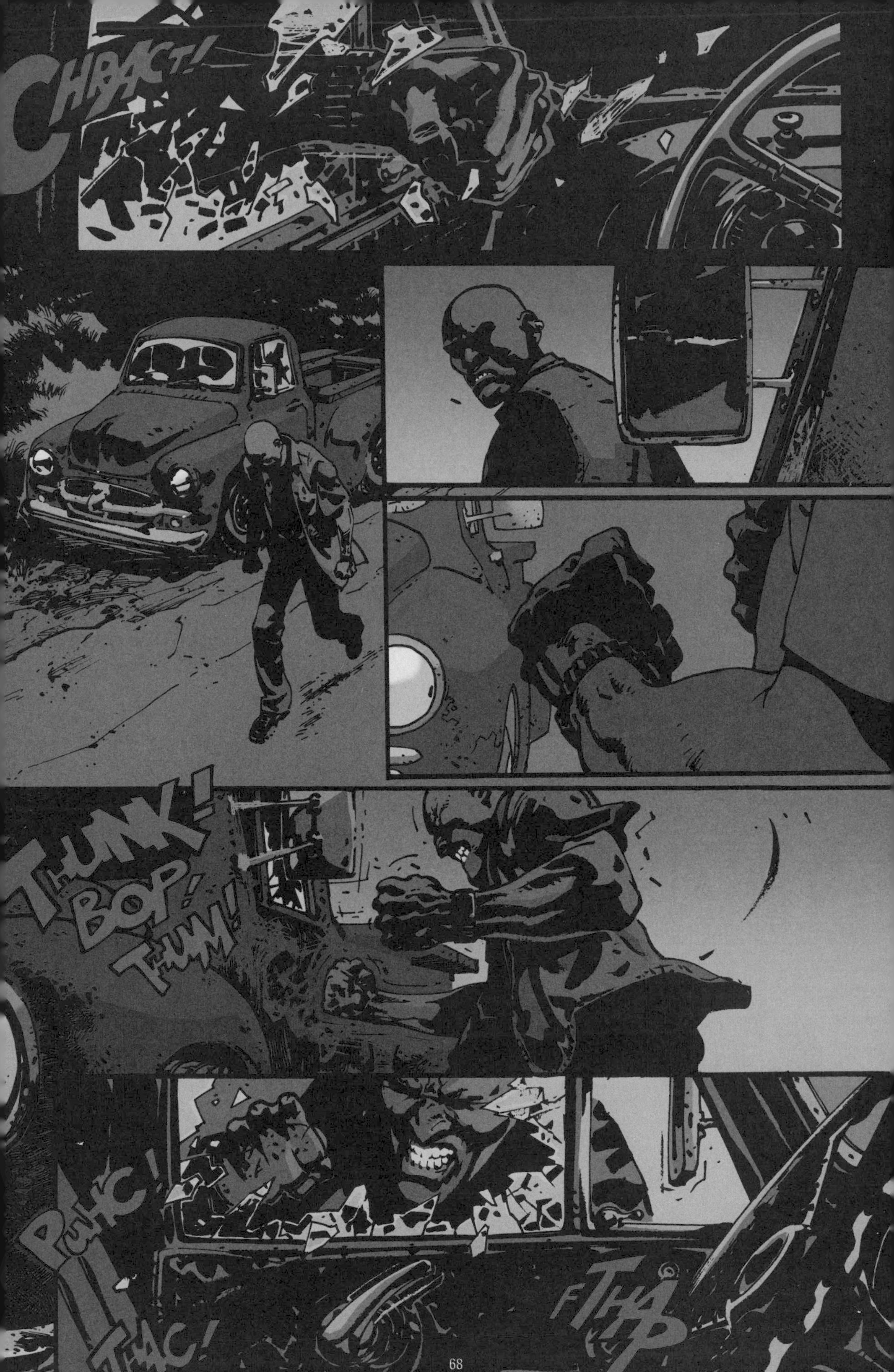
CHRACT!
THUNK!
BOP!
THUM!
PUHC!
THAC!
FTHAP

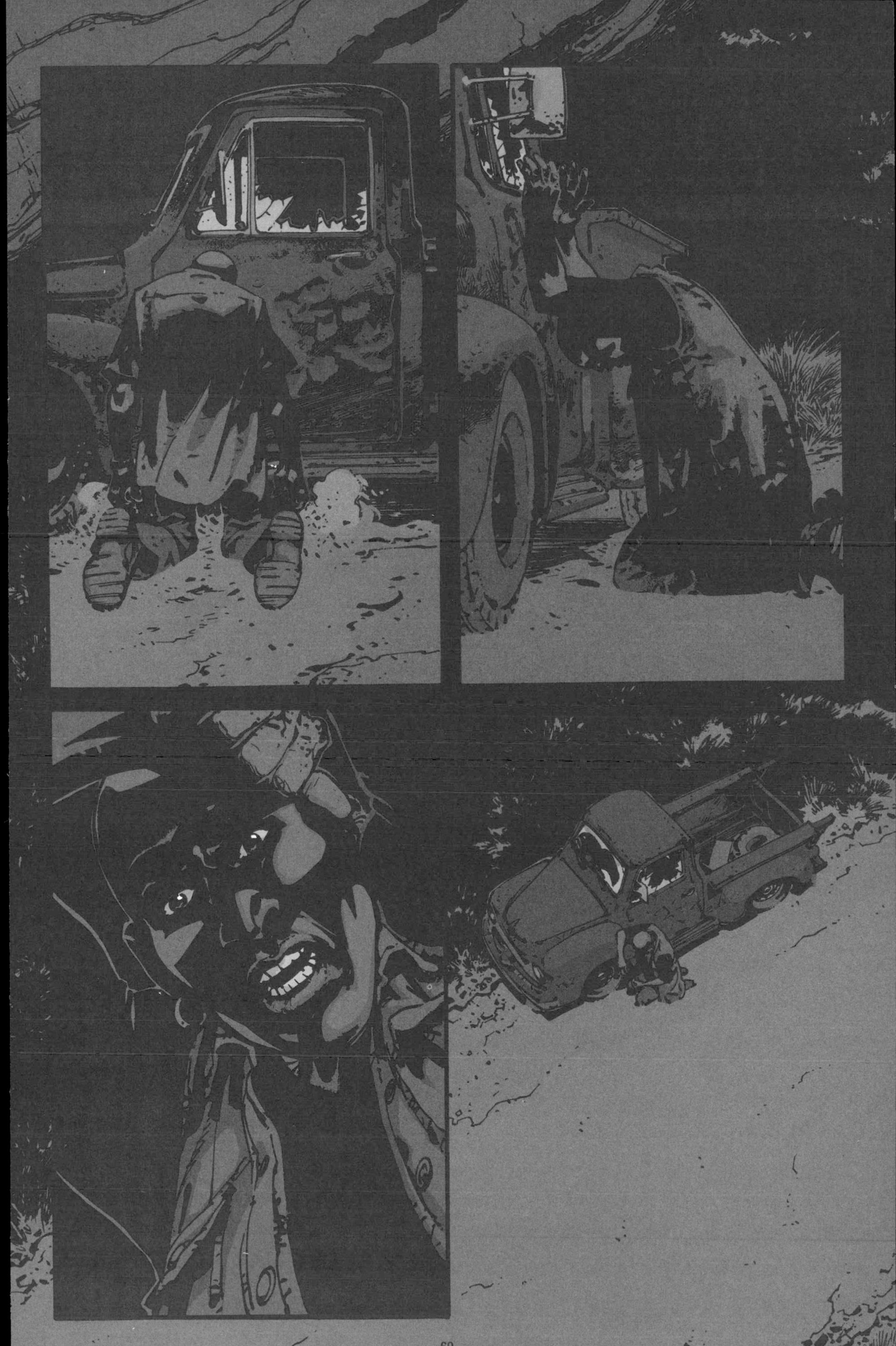

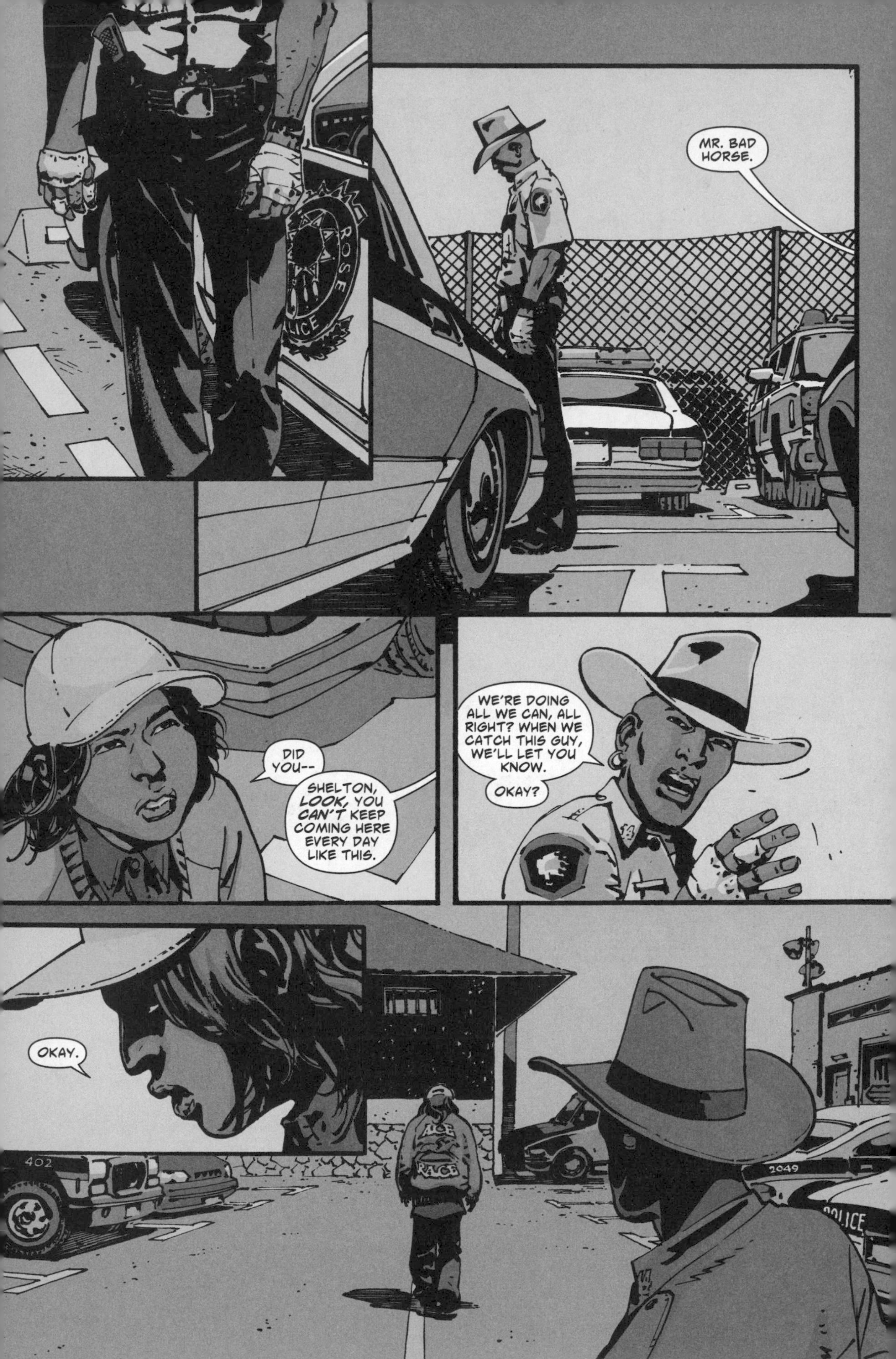
ROSE
POLICE
MR. BAD HORSE.
DID YOU--
SHELTON, LOOK, YOU CAN'T KEEP COMING HERE EVERY DAY LIKE THIS.
WE'RE DOING ALL WE CAN, ALL RIGHT? WHEN WE CATCH THIS GUY, WE'LL LET YOU KNOW.
OKAY?
OKAY.
402
RACE
RACE
2049
POLICE

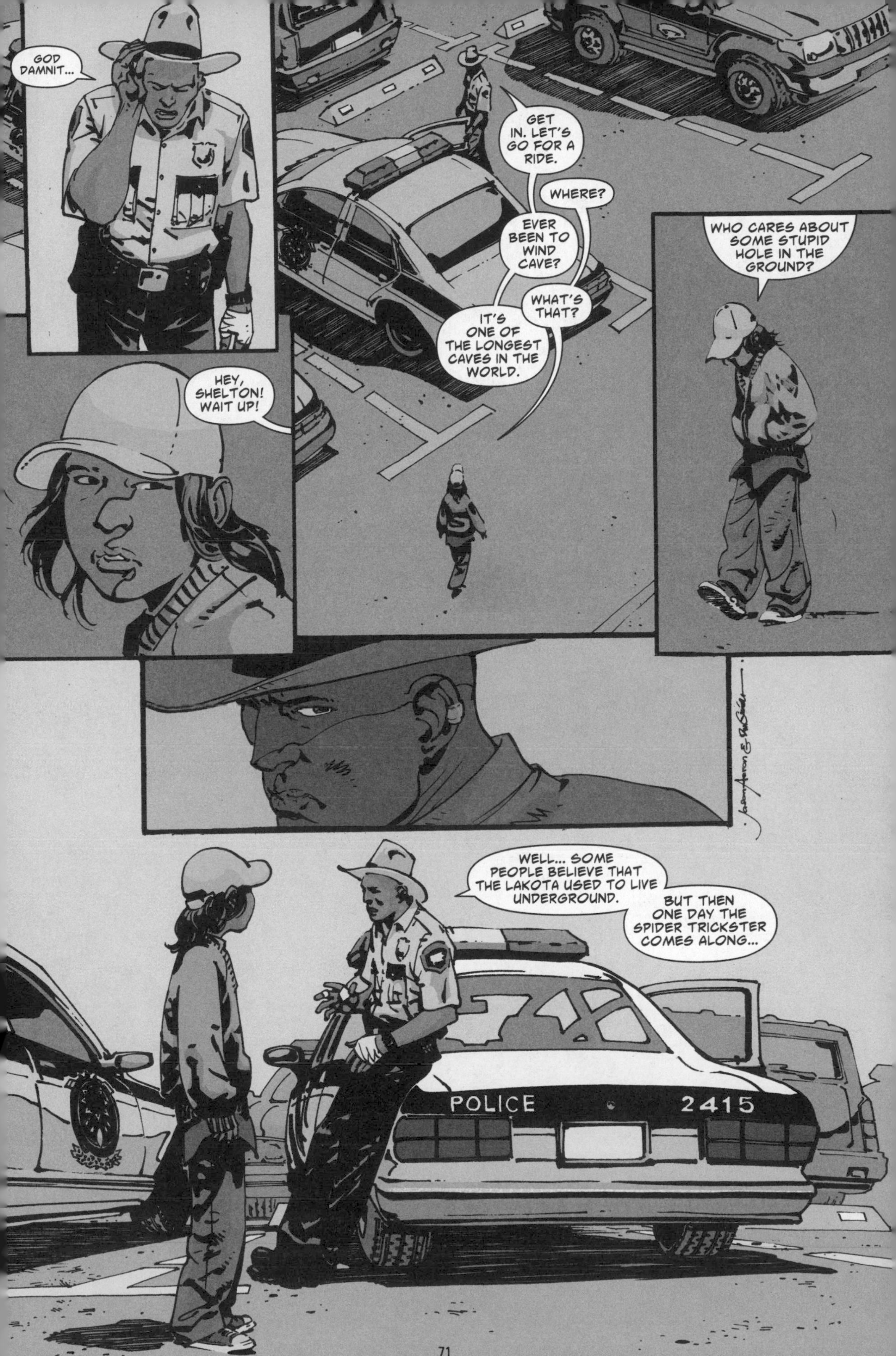
GOD DAMNIT...
GET IN. LET'S GO FOR A RIDE.
WHERE?
EVER BEEN TO WIND CAVE?
WHAT'S THAT?
IT'S ONE OF THE LONGEST CAVES IN THE WORLD.
HEY, SHELTON! WAIT UP!
WHO CARES ABOUT SOME STUPID HOLE IN THE GROUND?
WELL... SOME PEOPLE BELIEVE THAT THE LAKOTA USED TO LIVE UNDERGROUND.
BUT THEN ONE DAY THE SPIDER TRICKSTER COMES ALONG...
POLICE 2415

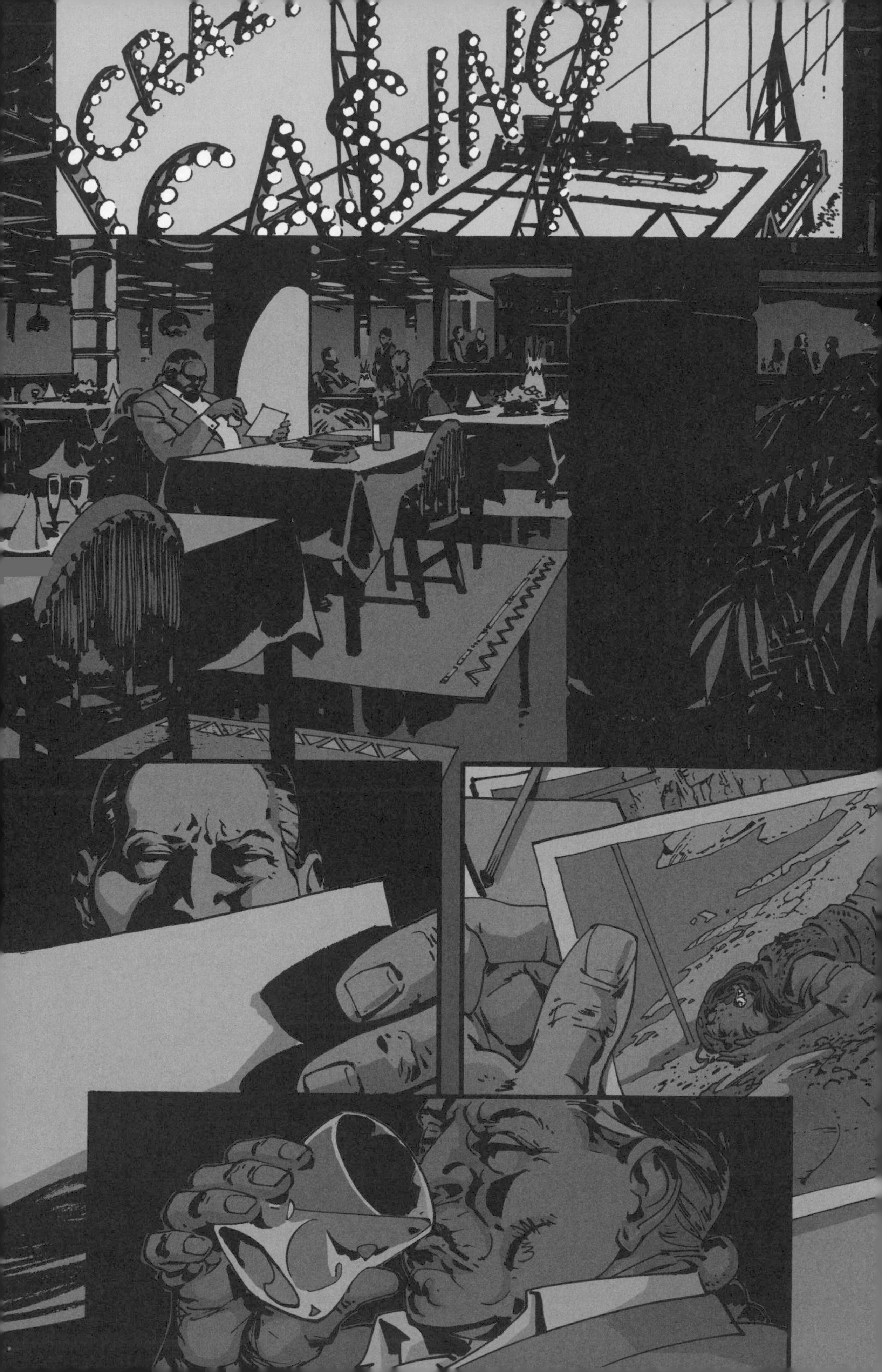
CASINO

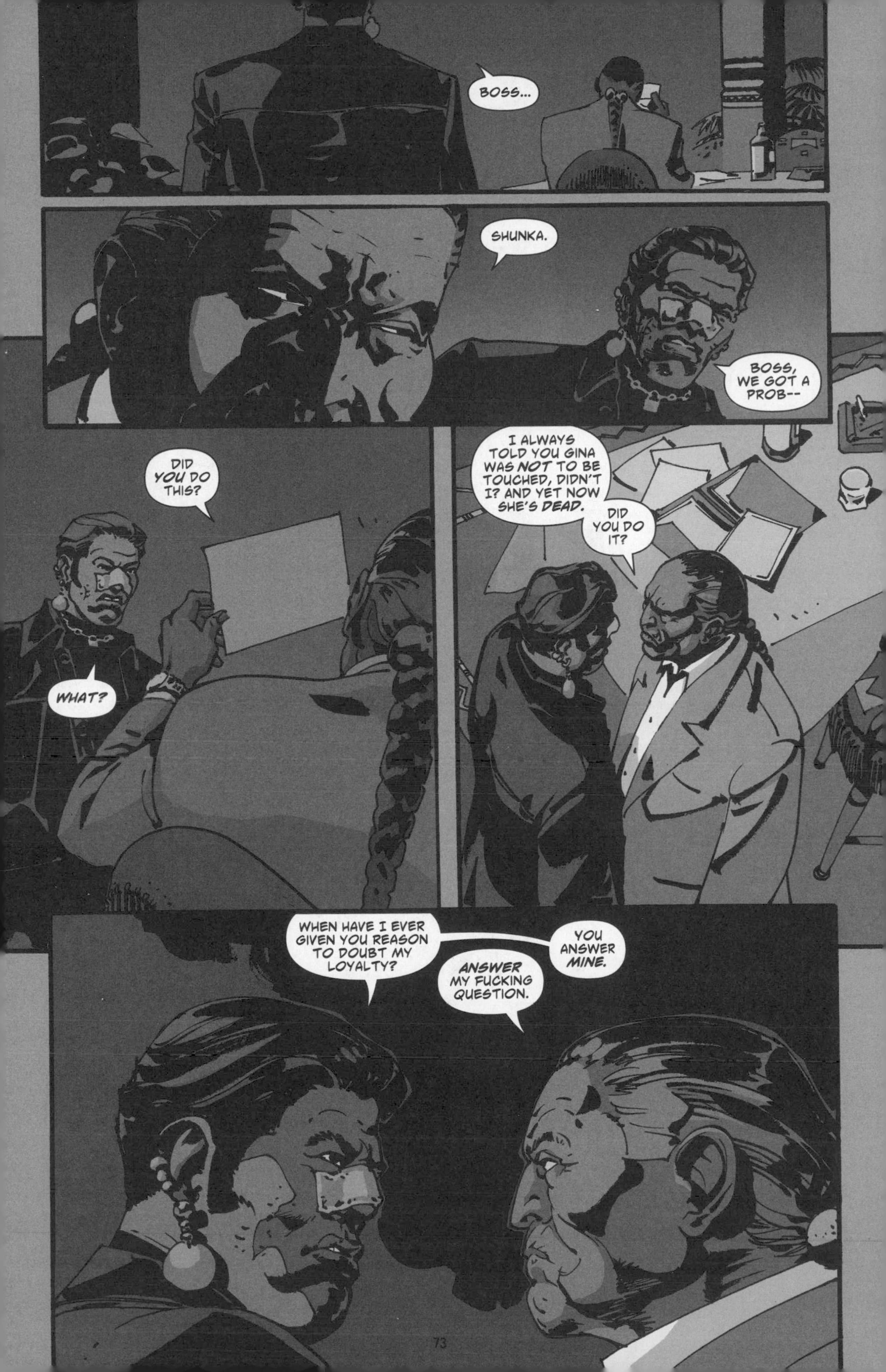
BOSS...
SHUNKA.
BOSS, WE GOT A PROB--
DID YOU DO THIS?
WHAT?
I ALWAYS TOLD YOU GINA WAS NOT TO BE TOUCHED, DIDN'T I? AND YET NOW SHE'S DEAD.
DID YOU DO IT?
WHEN HAVE I EVER GIVEN YOU REASON TO DOUBT MY LOYALTY?
YOU ANSWER MINE.
ANSWER MY FUCKING QUESTION.

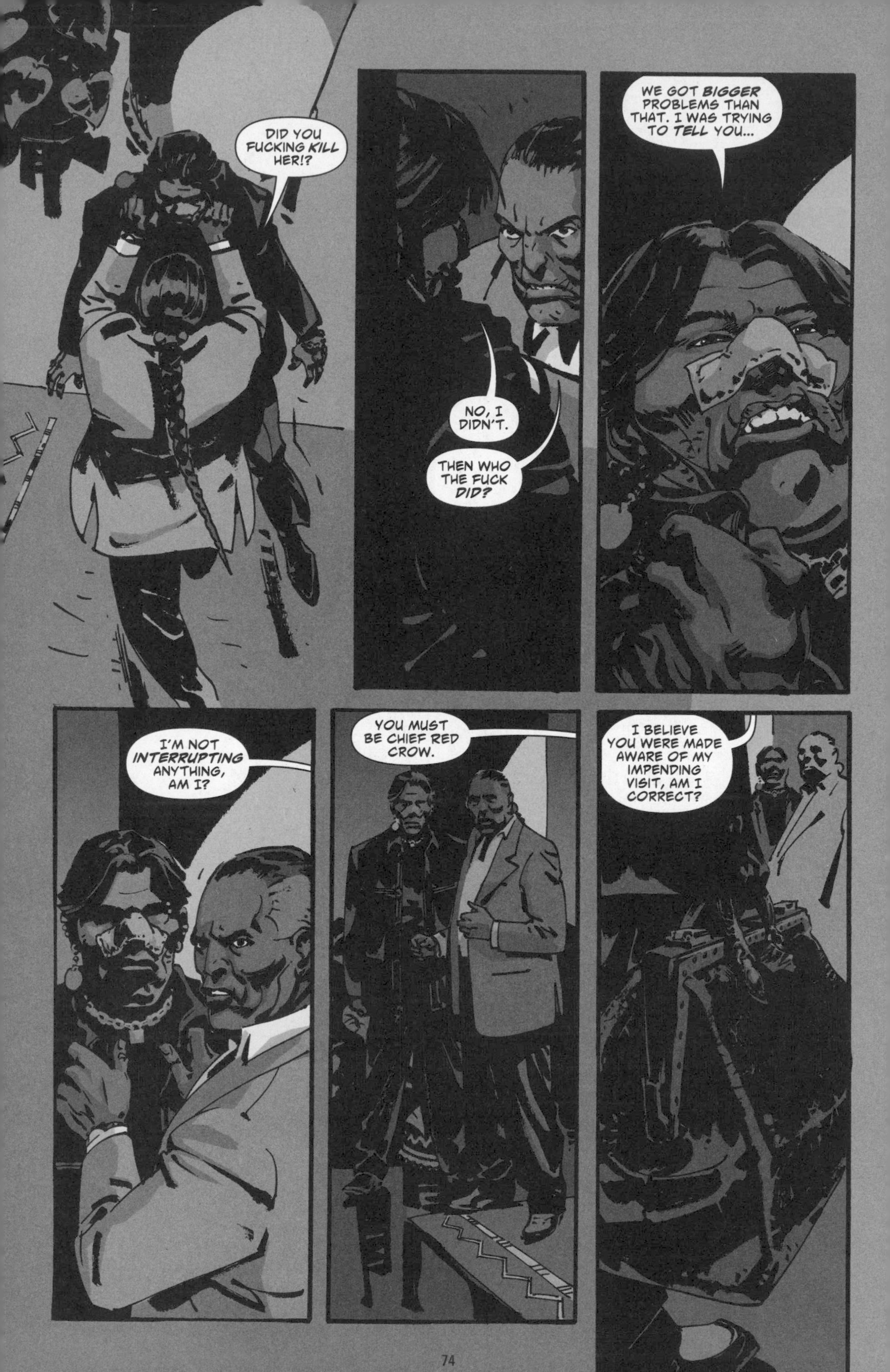
DID YOU FUCKING KILL HER!?
NO, I DIDN'T.
THEN WHO THE FUCK DID?
WE GOT BIGGER PROBLEMS THAN THAT. I WAS TRYING TO TELL YOU...
I'M NOT INTERRUPTING ANYTHING, AM I?
YOU MUST BE CHIEF RED CROW.
I BELIEVE YOU WERE MADE AWARE OF MY IMPENDING VISIT, AM I CORRECT?

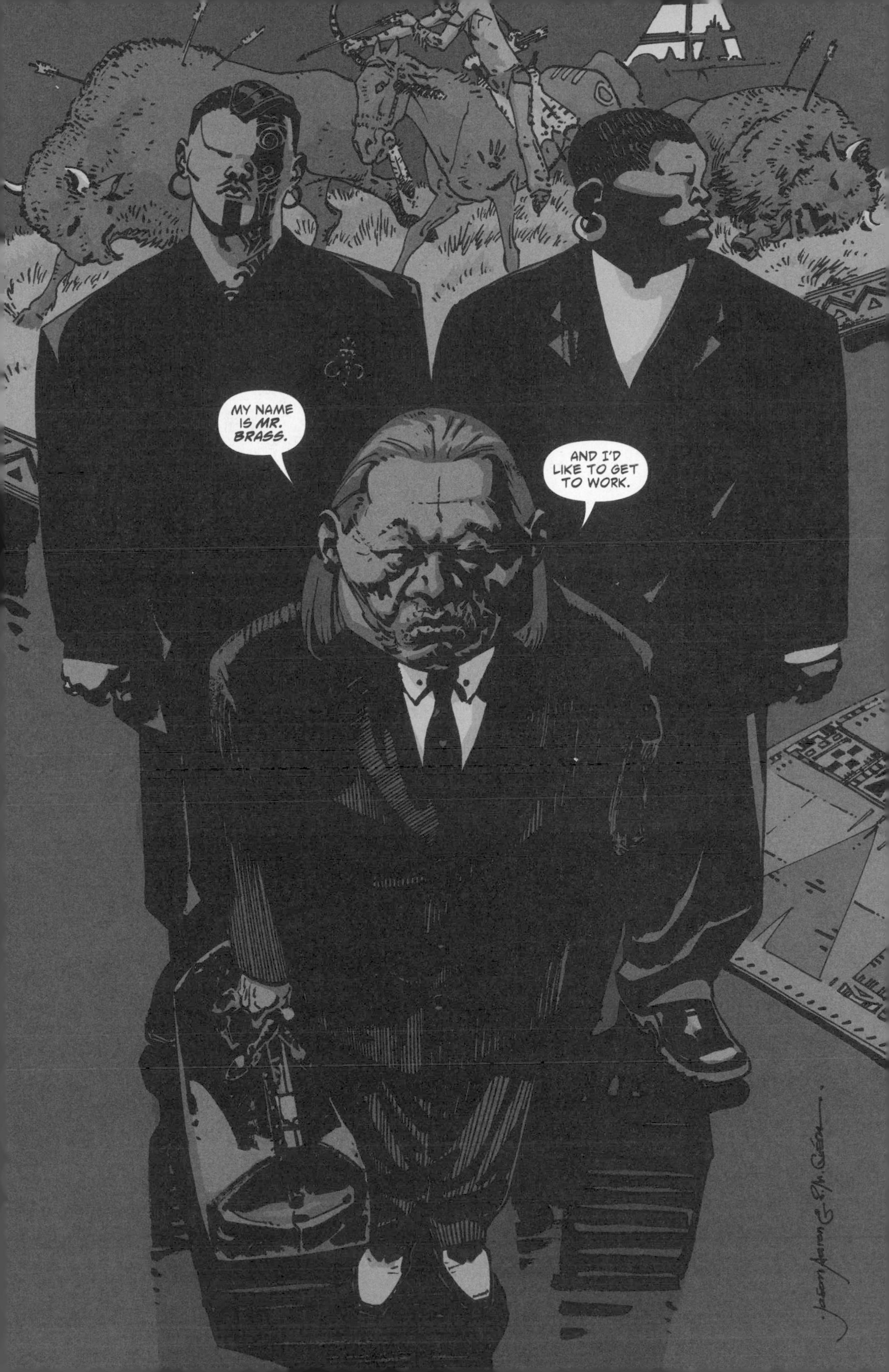
MY NAME IS MR. BRASS.
AND I'D LIKE TO GET TO WORK.

DEAD MOTHERS PART 3
COVER ART BY JOCK

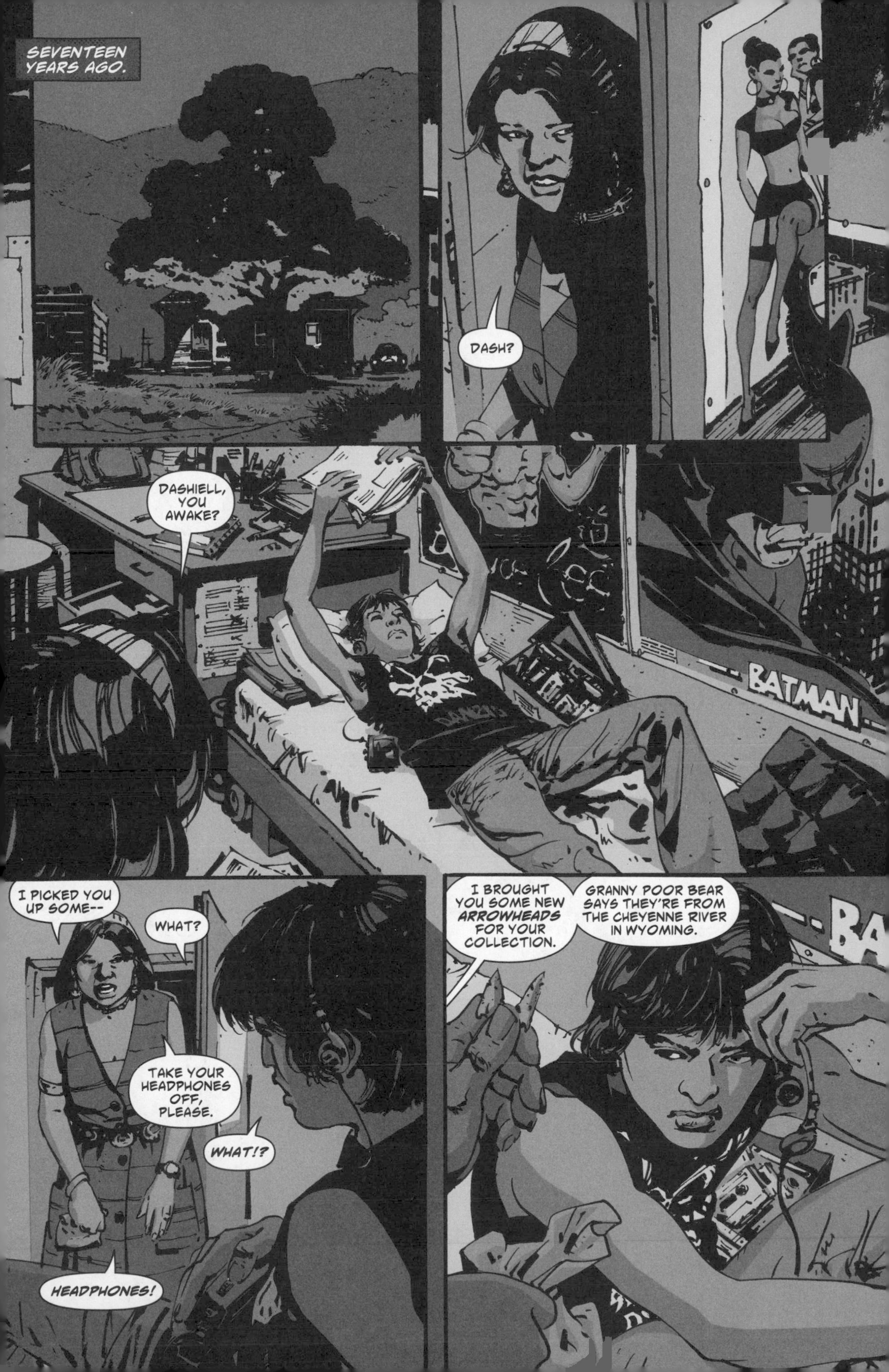
SEVENTEEN YEARS AGO.
DASH?
DASHIELL, YOU AWAKE?
BATMAN
I PICKED YOU UP SOME--
WHAT?
TAKE YOUR HEADPHONES OFF, PLEASE.
WHAT!?
HEADPHONES!
I BROUGHT YOU SOME NEW ARROWHEADS FOR YOUR COLLECTION.
GRANNY POOR BEAR SAYS THEY'RE FROM THE CHEYENNE RIVER IN WYOMING.

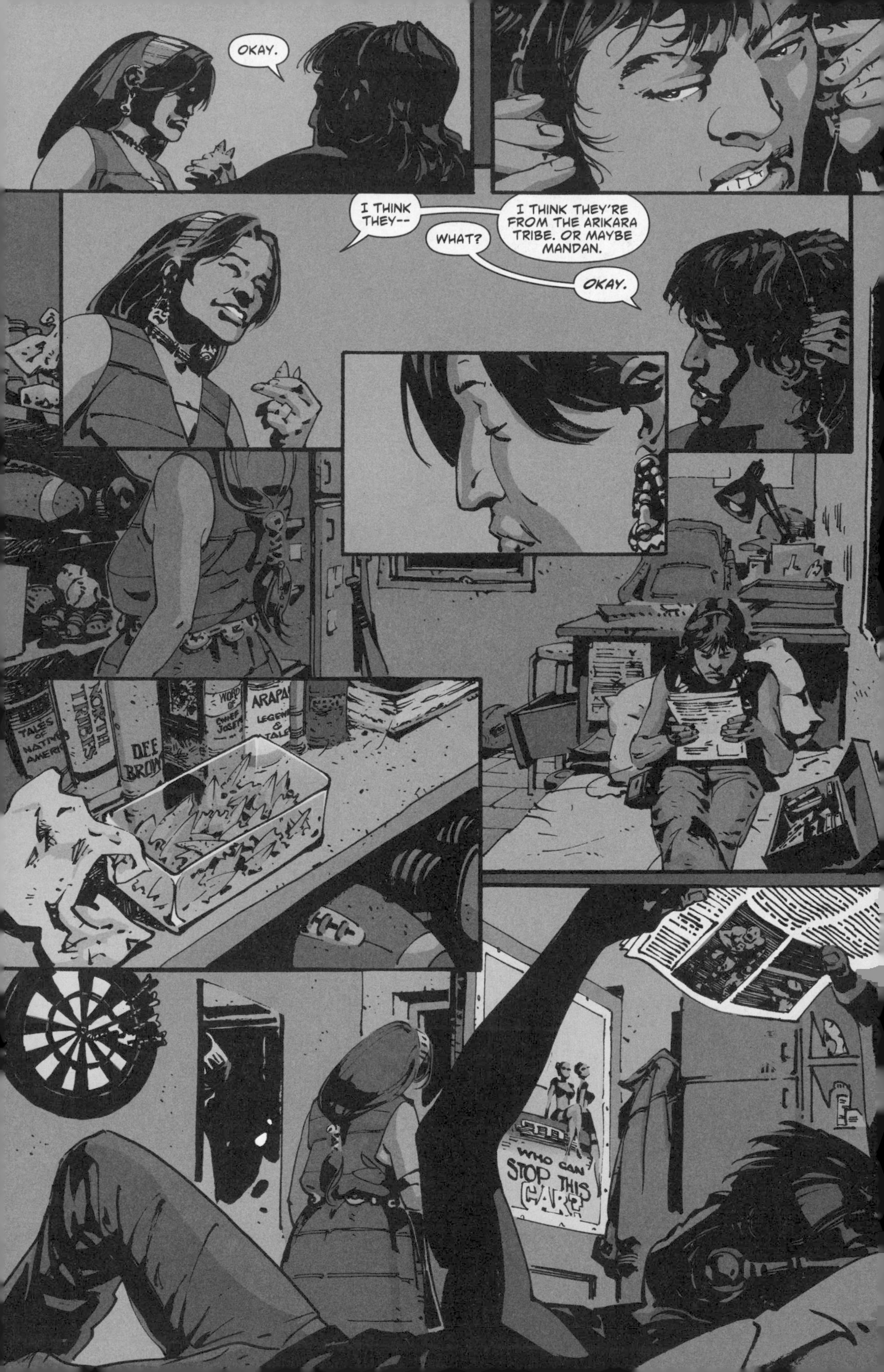

OKAY.
I THINK THEY--
I THINK THEY'RE FROM THE ARIKARA TRIBE. OR MAYBE MANDAN.
WHAT?
OKAY.
TALES OF NATIVE AMERICA
NORTH TRIBES
DEE BROWN
WORDS OF CHIEF JOSEPH
ARAPAHO LEGENDS & TALES
WHO CAN STOP THIS CAR?

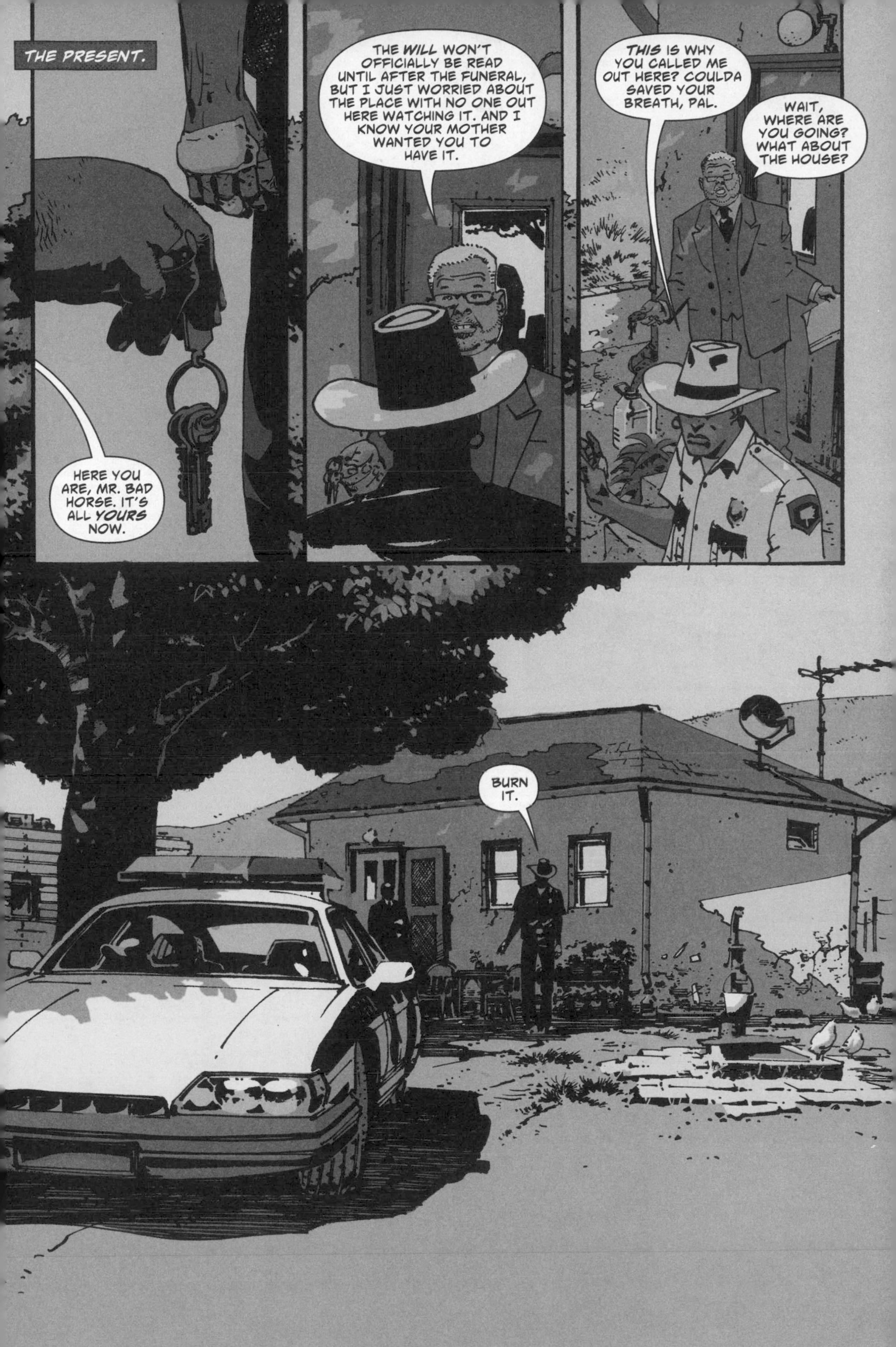
THE PRESENT.
HERE YOU ARE, MR. BAD HORSE. IT'S ALL YOURS NOW.
THE WILL WON'T OFFICIALLY BE READ UNTIL AFTER THE FUNERAL, BUT I JUST WORRIED ABOUT THE PLACE WITH NO ONE OUT HERE WATCHING IT. AND I KNOW YOUR MOTHER WANTED YOU TO HAVE IT.
THIS IS WHY YOU CALLED ME OUT HERE? COULDA SAVED YOUR BREATH, PAL.
WAIT, WHERE ARE YOU GOING? WHAT ABOUT THE HOUSE?
BURN IT.

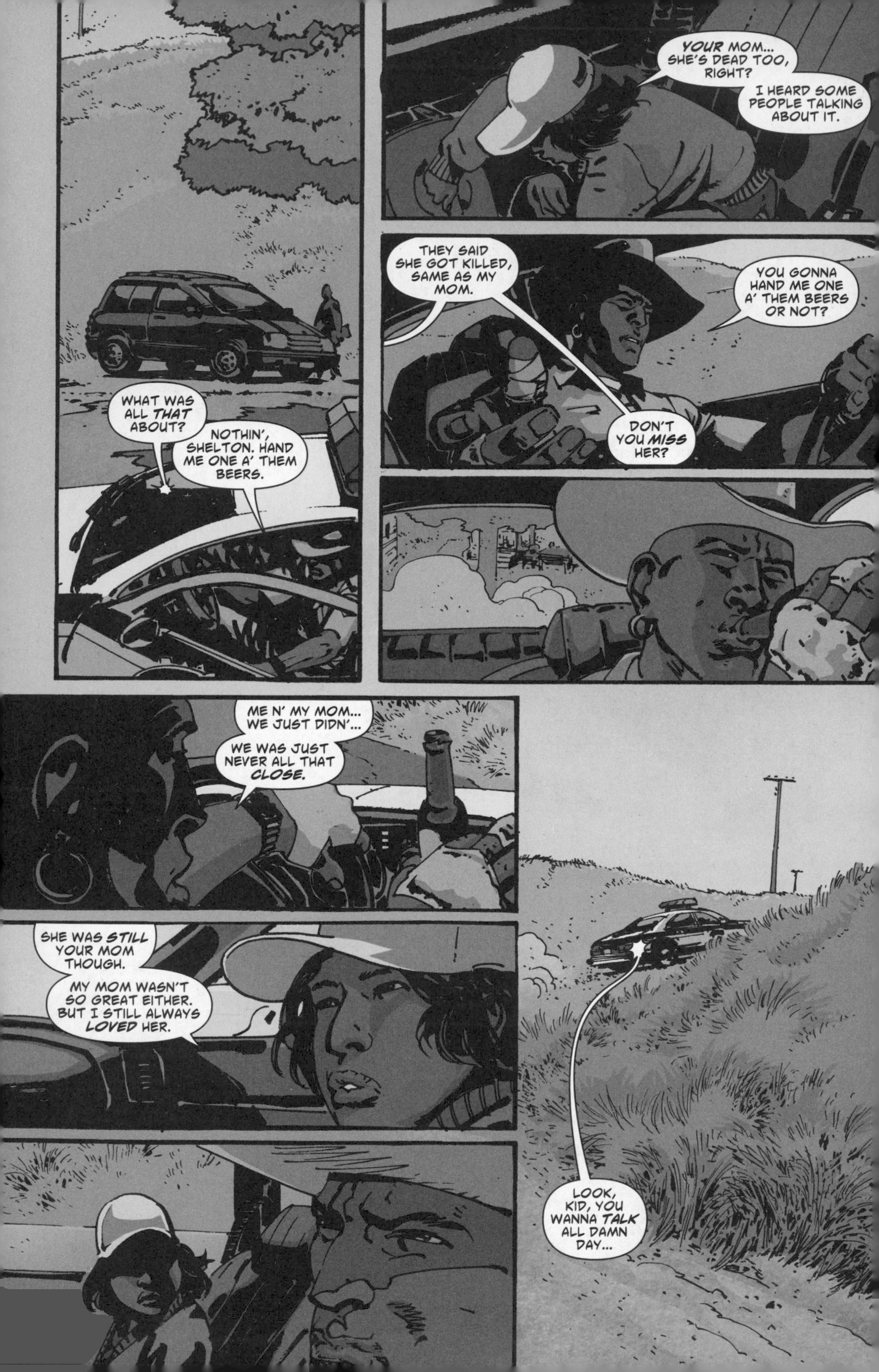
WHAT WAS ALL THAT ABOUT?
NOTHIN', SHELTON. HAND ME ONE A' THEM BEERS.
YOUR MOM... SHE'S DEAD TOO, RIGHT?
I HEARD SOME PEOPLE TALKING ABOUT IT.
THEY SAID SHE GOT KILLED, SAME AS MY MOM.
YOU GONNA HAND ME ONE A' THEM BEERS OR NOT?
DON'T YOU MISS HER?
ME N' MY MOM... WE JUST DIDN'...
WE WAS JUST NEVER ALL THAT CLOSE.
SHE WAS STILL YOUR MOM THOUGH.
MY MOM WASN'T SO GREAT EITHER. BUT I STILL ALWAYS LOVED HER.
LOOK, KID, YOU WANNA TALK ALL DAMN DAY...

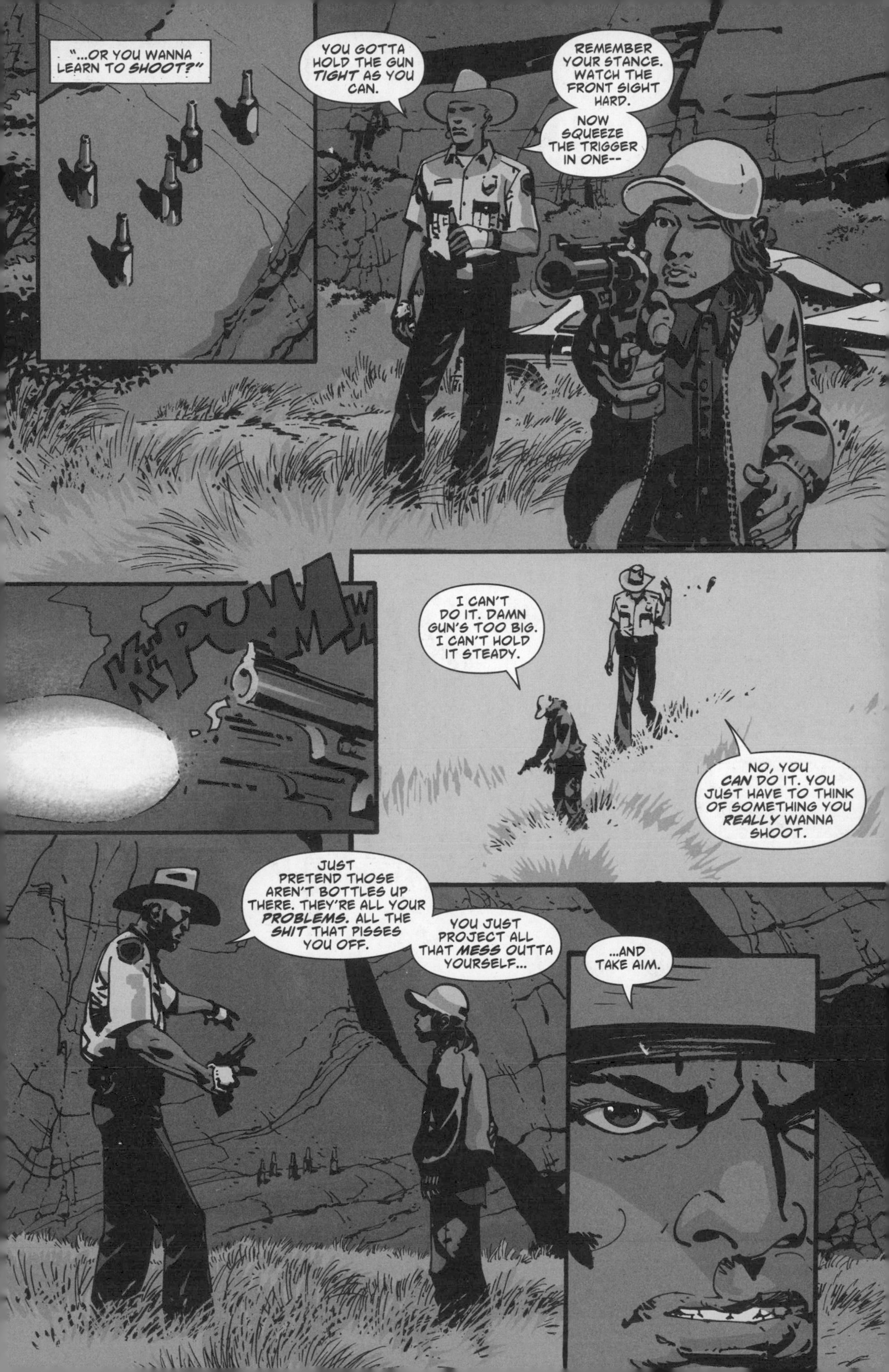
"...OR YOU WANNA LEARN TO SHOOT?"
YOU GOTTA HOLD THE GUN TIGHT AS YOU CAN.
REMEMBER YOUR STANCE. WATCH THE FRONT SIGHT HARD.
NOW SQUEEZE THE TRIGGER IN ONE--
K'PUM
I CAN'T DO IT. DAMN GUN'S TOO BIG. I CAN'T HOLD IT STEADY.
NO, YOU CAN DO IT. YOU JUST HAVE TO THINK OF SOMETHING YOU REALLY WANNA SHOOT.
JUST PRETEND THOSE AREN'T BOTTLES UP THERE. THEY'RE ALL YOUR PROBLEMS. ALL THE SHIT THAT PISSES YOU OFF.
YOU JUST PROJECT ALL THAT MESS OUTTA YOURSELF...
...AND TAKE AIM.

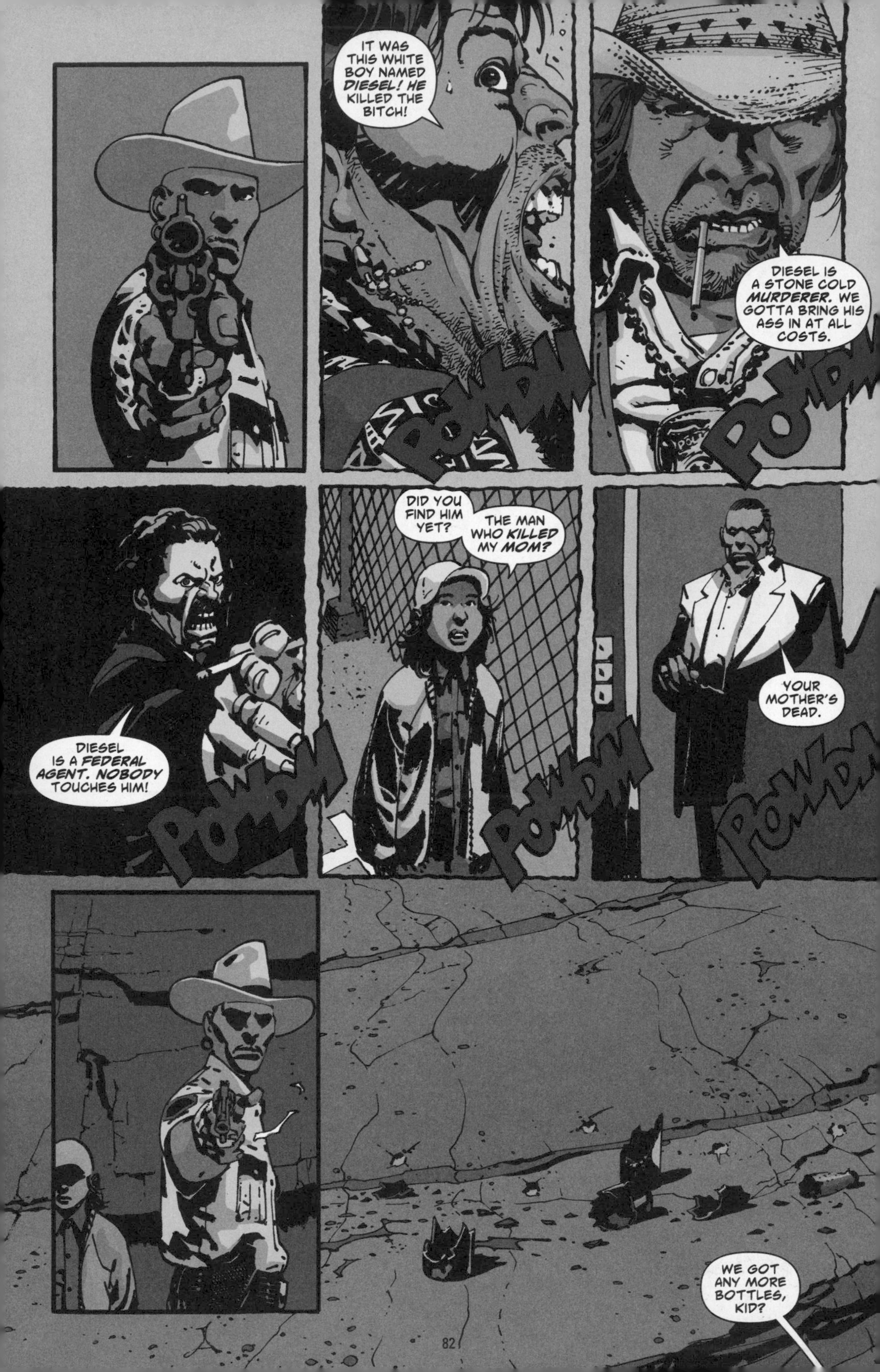
IT WAS THIS WHITE BOY NAMED DIESEL! HE KILLED THE BITCH!
POWDM
DIESEL IS A STONE COLD MURDERER. WE GOTTA BRING HIS ASS IN AT ALL COSTS.
POWDM
DIESEL IS A FEDERAL AGENT. NOBODY TOUCHES HIM!
POWDM
DID YOU FIND HIM YET?
THE MAN WHO KILLED MY MOM?
POWDM
YOUR MOTHER'S DEAD.
POWDM
WE GOT ANY MORE BOTTLES, KID?

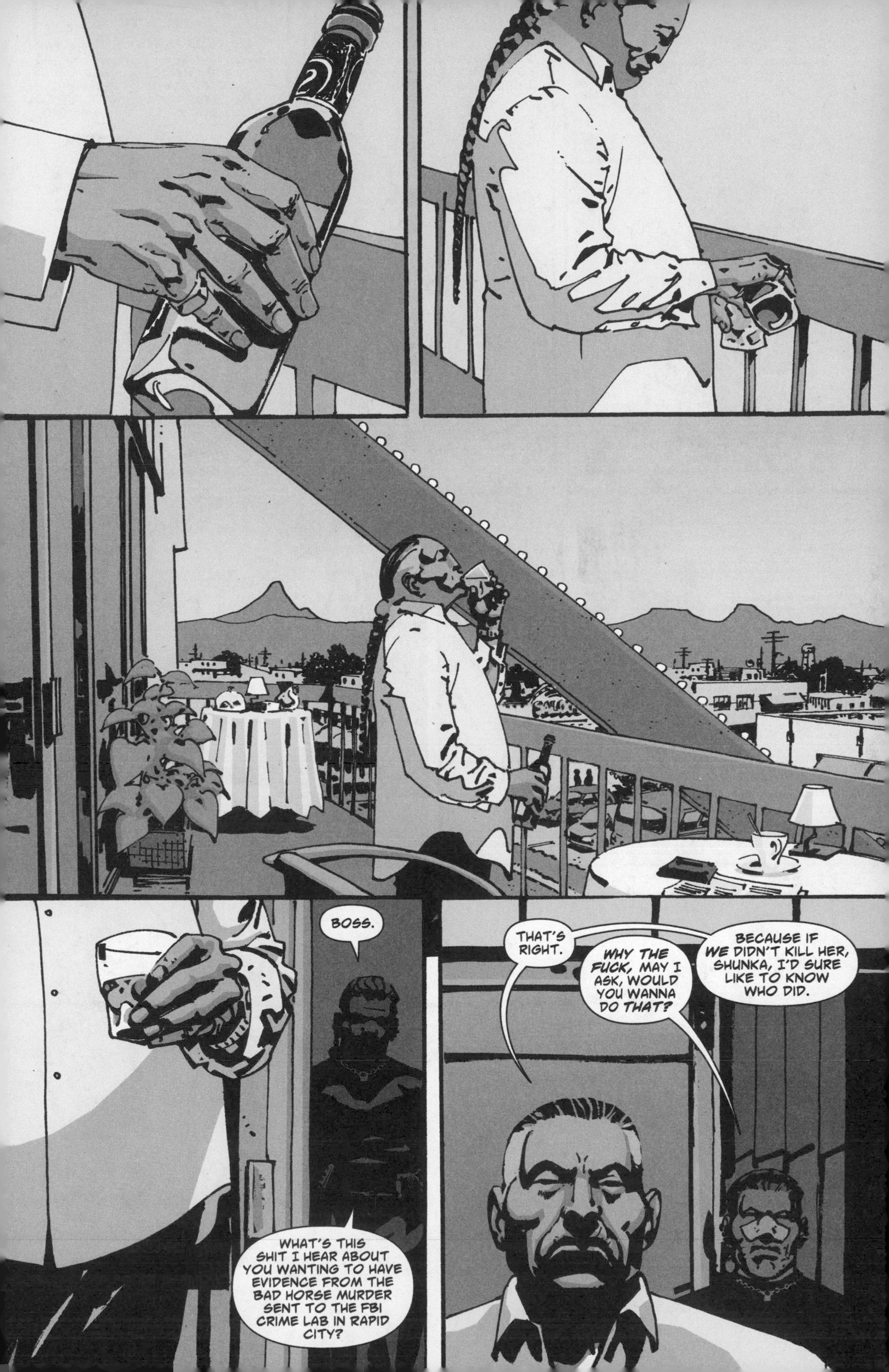
BOSS.
WHAT'S THIS SHIT I HEAR ABOUT YOU WANTING TO HAVE EVIDENCE FROM THE BAD HORSE MURDER SENT TO THE FBI CRIME LAB IN RAPID CITY?
THAT'S RIGHT.
WHY THE FUCK, MAY I ASK, WOULD YOU WANNA DO THAT?
BECAUSE IF WE DIDN'T KILL HER, SHUNKA, I'D SURE LIKE TO KNOW WHO DID.

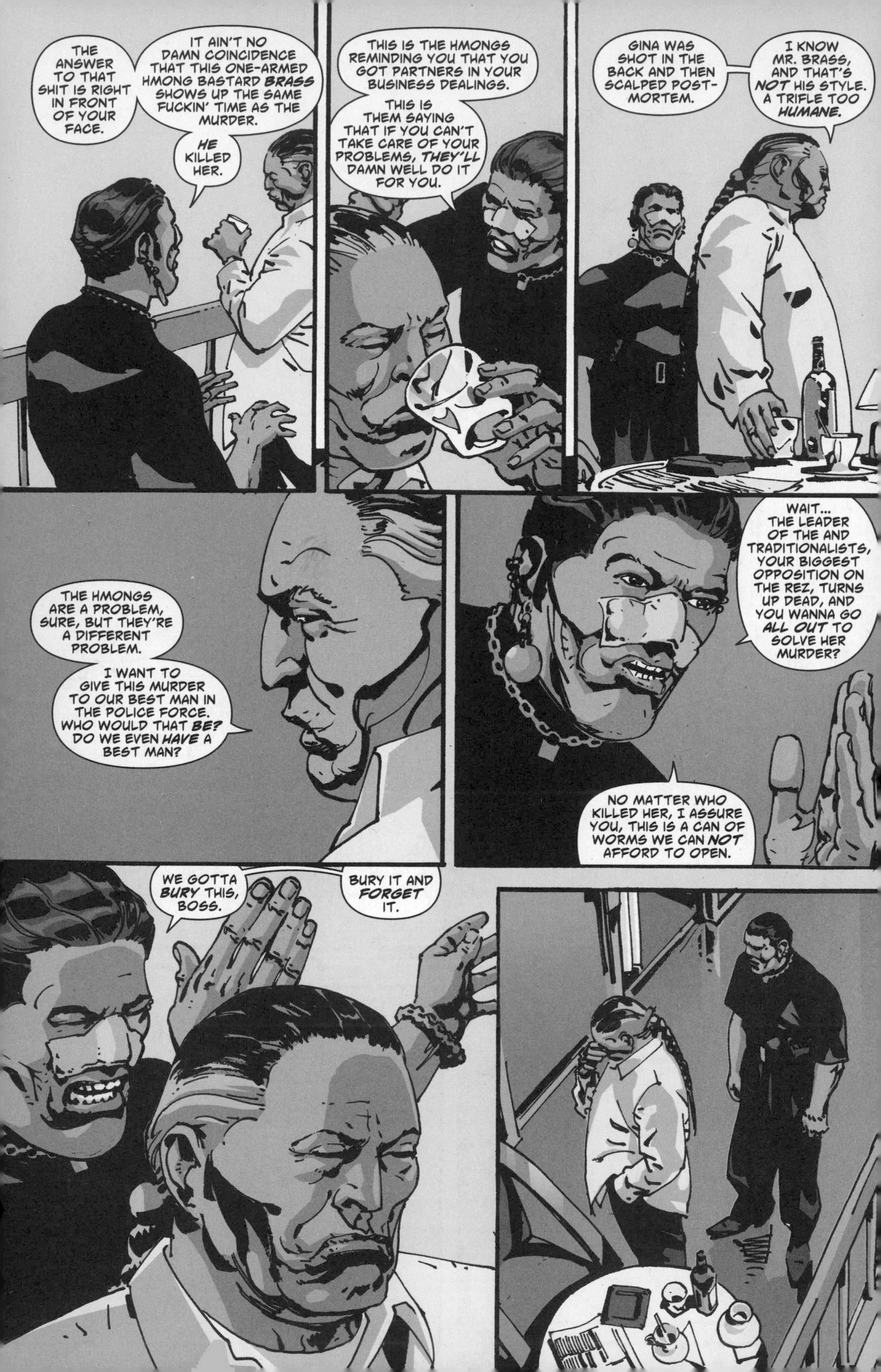
THE ANSWER TO THAT SHIT IS RIGHT IN FRONT OF YOUR FACE.
IT AIN'T NO DAMN COINCIDENCE THAT THIS ONE-ARMED HMONG BASTARD BRASS SHOWS UP THE SAME FUCKIN' TIME AS THE MURDER.
HE KILLED HER.
THIS IS THE HMONGS REMINDING YOU THAT YOU GOT PARTNERS IN YOUR BUSINESS DEALINGS.
THIS IS THEM SAYING THAT IF YOU CAN'T TAKE CARE OF YOUR PROBLEMS, THEY'LL DAMN WELL DO IT FOR YOU.
GINA WAS SHOT IN THE BACK AND THEN SCALPED POST-MORTEM.
I KNOW MR. BRASS, AND THAT'S NOT HIS STYLE. A TRIFLE TOO HUMANE.
THE HMONGS ARE A PROBLEM, SURE, BUT THEY'RE A DIFFERENT PROBLEM.
I WANT TO GIVE THIS MURDER TO OUR BEST MAN IN THE POLICE FORCE. WHO WOULD THAT BE? DO WE EVEN HAVE A BEST MAN?
WAIT... THE LEADER OF THE AND TRADITIONALISTS, YOUR BIGGEST OPPOSITION ON THE REZ, TURNS UP DEAD, AND YOU WANNA GO ALL OUT TO SOLVE HER MURDER?
NO MATTER WHO KILLED HER, I ASSURE YOU, THIS IS A CAN OF WORMS WE CAN NOT AFFORD TO OPEN.
WE GOTTA BURY THIS, BOSS.
BURY IT AND FORGET IT.

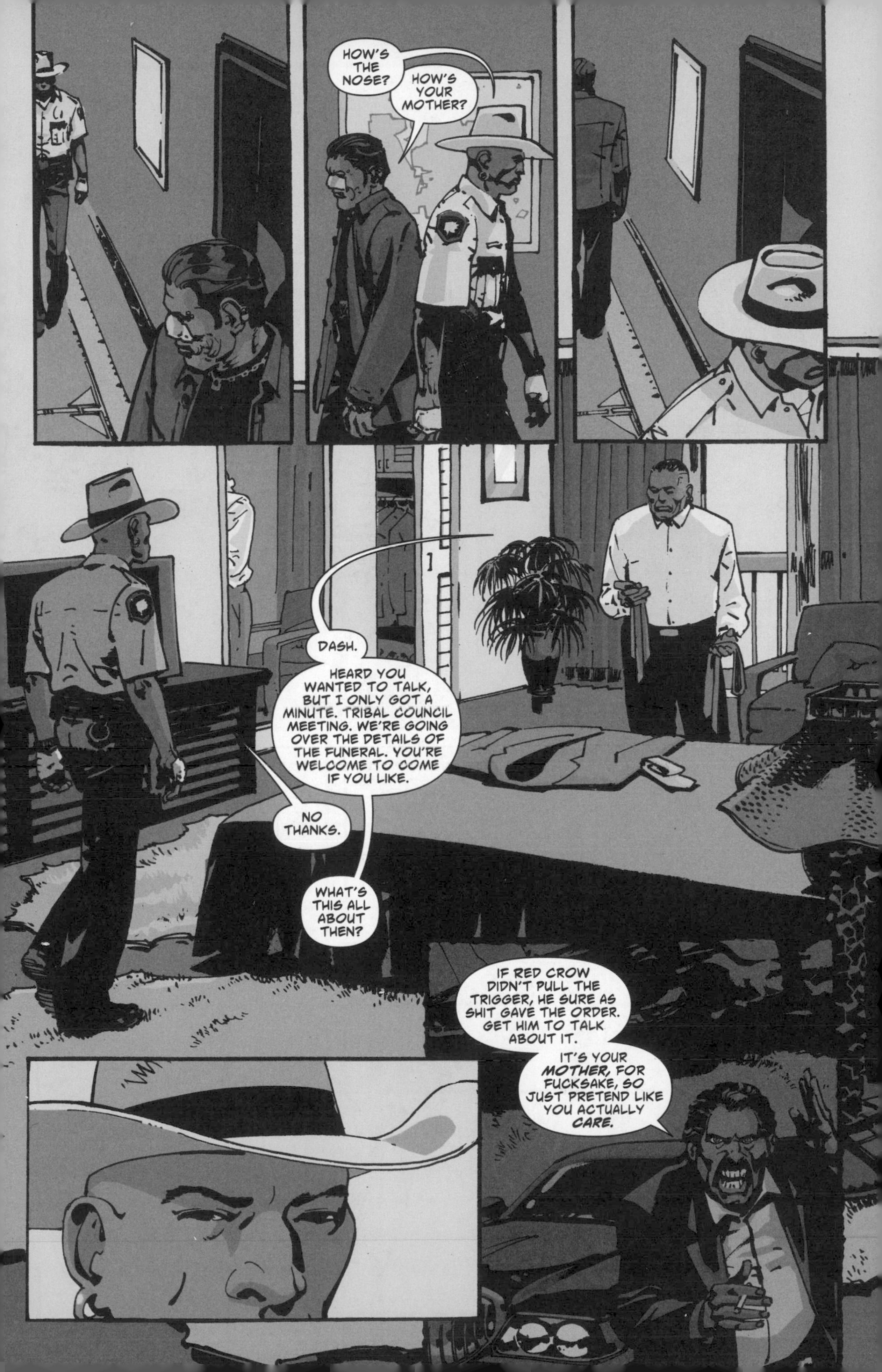
HOW'S THE NOSE?
HOW'S YOUR MOTHER?
DASH.
HEARD YOU WANTED TO TALK, BUT I ONLY GOT A MINUTE. TRIBAL COUNCIL MEETING. WE'RE GOING OVER THE DETAILS OF THE FUNERAL. YOU'RE WELCOME TO COME IF YOU LIKE.
NO THANKS.
WHAT'S THIS ALL ABOUT THEN?
IF RED CROW DIDN'T PULL THE TRIGGER, HE SURE AS SHIT GAVE THE ORDER. GET HIM TO TALK ABOUT IT.
IT'S YOUR MOTHER, FOR FUCKSAKE, SO JUST PRETEND LIKE YOU ACTUALLY CARE.

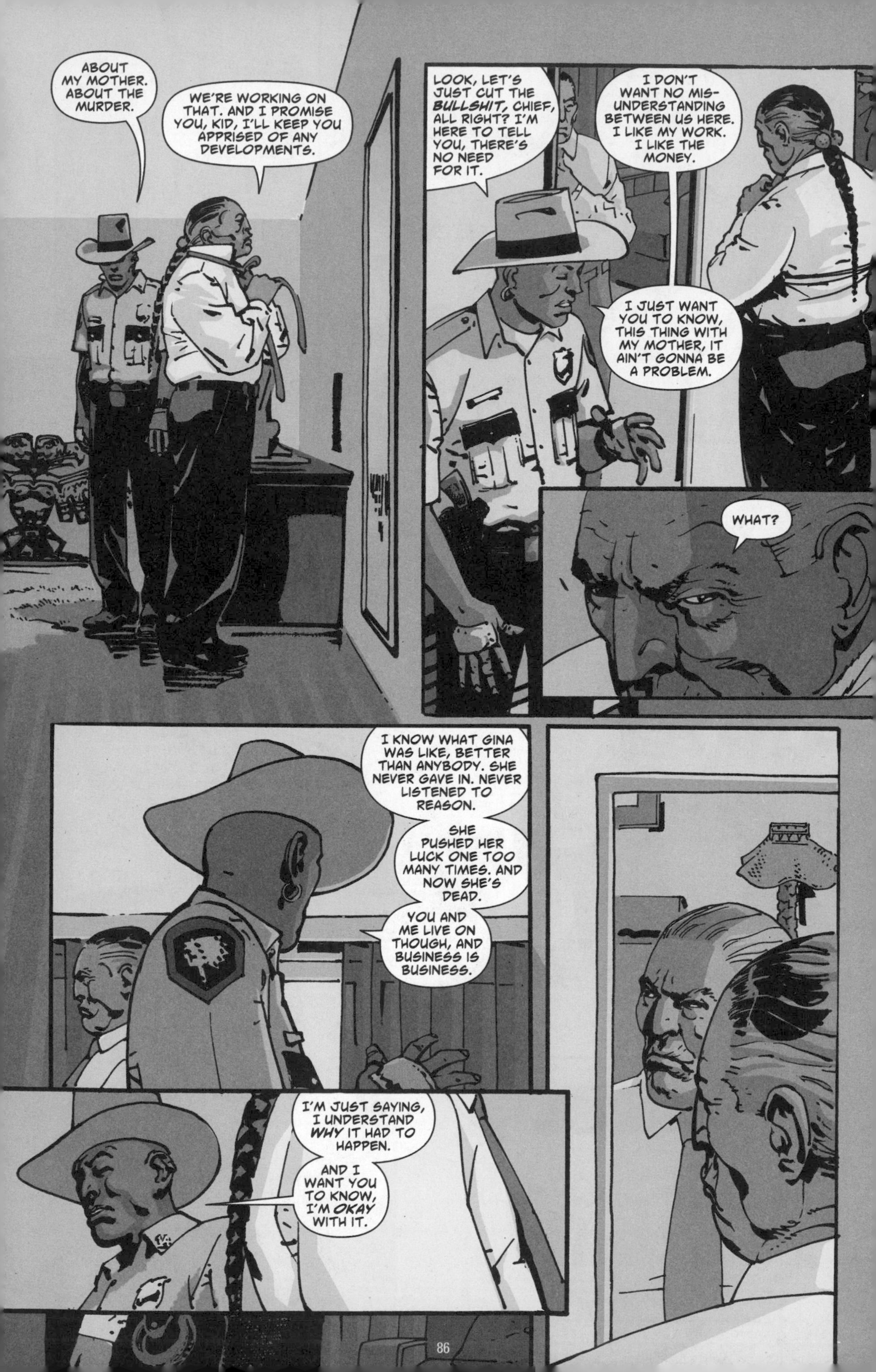
ABOUT MY MOTHER. ABOUT THE MURDER.
WE'RE WORKING ON THAT. AND I PROMISE YOU, KID, I'LL KEEP YOU APPRISED OF ANY DEVELOPMENTS.
LOOK, LET'S JUST CUT THE BULLSHIT, CHIEF, ALL RIGHT? I'M HERE TO TELL YOU, THERE'S NO NEED FOR IT.
I DON'T WANT NO MIS-UNDERSTANDING BETWEEN US HERE. I LIKE MY WORK. I LIKE THE MONEY.
I JUST WANT YOU TO KNOW, THIS THING WITH MY MOTHER, IT AIN'T GONNA BE A PROBLEM.
WHAT?
I KNOW WHAT GINA WAS LIKE, BETTER THAN ANYBODY. SHE NEVER GAVE IN. NEVER LISTENED TO REASON.
SHE PUSHED HER LUCK ONE TOO MANY TIMES. AND NOW SHE'S DEAD.
YOU AND ME LIVE ON THOUGH, AND BUSINESS IS BUSINESS.
I'M JUST SAYING, I UNDERSTAND WHY IT HAD TO HAPPEN.
AND I WANT YOU TO KNOW, I'M OKAY WITH IT.

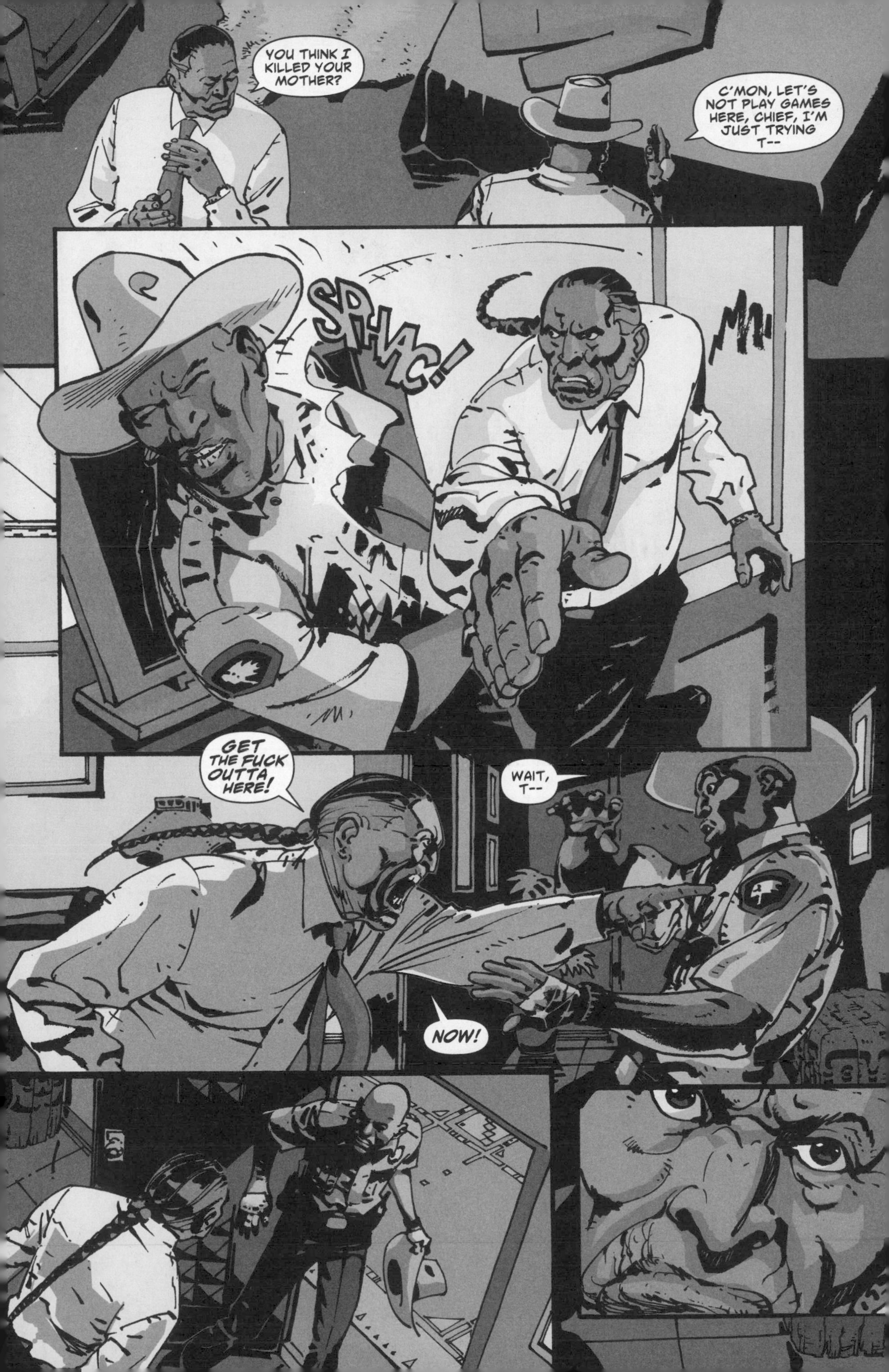
YOU THINK I KILLED YOUR MOTHER?
C'MON, LET'S NOT PLAY GAMES HERE, CHIEF, I'M JUST TRYING T--
SPHAC!
GET THE FUCK OUTTA HERE!
WAIT, T--
NOW!

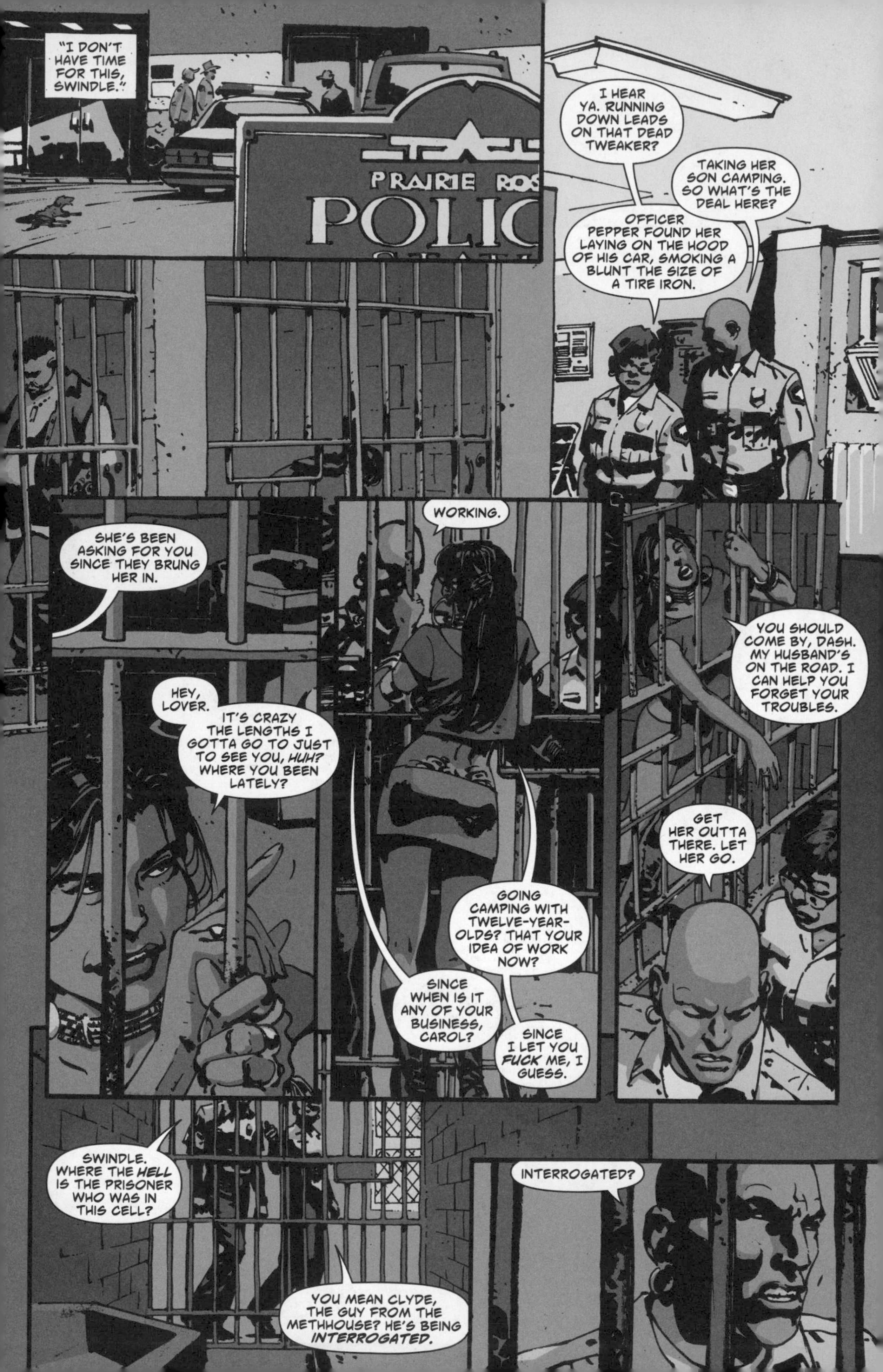
"I DON'T HAVE TIME FOR THIS, SWINDLE."
PRAIRIE ROS
POLIC
I HEAR YA. RUNNING DOWN LEADS ON THAT DEAD TWEAKER?
TAKING HER SON CAMPING. SO WHAT'S THE DEAL HERE?
OFFICER PEPPER FOUND HER LAYING ON THE HOOD OF HIS CAR, SMOKING A BLUNT THE SIZE OF A TIRE IRON.
SHE'S BEEN ASKING FOR YOU SINCE THEY BRUNG HER IN.
HEY, LOVER.
IT'S CRAZY THE LENGTHS I GOTTA GO TO JUST TO SEE YOU, *HUH?* WHERE YOU BEEN LATELY?
WORKING.
GOING CAMPING WITH TWELVE-YEAR-OLDS? THAT YOUR IDEA OF WORK NOW?
SINCE WHEN IS IT ANY OF YOUR BUSINESS, CAROL?
SINCE I LET YOU *FUCK* ME, I GUESS.
YOU SHOULD COME BY, DASH. MY HUSBAND'S ON THE ROAD. I CAN HELP YOU FORGET YOUR TROUBLES.
GET HER OUTTA THERE. LET HER GO.
SWINDLE. WHERE THE *HELL* IS THE PRISONER WHO WAS IN THIS CELL?
YOU MEAN CLYDE, THE GUY FROM THE METHHOUSE? HE'S BEING *INTERROGATED.*
INTERROGATED?

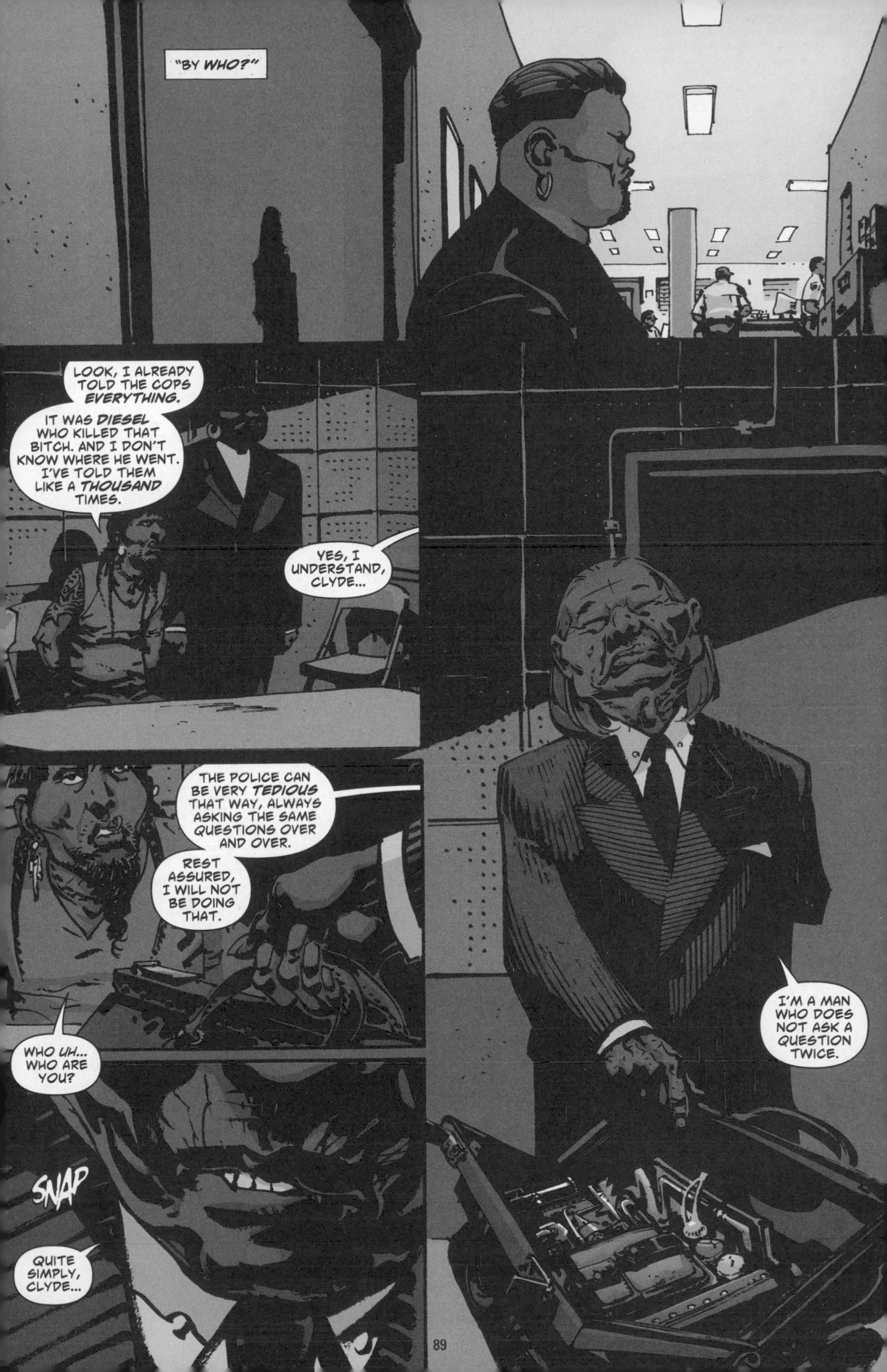
"BY WHO?"
LOOK, I ALREADY TOLD THE COPS EVERYTHING.
IT WAS DIESEL WHO KILLED THAT BITCH. AND I DON'T KNOW WHERE HE WENT. I'VE TOLD THEM LIKE A THOUSAND TIMES.
YES, I UNDERSTAND, CLYDE...
THE POLICE CAN BE VERY TEDIOUS THAT WAY, ALWAYS ASKING THE SAME QUESTIONS OVER AND OVER.
REST ASSURED, I WILL NOT BE DOING THAT.
WHO UH... WHO ARE YOU?
SNAP
QUITE SIMPLY, CLYDE...
I'M A MAN WHO DOES NOT ASK A QUESTION TWICE.

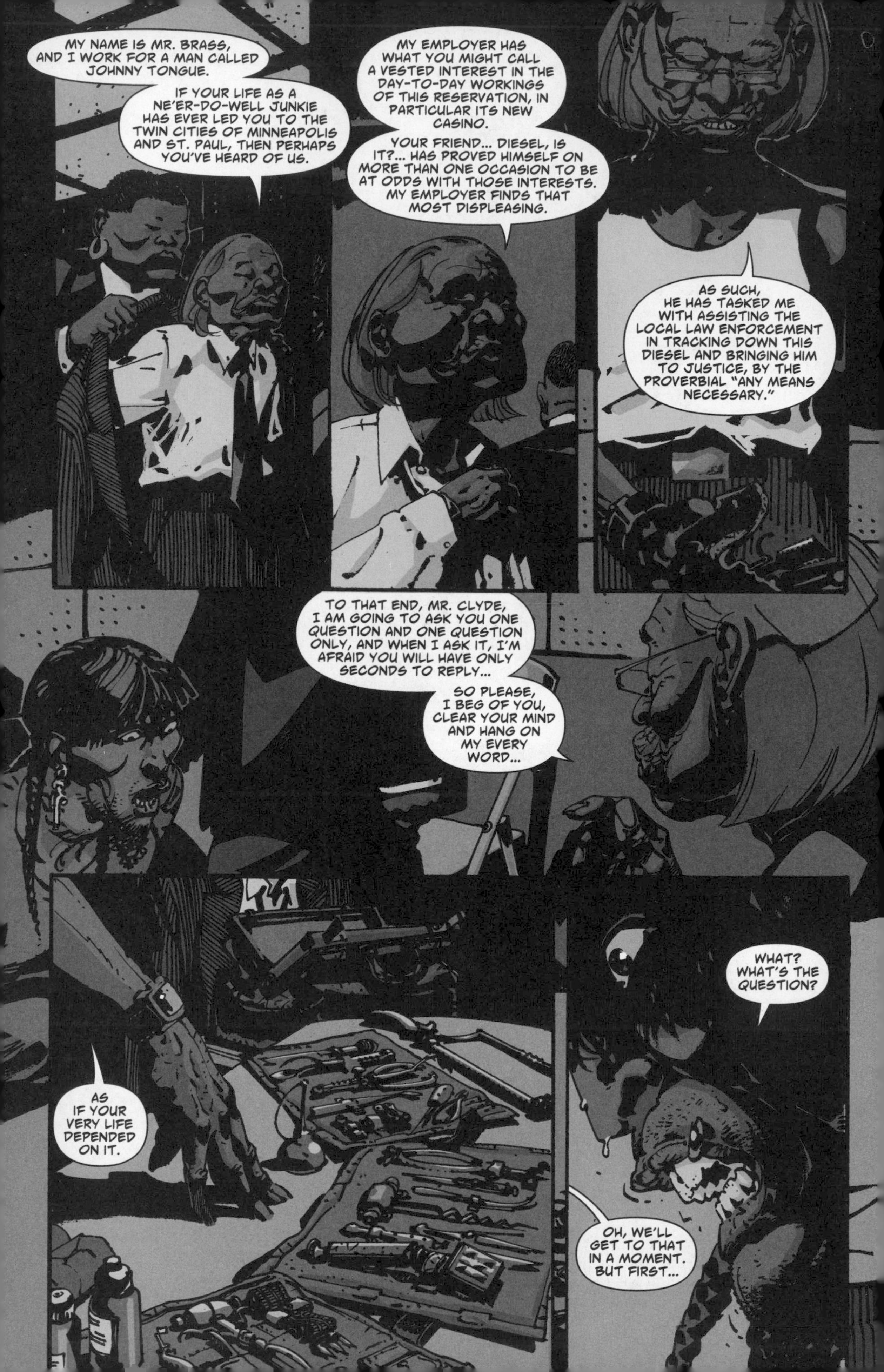
MY NAME IS MR. BRASS, AND I WORK FOR A MAN CALLED JOHNNY TONGUE.
IF YOUR LIFE AS A NE'ER-DO-WELL JUNKIE HAS EVER LED YOU TO THE TWIN CITIES OF MINNEAPOLIS AND ST. PAUL, THEN PERHAPS YOU'VE HEARD OF US.
MY EMPLOYER HAS WHAT YOU MIGHT CALL A VESTED INTEREST IN THE DAY-TO-DAY WORKINGS OF THIS RESERVATION, IN PARTICULAR ITS NEW CASINO.
YOUR FRIEND... DIESEL, IS IT?... HAS PROVED HIMSELF ON MORE THAN ONE OCCASION TO BE AT ODDS WITH THOSE INTERESTS. MY EMPLOYER FINDS THAT MOST DISPLEASING.
AS SUCH, HE HAS TASKED ME WITH ASSISTING THE LOCAL LAW ENFORCEMENT IN TRACKING DOWN THIS DIESEL AND BRINGING HIM TO JUSTICE, BY THE PROVERBIAL "ANY MEANS NECESSARY."
TO THAT END, MR. CLYDE, I AM GOING TO ASK YOU ONE QUESTION AND ONE QUESTION ONLY, AND WHEN I ASK IT, I'M AFRAID YOU WILL HAVE ONLY SECONDS TO REPLY...
SO PLEASE, I BEG OF YOU, CLEAR YOUR MIND AND HANG ON MY EVERY WORD...
AS IF YOUR VERY LIFE DEPENDED ON IT.
WHAT? WHAT'S THE QUESTION?
OH, WE'LL GET TO THAT IN A MOMENT. BUT FIRST...

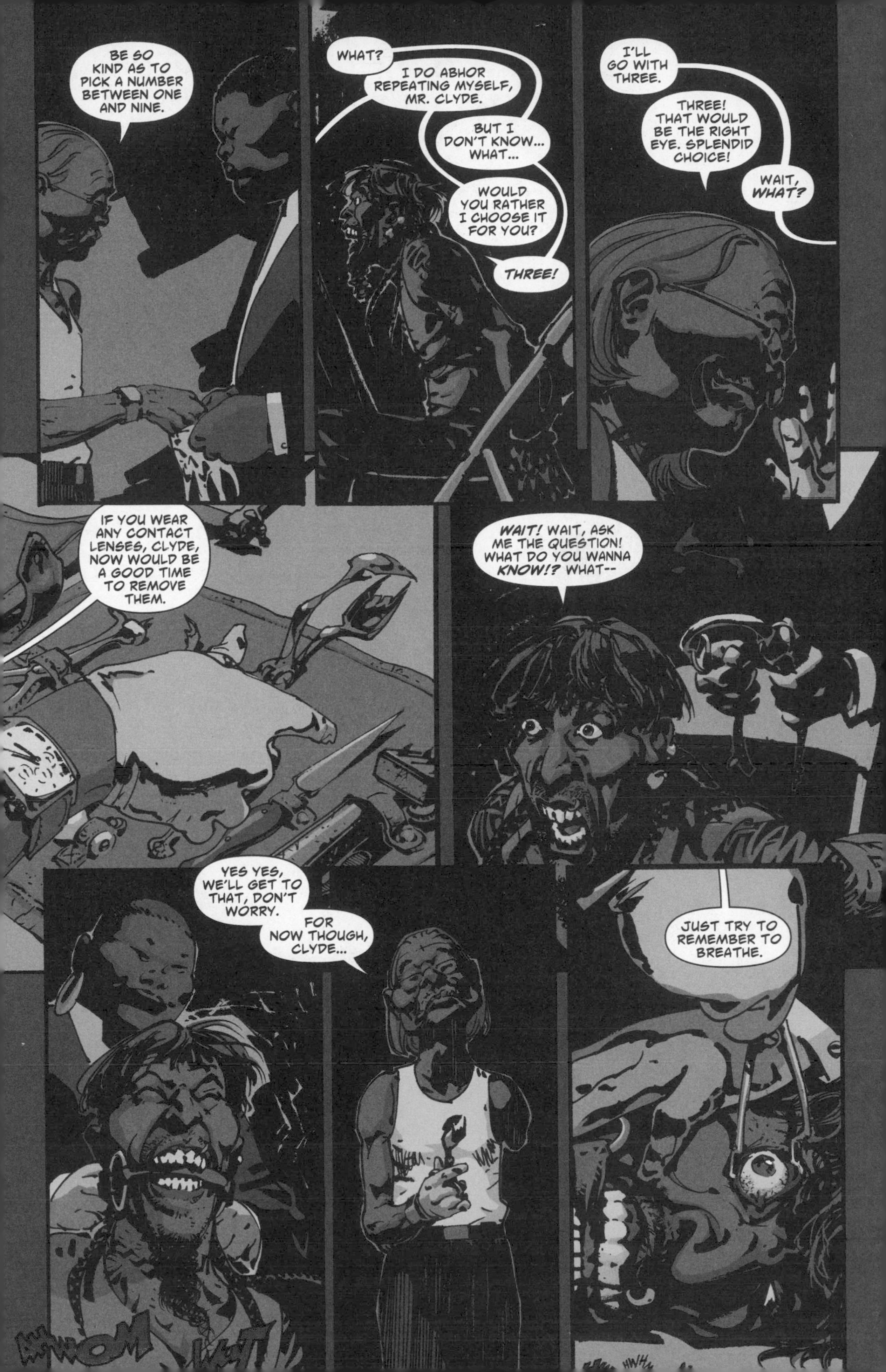
BE SO KIND AS TO PICK A NUMBER BETWEEN ONE AND NINE.
WHAT?
I DO ABHOR REPEATING MYSELF, MR. CLYDE.
BUT I DON'T KNOW... WHAT...
WOULD YOU RATHER I CHOOSE IT FOR YOU?
THREE!
I'LL GO WITH THREE.
THREE! THAT WOULD BE THE RIGHT EYE. SPLENDID CHOICE!
WAIT, WHAT?
IF YOU WEAR ANY CONTACT LENSES, CLYDE, NOW WOULD BE A GOOD TIME TO REMOVE THEM.
WAIT! WAIT, ASK ME THE QUESTION! WHAT DO YOU WANNA KNOW!? WHAT--
YES YES, WE'LL GET TO THAT, DON'T WORRY.
FOR NOW THOUGH, CLYDE...
JUST TRY TO REMEMBER TO BREATHE.

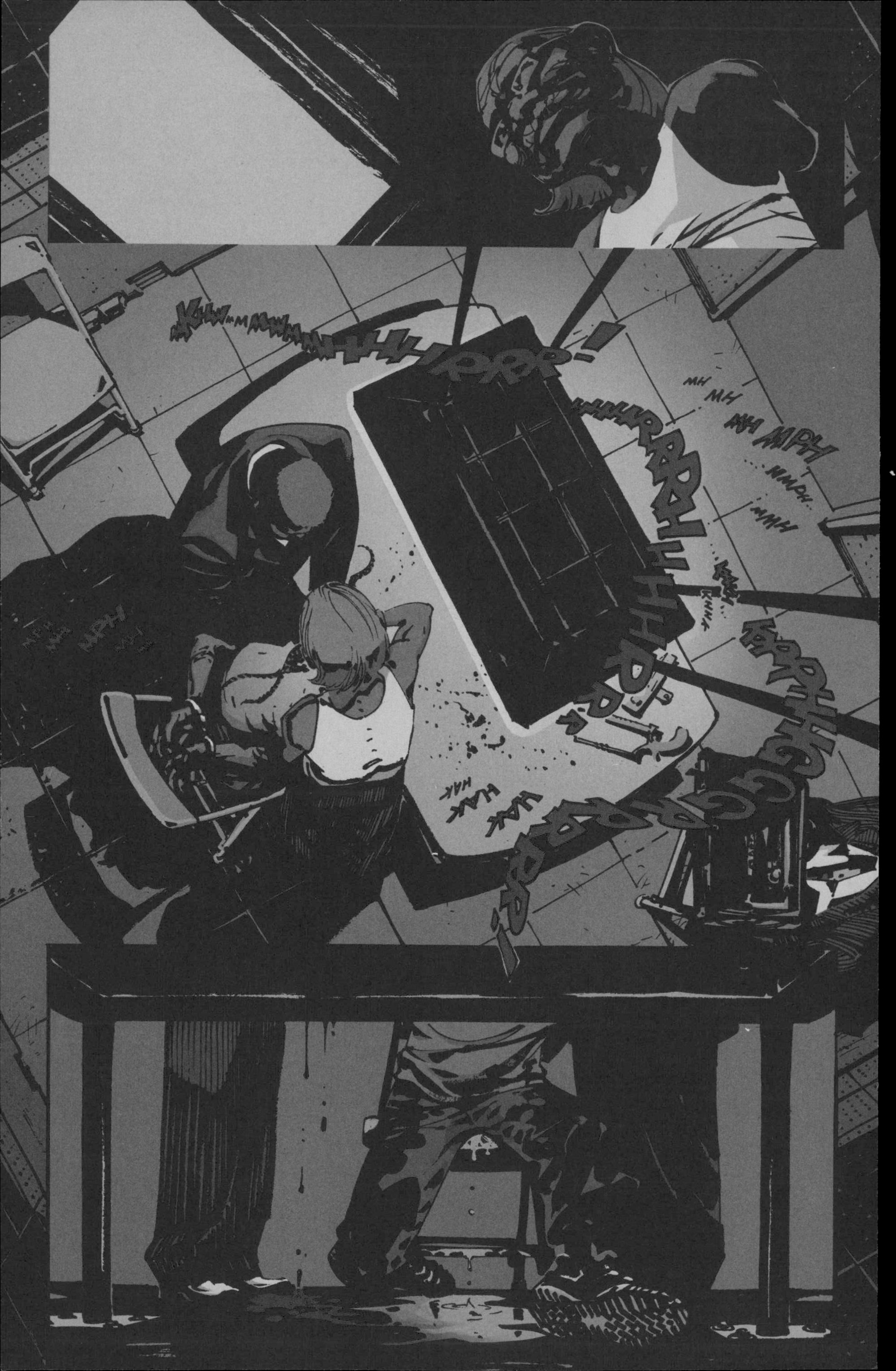
MH MH MH MPH
NMPH
MMH
KHHA
MPH
HAK HAK HAK

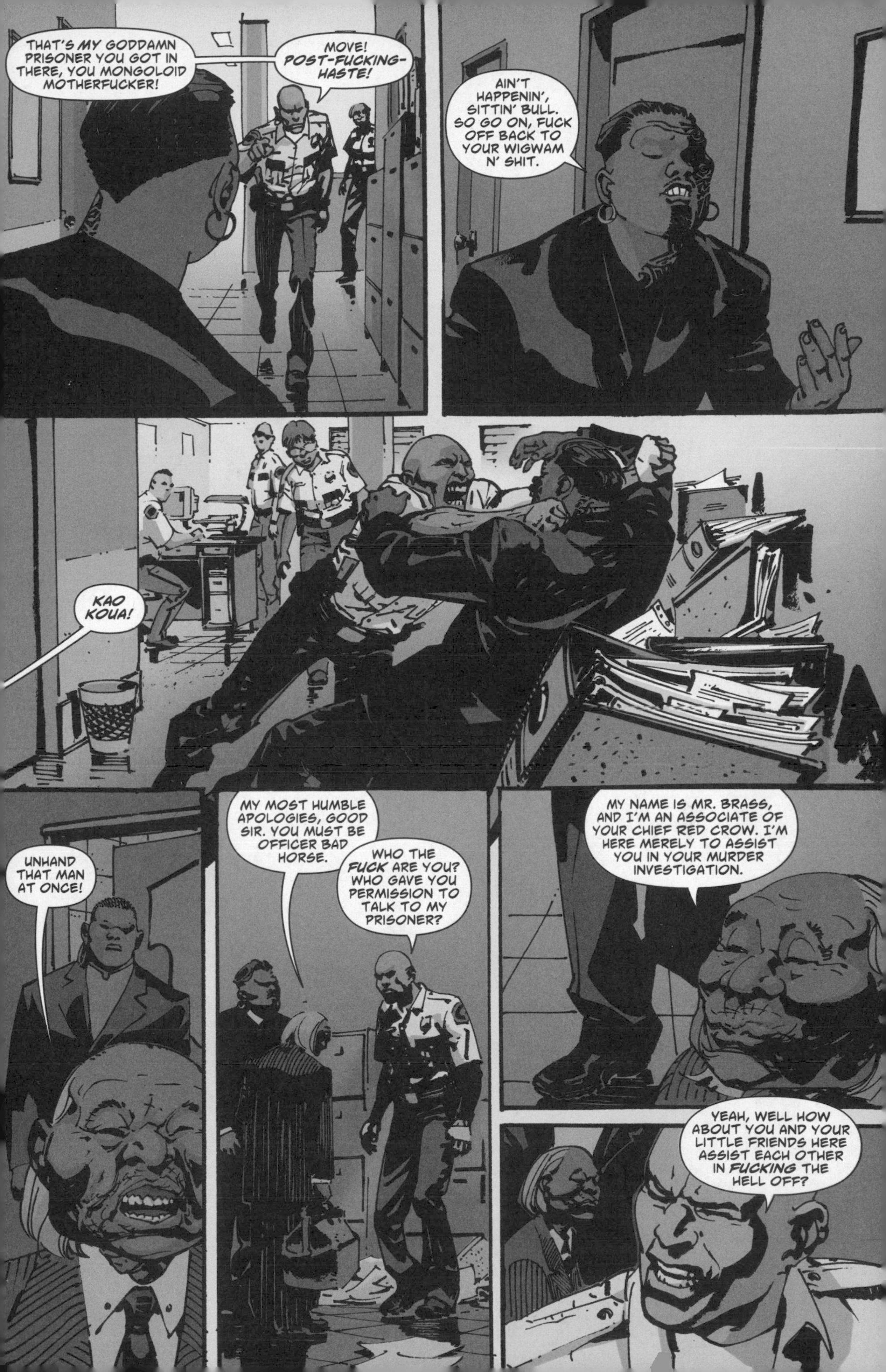

THAT'S MY GODDAMN PRISONER YOU GOT IN THERE, YOU MONGOLOID MOTHERFUCKER!
MOVE! POST-FUCKING-HASTE!
AIN'T HAPPENIN', SITTIN' BULL. SO GO ON, FUCK OFF BACK TO YOUR WIGWAM N' SHIT.
KAO KOUA!
UNHAND THAT MAN AT ONCE!
MY MOST HUMBLE APOLOGIES, GOOD SIR. YOU MUST BE OFFICER BAD HORSE.
WHO THE FUCK ARE YOU? WHO GAVE YOU PERMISSION TO TALK TO MY PRISONER?
MY NAME IS MR. BRASS, AND I'M AN ASSOCIATE OF YOUR CHIEF RED CROW. I'M HERE MERELY TO ASSIST YOU IN YOUR MURDER INVESTIGATION.
YEAH, WELL HOW ABOUT YOU AND YOUR LITTLE FRIENDS HERE ASSIST EACH OTHER IN FUCKING THE HELL OFF?

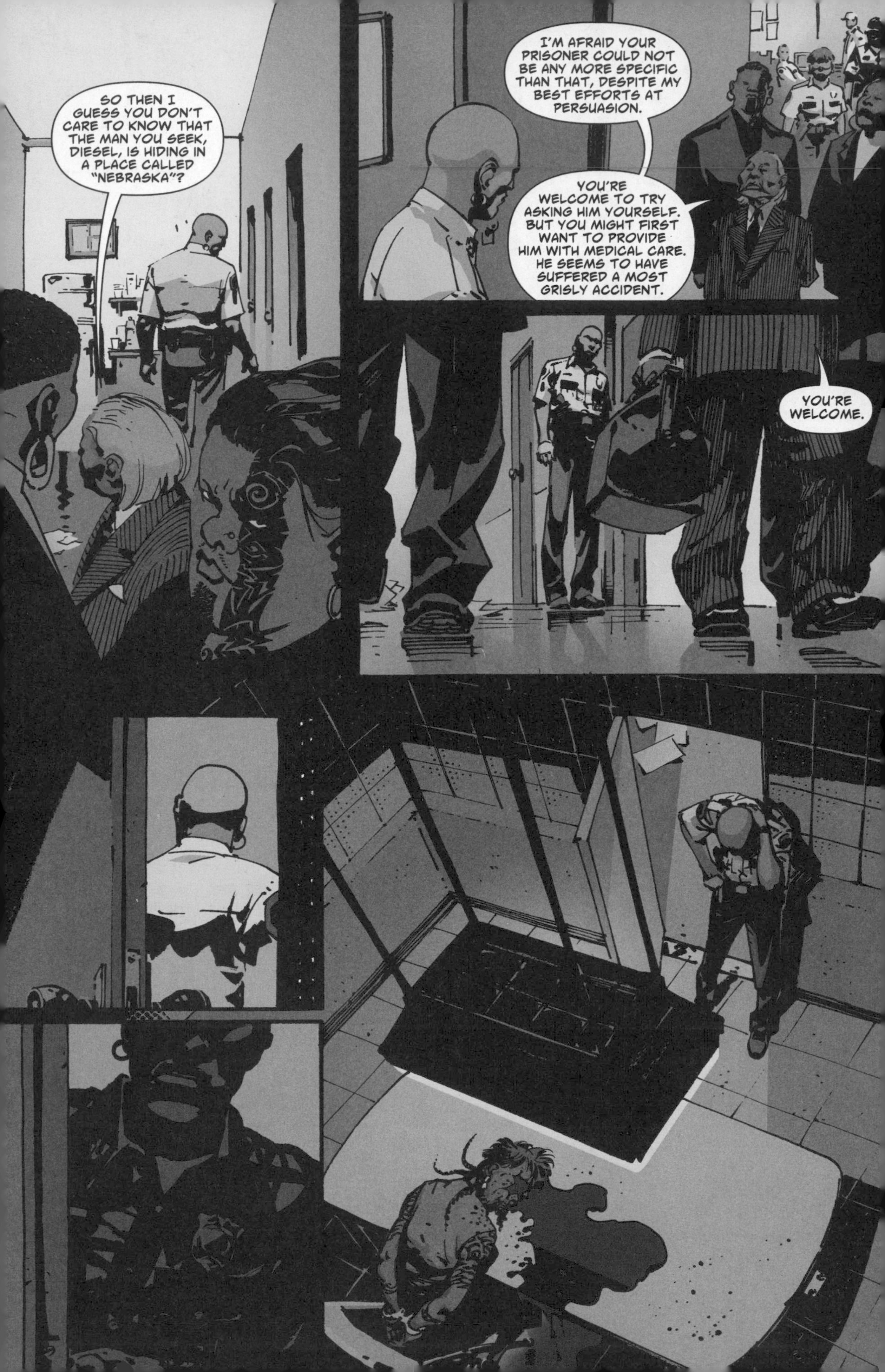
SO THEN I GUESS YOU DON'T CARE TO KNOW THAT THE MAN YOU SEEK, DIESEL, IS HIDING IN A PLACE CALLED "NEBRASKA"?
I'M AFRAID YOUR PRISONER COULD NOT BE ANY MORE SPECIFIC THAN THAT, DESPITE MY BEST EFFORTS AT PERSUASION.
YOU'RE WELCOME TO TRY ASKING HIM YOURSELF. BUT YOU MIGHT FIRST WANT TO PROVIDE HIM WITH MEDICAL CARE. HE SEEMS TO HAVE SUFFERED A MOST GRISLY ACCIDENT.
YOU'RE WELCOME.

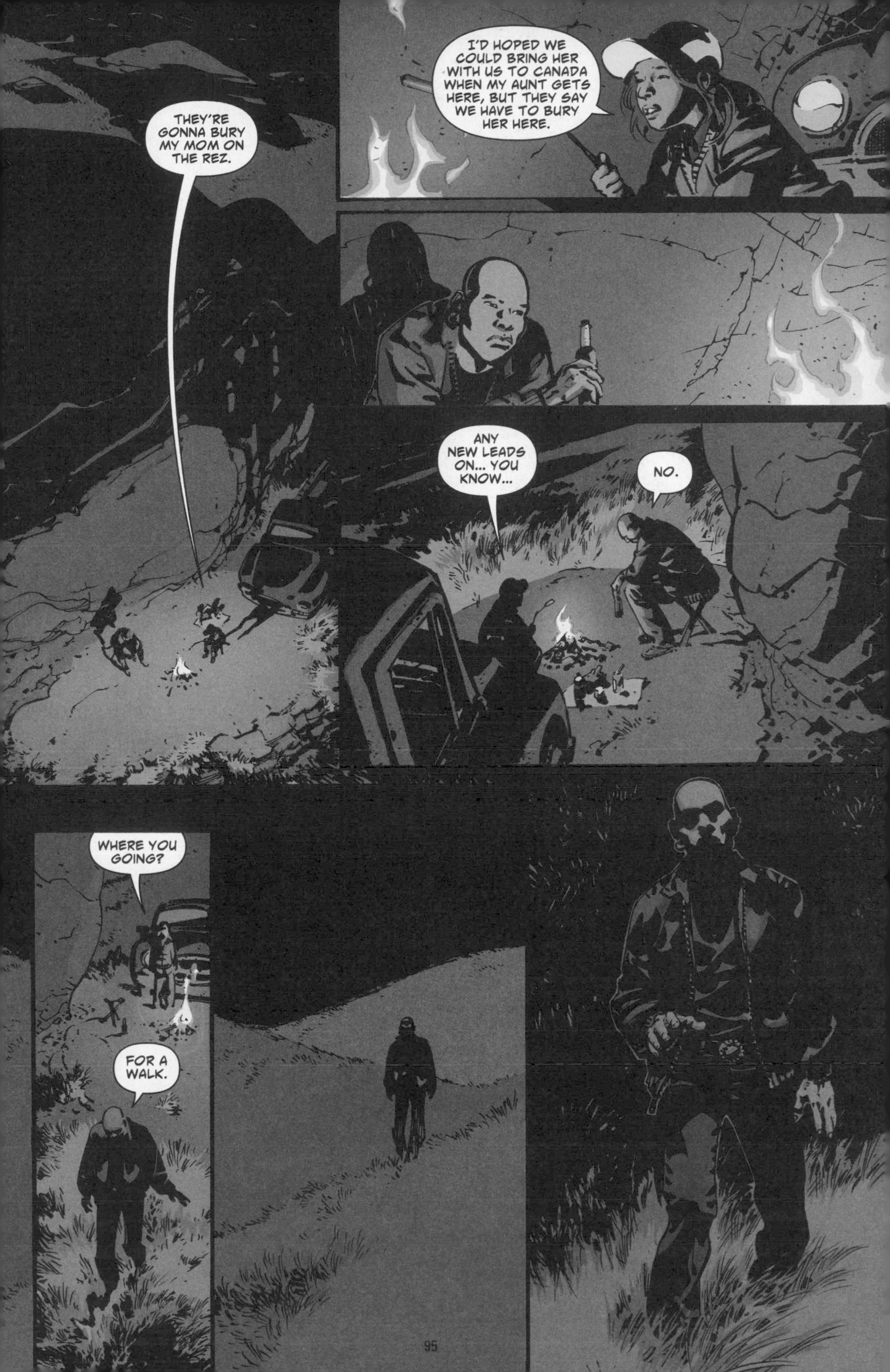
THEY'RE GONNA BURY MY MOM ON THE REZ.
I'D HOPED WE COULD BRING HER WITH US TO CANADA WHEN MY AUNT GETS HERE, BUT THEY SAY WE HAVE TO BURY HER HERE.
ANY NEW LEADS ON... YOU KNOW...
NO.
WHERE YOU GOING?
FOR A WALK.

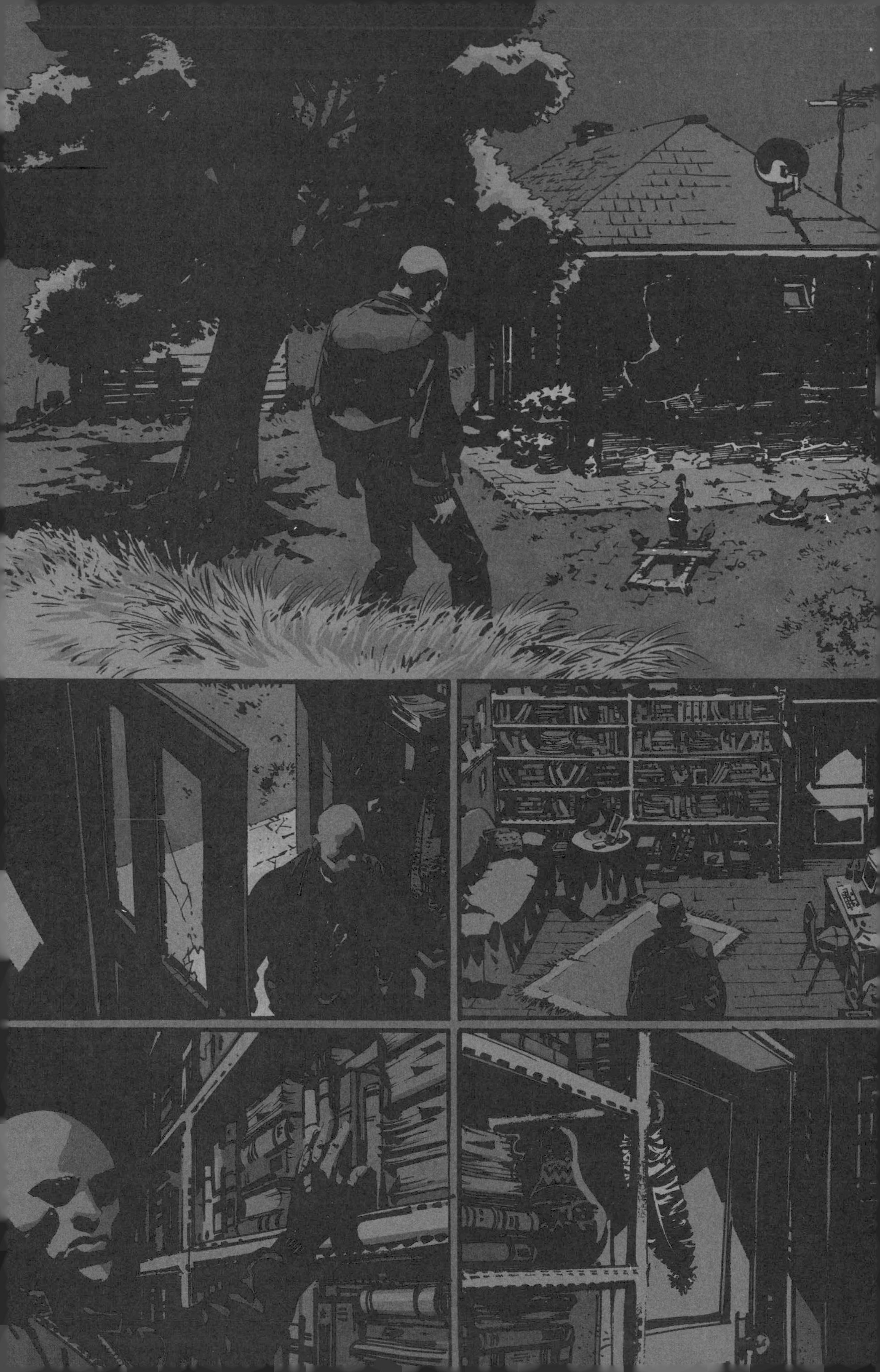

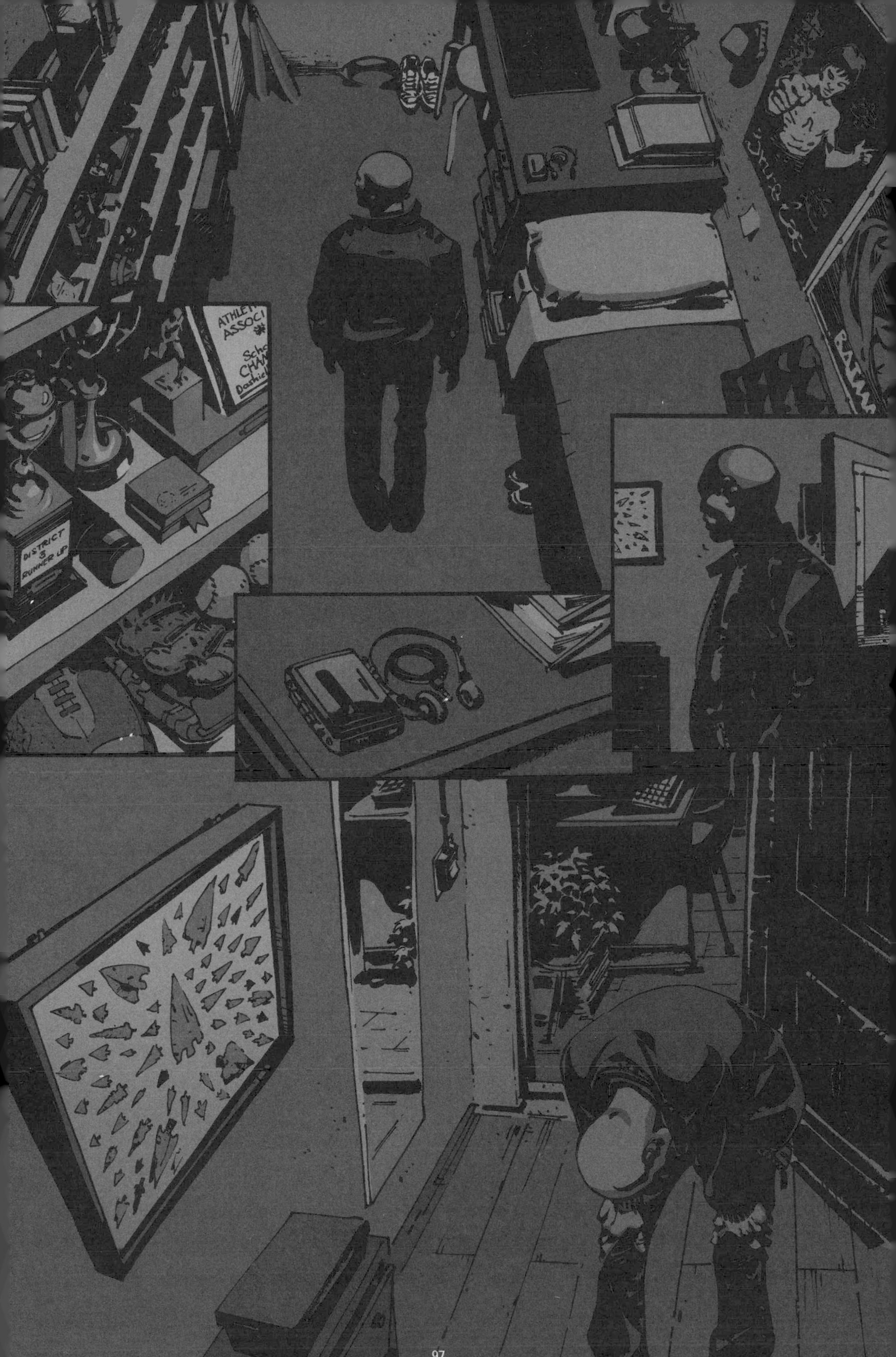
DISTRICT 3 RUNNER UP

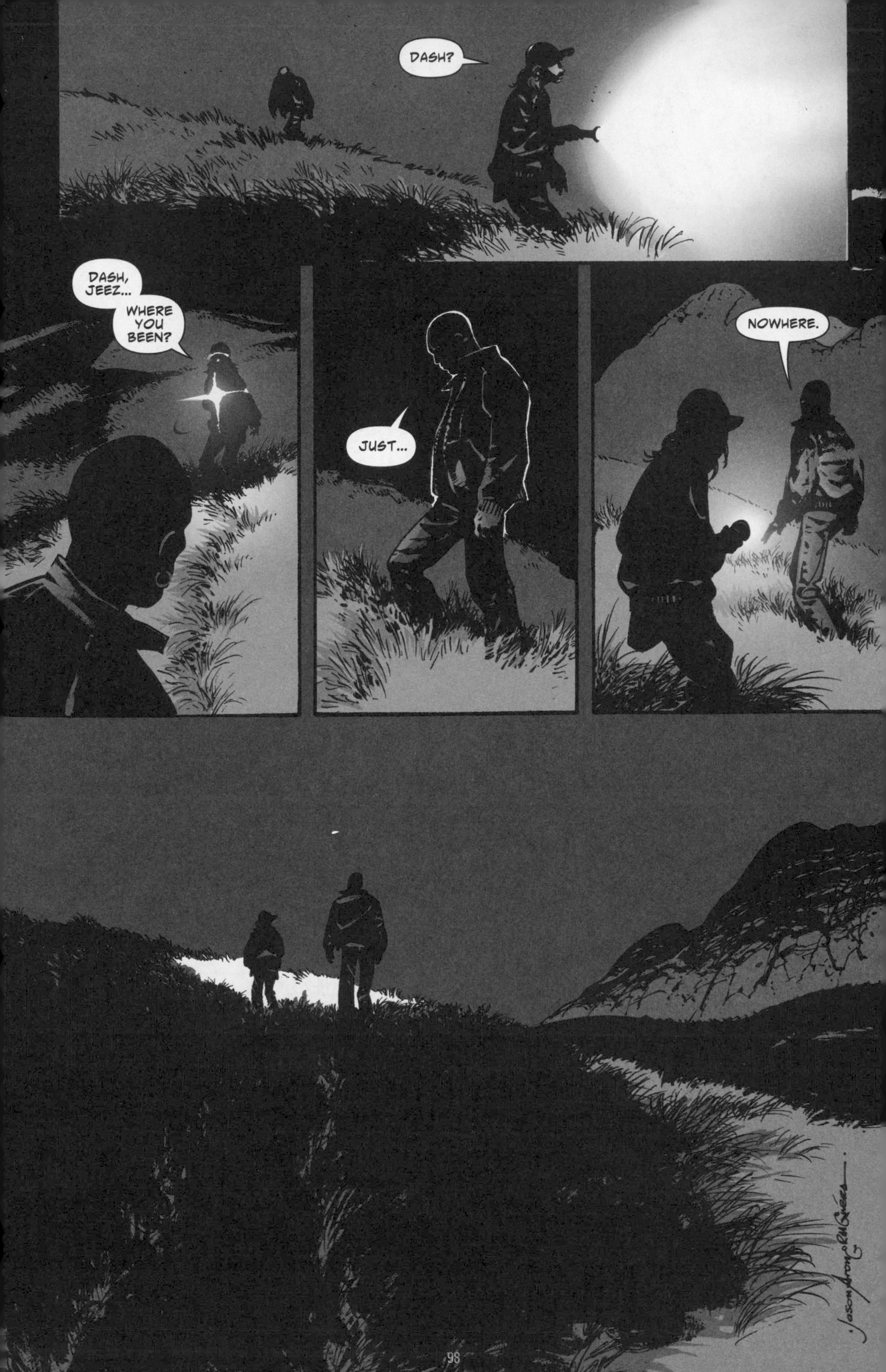
DASH?
DASH, JEEZ...
WHERE YOU BEEN?
JUST...
NOWHERE.

DEAD MOTHERS PART 4

COVER ART BY JOCK

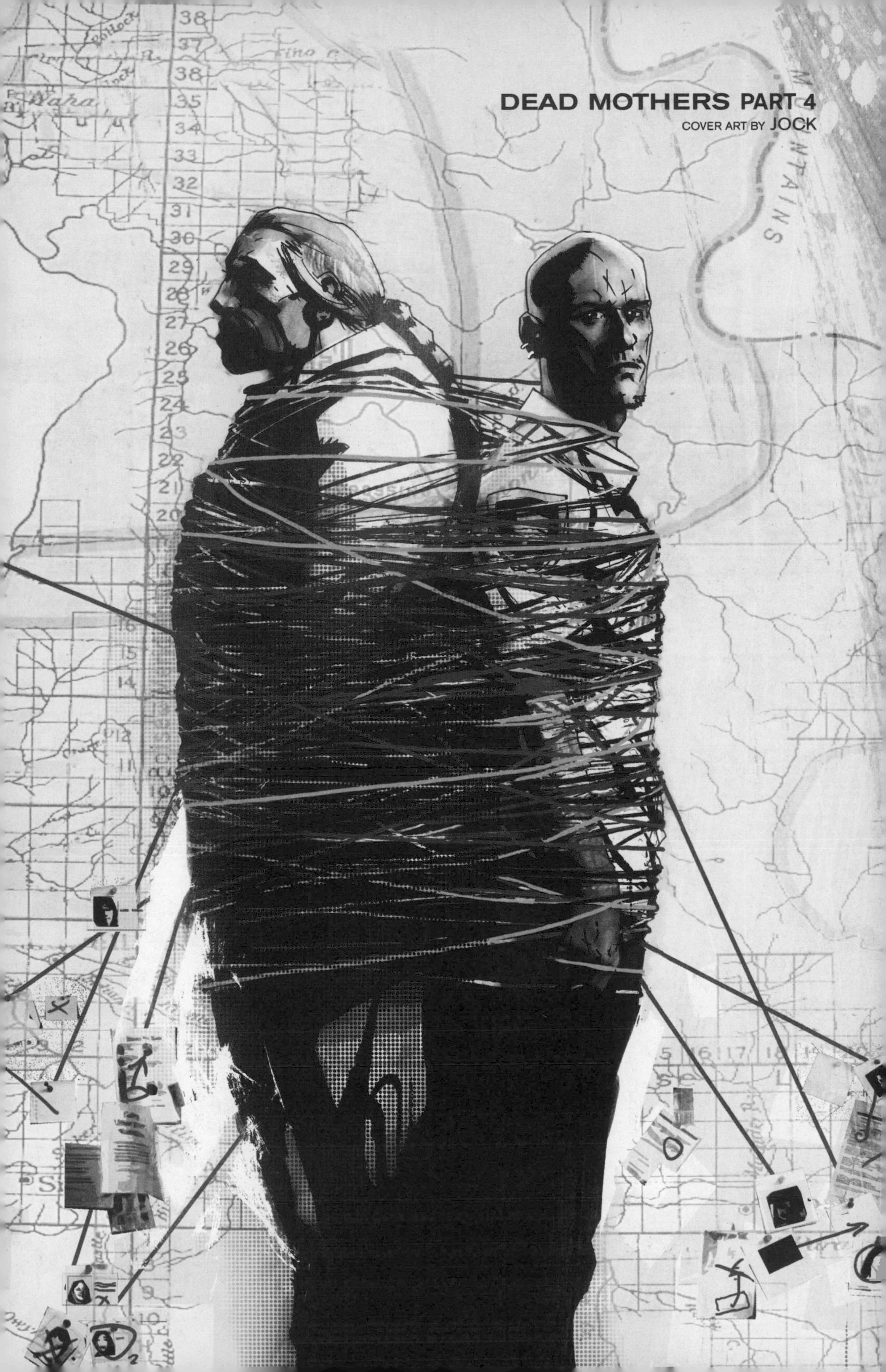

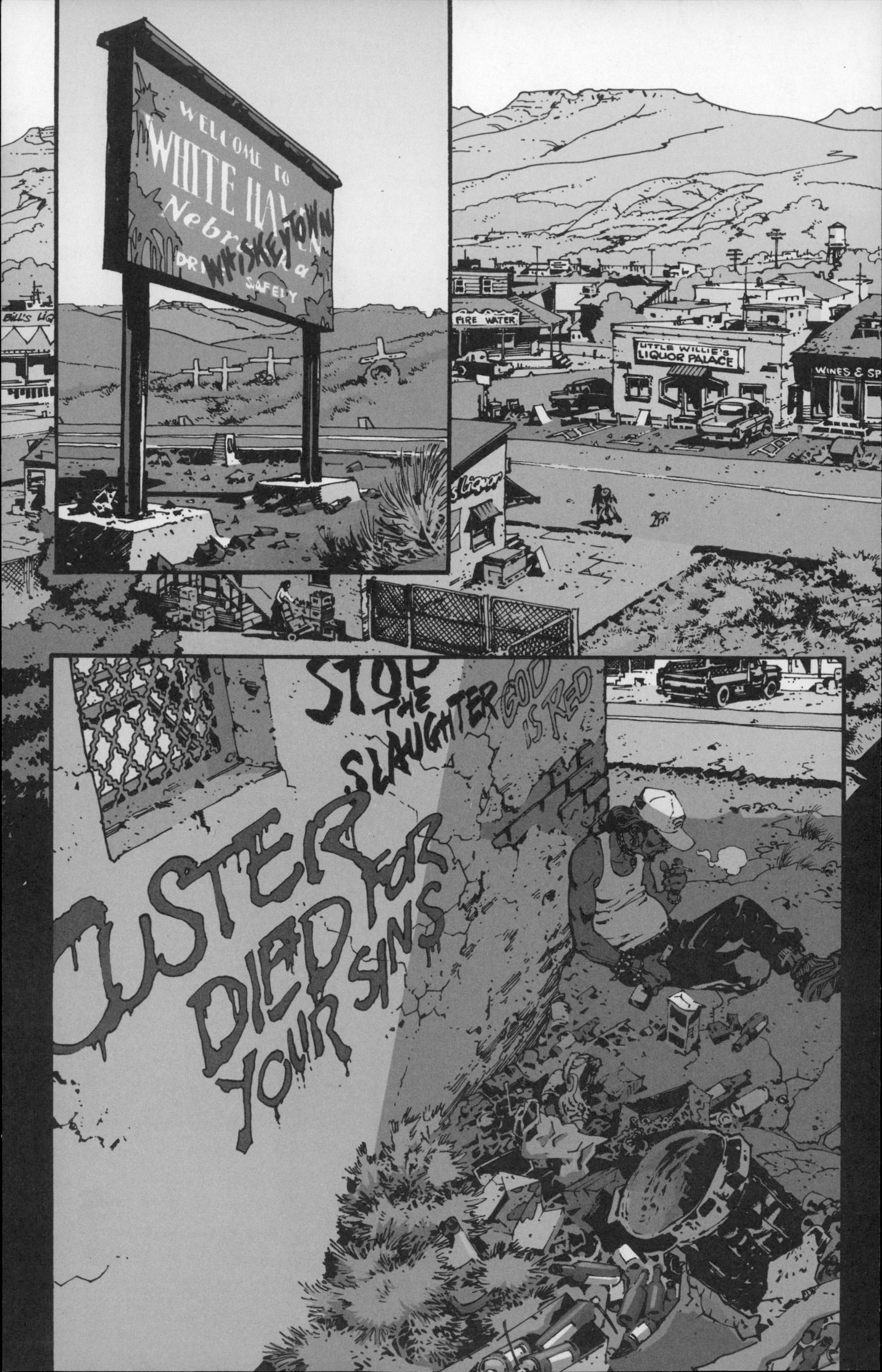
WELCOME TO
WHITE HAV
Nebr
WHISKEYTOWN
SAFELY
BILL'S LIQ
FIRE WATER
LITTLE WILLIE'S LIQUOR PALACE
WINES & SP
'S Liquor
STOP THE SLAUGHTER
GOD IS RED
CUSTER DIED FOR YOUR SINS

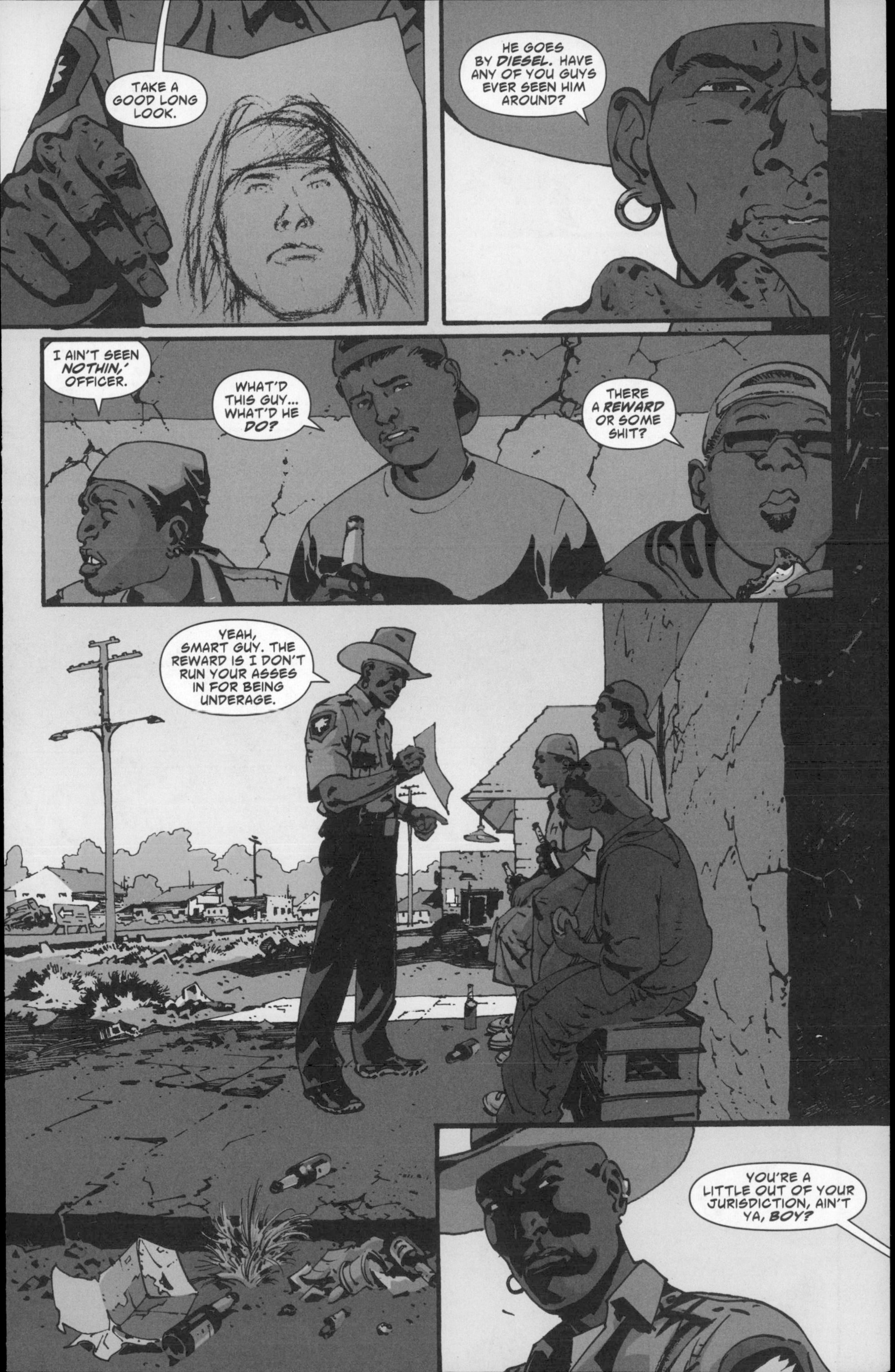
TAKE A GOOD LONG LOOK.
HE GOES BY DIESEL. HAVE ANY OF YOU GUYS EVER SEEN HIM AROUND?
I AIN'T SEEN NOTHIN,' OFFICER.
WHAT'D THIS GUY... WHAT'D HE DO?
THERE A REWARD OR SOME SHIT?
YEAH, SMART GUY. THE REWARD IS I DON'T RUN YOUR ASSES IN FOR BEING UNDERAGE.
YOU'RE A LITTLE OUT OF YOUR JURISDICTION, AIN'T YA, BOY?

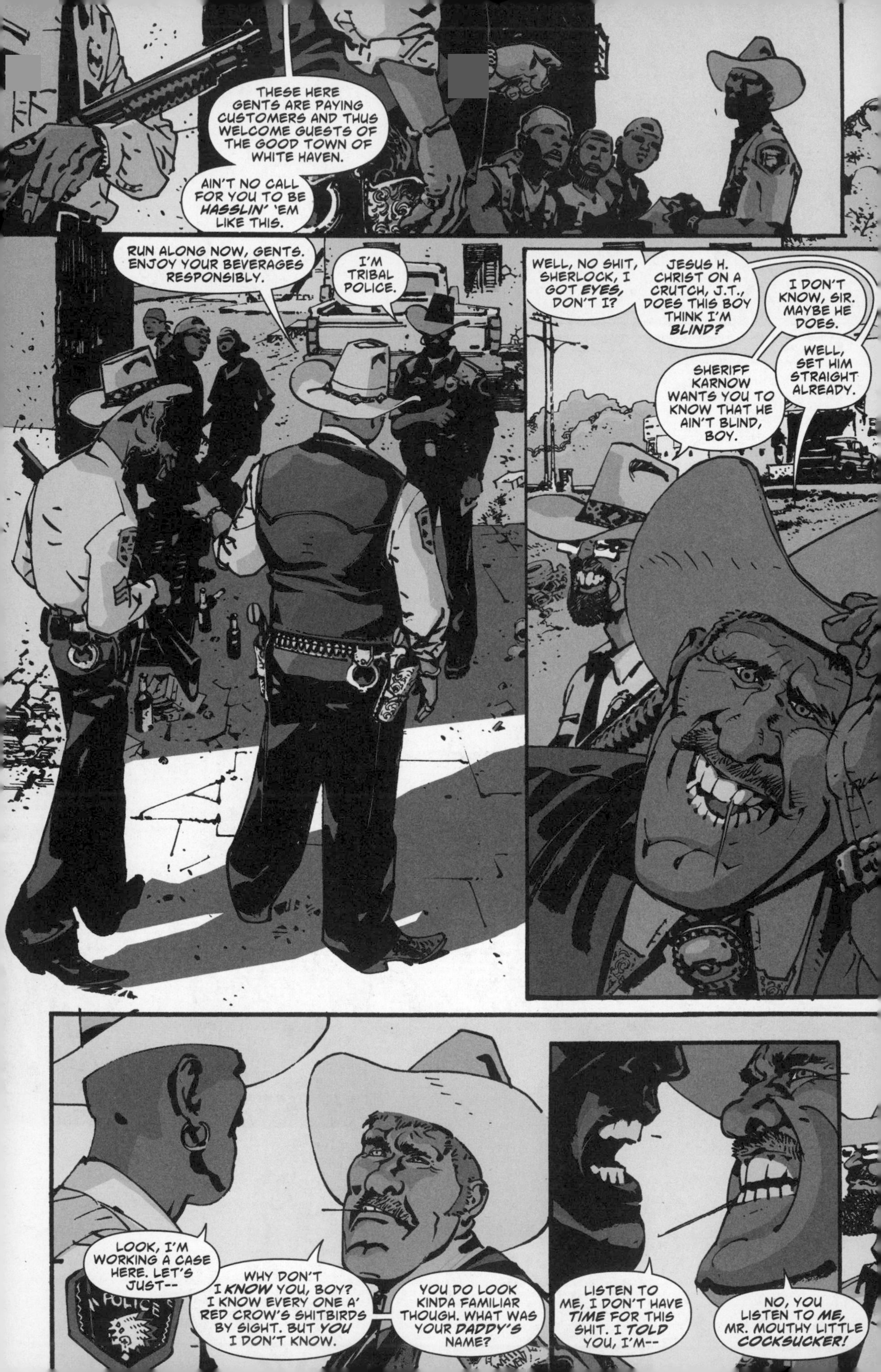

THESE HERE GENTS ARE PAYING CUSTOMERS AND THUS WELCOME GUESTS OF THE GOOD TOWN OF WHITE HAVEN.
AIN'T NO CALL FOR YOU TO BE *HASSLIN'* 'EM LIKE THIS.
RUN ALONG NOW, GENTS. ENJOY YOUR BEVERAGES RESPONSIBLY.
I'M TRIBAL POLICE.
WELL, NO SHIT, SHERLOCK, I GOT *EYES,* DON'T I?
JESUS H. CHRIST ON A CRUTCH, J.T., DOES THIS BOY THINK I'M *BLIND?*
I DON'T KNOW, SIR. MAYBE HE DOES.
WELL, SET HIM STRAIGHT ALREADY.
SHERIFF KARNOW WANTS YOU TO KNOW THAT HE AIN'T BLIND, BOY.
LOOK, I'M WORKING A CASE HERE. LET'S JUST--
WHY DON'T I *KNOW* YOU, BOY? I KNOW EVERY ONE A' RED CROW'S SHITBIRDS BY SIGHT. BUT *YOU* I DON'T KNOW.
YOU DO LOOK KINDA FAMILIAR THOUGH. WHAT WAS YOUR *DADDY'S* NAME?
LISTEN TO ME, I DON'T HAVE *TIME* FOR THIS SHIT. I *TOLD* YOU, I'M--
NO, YOU LISTEN TO *ME,* MR. MOUTHY LITTLE *COCKSUCKER!*
POLICE

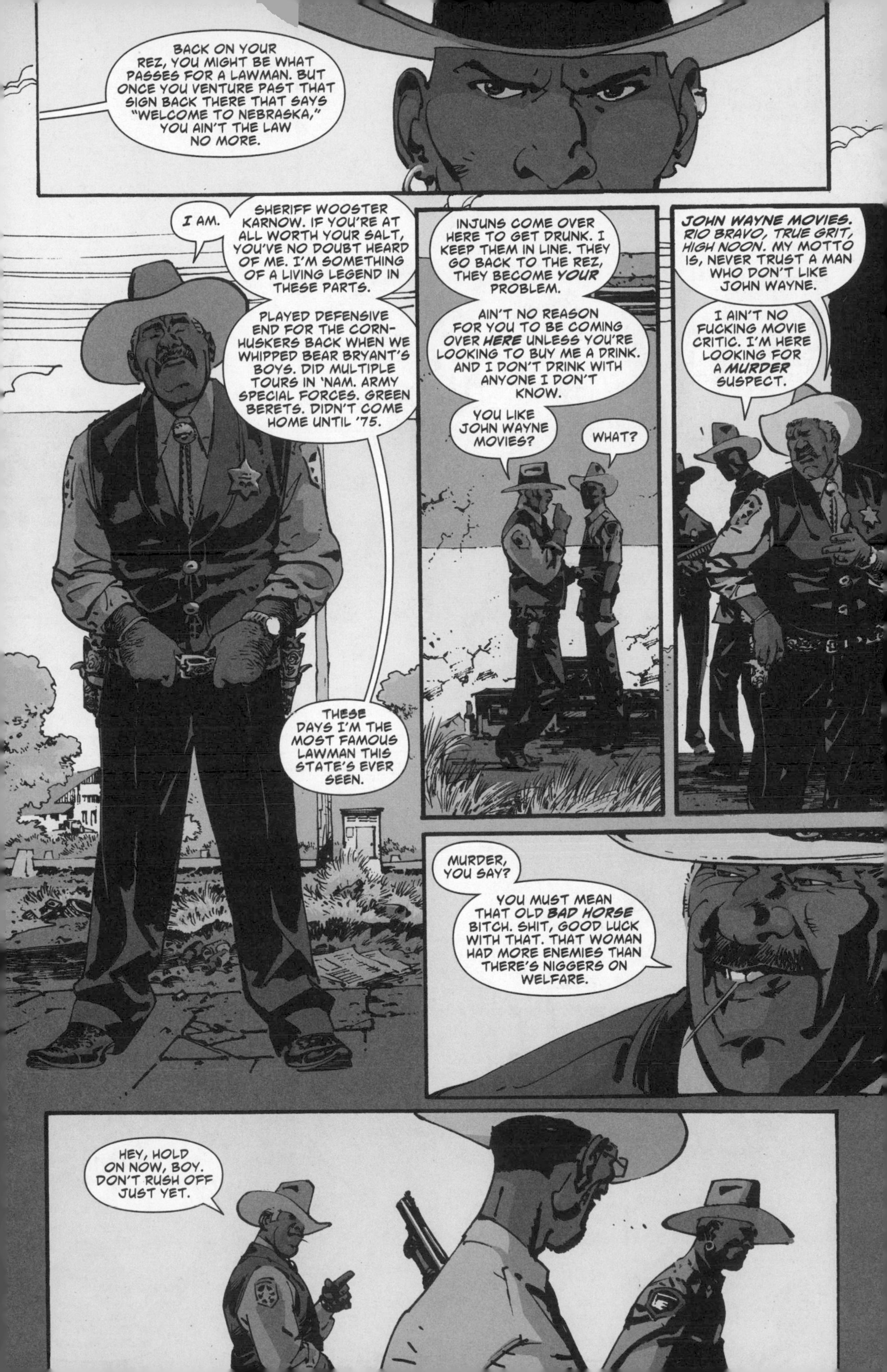
BACK ON YOUR REZ, YOU MIGHT BE WHAT PASSES FOR A LAWMAN. BUT ONCE YOU VENTURE PAST THAT SIGN BACK THERE THAT SAYS "WELCOME TO NEBRASKA," YOU AIN'T THE LAW NO MORE.
I AM.
SHERIFF WOOSTER KARNOW. IF YOU'RE AT ALL WORTH YOUR SALT, YOU'VE NO DOUBT HEARD OF ME. I'M SOMETHING OF A LIVING LEGEND IN THESE PARTS.
PLAYED DEFENSIVE END FOR THE CORN-HUSKERS BACK WHEN WE WHIPPED BEAR BRYANT'S BOYS. DID MULTIPLE TOURS IN 'NAM. ARMY SPECIAL FORCES. GREEN BERETS. DIDN'T COME HOME UNTIL '75.
THESE DAYS I'M THE MOST FAMOUS LAWMAN THIS STATE'S EVER SEEN.
INJUNS COME OVER HERE TO GET DRUNK. I KEEP THEM IN LINE. THEY GO BACK TO THE REZ, THEY BECOME *YOUR* PROBLEM.
AIN'T NO REASON FOR YOU TO BE COMING OVER *HERE* UNLESS YOU'RE LOOKING TO BUY ME A DRINK. AND I DON'T DRINK WITH ANYONE I DON'T KNOW.
YOU LIKE JOHN WAYNE MOVIES?
WHAT?
JOHN WAYNE MOVIES. RIO BRAVO, TRUE GRIT, HIGH NOON. MY MOTTO IS, NEVER TRUST A MAN WHO DON'T LIKE JOHN WAYNE.
I AIN'T NO FUCKING MOVIE CRITIC. I'M HERE LOOKING FOR A *MURDER* SUSPECT.
MURDER, YOU SAY?
YOU MUST MEAN THAT OLD *BAD HORSE* BITCH. SHIT, GOOD LUCK WITH THAT. THAT WOMAN HAD MORE ENEMIES THAN THERE'S NIGGERS ON WELFARE.
HEY, HOLD ON NOW, BOY. DON'T RUSH OFF JUST YET.

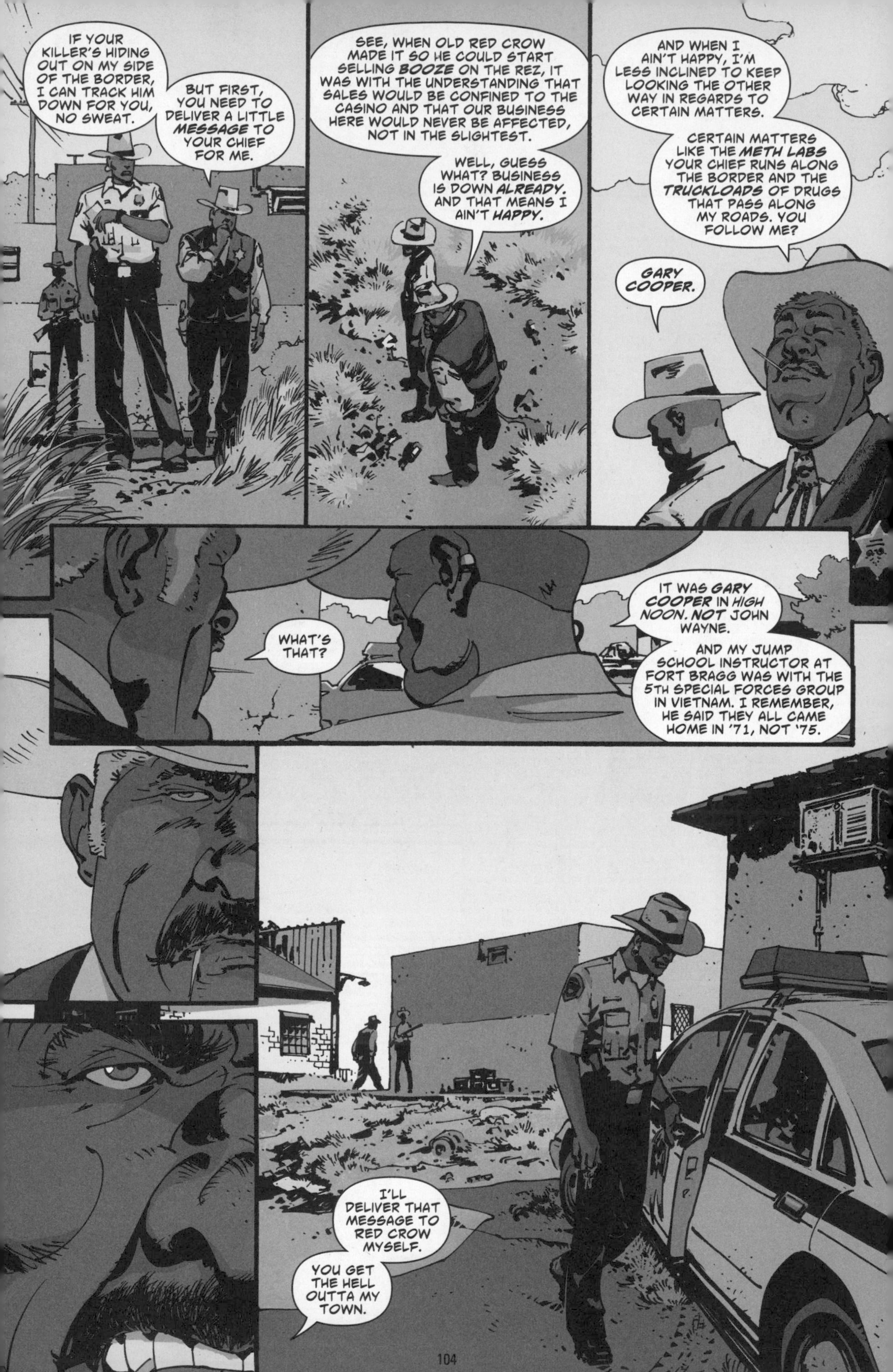
IF YOUR KILLER'S HIDING OUT ON MY SIDE OF THE BORDER, I CAN TRACK HIM DOWN FOR YOU, NO SWEAT.
BUT FIRST, YOU NEED TO DELIVER A LITTLE MESSAGE TO YOUR CHIEF FOR ME.
SEE, WHEN OLD RED CROW MADE IT SO HE COULD START SELLING BOOZE ON THE REZ, IT WAS WITH THE UNDERSTANDING THAT SALES WOULD BE CONFINED TO THE CASINO AND THAT OUR BUSINESS HERE WOULD NEVER BE AFFECTED, NOT IN THE SLIGHTEST.
WELL, GUESS WHAT? BUSINESS IS DOWN ALREADY. AND THAT MEANS I AIN'T HAPPY.
AND WHEN I AIN'T HAPPY, I'M LESS INCLINED TO KEEP LOOKING THE OTHER WAY IN REGARDS TO CERTAIN MATTERS.
CERTAIN MATTERS LIKE THE METH LABS YOUR CHIEF RUNS ALONG THE BORDER AND THE TRUCKLOADS OF DRUGS THAT PASS ALONG MY ROADS. YOU FOLLOW ME?
GARY COOPER.
WHAT'S THAT?
IT WAS GARY COOPER IN HIGH NOON. NOT JOHN WAYNE.
AND MY JUMP SCHOOL INSTRUCTOR AT FORT BRAGG WAS WITH THE 5TH SPECIAL FORCES GROUP IN VIETNAM. I REMEMBER, HE SAID THEY ALL CAME HOME IN '71, NOT '75.
I'LL DELIVER THAT MESSAGE TO RED CROW MYSELF.
YOU GET THE HELL OUTTA MY TOWN.

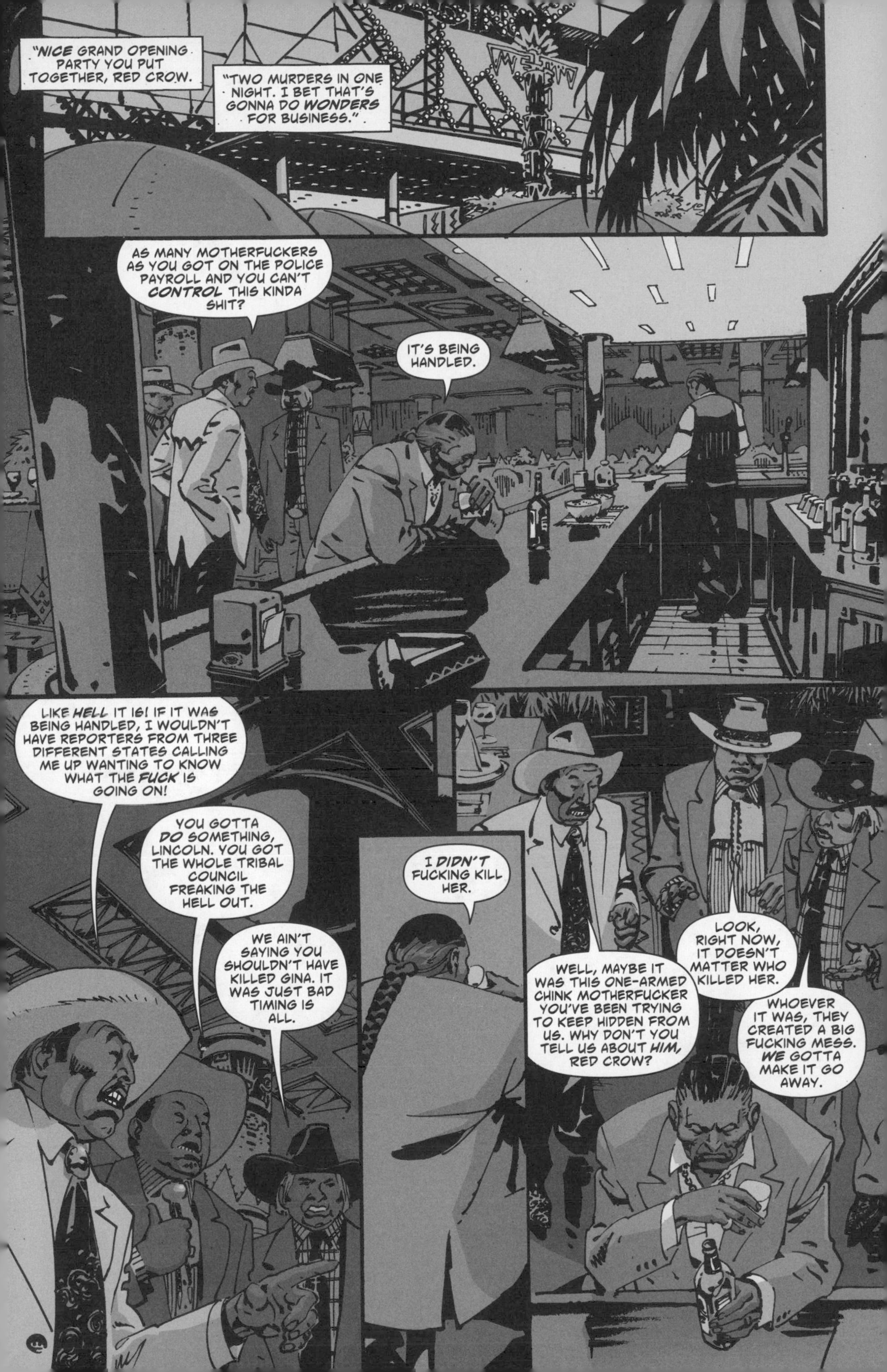
"NICE GRAND OPENING PARTY YOU PUT TOGETHER, RED CROW.
"TWO MURDERS IN ONE NIGHT. I BET THAT'S GONNA DO WONDERS FOR BUSINESS."
AS MANY MOTHERFUCKERS AS YOU GOT ON THE POLICE PAYROLL AND YOU CAN'T CONTROL THIS KINDA SHIT?
IT'S BEING HANDLED.
LIKE HELL IT IS! IF IT WAS BEING HANDLED, I WOULDN'T HAVE REPORTERS FROM THREE DIFFERENT STATES CALLING ME UP WANTING TO KNOW WHAT THE FUCK IS GOING ON!
YOU GOTTA DO SOMETHING, LINCOLN. YOU GOT THE WHOLE TRIBAL COUNCIL FREAKING THE HELL OUT.
WE AIN'T SAYING YOU SHOULDN'T HAVE KILLED GINA. IT WAS JUST BAD TIMING IS ALL.
I DIDN'T FUCKING KILL HER.
WELL, MAYBE IT WAS THIS ONE-ARMED CHINK MOTHERFUCKER YOU'VE BEEN TRYING TO KEEP HIDDEN FROM US. WHY DON'T YOU TELL US ABOUT HIM, RED CROW?
LOOK, RIGHT NOW, IT DOESN'T MATTER WHO KILLED HER.
WHOEVER IT WAS, THEY CREATED A BIG FUCKING MESS. WE GOTTA MAKE IT GO AWAY.

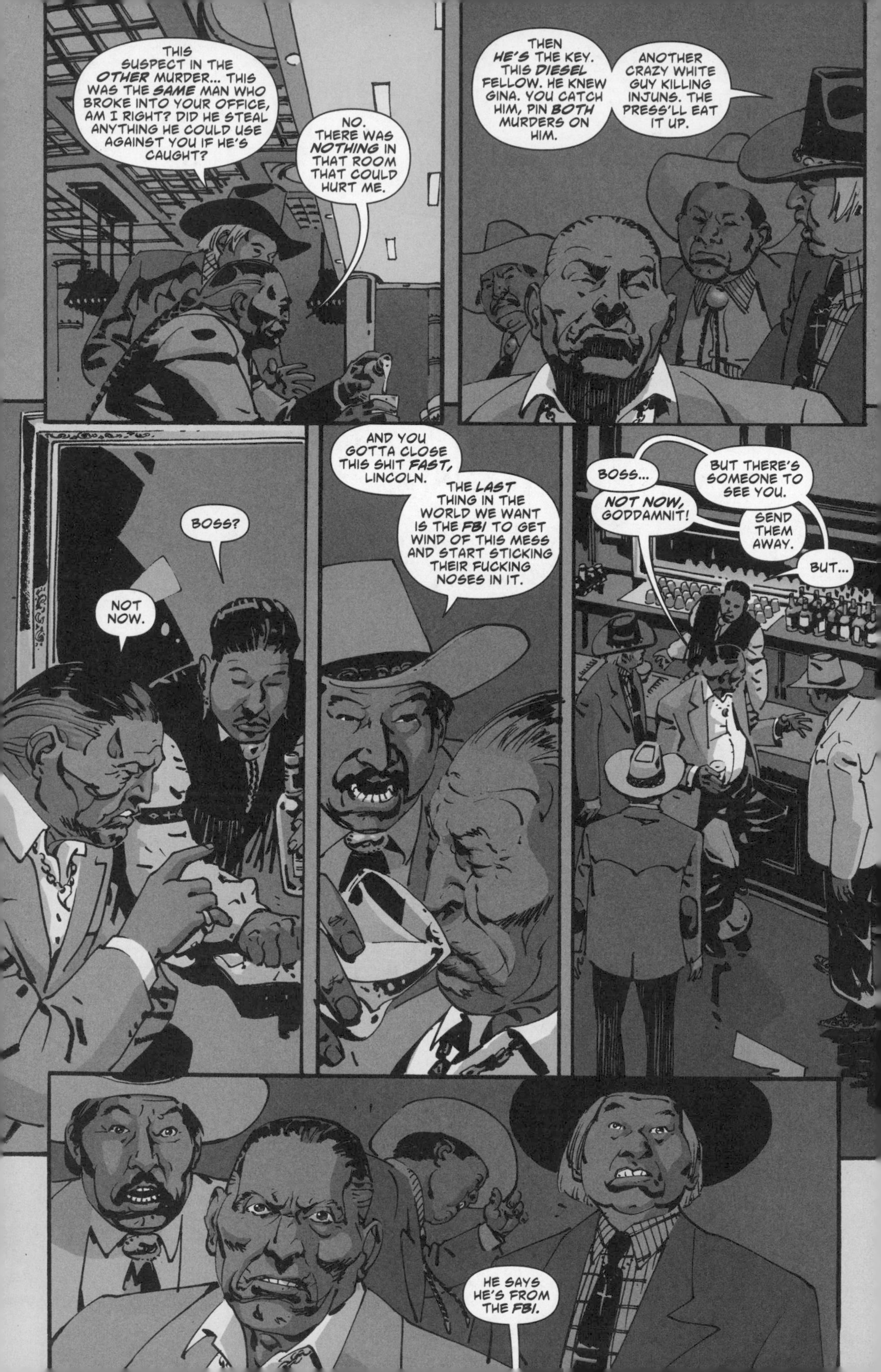
THIS SUSPECT IN THE OTHER MURDER... THIS WAS THE SAME MAN WHO BROKE INTO YOUR OFFICE, AM I RIGHT? DID HE STEAL ANYTHING HE COULD USE AGAINST YOU IF HE'S CAUGHT?
NO. THERE WAS NOTHING IN THAT ROOM THAT COULD HURT ME.
THEN HE'S THE KEY. THIS DIESEL FELLOW. HE KNEW GINA. YOU CATCH HIM, PIN BOTH MURDERS ON HIM.
ANOTHER CRAZY WHITE GUY KILLING INJUNS. THE PRESS'LL EAT IT UP.
BOSS?
NOT NOW.
AND YOU GOTTA CLOSE THIS SHIT FAST, LINCOLN.
THE LAST THING IN THE WORLD WE WANT IS THE FBI TO GET WIND OF THIS MESS AND START STICKING THEIR FUCKING NOSES IN IT.
BOSS...
BUT THERE'S SOMEONE TO SEE YOU.
NOT NOW, GODDAMNIT!
SEND THEM AWAY.
BUT...
HE SAYS HE'S FROM THE FBI.

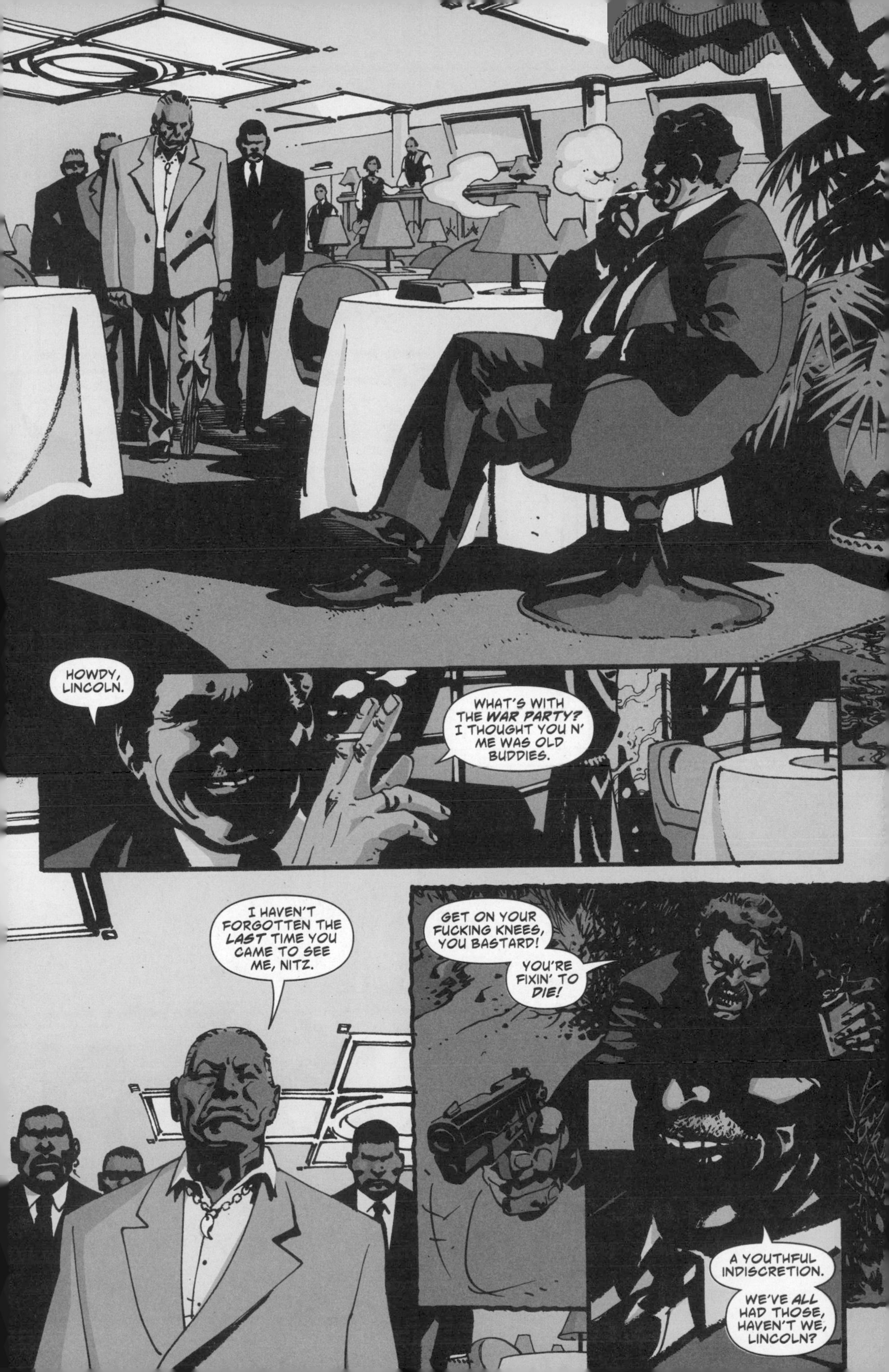
HOWDY, LINCOLN.
WHAT'S WITH THE *WAR PARTY?* I THOUGHT YOU N' ME WAS OLD BUDDIES.
I HAVEN'T FORGOTTEN THE *LAST* TIME YOU CAME TO SEE ME, NITZ.
GET ON YOUR FUCKING KNEES, YOU BASTARD!
YOU'RE FIXIN' TO *DIE!*
A YOUTHFUL INDISCRETION.
WE'VE *ALL* HAD THOSE, HAVEN'T WE, LINCOLN?

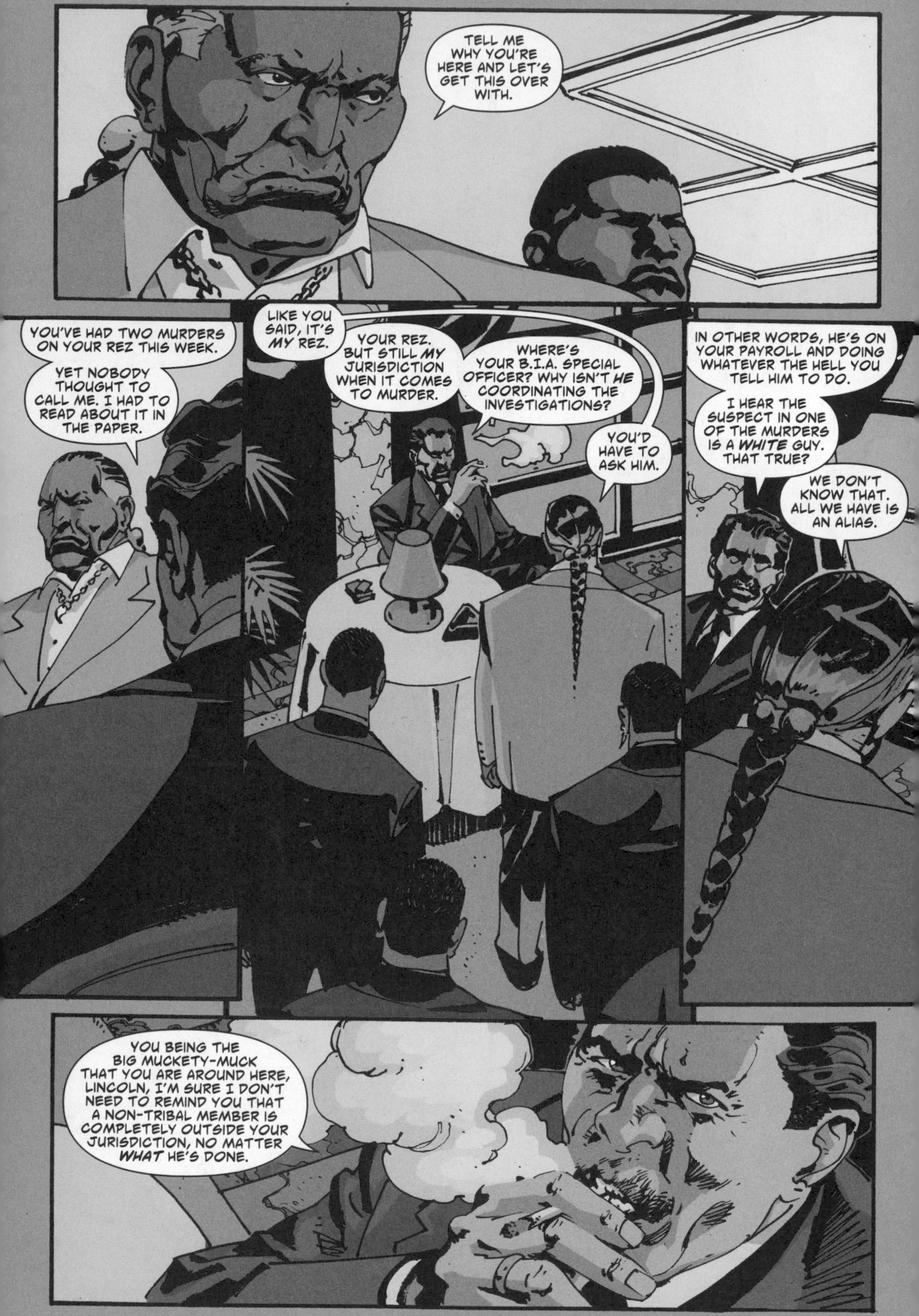
TELL ME WHY YOU'RE HERE AND LET'S GET THIS OVER WITH.
YOU'VE HAD TWO MURDERS ON YOUR REZ THIS WEEK.
YET NOBODY THOUGHT TO CALL ME. I HAD TO READ ABOUT IT IN THE PAPER.
LIKE YOU SAID, IT'S *MY* REZ.
YOUR REZ. BUT STILL *MY* JURISDICTION WHEN IT COMES TO MURDER.
WHERE'S YOUR B.I.A. SPECIAL OFFICER? WHY ISN'T *HE* COORDINATING THE INVESTIGATIONS?
YOU'D HAVE TO ASK HIM.
IN OTHER WORDS, HE'S ON YOUR PAYROLL AND DOING WHATEVER THE HELL YOU TELL HIM TO DO.
I HEAR THE SUSPECT IN ONE OF THE MURDERS IS A *WHITE* GUY. THAT TRUE?
WE DON'T KNOW THAT. ALL WE HAVE IS AN ALIAS.
YOU BEING THE BIG MUCKETY-MUCK THAT YOU ARE AROUND HERE, LINCOLN, I'M SURE I DON'T NEED TO REMIND YOU THAT A NON-TRIBAL MEMBER IS COMPLETELY OUTSIDE YOUR JURISDICTION, NO MATTER *WHAT* HE'S DONE.

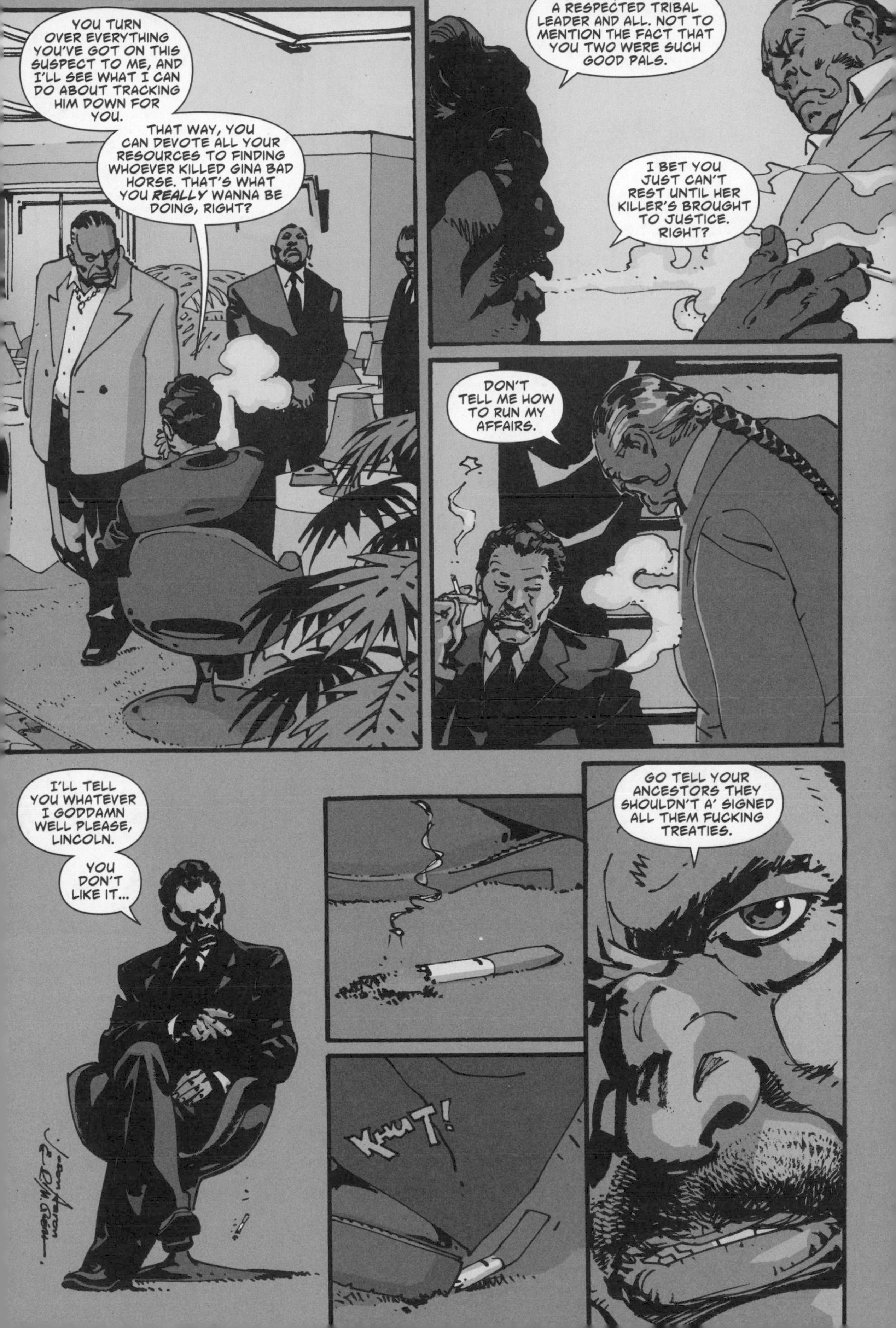
YOU TURN OVER EVERYTHING YOU'VE GOT ON THIS SUSPECT TO ME, AND I'LL SEE WHAT I CAN DO ABOUT TRACKING HIM DOWN FOR YOU.
THAT WAY, YOU CAN DEVOTE ALL YOUR RESOURCES TO FINDING WHOEVER KILLED GINA BAD HORSE. THAT'S WHAT YOU *REALLY* WANNA BE DOING, RIGHT?
I MEAN, SHE WAS A RESPECTED TRIBAL LEADER AND ALL. NOT TO MENTION THE FACT THAT YOU TWO WERE SUCH GOOD PALS.
I BET YOU JUST CAN'T REST UNTIL HER KILLER'S BROUGHT TO JUSTICE. RIGHT?
DON'T TELL ME HOW TO RUN MY AFFAIRS.
I'LL TELL YOU WHATEVER I GODDAMN WELL PLEASE, LINCOLN.
YOU DON'T LIKE IT...
GO TELL YOUR ANCESTORS THEY SHOULDN'T A' SIGNED ALL THEM FUCKING TREATIES.

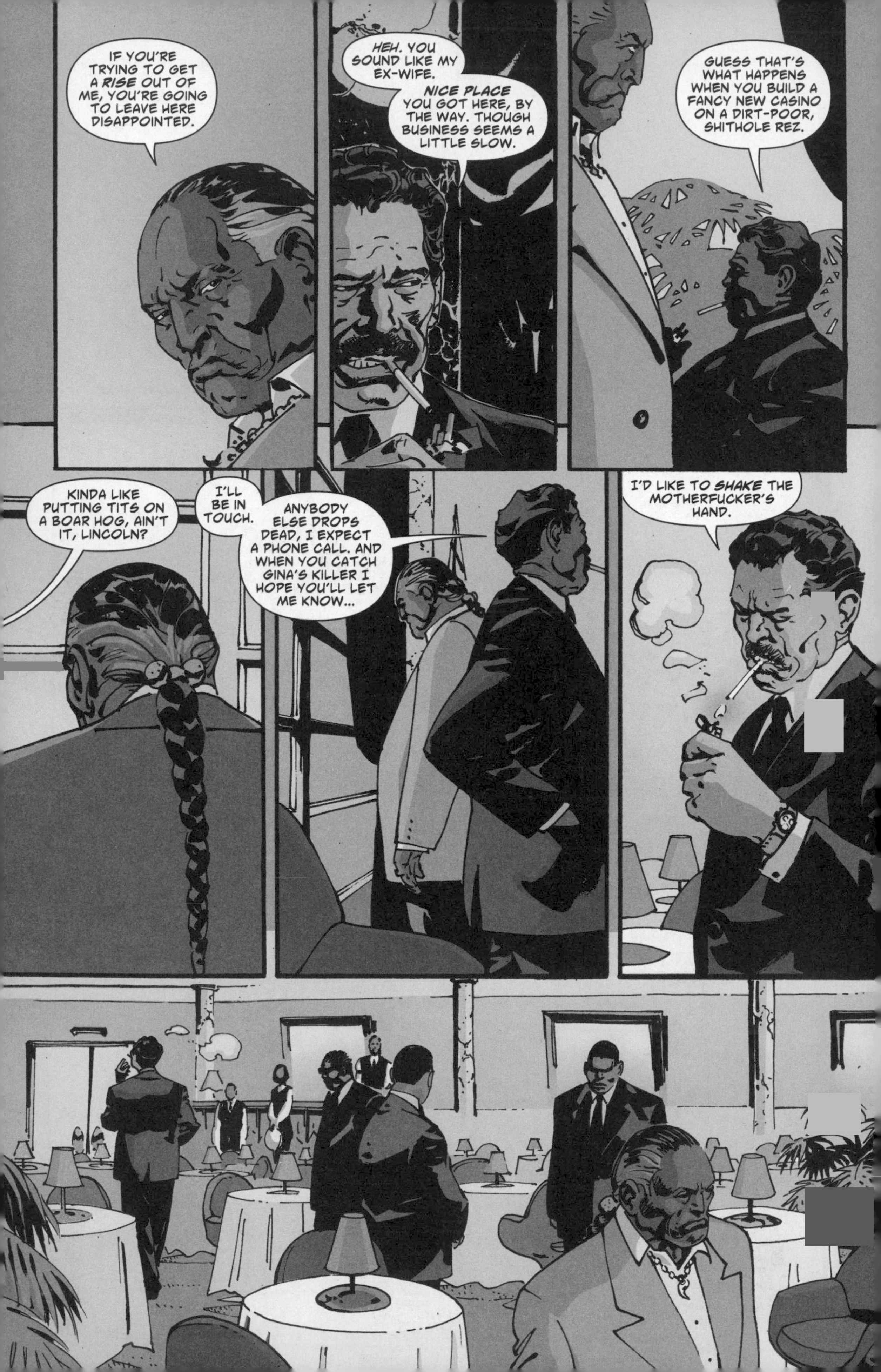

IF YOU'RE TRYING TO GET A *RISE* OUT OF ME, YOU'RE GOING TO LEAVE HERE DISAPPOINTED.
HEH. YOU SOUND LIKE MY EX-WIFE.
NICE PLACE YOU GOT HERE, BY THE WAY. THOUGH BUSINESS SEEMS A LITTLE SLOW.
GUESS THAT'S WHAT HAPPENS WHEN YOU BUILD A FANCY NEW CASINO ON A DIRT-POOR, SHITHOLE REZ.
KINDA LIKE PUTTING TITS ON A BOAR HOG, AIN'T IT, LINCOLN?
I'LL BE IN TOUCH.
ANYBODY ELSE DROPS DEAD, I EXPECT A PHONE CALL. AND WHEN YOU CATCH GINA'S KILLER I HOPE YOU'LL LET ME KNOW...
I'D LIKE TO *SHAKE* THE MOTHERFUCKER'S HAND.

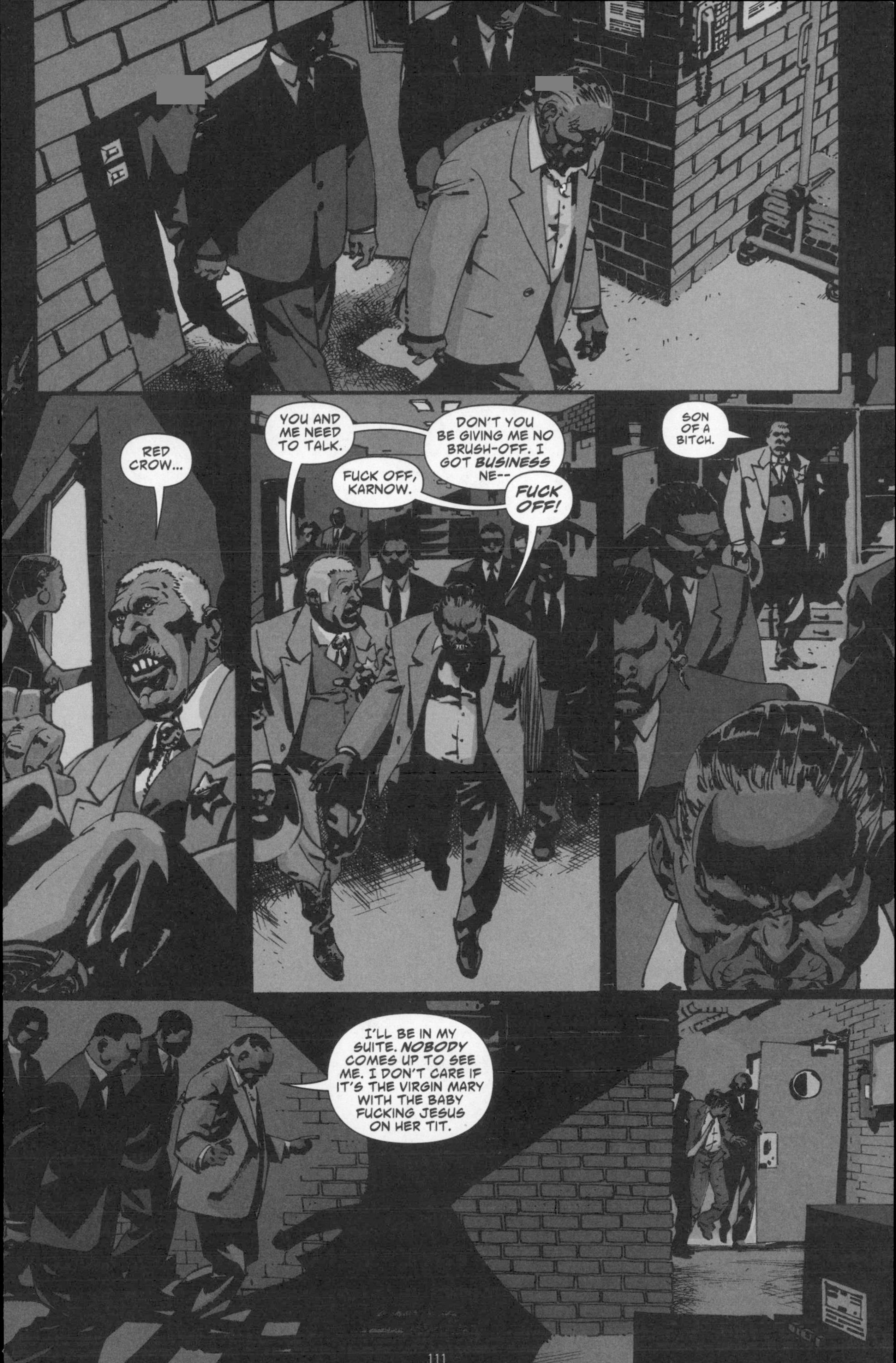
RED CROW...
YOU AND ME NEED TO TALK.
FUCK OFF, KARNOW.
DON'T YOU BE GIVING ME NO BRUSH-OFF. I GOT *BUSINESS* NE--
FUCK OFF!
SON OF A BITCH.
I'LL BE IN MY SUITE. *NOBODY* COMES UP TO SEE ME. I DON'T CARE IF IT'S THE VIRGIN MARY WITH THE BABY FUCKING JESUS ON HER TIT.

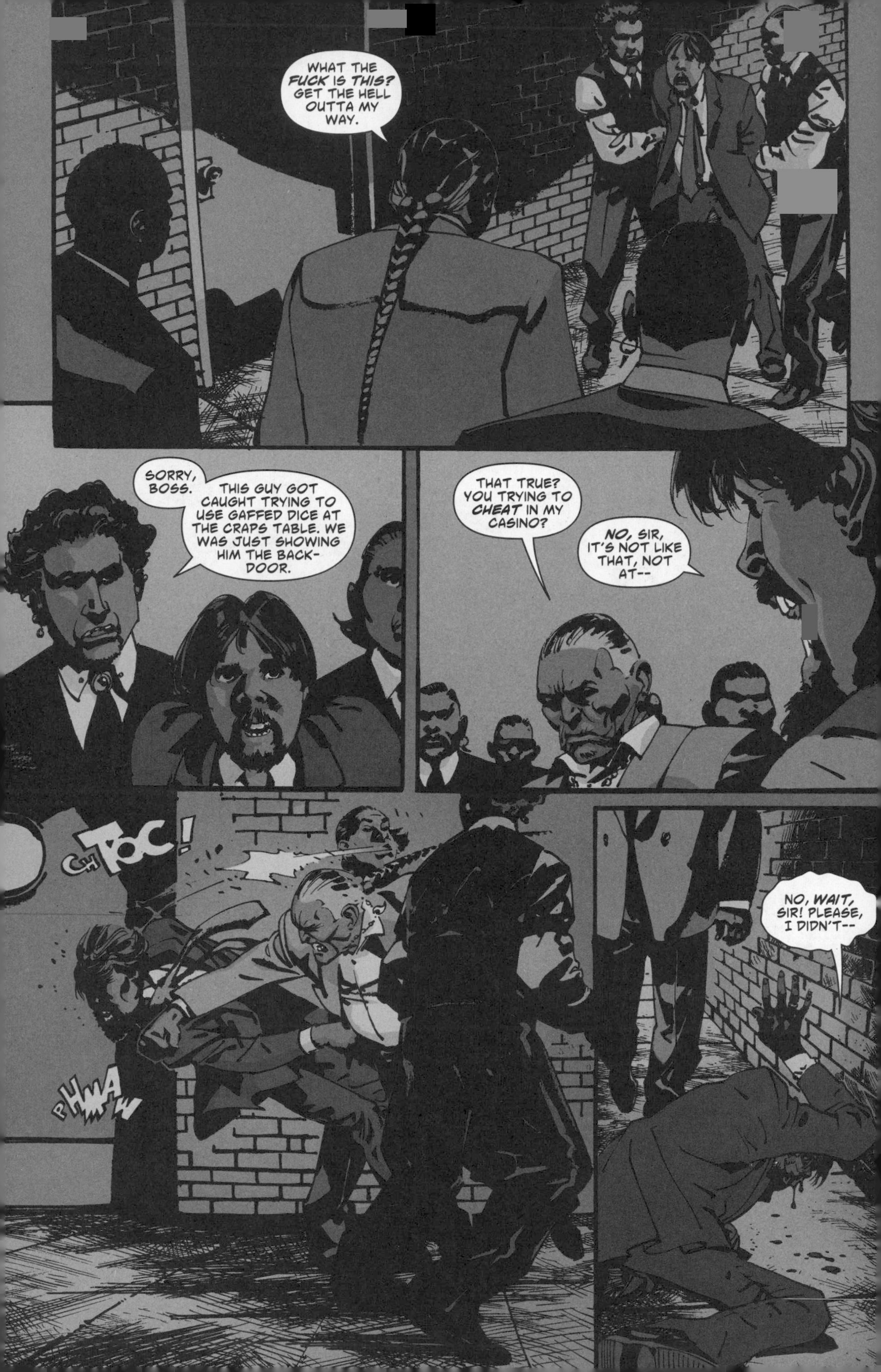

WHAT THE *FUCK* IS *THIS?* GET THE HELL OUTTA MY WAY.
SORRY, BOSS.
THIS GUY GOT CAUGHT TRYING TO USE GAFFED DICE AT THE CRAPS TABLE. WE WAS JUST SHOWING HIM THE BACK-DOOR.
THAT TRUE? YOU TRYING TO *CHEAT* IN MY CASINO?
NO, SIR, IT'S NOT LIKE THAT, NOT AT--
CHTOC!
PHWAW
NO, *WAIT*, SIR! PLEASE, I DIDN'T--

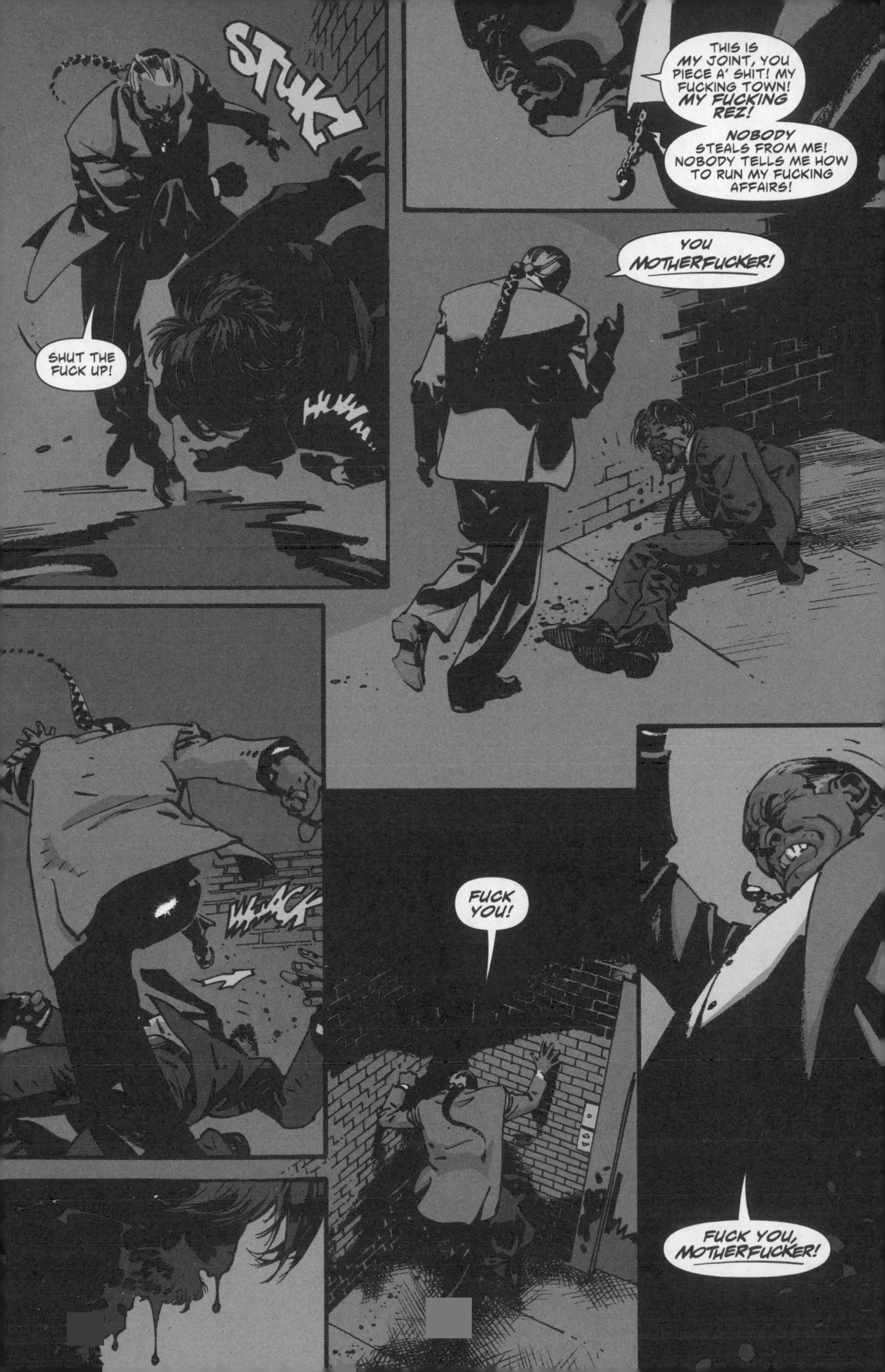
STUK
SHUT THE FUCK UP!
THIS IS MY JOINT, YOU PIECE A' SHIT! MY FUCKING TOWN! MY FUCKING REZ!
NOBODY STEALS FROM ME! NOBODY TELLS ME HOW TO RUN MY FUCKING AFFAIRS!
YOU MOTHERFUCKER!
WHACK
FUCK YOU!
FUCK YOU, MOTHERFUCKER!

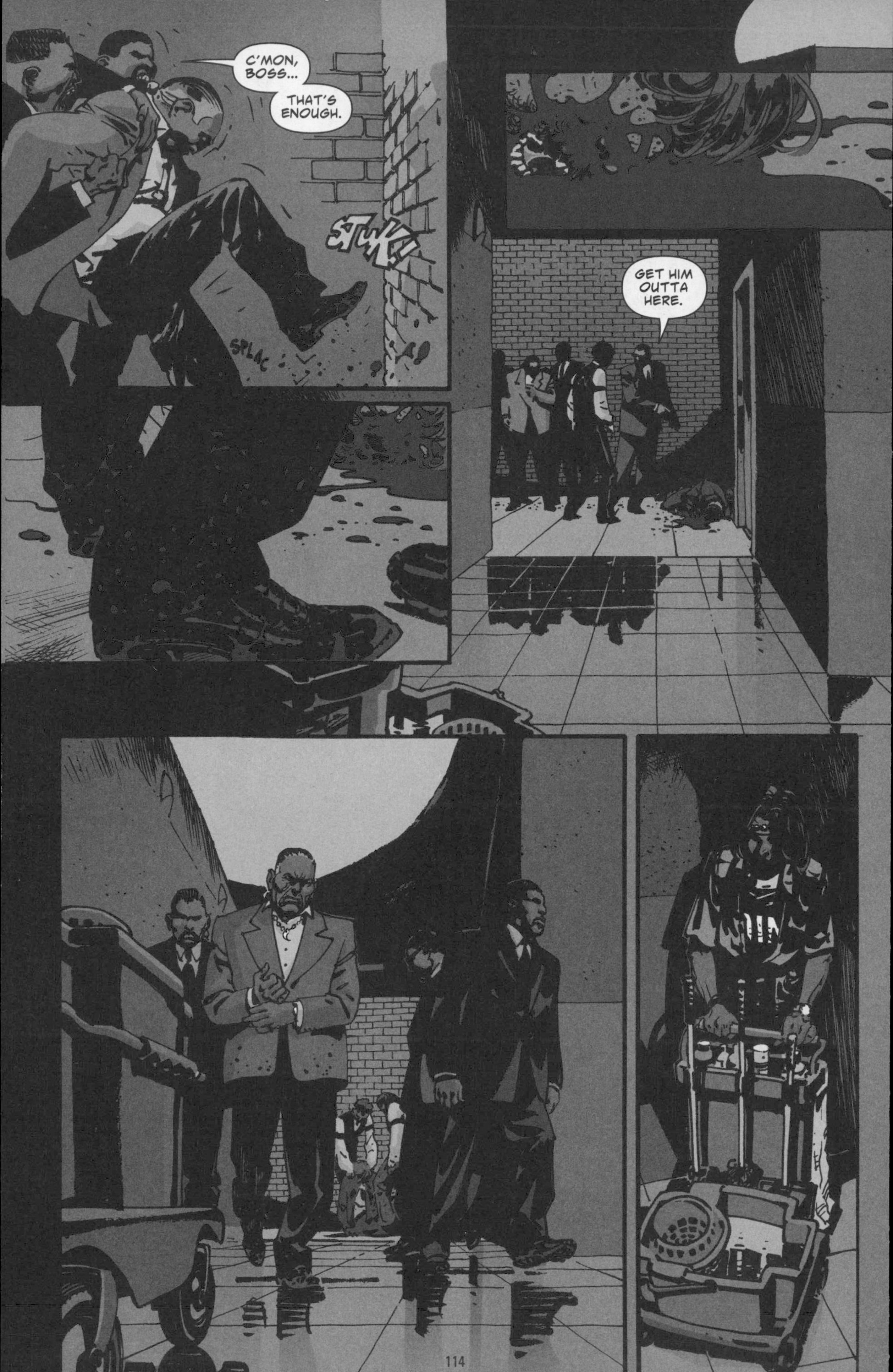
C'MON, BOSS...
THAT'S ENOUGH.
STUK!!
SPLAC
GET HIM OUTTA HERE.

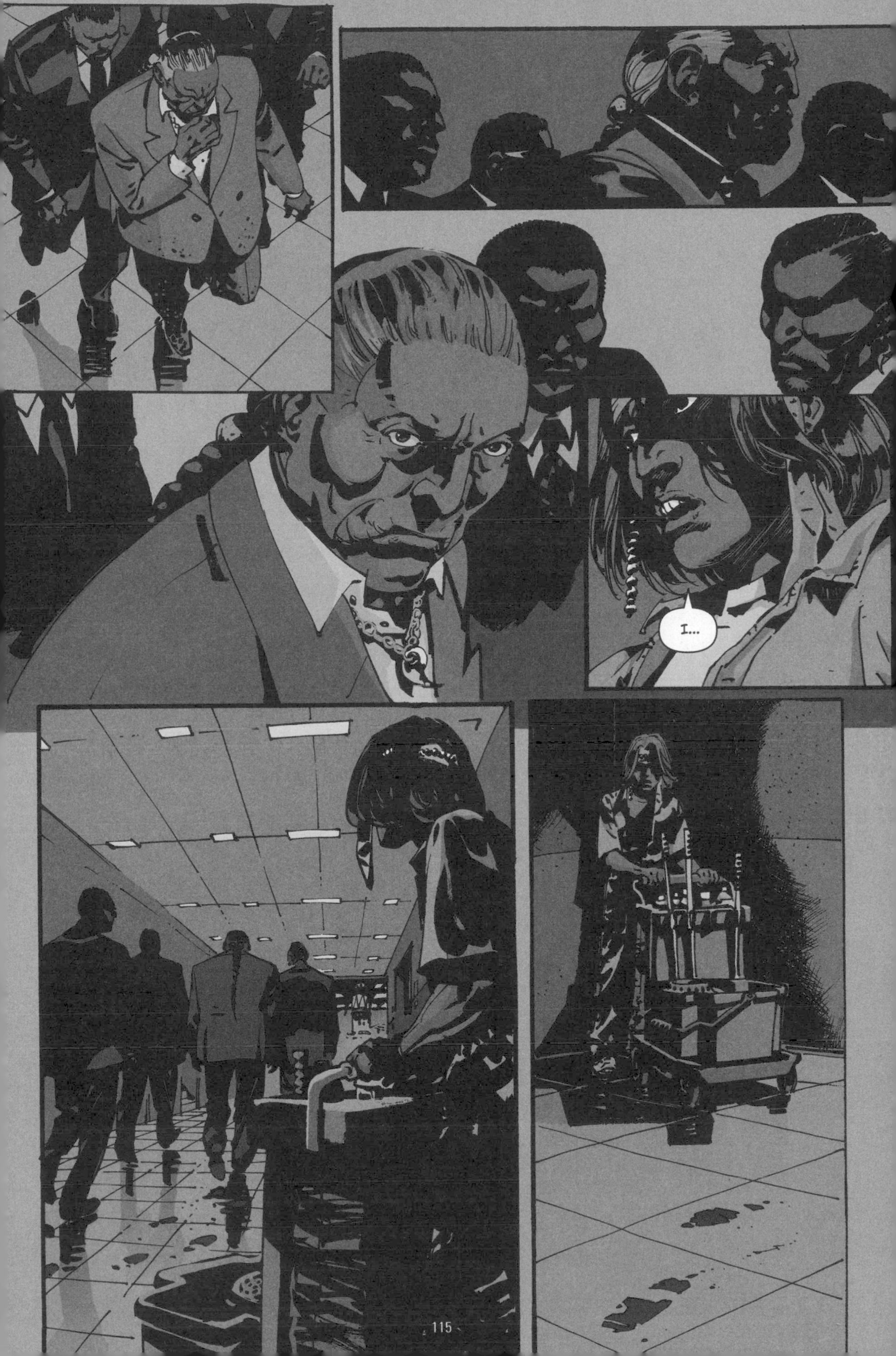
I...

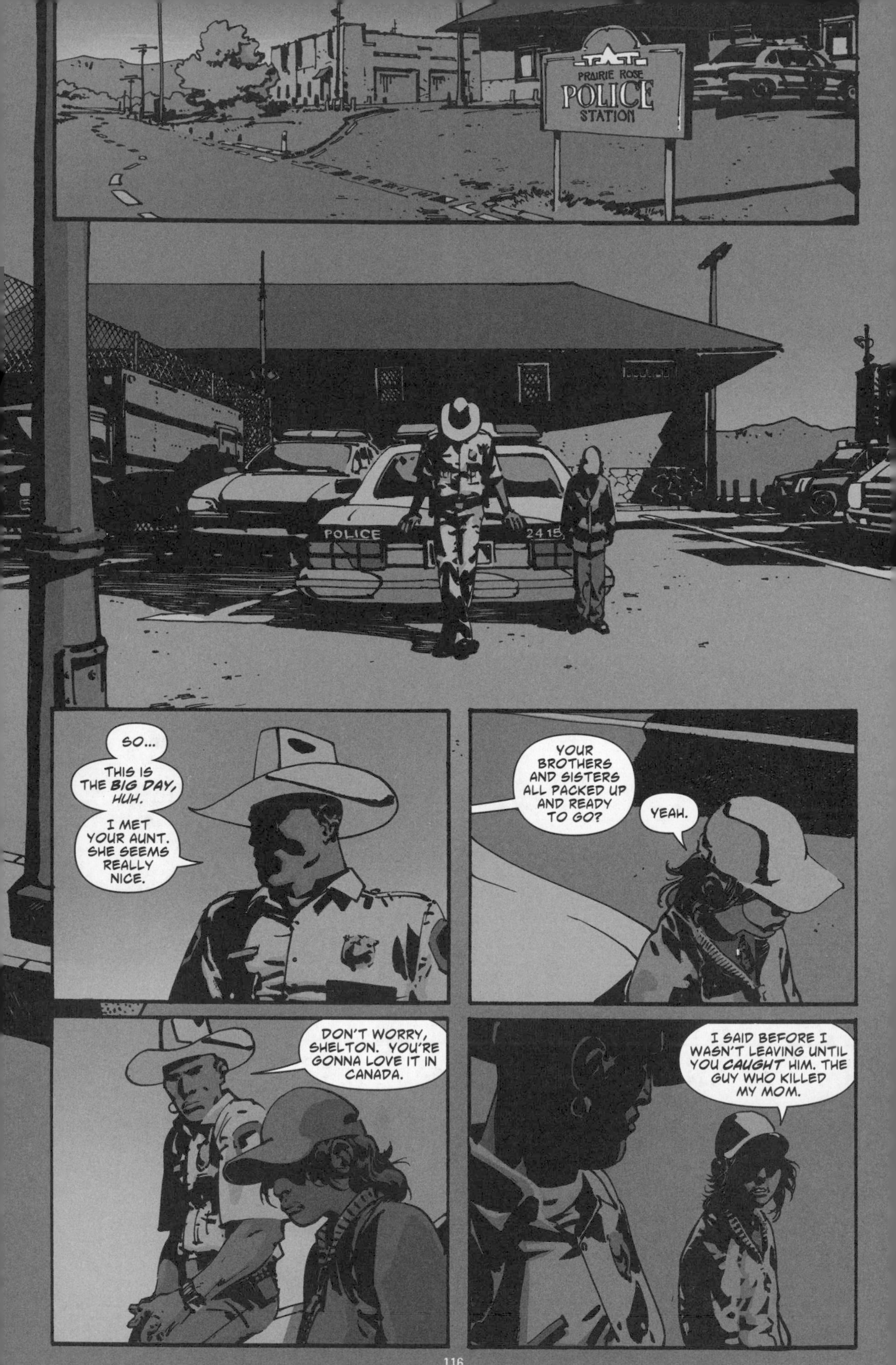
PRAIRIE ROSE POLICE STATION
POLICE 2415
SO...
THIS IS THE BIG DAY, HUH.
I MET YOUR AUNT. SHE SEEMS REALLY NICE.
YOUR BROTHERS AND SISTERS ALL PACKED UP AND READY TO GO?
YEAH.
DON'T WORRY, SHELTON. YOU'RE GONNA LOVE IT IN CANADA.
I SAID BEFORE I WASN'T LEAVING UNTIL YOU CAUGHT HIM. THE GUY WHO KILLED MY MOM.

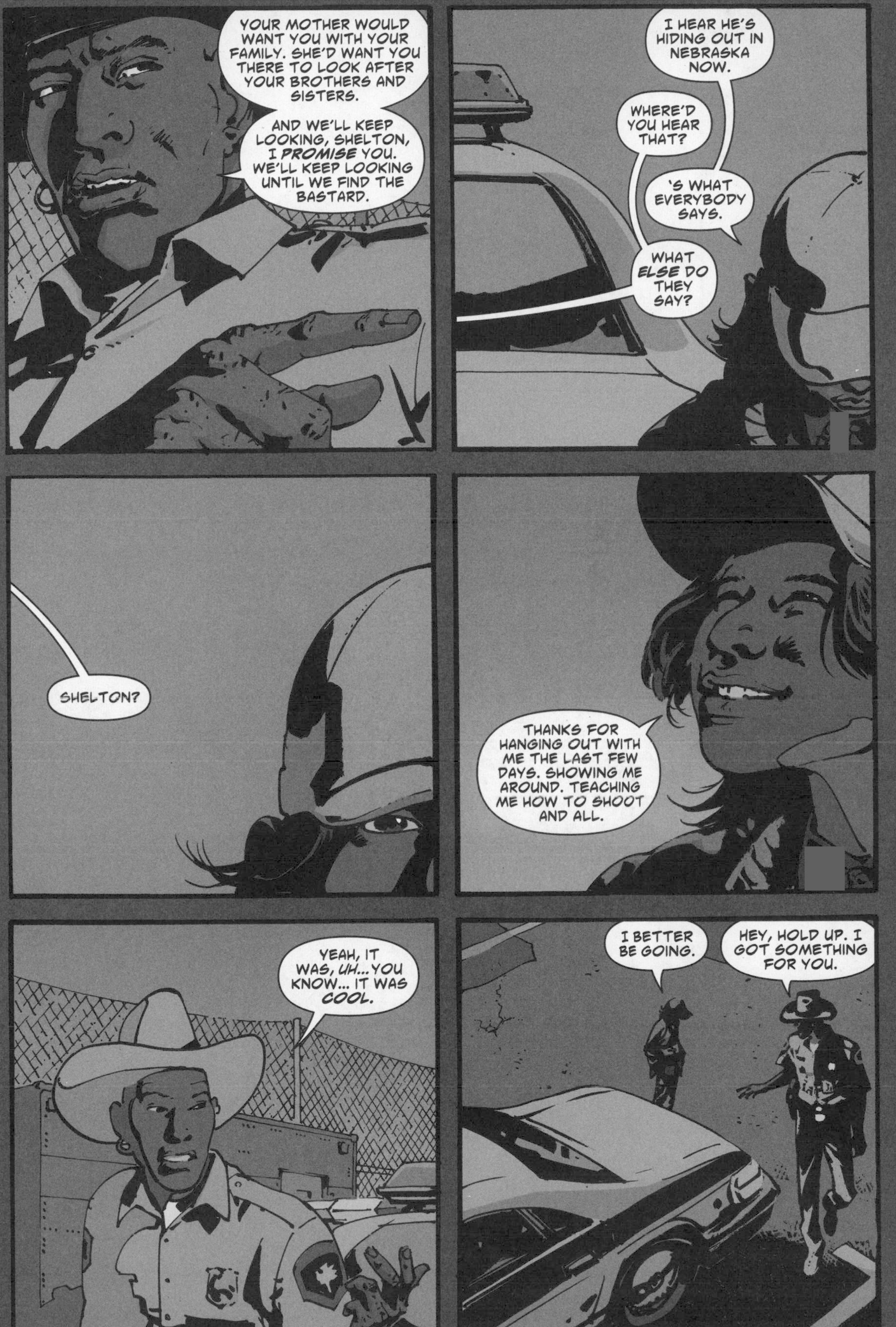
YOUR MOTHER WOULD WANT YOU WITH YOUR FAMILY. SHE'D WANT YOU THERE TO LOOK AFTER YOUR BROTHERS AND SISTERS.
AND WE'LL KEEP LOOKING, SHELTON, I *PROMISE* YOU. WE'LL KEEP LOOKING UNTIL WE FIND THE BASTARD.
I HEAR HE'S HIDING OUT IN NEBRASKA NOW.
WHERE'D YOU HEAR THAT?
'S WHAT EVERYBODY SAYS.
WHAT *ELSE* DO THEY SAY?
SHELTON?
THANKS FOR HANGING OUT WITH ME THE LAST FEW DAYS. SHOWING ME AROUND. TEACHING ME HOW TO SHOOT AND ALL.
YEAH, IT WAS, *UH*... YOU KNOW... IT WAS *COOL.*
I BETTER BE GOING.
HEY, HOLD UP. I GOT SOMETHING FOR YOU.

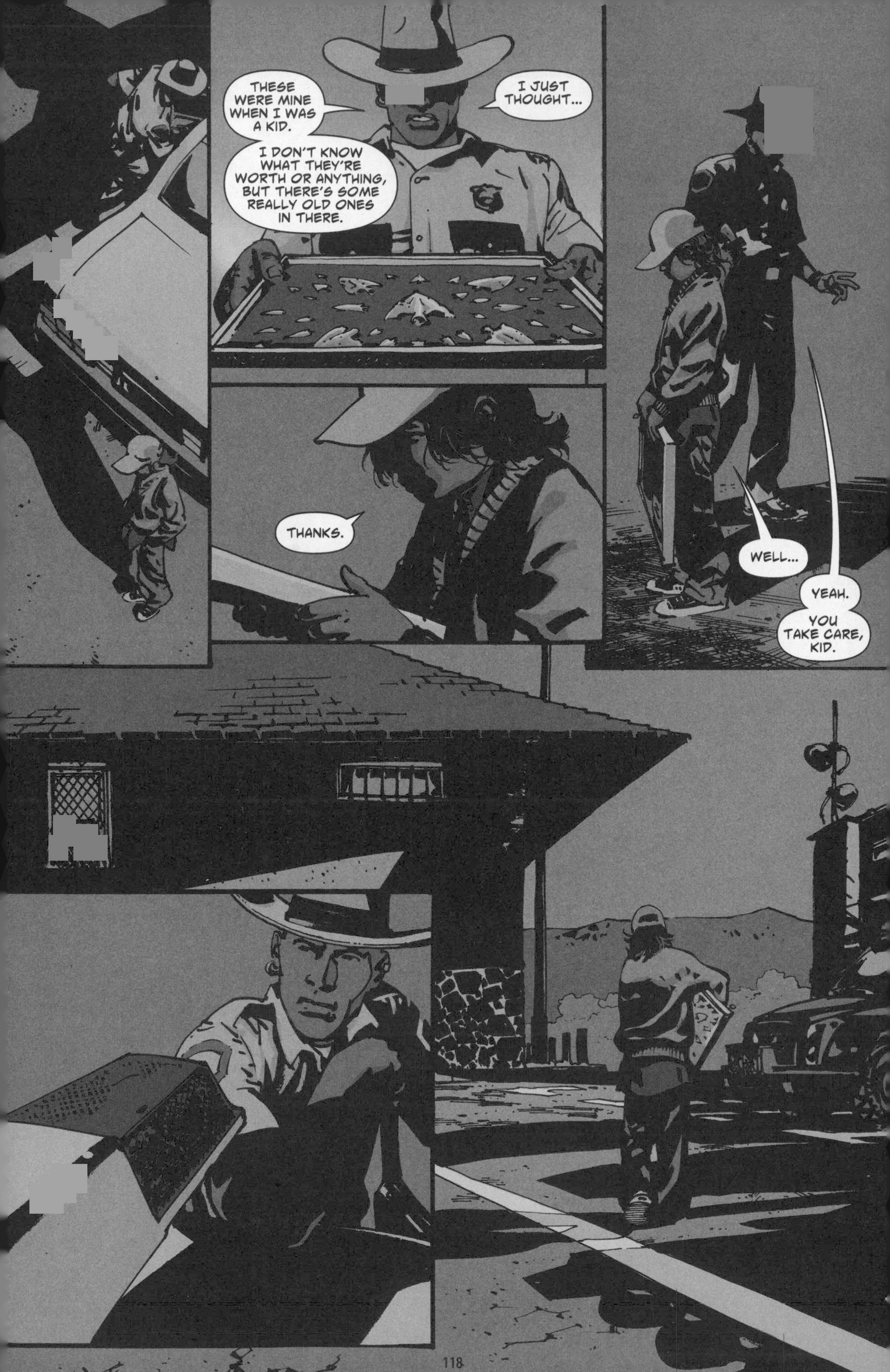

THESE WERE MINE WHEN I WAS A KID.
I DON'T KNOW WHAT THEY'RE WORTH OR ANYTHING, BUT THERE'S SOME REALLY OLD ONES IN THERE.
I JUST THOUGHT...
THANKS.
WELL...
YEAH.
YOU TAKE CARE, KID.

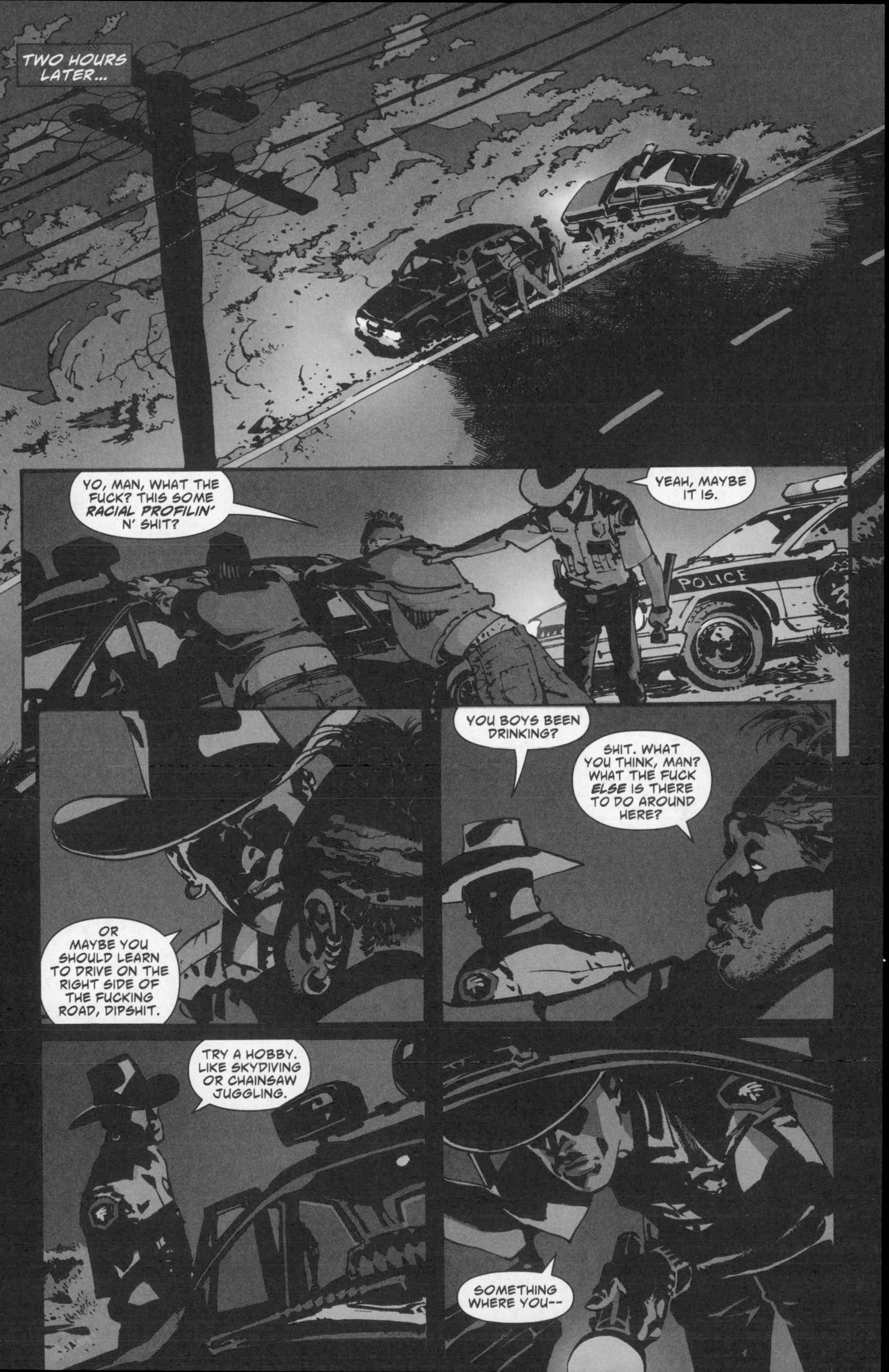
TWO HOURS LATER...
YO, MAN, WHAT THE FUCK? THIS SOME RACIAL PROFILIN' N' SHIT?
YEAH, MAYBE IT IS.
POLICE
OR MAYBE YOU SHOULD LEARN TO DRIVE ON THE RIGHT SIDE OF THE FUCKING ROAD, DIPSHIT.
YOU BOYS BEEN DRINKING?
SHIT. WHAT YOU THINK, MAN? WHAT THE FUCK ELSE IS THERE TO DO AROUND HERE?
TRY A HOBBY. LIKE SKYDIVING OR CHAINSAW JUGGLING.
SOMETHING WHERE YOU--

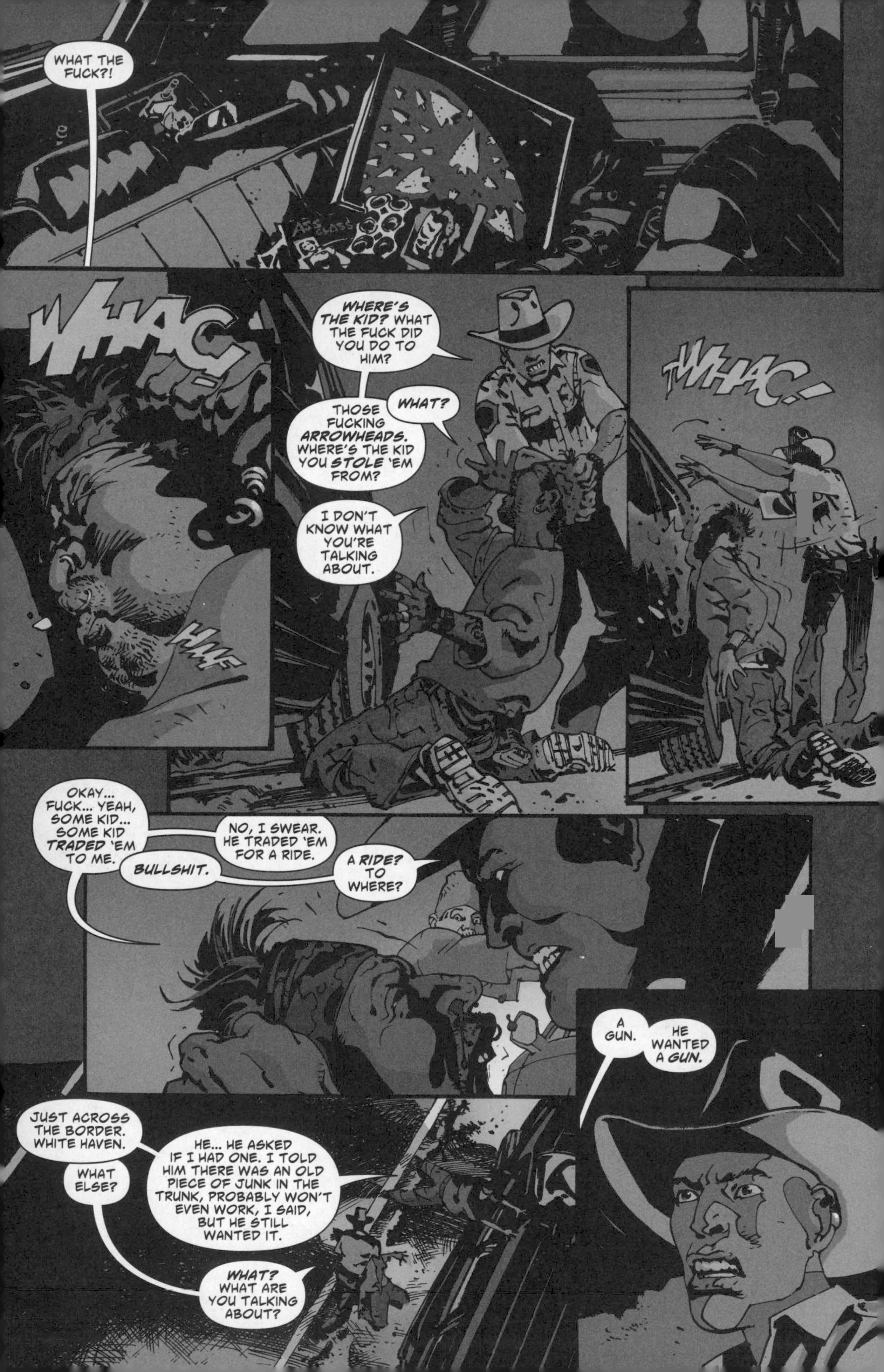

WHAT THE FUCK?!
WHAC
WHERE'S THE KID? WHAT THE FUCK DID YOU DO TO HIM?
WHAT?
THOSE FUCKING ARROWHEADS. WHERE'S THE KID YOU STOLE 'EM FROM?
I DON'T KNOW WHAT YOU'RE TALKING ABOUT.
HUF
TWHAC!
OKAY... FUCK... YEAH, SOME KID... SOME KID TRADED 'EM TO ME.
BULLSHIT.
NO, I SWEAR. HE TRADED 'EM FOR A RIDE.
A RIDE? TO WHERE?
JUST ACROSS THE BORDER. WHITE HAVEN.
WHAT ELSE?
A GUN.
HE WANTED A GUN.
HE... HE ASKED IF I HAD ONE. I TOLD HIM THERE WAS AN OLD PIECE OF JUNK IN THE TRUNK, PROBABLY WON'T EVEN WORK, I SAID, BUT HE STILL WANTED IT.
WHAT? WHAT ARE YOU TALKING ABOUT?

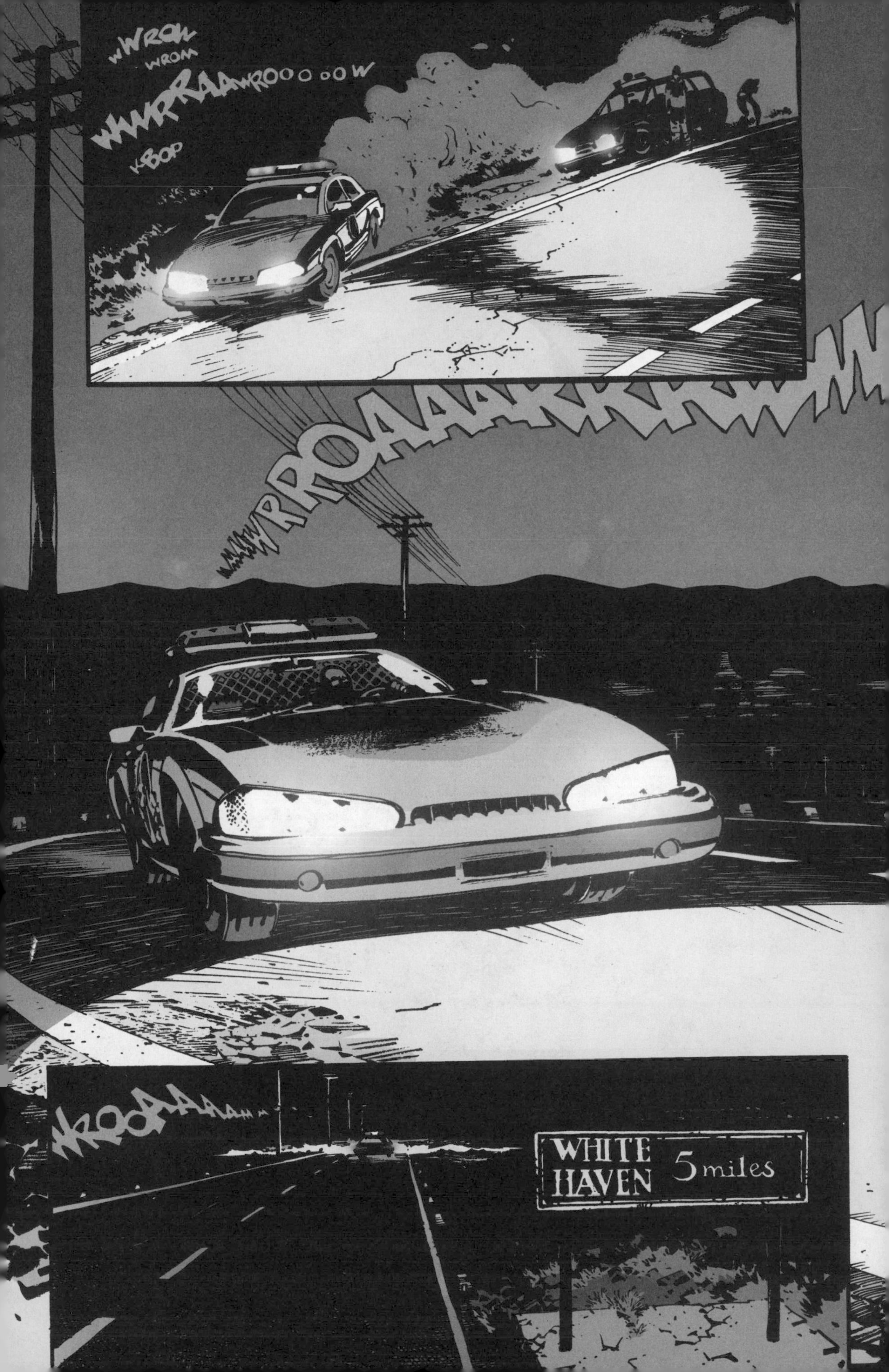
wWROM
WROM
WWWRRAAWROOOOOOW
K-BOP
WWWRROAAAKKKWWWM
WROOAAAAAA
WHITE HAVEN 5 miles

DEAD MOTHERS PART 5

COVER ART BY JOCK

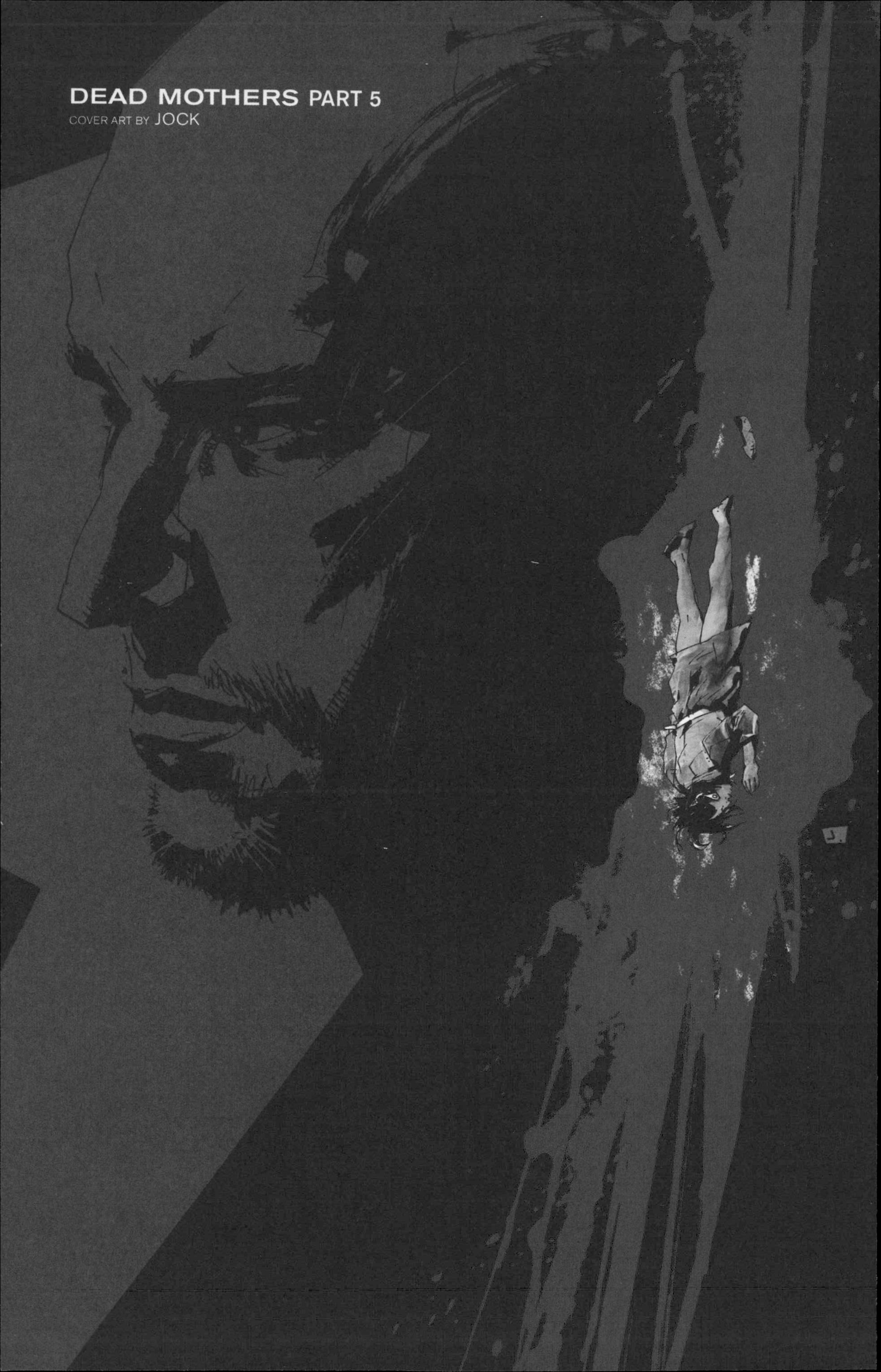

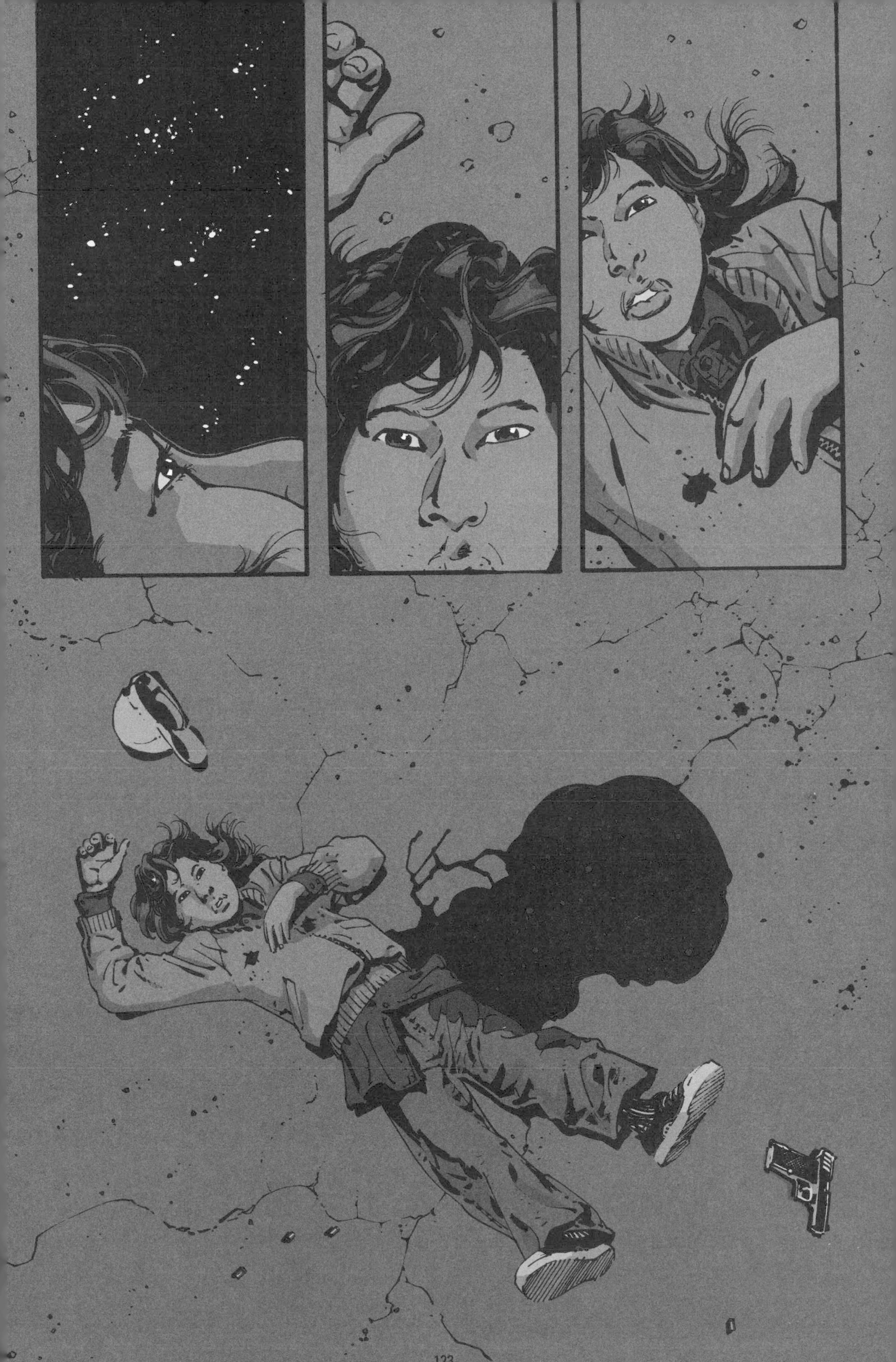

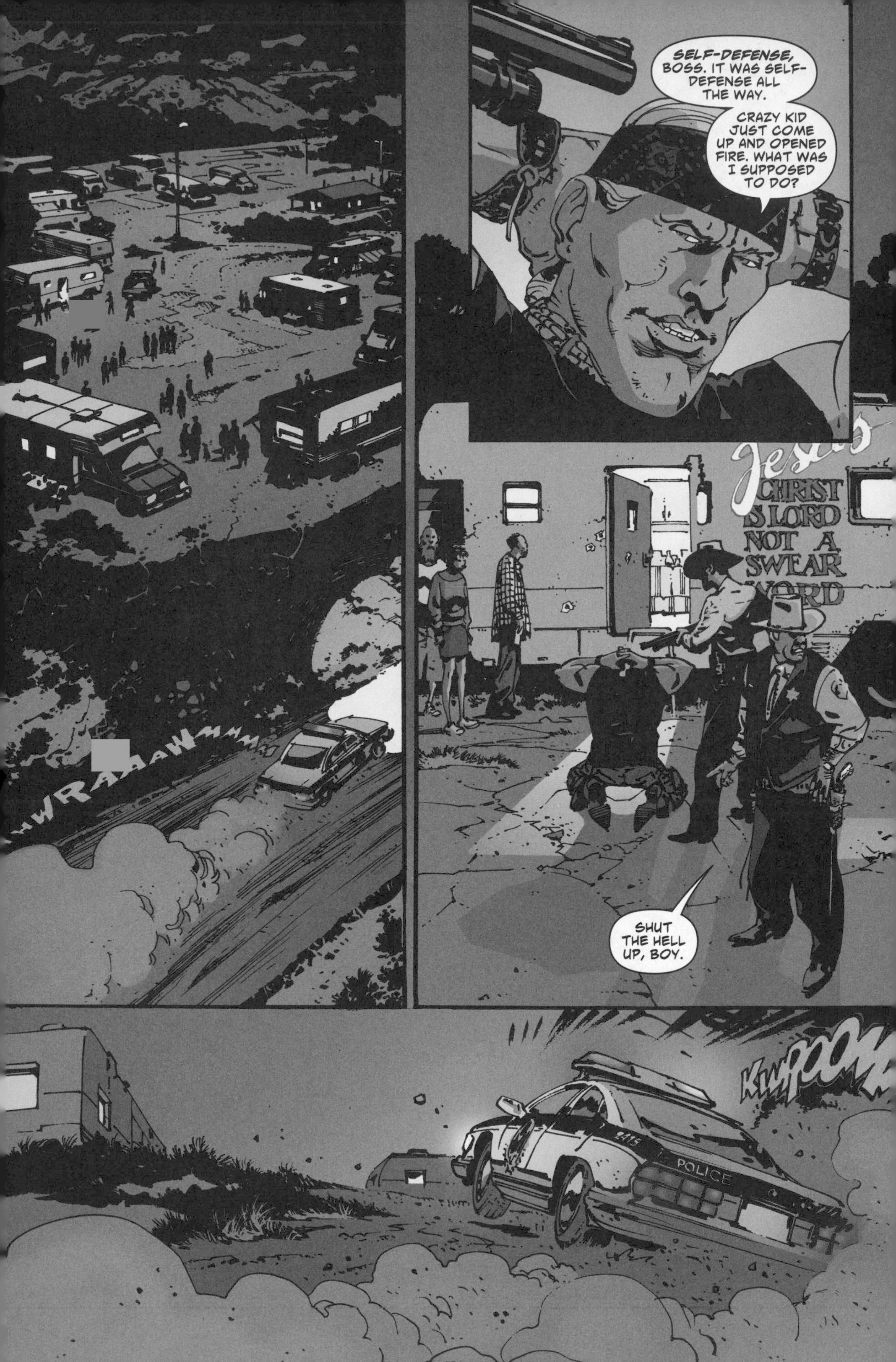
SELF-DEFENSE, BOSS. IT WAS SELF-DEFENSE ALL THE WAY.
CRAZY KID JUST COME UP AND OPENED FIRE. WHAT WAS I SUPPOSED TO DO?
CHRIST IS LORD NOT A SWEAR WORD
SHUT THE HELL UP, BOY.

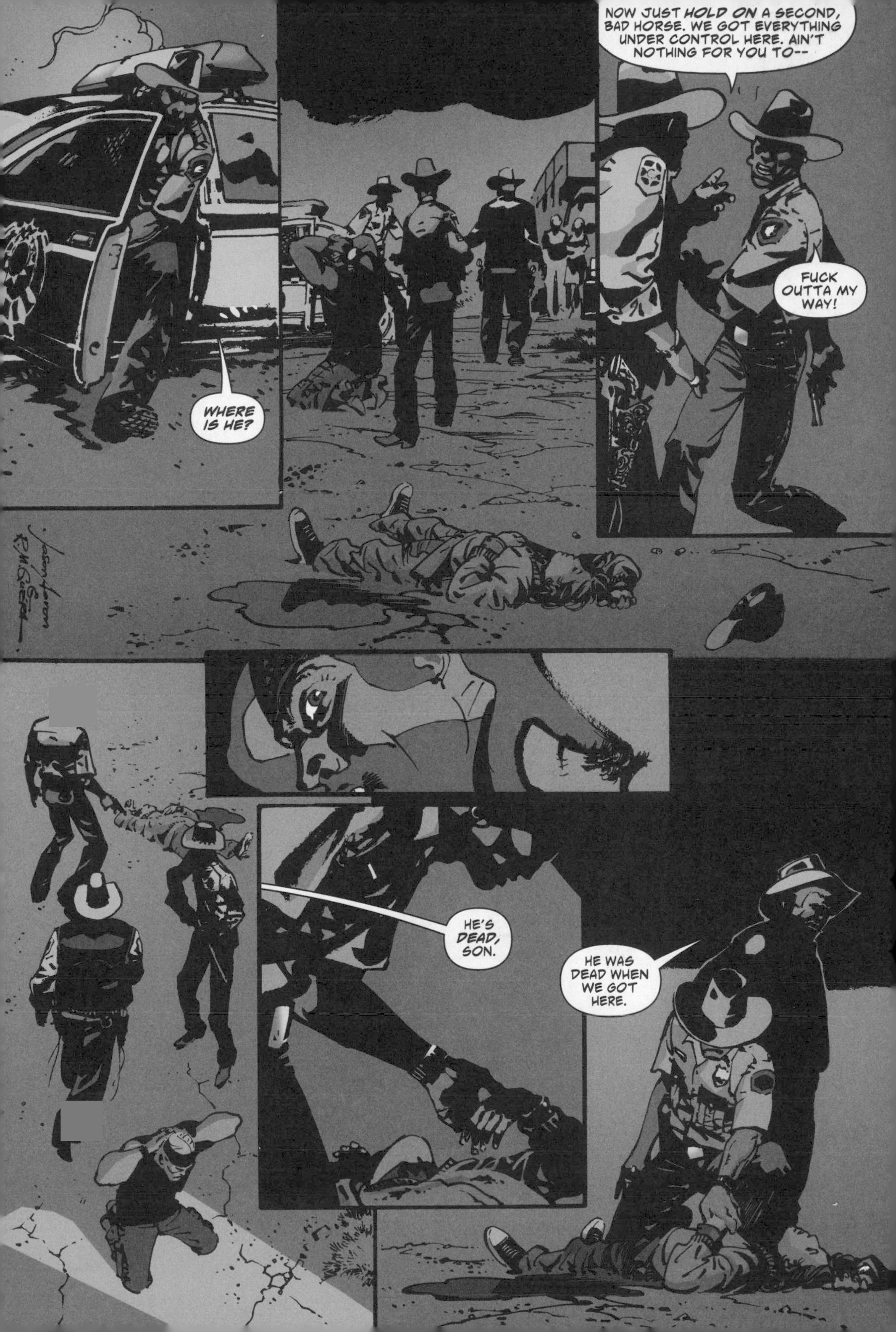
WHERE IS HE?
NOW JUST HOLD ON A SECOND, BAD HORSE. WE GOT EVERYTHING UNDER CONTROL HERE. AIN'T NOTHING FOR YOU TO--
FUCK OUTTA MY WAY!
HE'S DEAD, SON.
HE WAS DEAD WHEN WE GOT HERE.

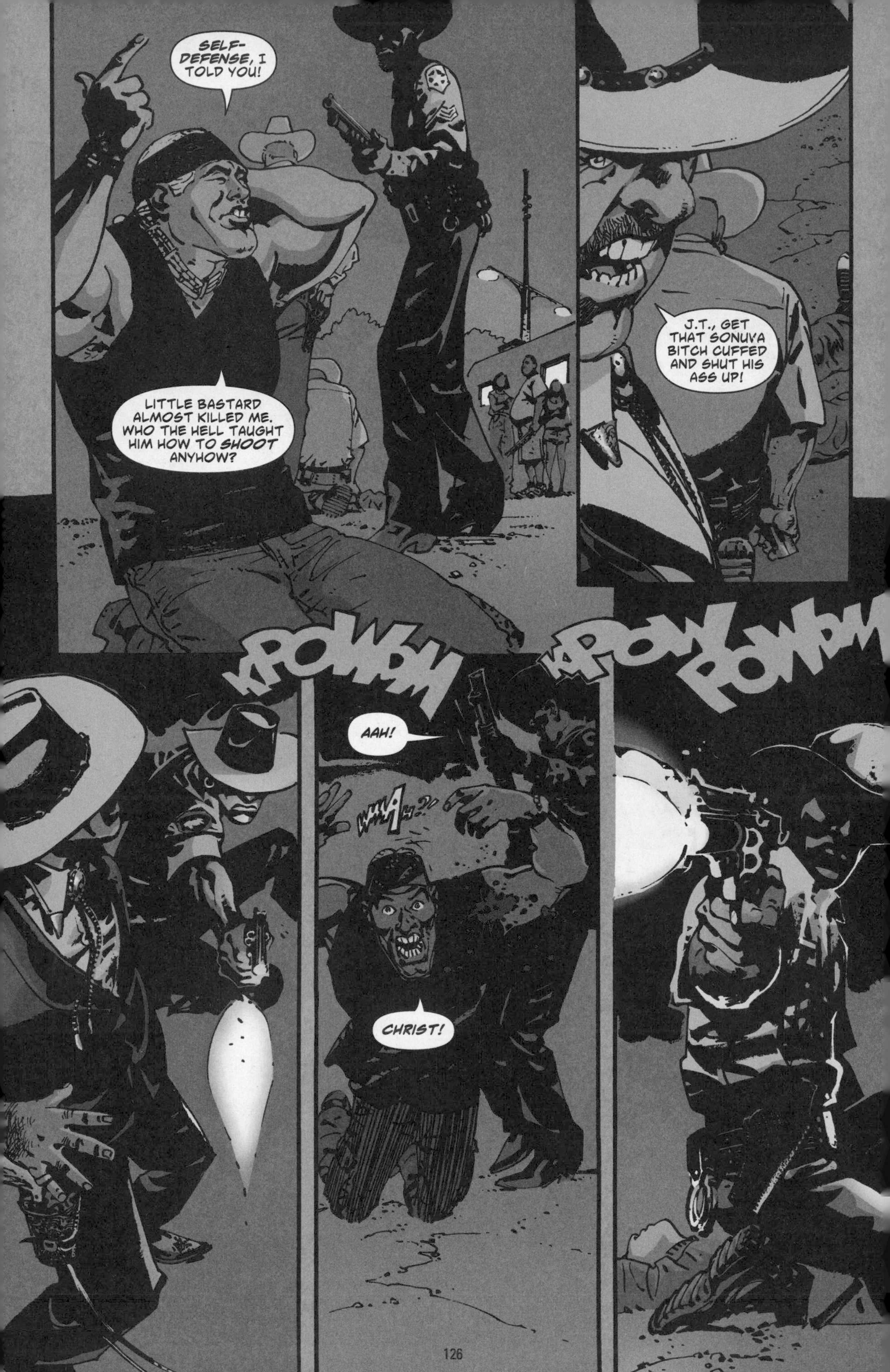
SELF-DEFENSE, I TOLD YOU!
LITTLE BASTARD ALMOST KILLED ME. WHO THE HELL TAUGHT HIM HOW TO *SHOOT* ANYHOW?
J.T., GET THAT SONUVA BITCH CUFFED AND SHUT HIS ASS UP!
KPOWM
AAH!
CHRIST!
KPOW
POWM

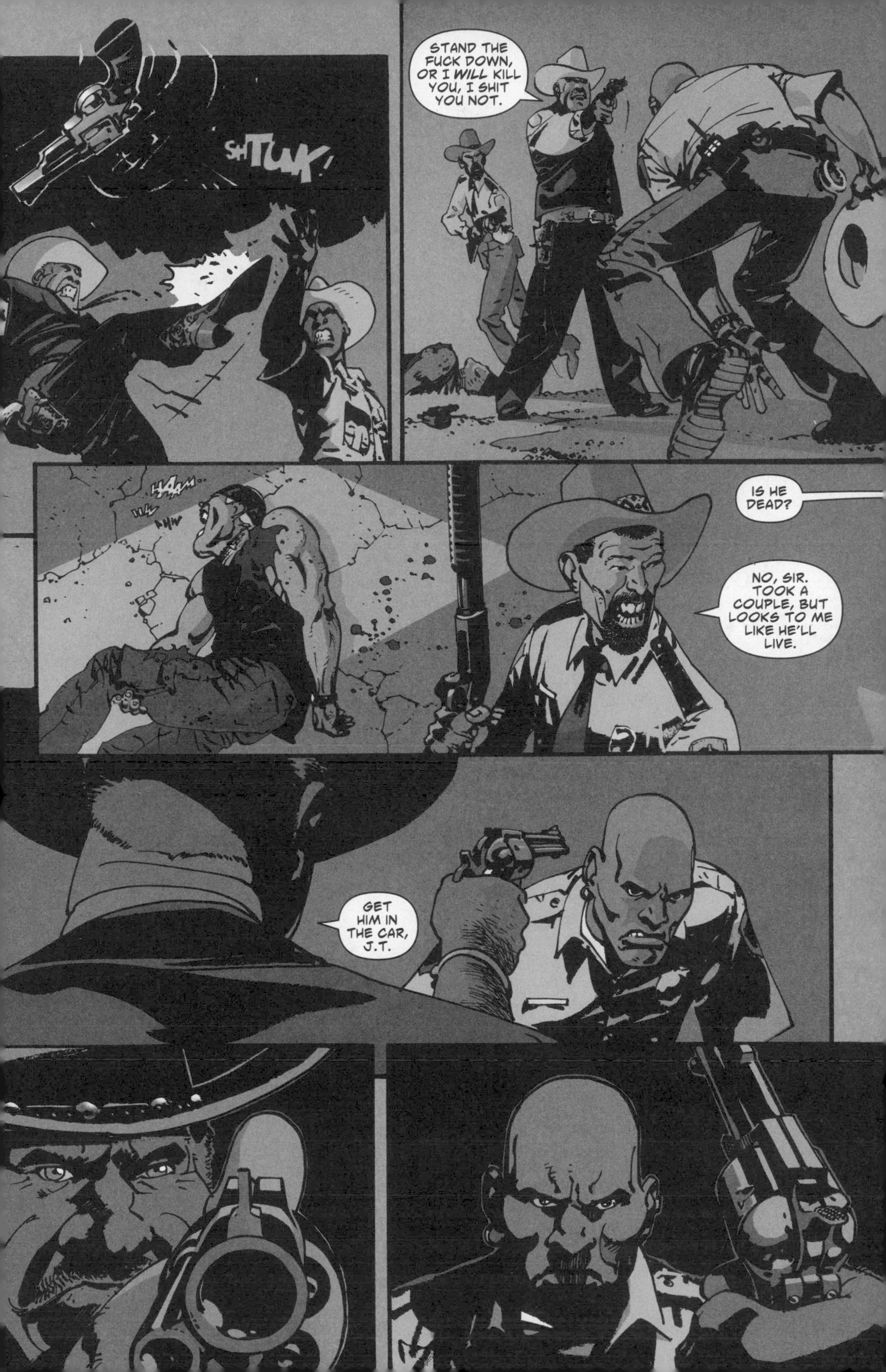
SHTUNK!
STAND THE FUCK DOWN, OR I WILL KILL YOU, I SHIT YOU NOT.
HAAAAA
IS HE DEAD?
NO, SIR. TOOK A COUPLE, BUT LOOKS TO ME LIKE HE'LL LIVE.
GET HIM IN THE CAR, J.T.

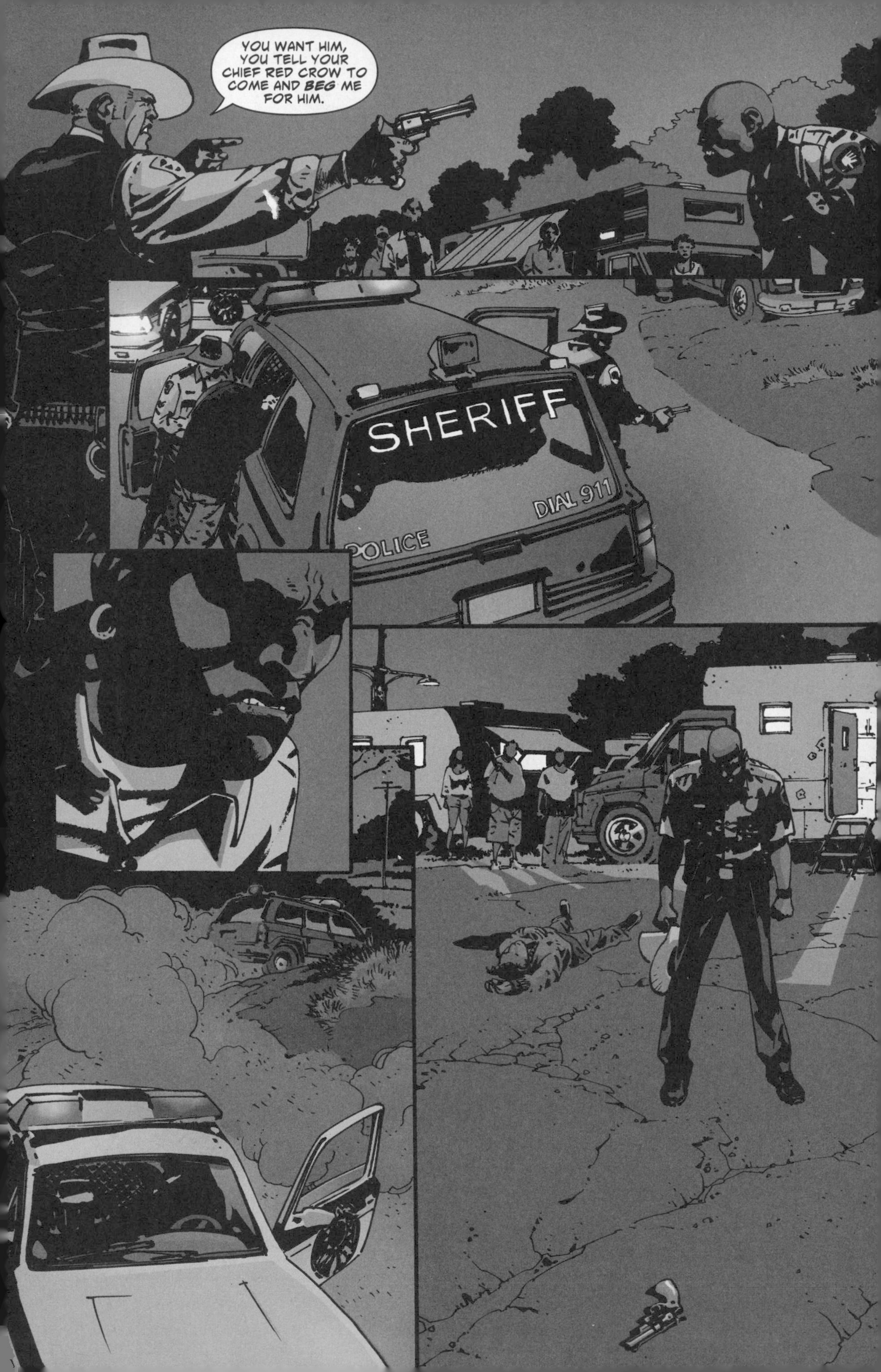
YOU WANT HIM, YOU TELL YOUR CHIEF RED CROW TO COME AND BEG ME FOR HIM.
SHERIFF
DIAL 911
POLICE

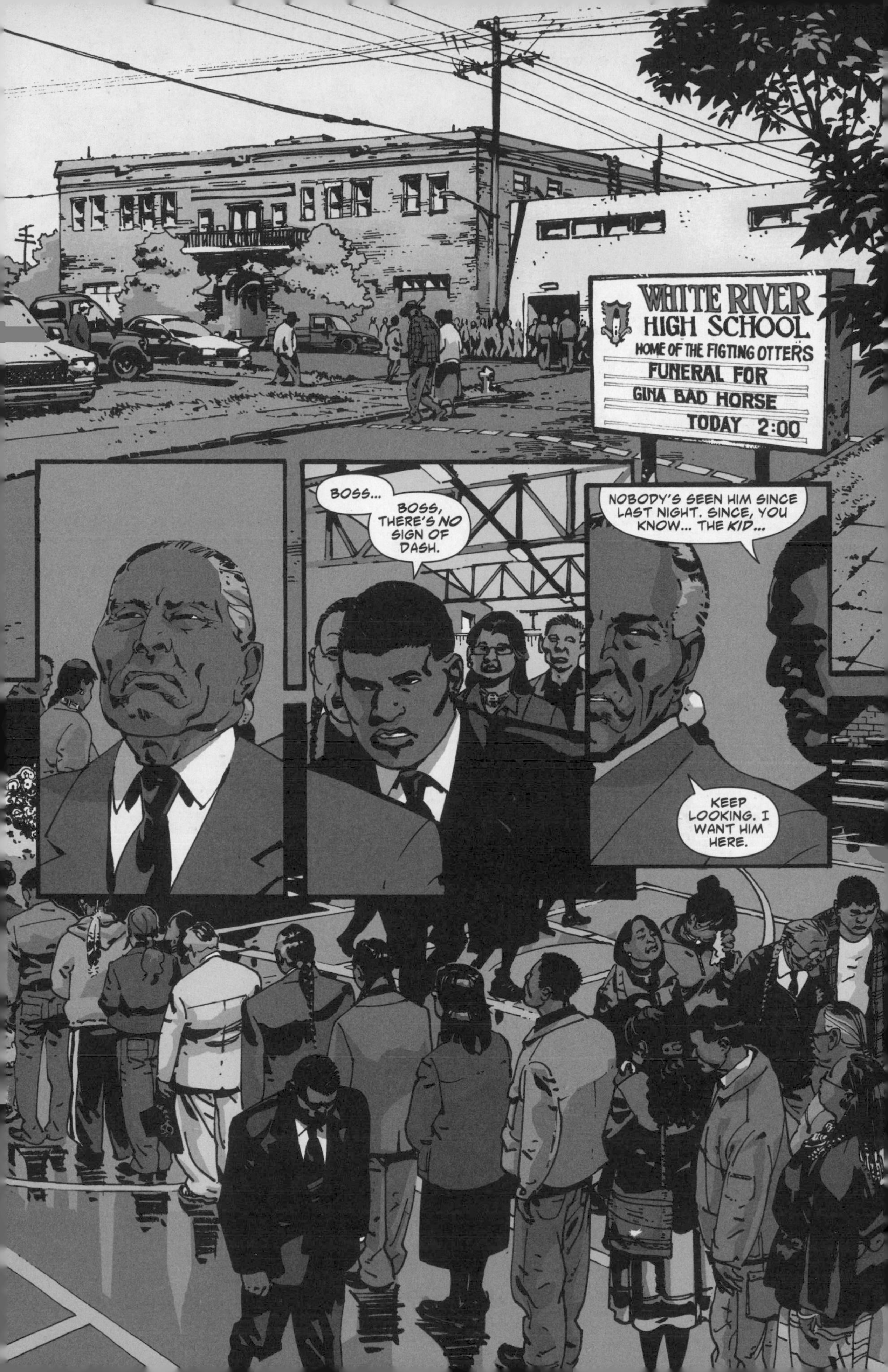
WHITE RIVER
HIGH SCHOOL
HOME OF THE FIGTING OTTERS
FUNERAL FOR
GINA BAD HORSE
TODAY 2:00
BOSS...
BOSS, THERE'S NO SIGN OF DASH.
NOBODY'S SEEN HIM SINCE LAST NIGHT. SINCE, YOU KNOW... THE KID...
KEEP LOOKING. I WANT HIM HERE.

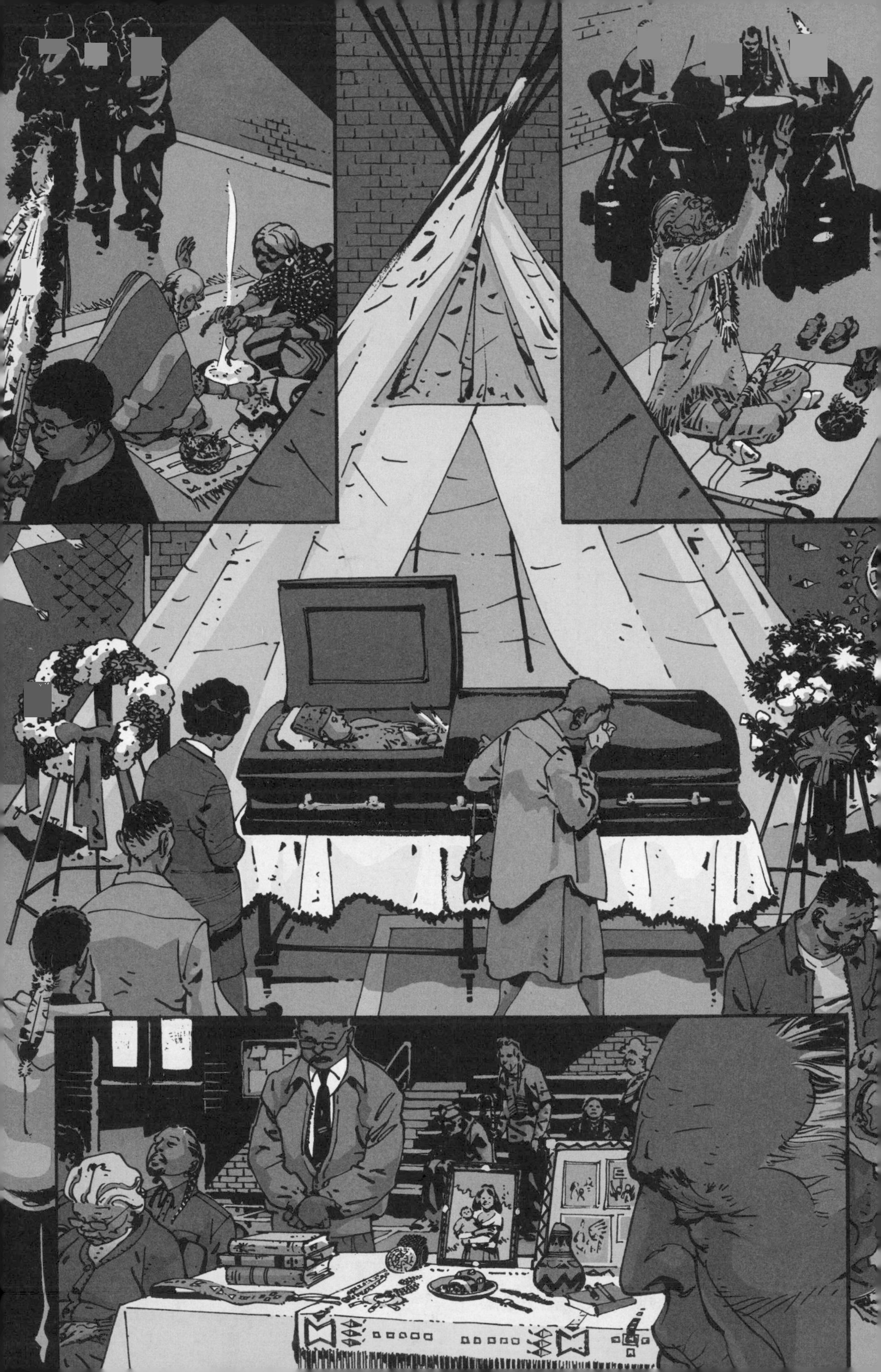

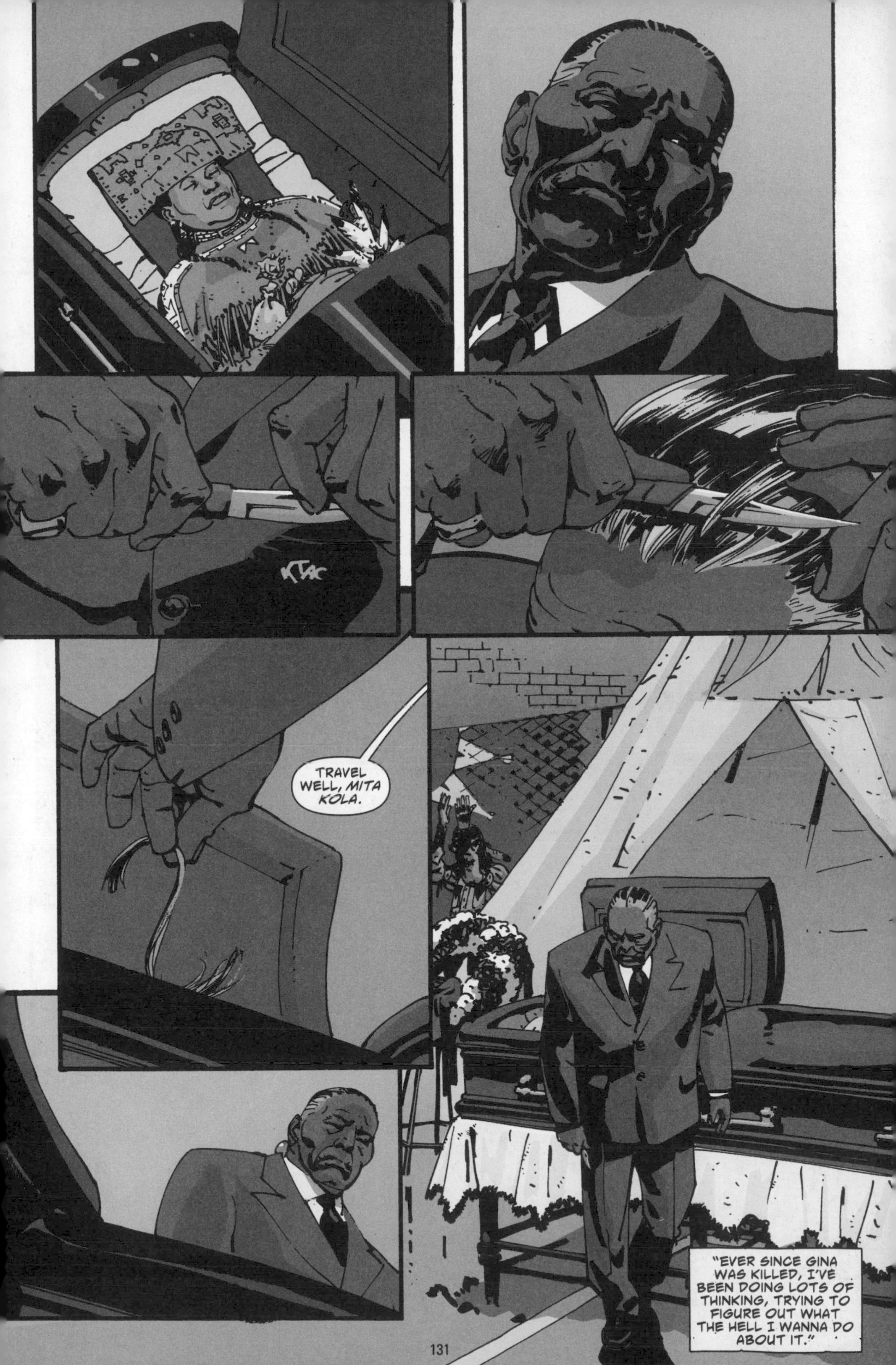
TRAVEL WELL, MITA KOLA.
"EVER SINCE GINA WAS KILLED, I'VE BEEN DOING LOTS OF THINKING, TRYING TO FIGURE OUT WHAT THE HELL I WANNA DO ABOUT IT."

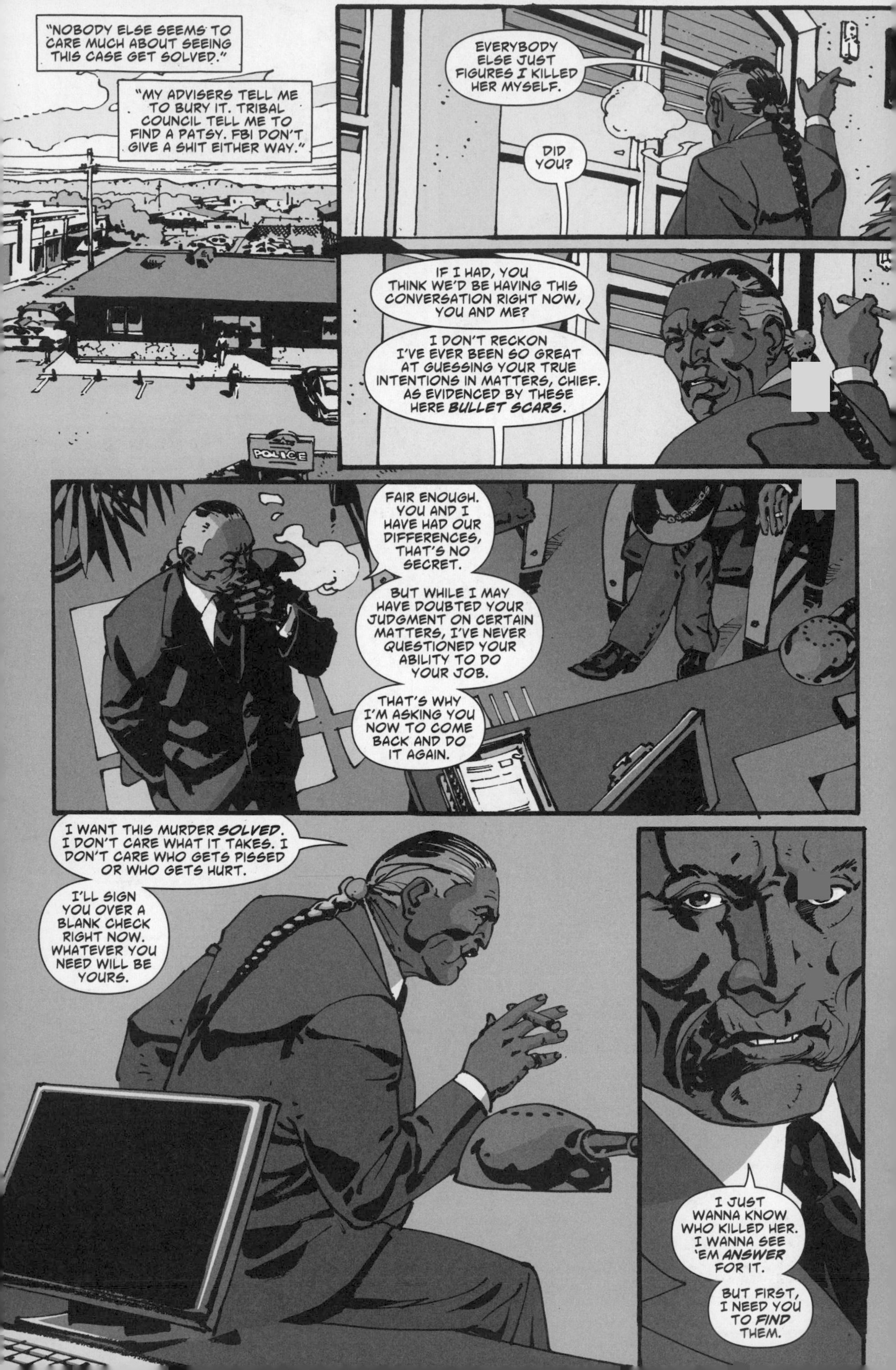
"NOBODY ELSE SEEMS TO CARE MUCH ABOUT SEEING THIS CASE GET SOLVED."
"MY ADVISERS TELL ME TO BURY IT. TRIBAL COUNCIL TELL ME TO FIND A PATSY. FBI DON'T GIVE A SHIT EITHER WAY."
POLICE
EVERYBODY ELSE JUST FIGURES I KILLED HER MYSELF.
DID YOU?
IF I HAD, YOU THINK WE'D BE HAVING THIS CONVERSATION RIGHT NOW, YOU AND ME?
I DON'T RECKON I'VE EVER BEEN SO GREAT AT GUESSING YOUR TRUE INTENTIONS IN MATTERS, CHIEF. AS EVIDENCED BY THESE HERE BULLET SCARS.
FAIR ENOUGH. YOU AND I HAVE HAD OUR DIFFERENCES, THAT'S NO SECRET.
BUT WHILE I MAY HAVE DOUBTED YOUR JUDGMENT ON CERTAIN MATTERS, I'VE NEVER QUESTIONED YOUR ABILITY TO DO YOUR JOB.
THAT'S WHY I'M ASKING YOU NOW TO COME BACK AND DO IT AGAIN.
I WANT THIS MURDER SOLVED. I DON'T CARE WHAT IT TAKES. I DON'T CARE WHO GETS PISSED OR WHO GETS HURT.
I'LL SIGN YOU OVER A BLANK CHECK RIGHT NOW. WHATEVER YOU NEED WILL BE YOURS.
I JUST WANNA KNOW WHO KILLED HER. I WANNA SEE 'EM ANSWER FOR IT.
BUT FIRST, I NEED YOU TO FIND THEM.

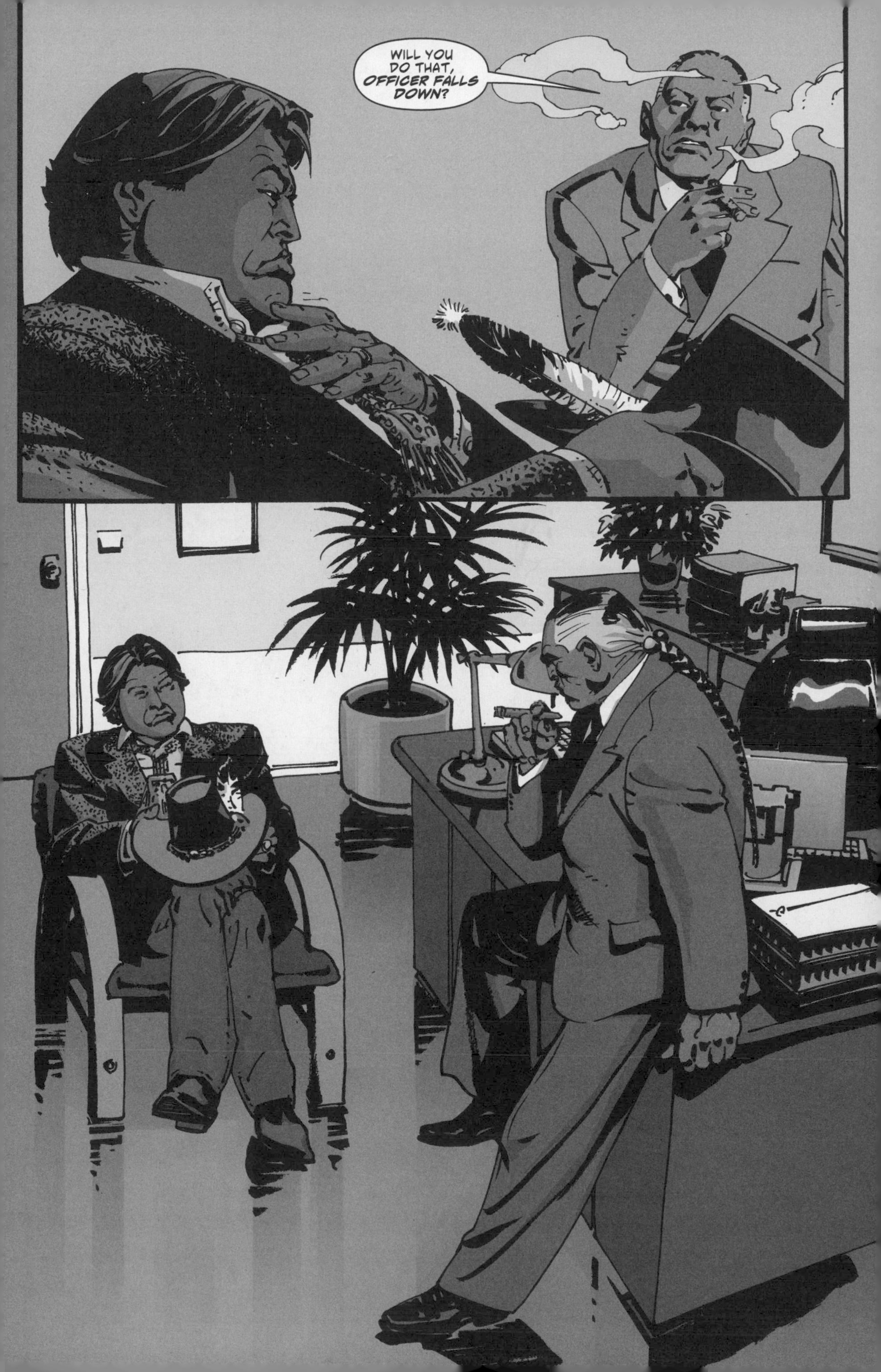
WILL YOU DO THAT, OFFICER FALLS DOWN?

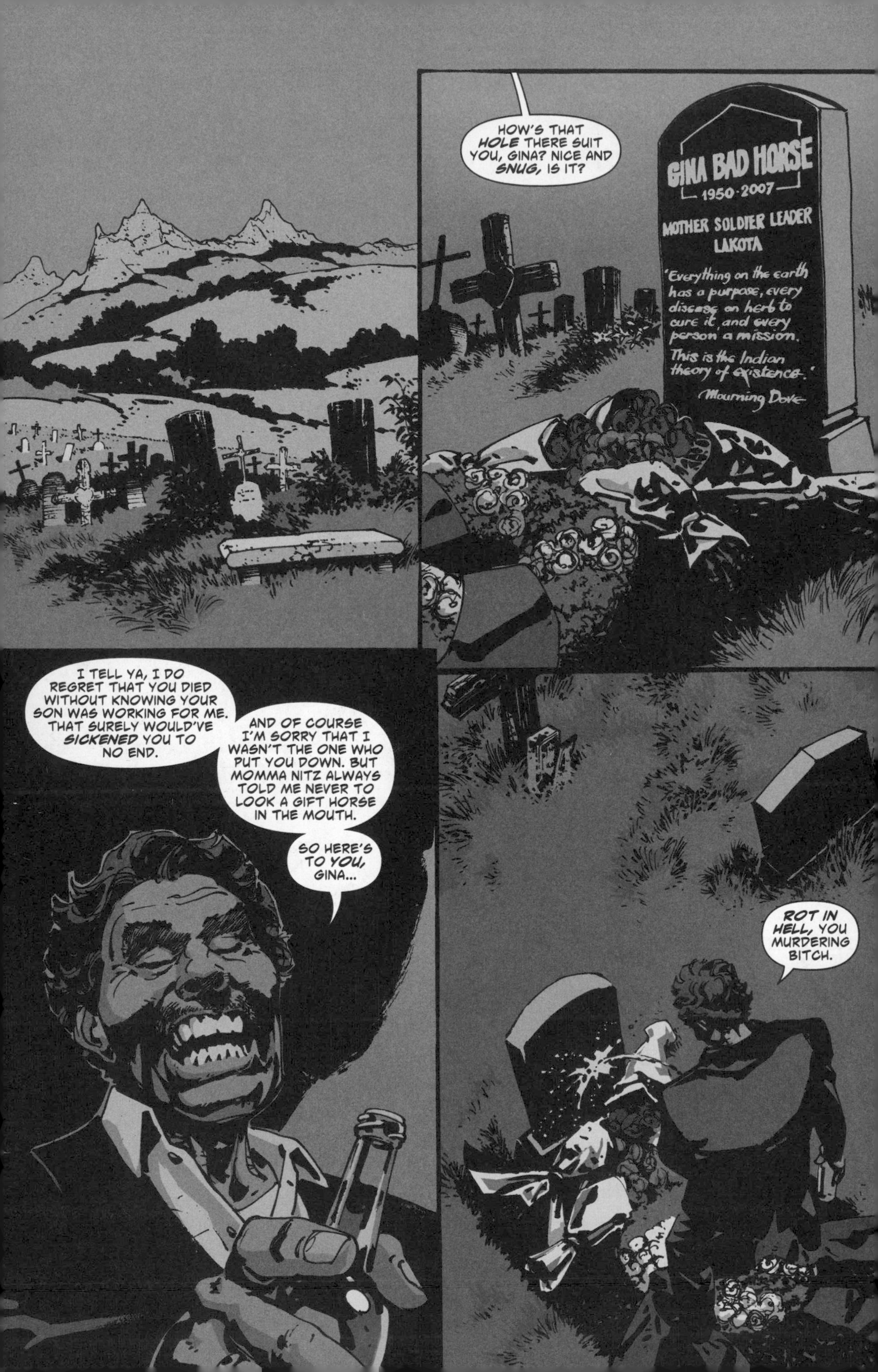
HOW'S THAT HOLE THERE SUIT YOU, GINA? NICE AND SNUG, IS IT?
GINA BAD HORSE
1950-2007
MOTHER SOLDIER LEADER
LAKOTA
"Everything on the earth has a purpose, every disease an herb to cure it, and every person a mission.
This is the Indian theory of existence."
Mourning Dove
I TELL YA, I DO REGRET THAT YOU DIED WITHOUT KNOWING YOUR SON WAS WORKING FOR ME. THAT SURELY WOULD'VE SICKENED YOU TO NO END.
AND OF COURSE I'M SORRY THAT I WASN'T THE ONE WHO PUT YOU DOWN. BUT MOMMA NITZ ALWAYS TOLD ME NEVER TO LOOK A GIFT HORSE IN THE MOUTH.
SO HERE'S TO YOU, GINA...
ROT IN HELL, YOU MURDERING BITCH.

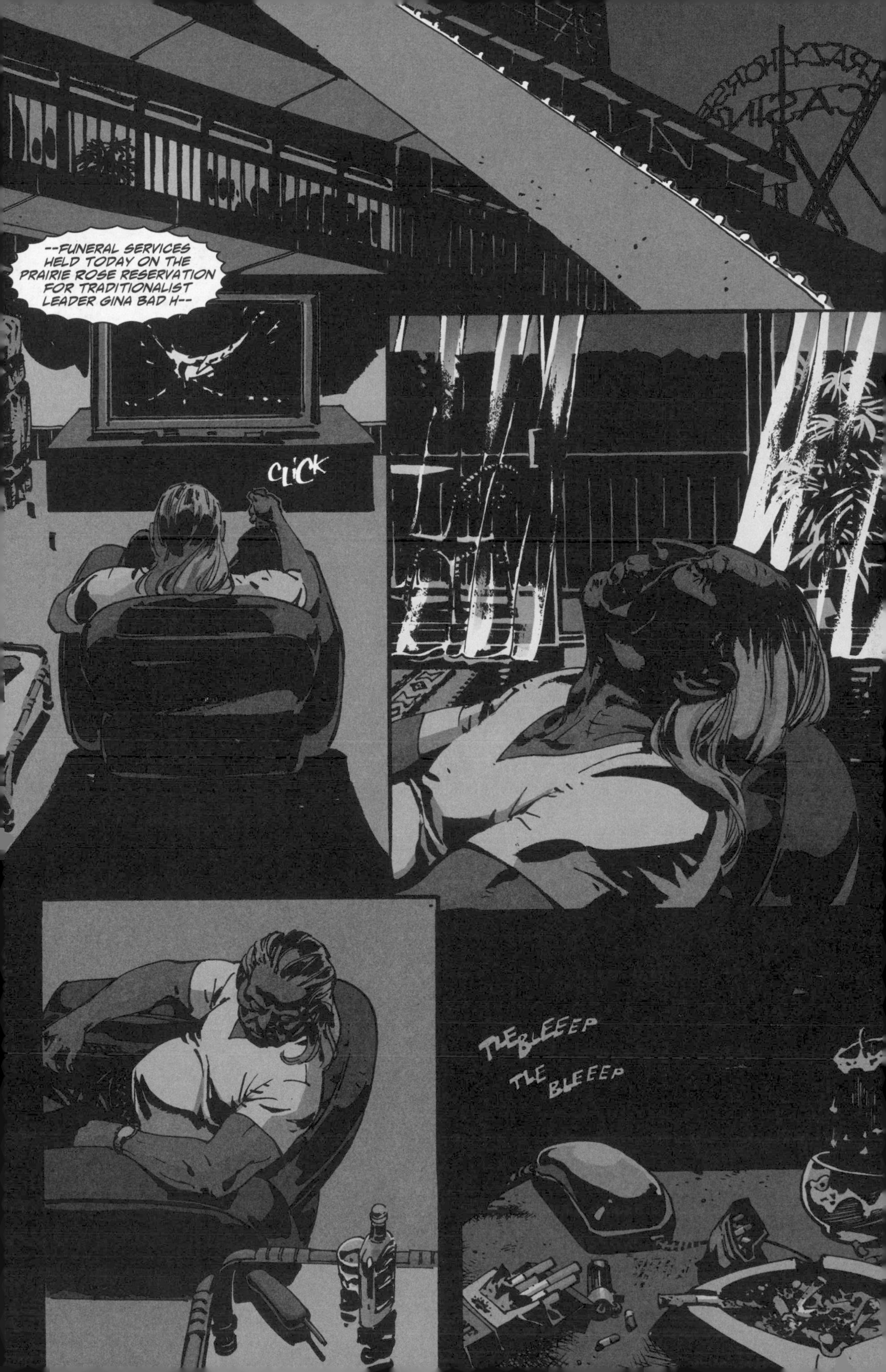
CRAZY HORSE CASINO
--FUNERAL SERVICES HELD TODAY ON THE PRAIRIE ROSE RESERVATION FOR TRADITIONALIST LEADER GINA BAD H--
CLICK
TLE BLEEEP
TLE BLEEEP

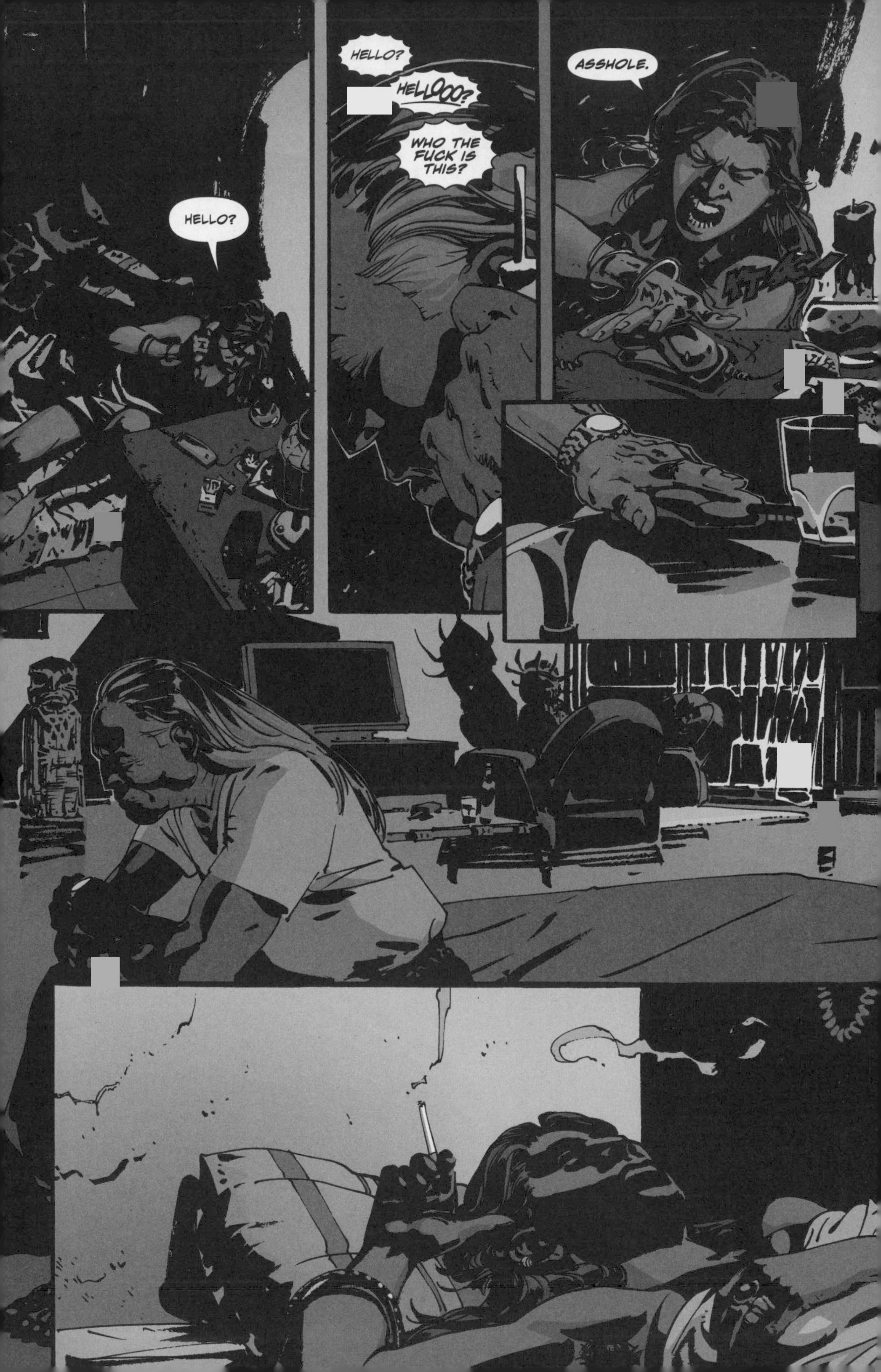
HELLO?
HELLO?
HELLOOO?
WHO THE FUCK IS THIS?
ASSHOLE.
KTAK!

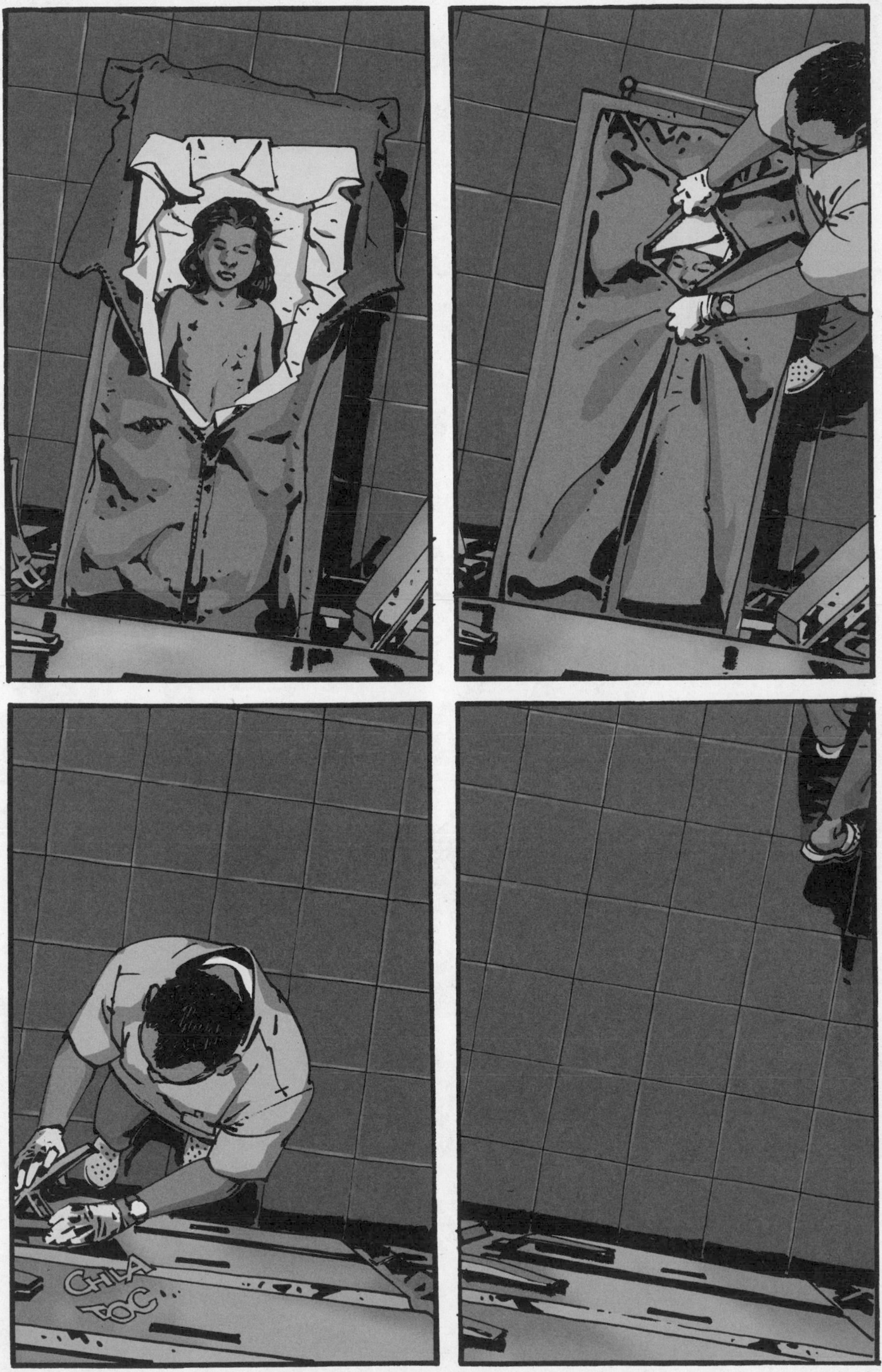

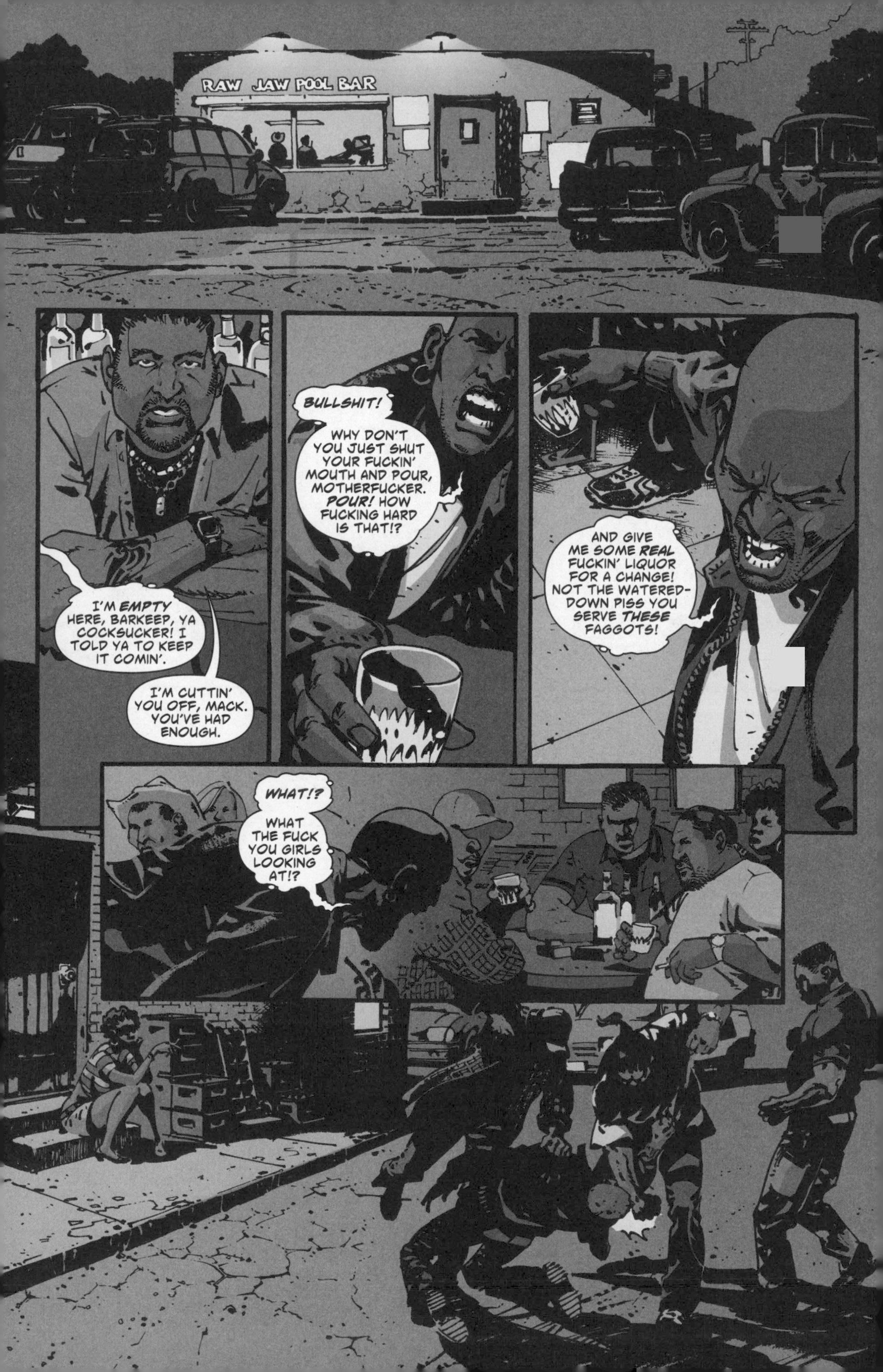
RAW JAW POOL BAR
I'M EMPTY HERE, BARKEEP, YA COCKSUCKER! I TOLD YA TO KEEP IT COMIN'.
I'M CUTTIN' YOU OFF, MACK. YOU'VE HAD ENOUGH.
BULLSHIT!
WHY DON'T YOU JUST SHUT YOUR FUCKIN' MOUTH AND POUR, MOTHERFUCKER. POUR! HOW FUCKING HARD IS THAT!?
AND GIVE ME SOME REAL FUCKIN' LIQUOR FOR A CHANGE! NOT THE WATERED-DOWN PISS YOU SERVE THESE FAGGOTS!
WHAT!?
WHAT THE FUCK YOU GIRLS LOOKING AT!?

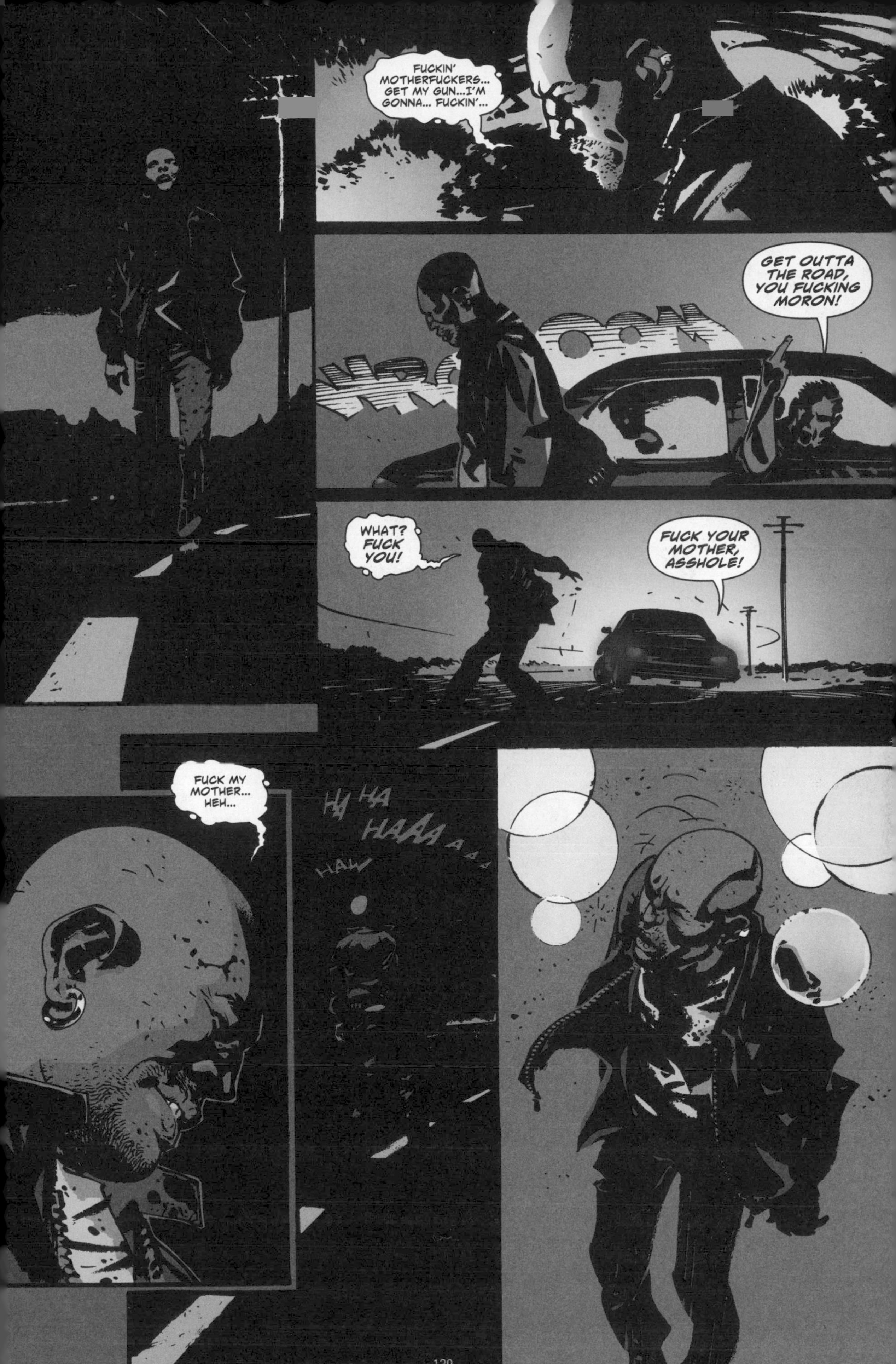
FUCKIN' MOTHERFUCKERS... GET MY GUN...I'M GONNA... FUCKIN'...
GET OUTTA THE ROAD, YOU FUCKING MORON!
WHAT? FUCK YOU!
FUCK YOUR MOTHER, ASSHOLE!
FUCK MY MOTHER... HEH...
HA HA HAAAAAAA
HAW

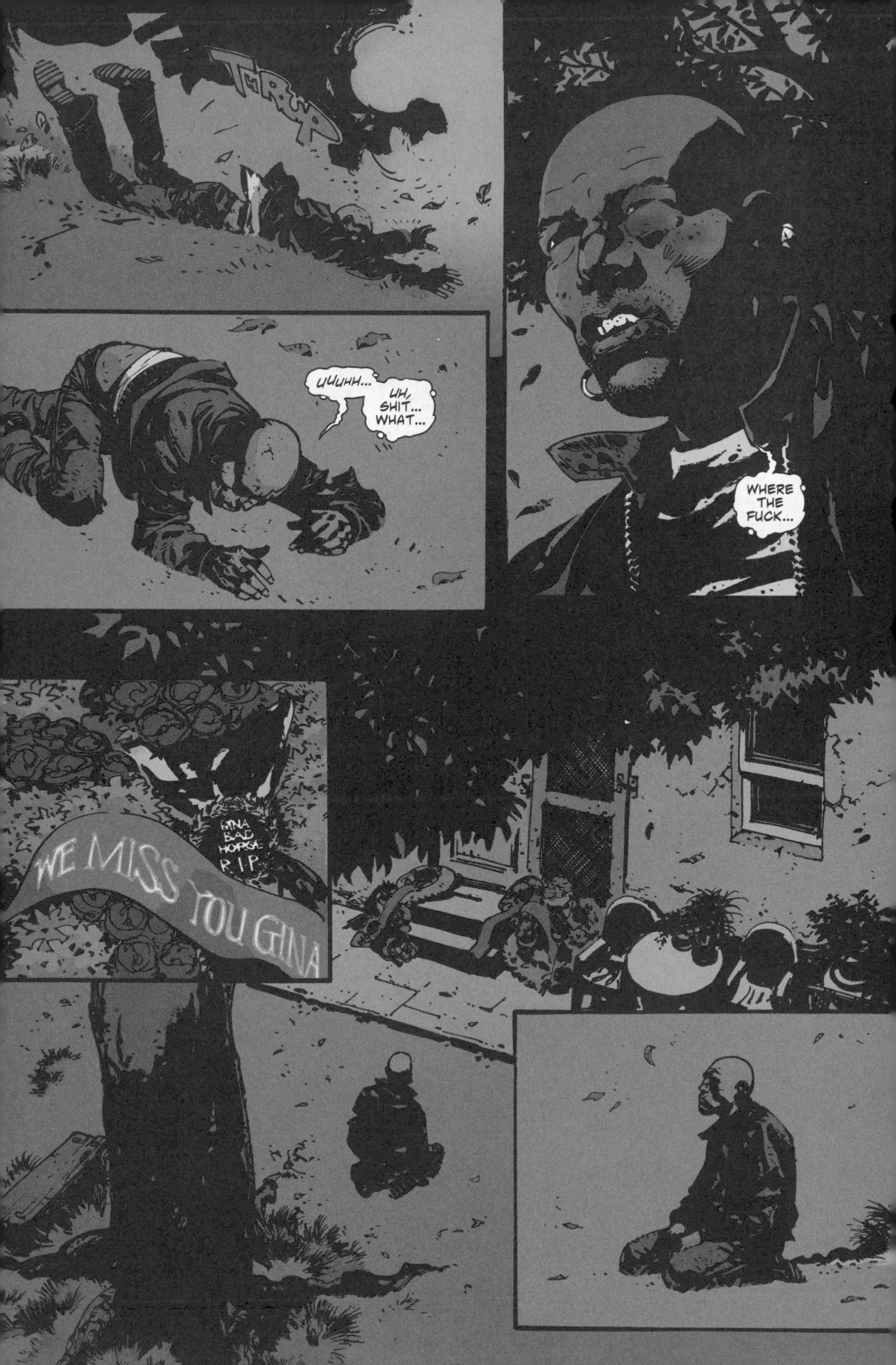
THRUP
UUUHH...
UH, SHIT... WHAT...
WHERE THE FUCK...
GINA BAD HORSE R.I.P.
WE MISS YOU GINA

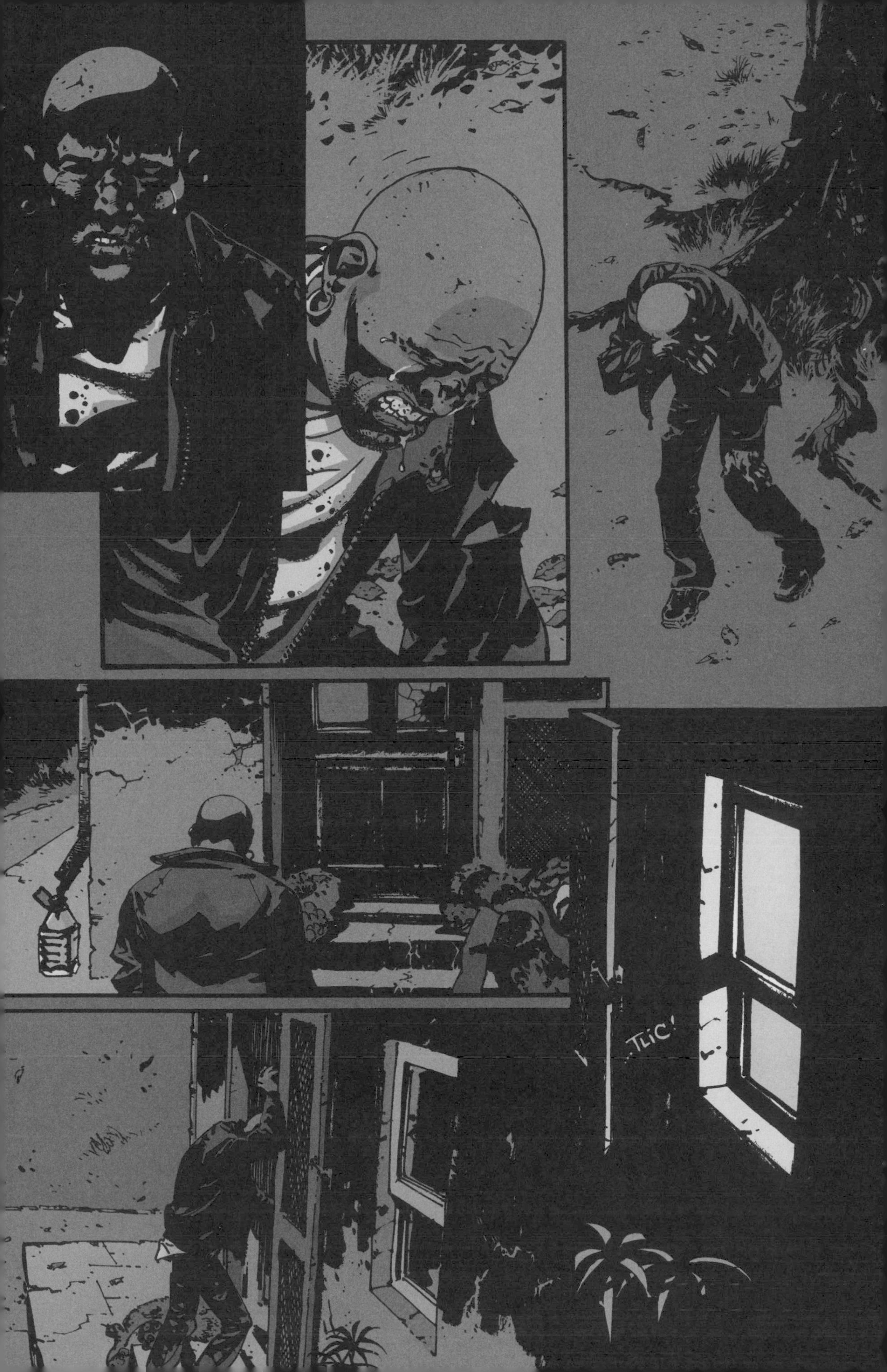
TLIC

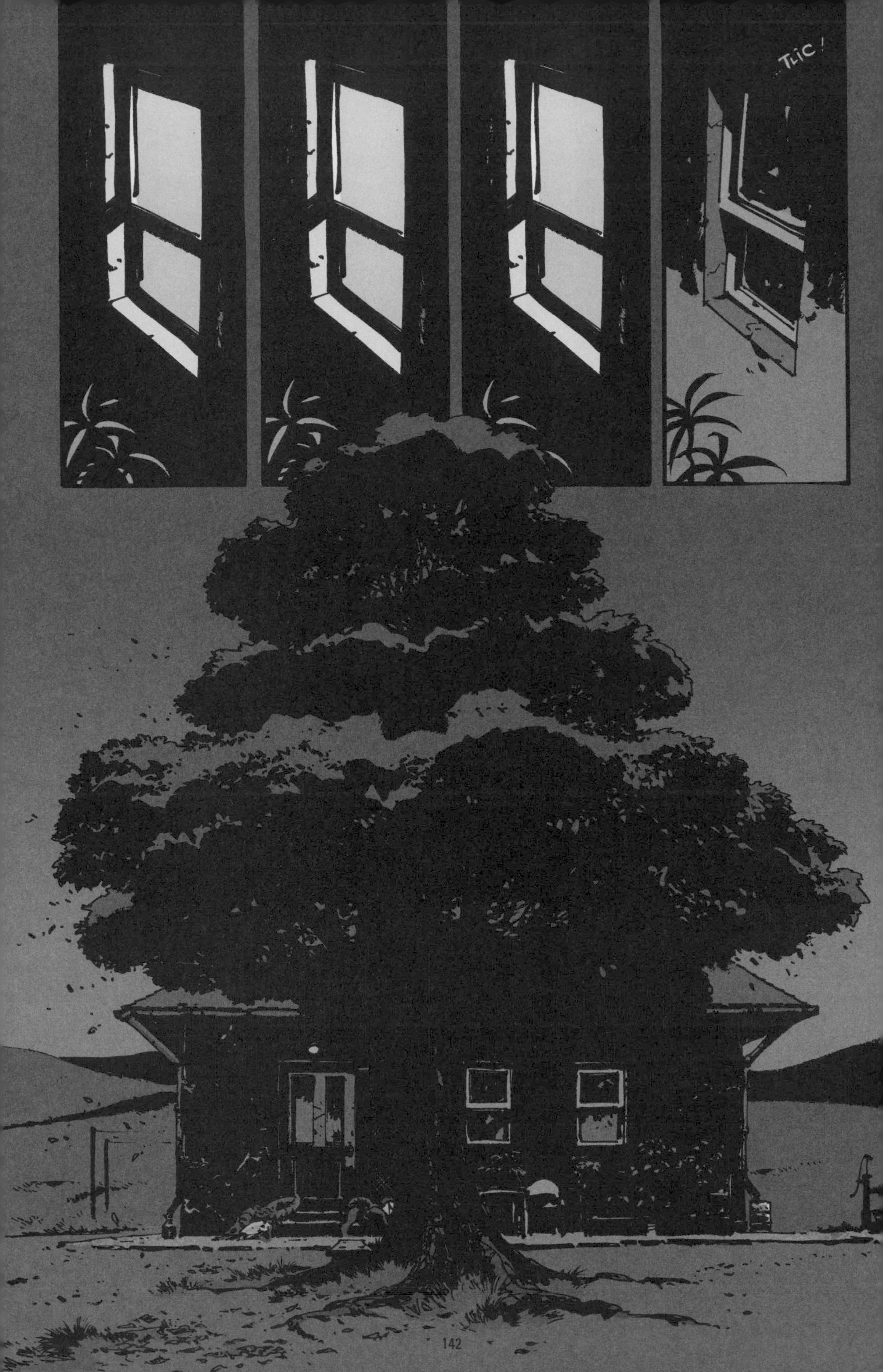
TLIC!

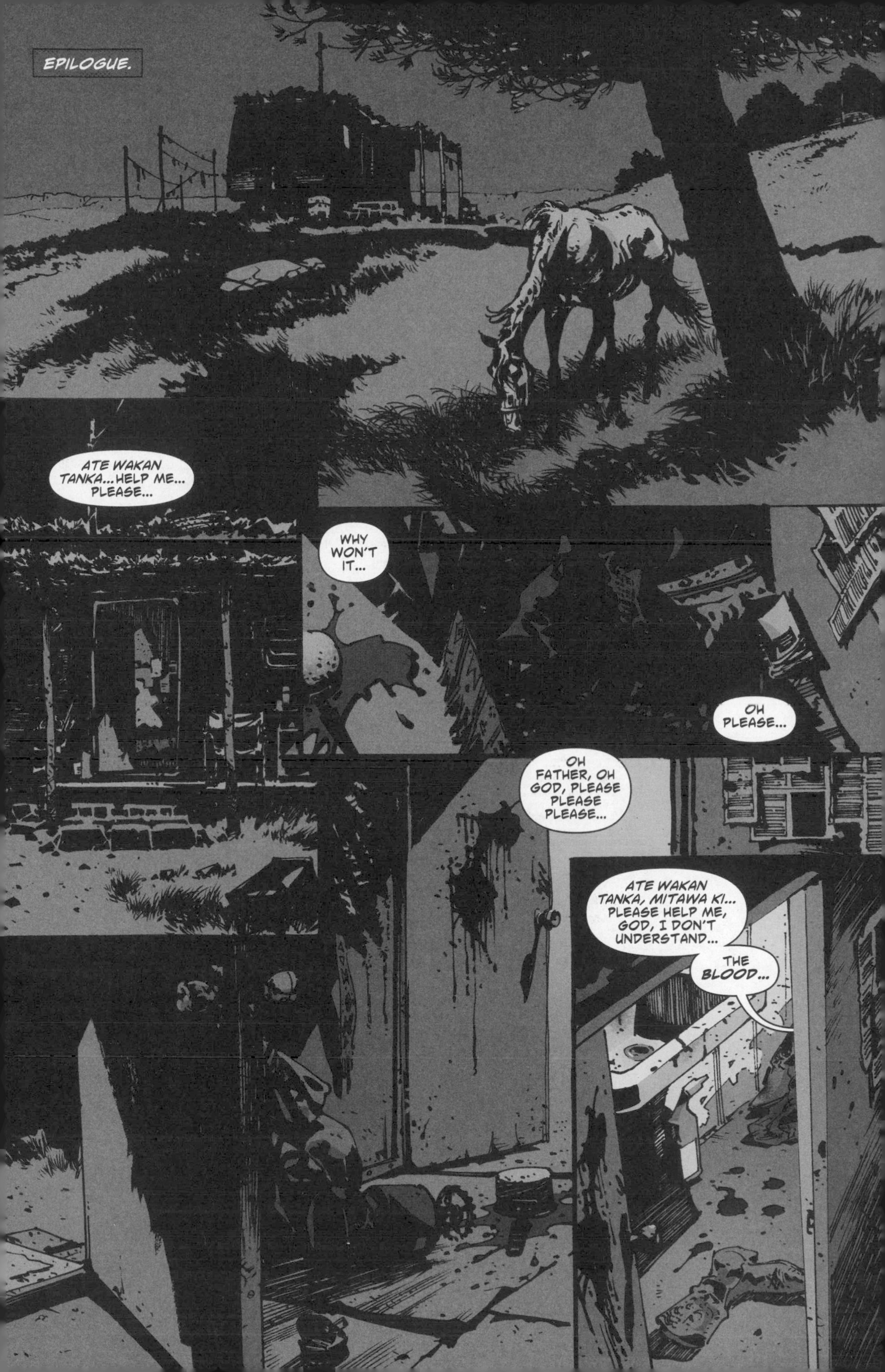
EPILOGUE.
ATE WAKAN TANKA... HELP ME... PLEASE...
WHY WON'T IT...
OH PLEASE...
OH FATHER, OH GOD, PLEASE PLEASE PLEASE...
ATE WAKAN TANKA, MITAWA KI... PLEASE HELP ME, GOD, I DON'T UNDERSTAND...
THE *BLOOD*...

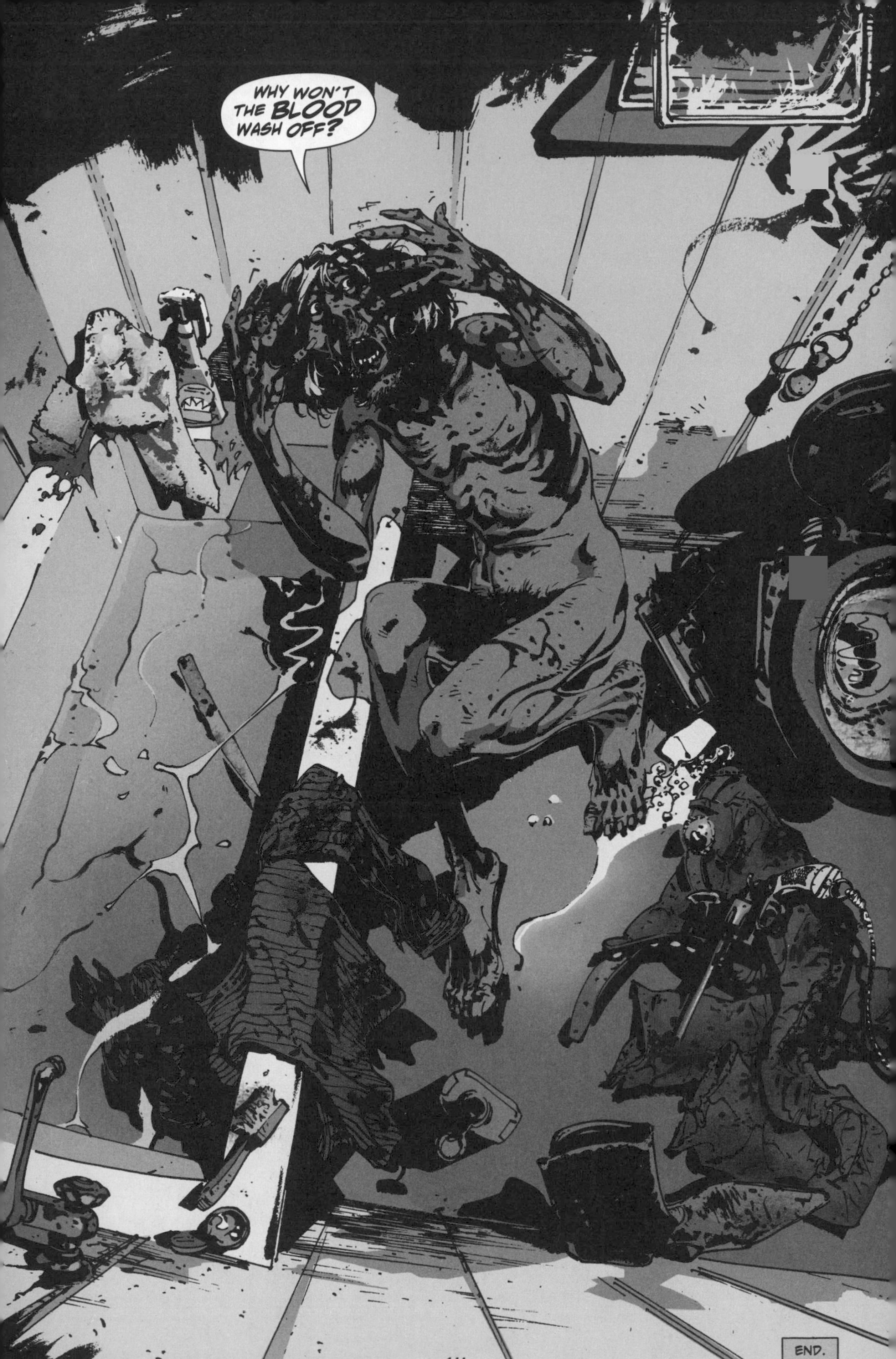
WHY WON'T THE BLOOD WASH OFF?
END.

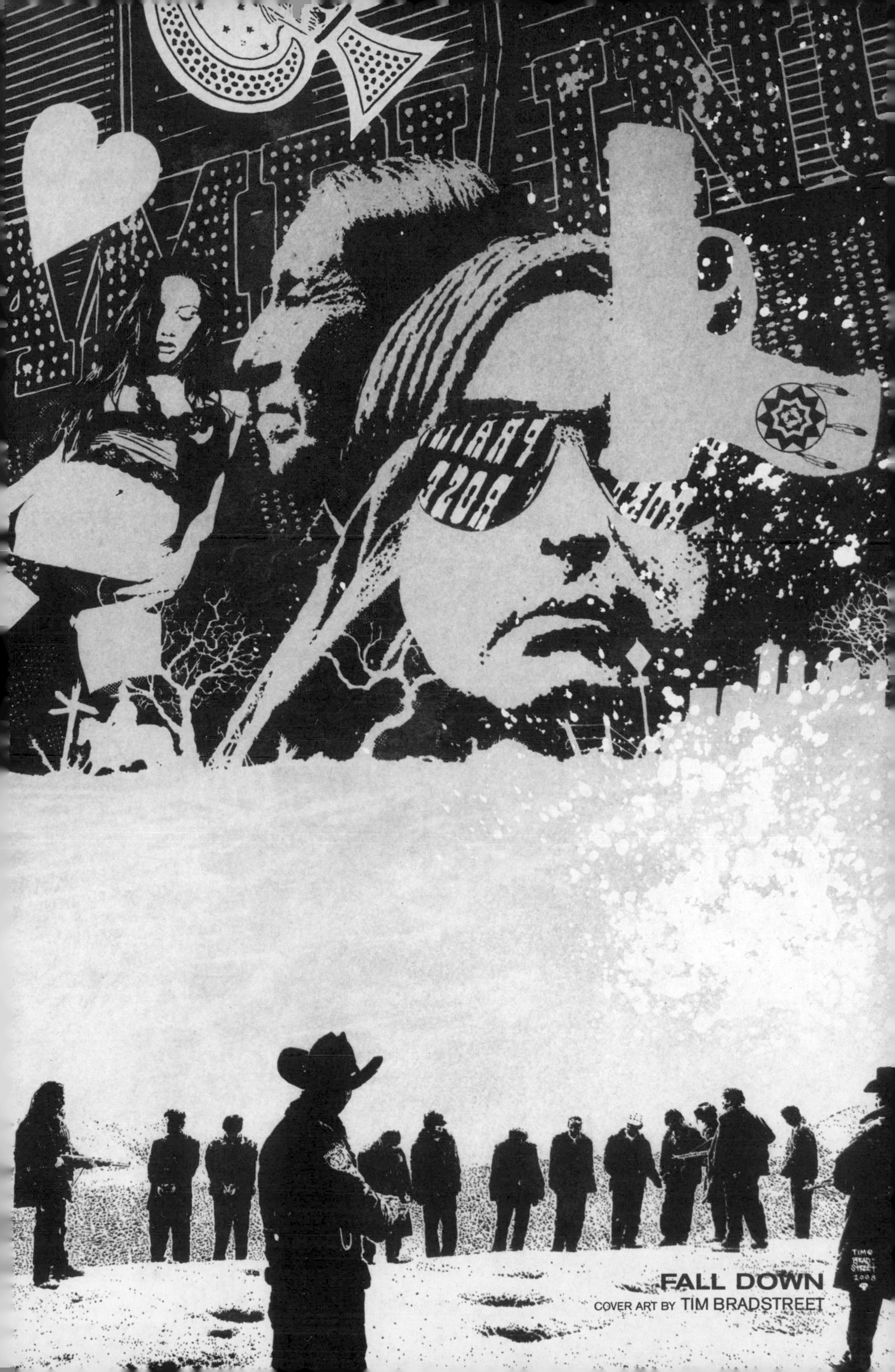

FALL DOWN
COVER ART BY TIM BRADSTREET

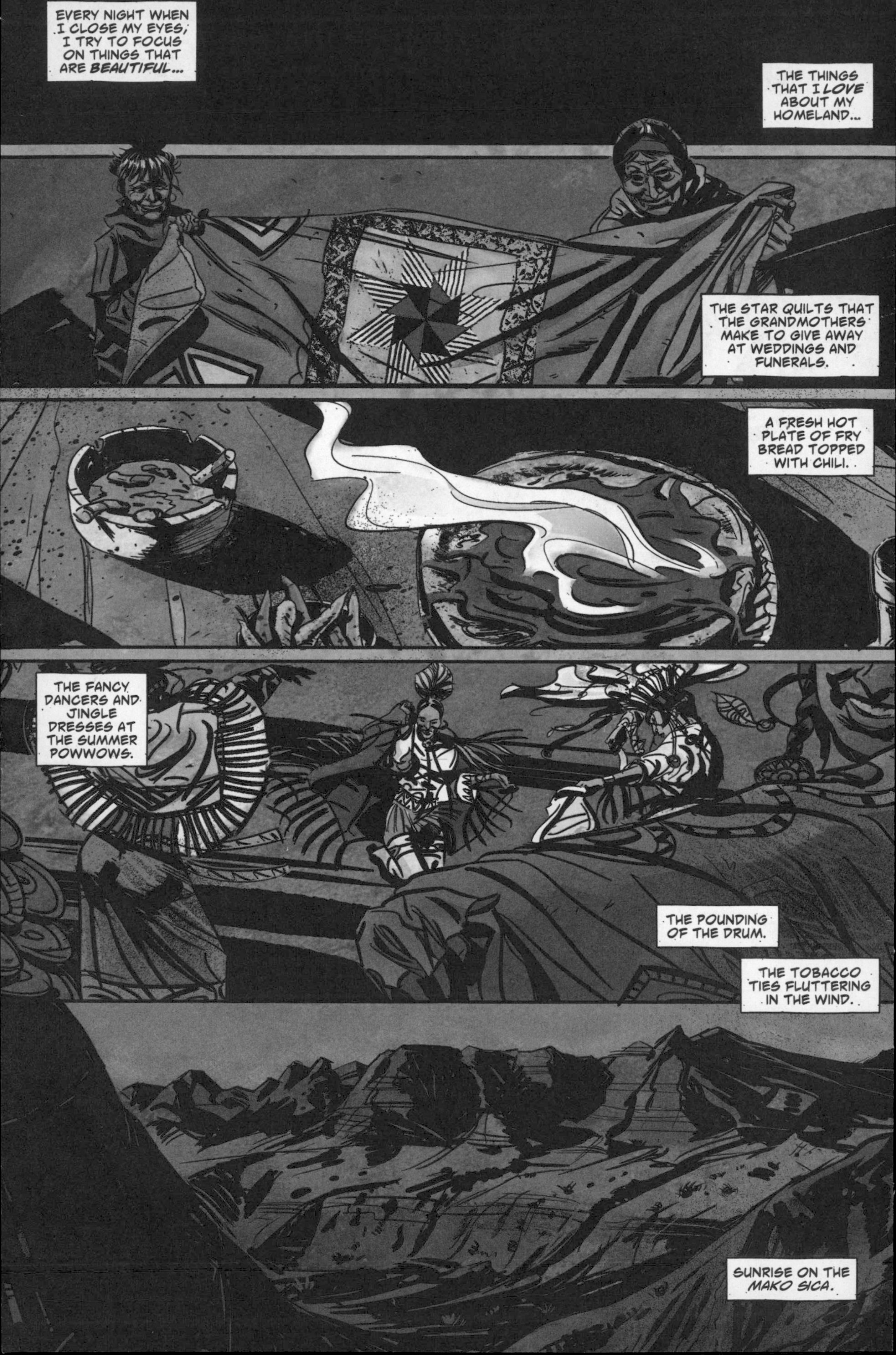
EVERY NIGHT WHEN I CLOSE MY EYES, I TRY TO FOCUS ON THINGS THAT ARE *BEAUTIFUL*...
THE THINGS THAT I *LOVE* ABOUT MY HOMELAND...
THE STAR QUILTS THAT THE GRANDMOTHERS MAKE TO GIVE AWAY AT WEDDINGS AND FUNERALS.
A FRESH HOT PLATE OF FRY BREAD TOPPED WITH CHILI.
THE FANCY DANCERS AND JINGLE DRESSES AT THE SUMMER POWWOWS.
THE POUNDING OF THE DRUM.
THE TOBACCO TIES FLUTTERING IN THE WIND.
SUNRISE ON THE *MAKO SICA*.

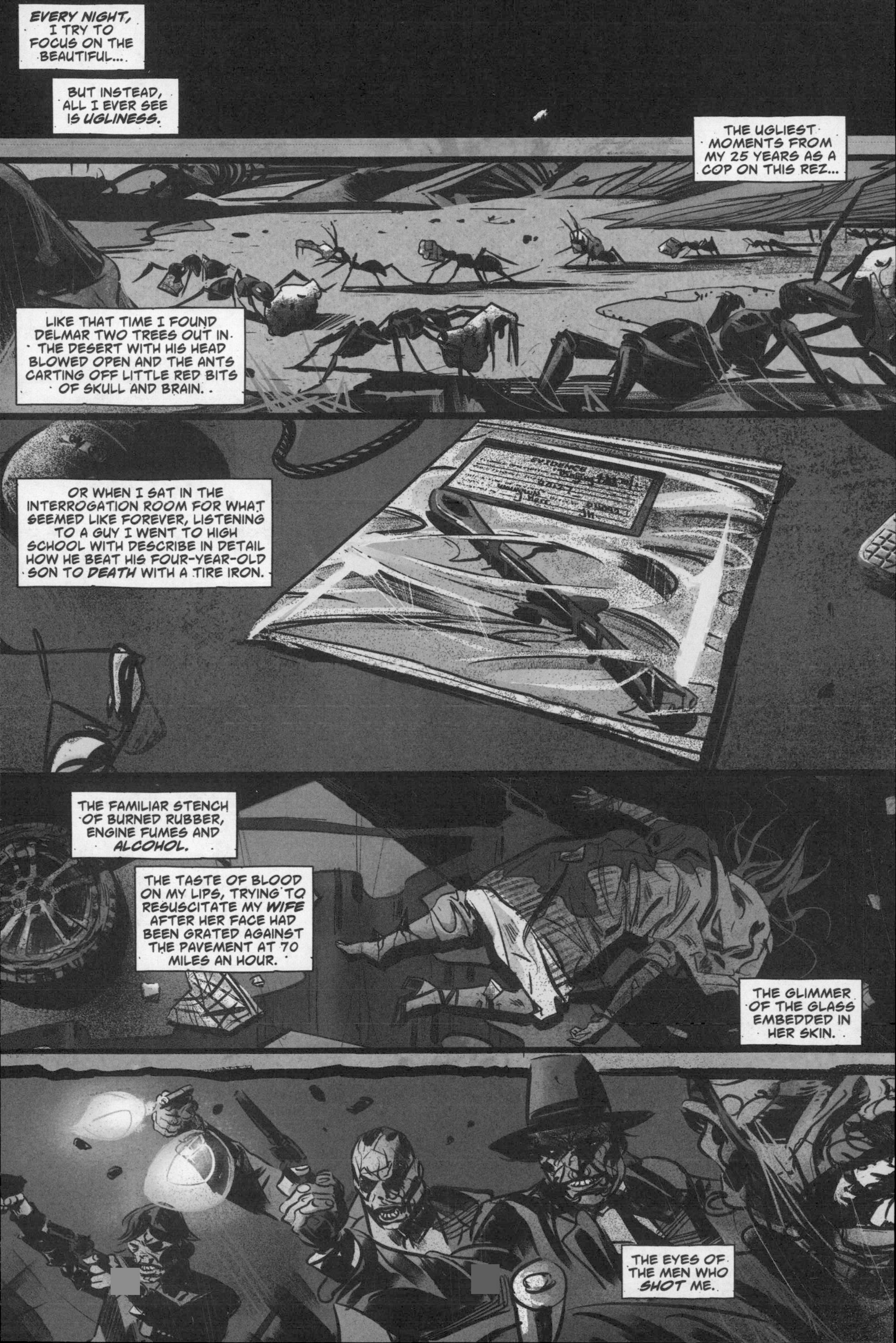
EVERY NIGHT, I TRY TO FOCUS ON THE BEAUTIFUL...
BUT INSTEAD, ALL I EVER SEE IS UGLINESS.
THE UGLIEST MOMENTS FROM MY 25 YEARS AS A COP ON THIS REZ...
LIKE THAT TIME I FOUND DELMAR TWO TREES OUT IN THE DESERT WITH HIS HEAD BLOWED OPEN AND THE ANTS CARTING OFF LITTLE RED BITS OF SKULL AND BRAIN.
OR WHEN I SAT IN THE INTERROGATION ROOM FOR WHAT SEEMED LIKE FOREVER, LISTENING TO A GUY I WENT TO HIGH SCHOOL WITH DESCRIBE IN DETAIL HOW HE BEAT HIS FOUR-YEAR-OLD SON TO DEATH WITH A TIRE IRON.
THE FAMILIAR STENCH OF BURNED RUBBER, ENGINE FUMES AND ALCOHOL.
THE TASTE OF BLOOD ON MY LIPS, TRYING TO RESUSCITATE MY WIFE AFTER HER FACE HAD BEEN GRATED AGAINST THE PAVEMENT AT 70 MILES AN HOUR.
THE GLIMMER OF THE GLASS EMBEDDED IN HER SKIN.
THE EYES OF THE MEN WHO SHOT ME.

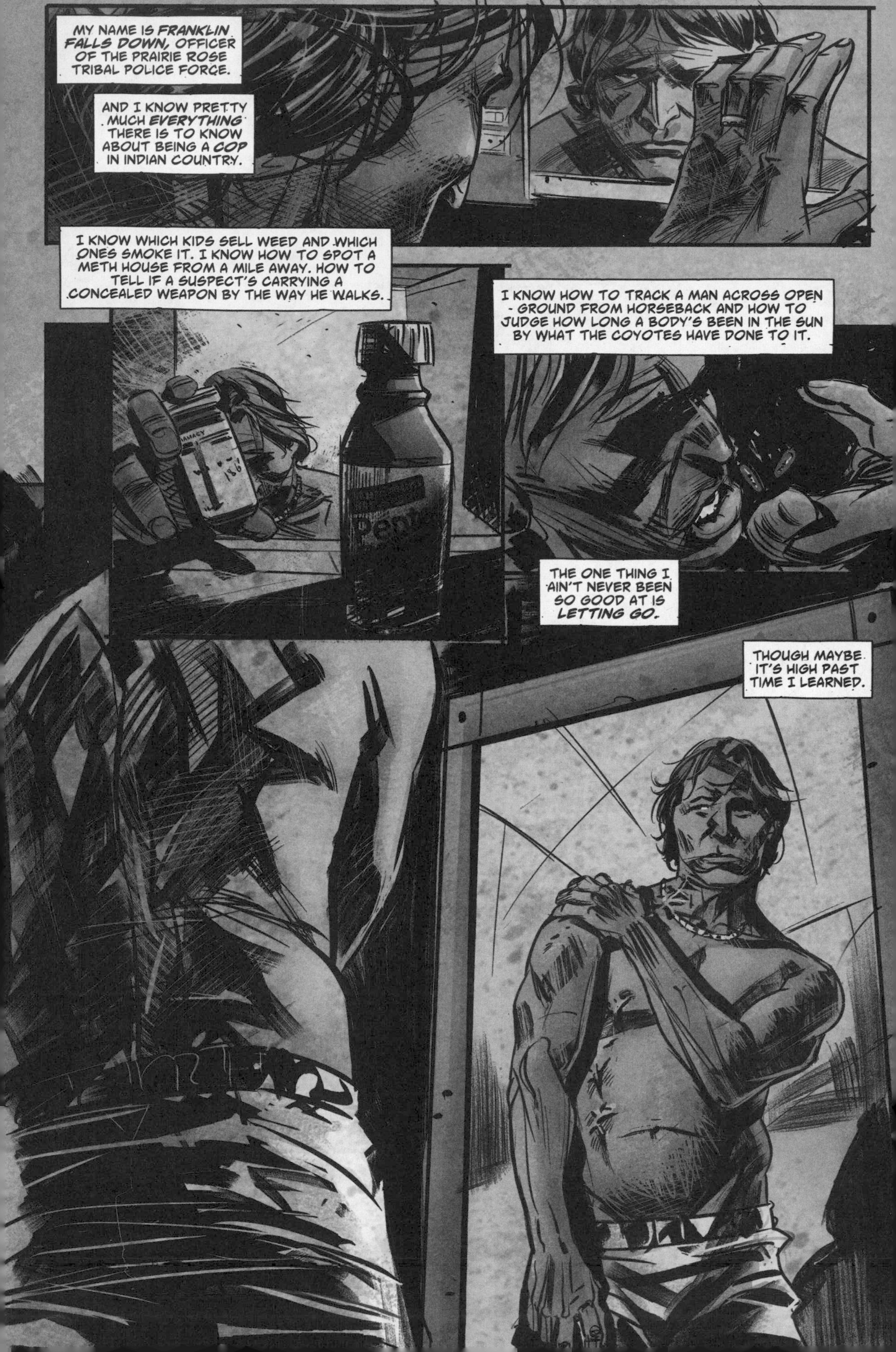
MY NAME IS FRANKLIN FALLS DOWN, OFFICER OF THE PRAIRIE ROSE TRIBAL POLICE FORCE.
AND I KNOW PRETTY MUCH EVERYTHING THERE IS TO KNOW ABOUT BEING A COP IN INDIAN COUNTRY.
I KNOW WHICH KIDS SELL WEED AND WHICH ONES SMOKE IT. I KNOW HOW TO SPOT A METH HOUSE FROM A MILE AWAY. HOW TO TELL IF A SUSPECT'S CARRYING A CONCEALED WEAPON BY THE WAY HE WALKS.
I KNOW HOW TO TRACK A MAN ACROSS OPEN GROUND FROM HORSEBACK AND HOW TO JUDGE HOW LONG A BODY'S BEEN IN THE SUN BY WHAT THE COYOTES HAVE DONE TO IT.
THE ONE THING I AIN'T NEVER BEEN SO GOOD AT IS LETTING GO.
THOUGH MAYBE IT'S HIGH PAST TIME I LEARNED.

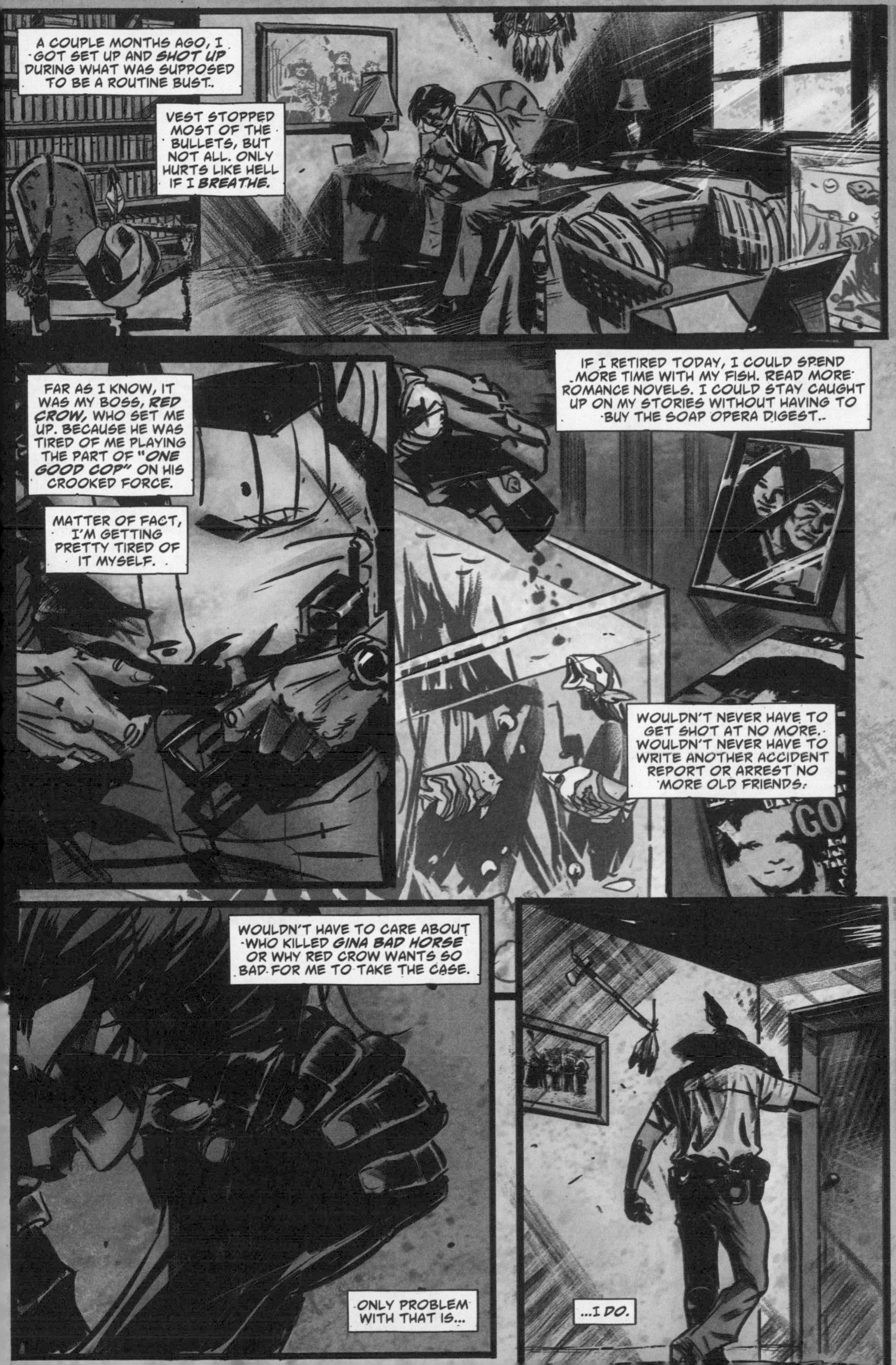
A COUPLE MONTHS AGO, I GOT SET UP AND SHOT UP DURING WHAT WAS SUPPOSED TO BE A ROUTINE BUST.
VEST STOPPED MOST OF THE BULLETS, BUT NOT ALL. ONLY HURTS LIKE HELL IF I BREATHE.
FAR AS I KNOW, IT WAS MY BOSS, RED CROW, WHO SET ME UP. BECAUSE HE WAS TIRED OF ME PLAYING THE PART OF "ONE GOOD COP" ON HIS CROOKED FORCE.
MATTER OF FACT, I'M GETTING PRETTY TIRED OF IT MYSELF.
IF I RETIRED TODAY, I COULD SPEND MORE TIME WITH MY FISH. READ MORE ROMANCE NOVELS. I COULD STAY CAUGHT UP ON MY STORIES WITHOUT HAVING TO BUY THE SOAP OPERA DIGEST.
WOULDN'T NEVER HAVE TO GET SHOT AT NO MORE. WOULDN'T NEVER HAVE TO WRITE ANOTHER ACCIDENT REPORT OR ARREST NO MORE OLD FRIENDS.
WOULDN'T HAVE TO CARE ABOUT WHO KILLED GINA BAD HORSE OR WHY RED CROW WANTS SO BAD FOR ME TO TAKE THE CASE.
ONLY PROBLEM WITH THAT IS...
...I DO.

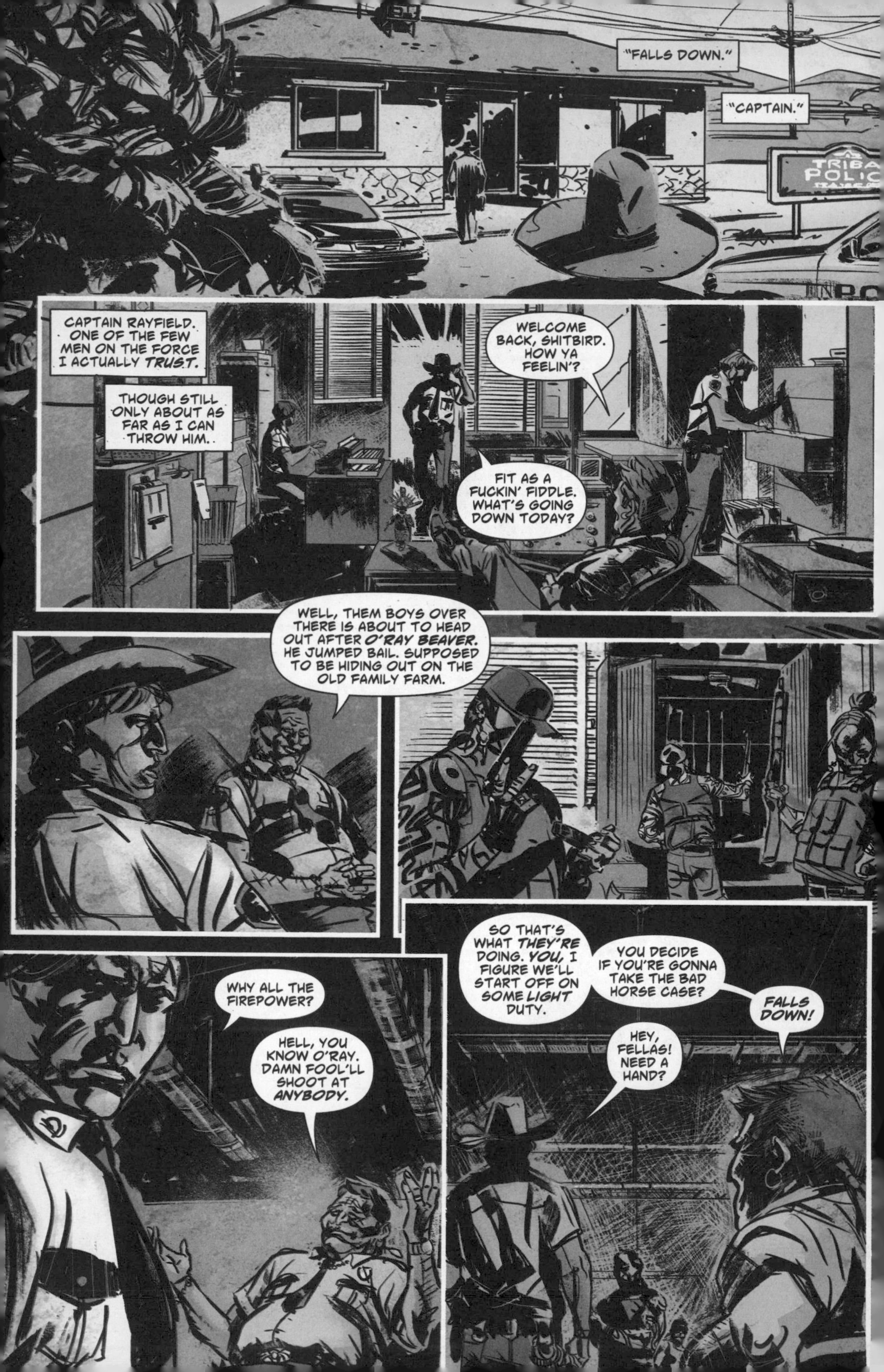
"FALLS DOWN."
"CAPTAIN."
CAPTAIN RAYFIELD. ONE OF THE FEW MEN ON THE FORCE I ACTUALLY TRUST.
THOUGH STILL ONLY ABOUT AS FAR AS I CAN THROW HIM.
WELCOME BACK, SHITBIRD. HOW YA FEELIN'?
FIT AS A FUCKIN' FIDDLE. WHAT'S GOING DOWN TODAY?
WELL, THEM BOYS OVER THERE IS ABOUT TO HEAD OUT AFTER O'RAY BEAVER. HE JUMPED BAIL. SUPPOSED TO BE HIDING OUT ON THE OLD FAMILY FARM.
WHY ALL THE FIREPOWER?
HELL, YOU KNOW O'RAY. DAMN FOOL'LL SHOOT AT ANYBODY.
SO THAT'S WHAT THEY'RE DOING. YOU, I FIGURE WE'LL START OFF ON SOME LIGHT DUTY.
YOU DECIDE IF YOU'RE GONNA TAKE THE BAD HORSE CASE?
FALLS DOWN!
HEY, FELLAS! NEED A HAND?

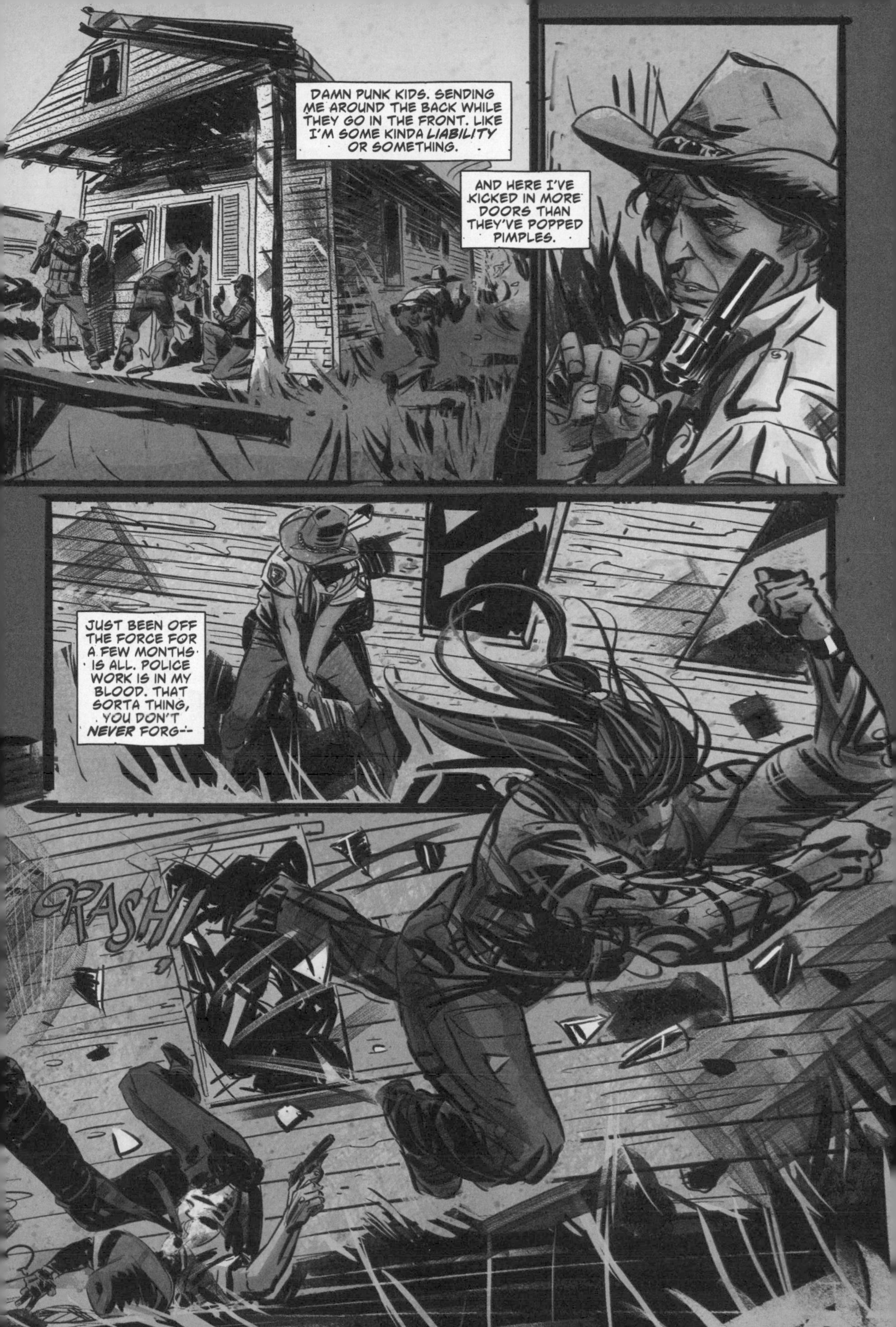
DAMN PUNK KIDS. SENDING ME AROUND THE BACK WHILE THEY GO IN THE FRONT. LIKE I'M SOME KINDA *LIABILITY* OR SOMETHING.
AND HERE I'VE KICKED IN MORE DOORS THAN THEY'VE POPPED PIMPLES.
JUST BEEN OFF THE FORCE FOR A FEW MONTHS IS ALL. POLICE WORK IS IN MY BLOOD. THAT SORTA THING, YOU DON'T *NEVER* FORG--
CRASH!

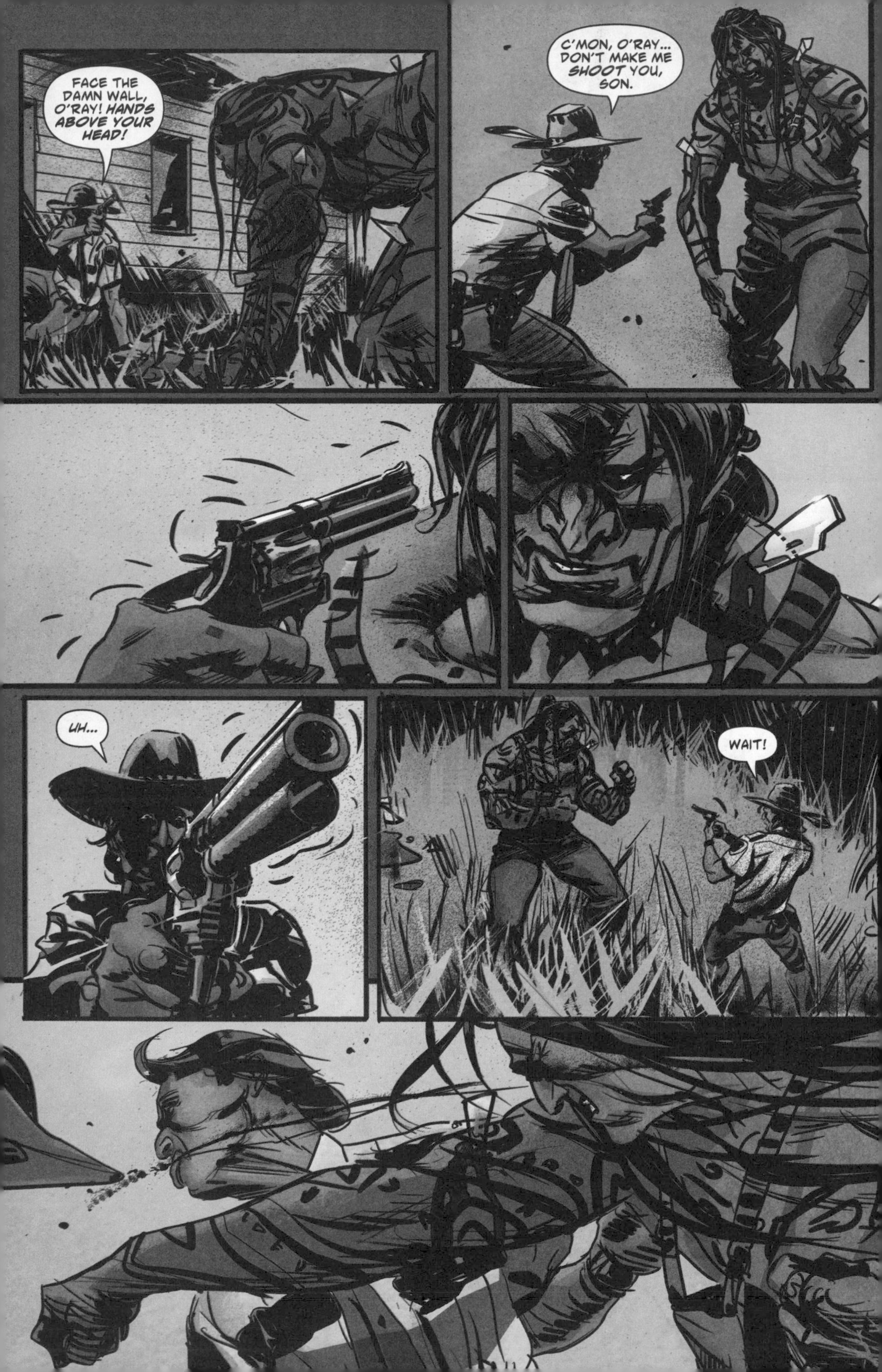
FACE THE DAMN WALL, O'RAY! HANDS ABOVE YOUR HEAD!
C'MON, O'RAY... DON'T MAKE ME SHOOT YOU, SON.
UH...
WAIT!

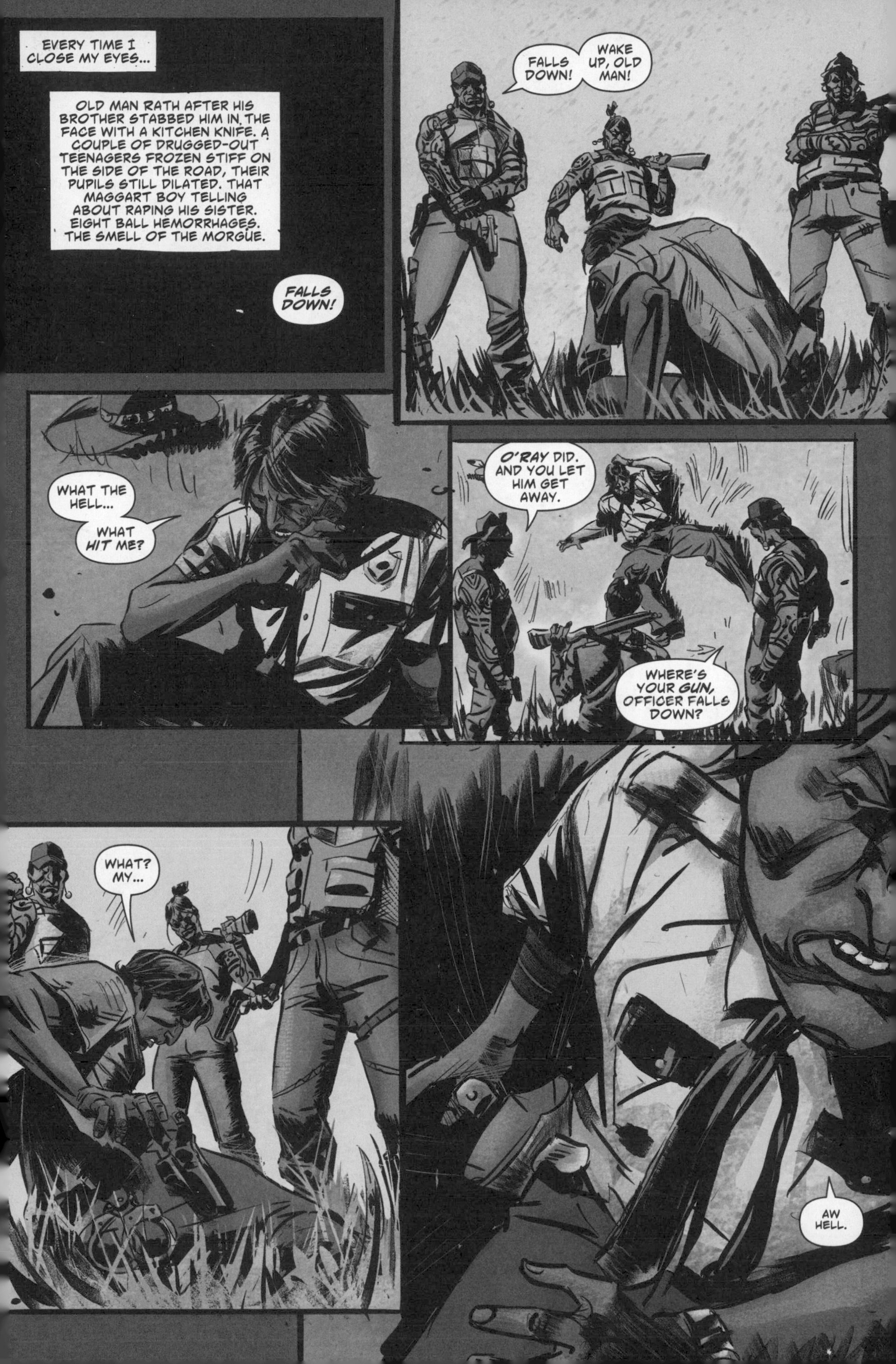
EVERY TIME I CLOSE MY EYES...
OLD MAN RATH AFTER HIS BROTHER STABBED HIM IN THE FACE WITH A KITCHEN KNIFE. A COUPLE OF DRUGGED-OUT TEENAGERS FROZEN STIFF ON THE SIDE OF THE ROAD, THEIR PUPILS STILL DILATED. THAT MAGGART BOY TELLING ABOUT RAPING HIS SISTER. EIGHT BALL HEMORRHAGES. THE SMELL OF THE MORGUE.
FALLS DOWN!
FALLS DOWN!
WAKE UP, OLD MAN!
WHAT THE HELL...
WHAT HIT ME?
O'RAY DID. AND YOU LET HIM GET AWAY.
WHERE'S YOUR GUN, OFFICER FALLS DOWN?
WHAT? MY...
AW HELL.

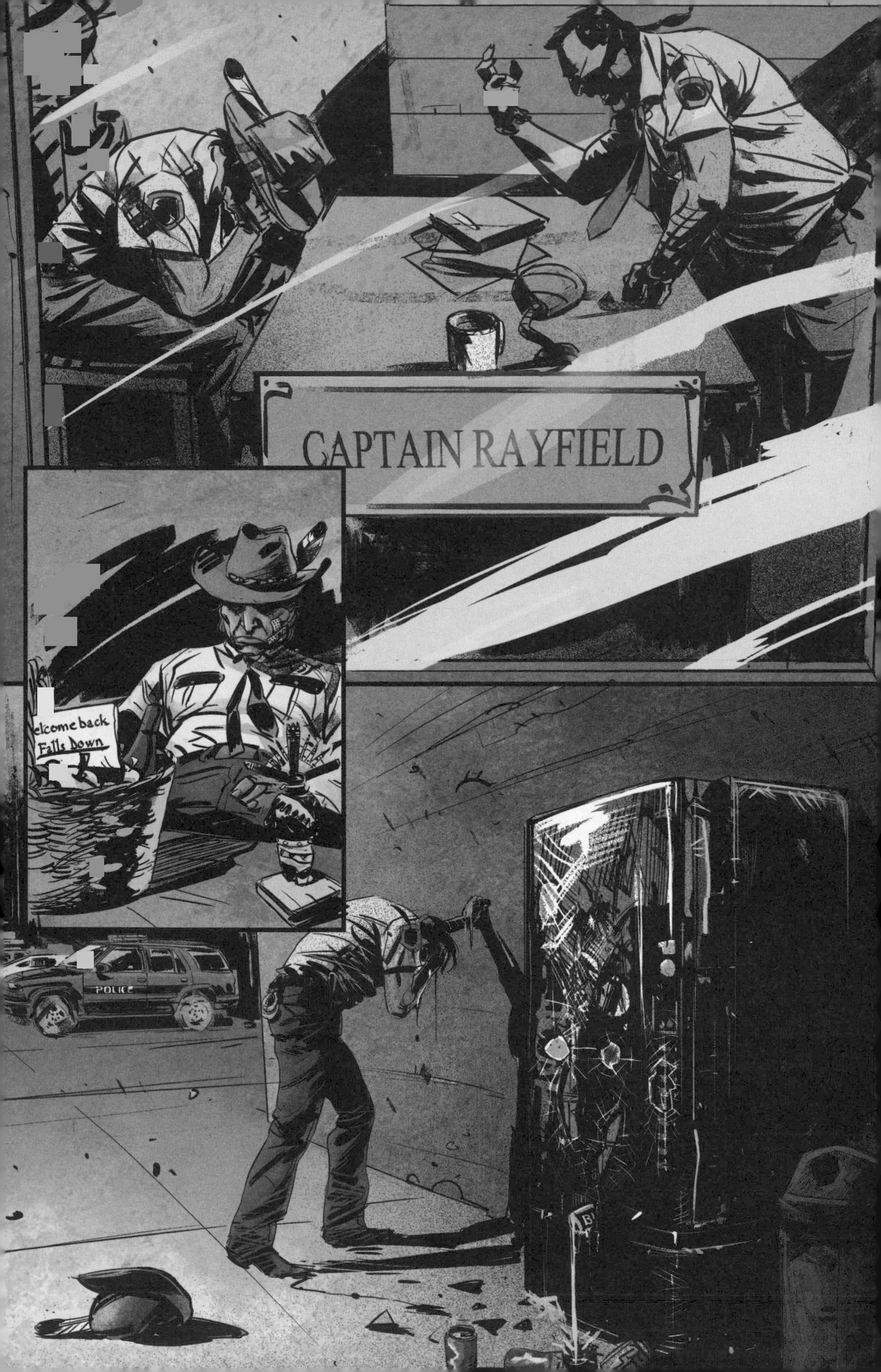
CAPTAIN RAYFIELD
elcome back
Falls Down
POLICE

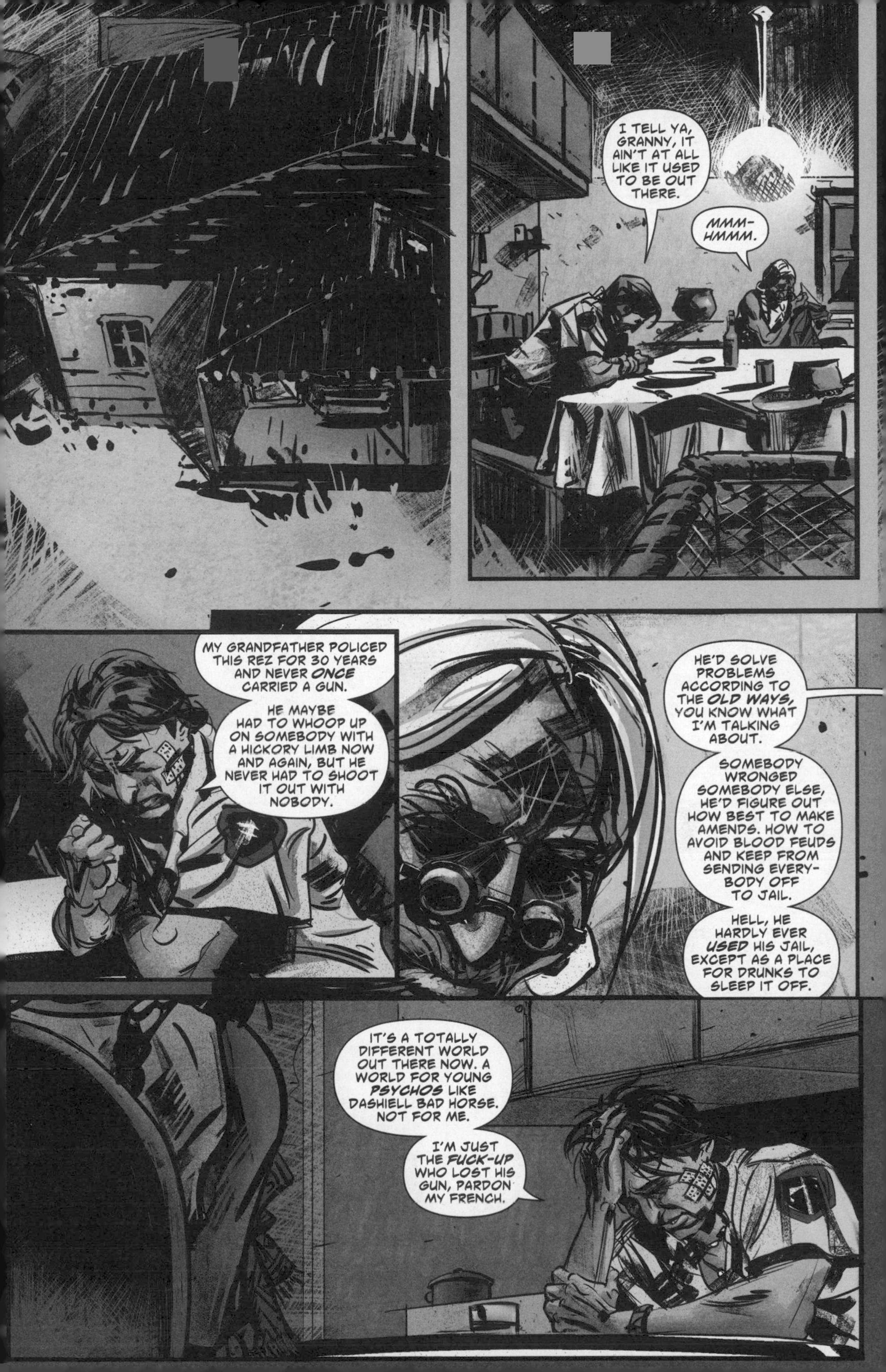
I TELL YA, GRANNY, IT AIN'T AT ALL LIKE IT USED TO BE OUT THERE.
MMM-HMMM.
MY GRANDFATHER POLICED THIS REZ FOR 30 YEARS AND NEVER ONCE CARRIED A GUN.
HE MAYBE HAD TO WHOOP UP ON SOMEBODY WITH A HICKORY LIMB NOW AND AGAIN, BUT HE NEVER HAD TO SHOOT IT OUT WITH NOBODY.
HE'D SOLVE PROBLEMS ACCORDING TO THE OLD WAYS, YOU KNOW WHAT I'M TALKING ABOUT.
SOMEBODY WRONGED SOMEBODY ELSE, HE'D FIGURE OUT HOW BEST TO MAKE AMENDS. HOW TO AVOID BLOOD FEUDS AND KEEP FROM SENDING EVERY-BODY OFF TO JAIL.
HELL, HE HARDLY EVER USED HIS JAIL, EXCEPT AS A PLACE FOR DRUNKS TO SLEEP IT OFF.
IT'S A TOTALLY DIFFERENT WORLD OUT THERE NOW. A WORLD FOR YOUNG PSYCHOS LIKE DASHIELL BAD HORSE. NOT FOR ME.
I'M JUST THE FUCK-UP WHO LOST HIS GUN, PARDON MY FRENCH.

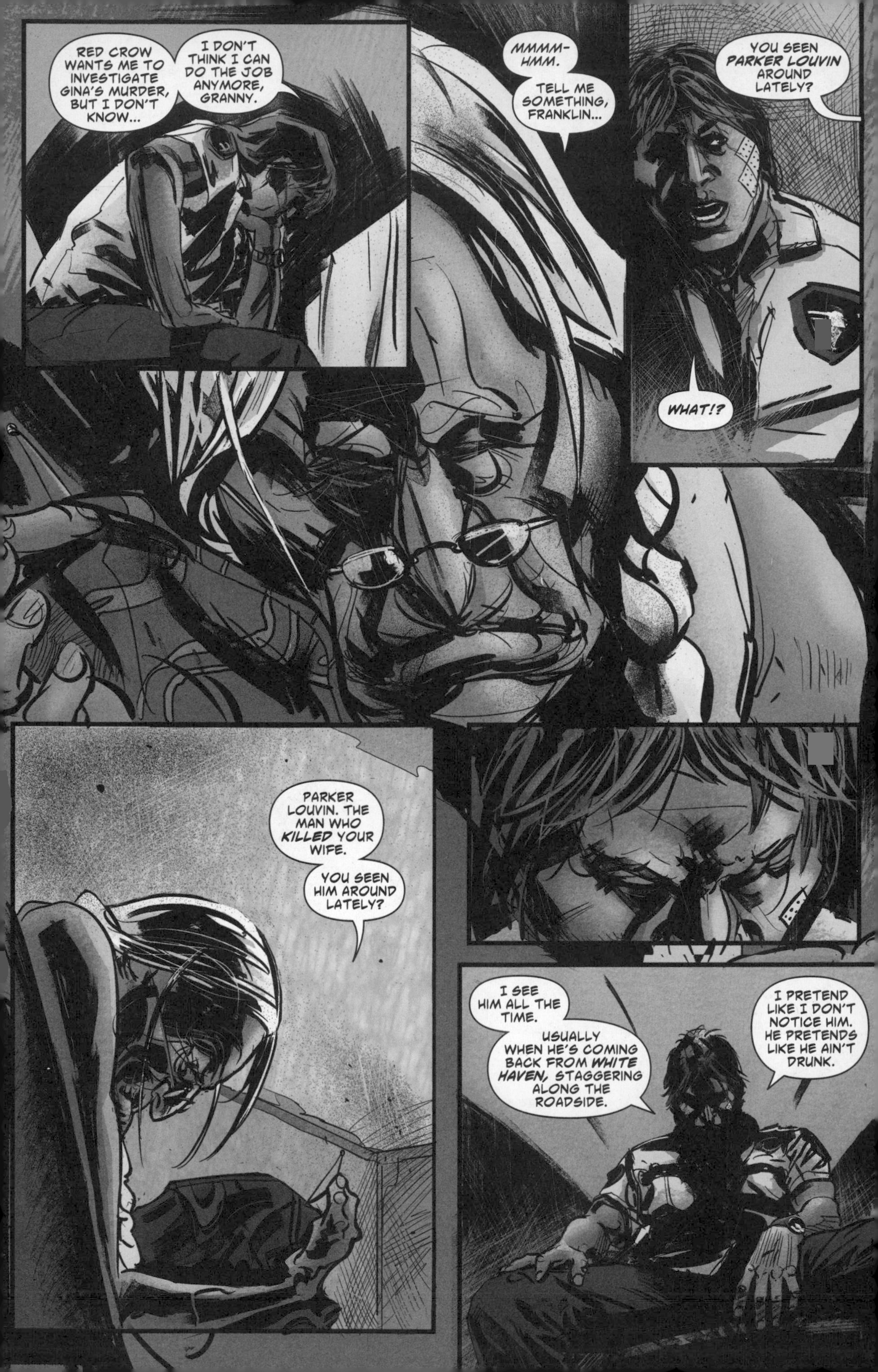
RED CROW WANTS ME TO INVESTIGATE GINA'S MURDER, BUT I DON'T KNOW...
I DON'T THINK I CAN DO THE JOB ANYMORE, GRANNY.
MMMM-HMM.
TELL ME SOMETHING, FRANKLIN...
YOU SEEN PARKER LOUVIN AROUND LATELY?
WHAT!?
PARKER LOUVIN. THE MAN WHO KILLED YOUR WIFE.
YOU SEEN HIM AROUND LATELY?
I SEE HIM ALL THE TIME.
USUALLY WHEN HE'S COMING BACK FROM WHITE HAVEN, STAGGERING ALONG THE ROADSIDE.
I PRETEND LIKE I DON'T NOTICE HIM. HE PRETENDS LIKE HE AIN'T DRUNK.

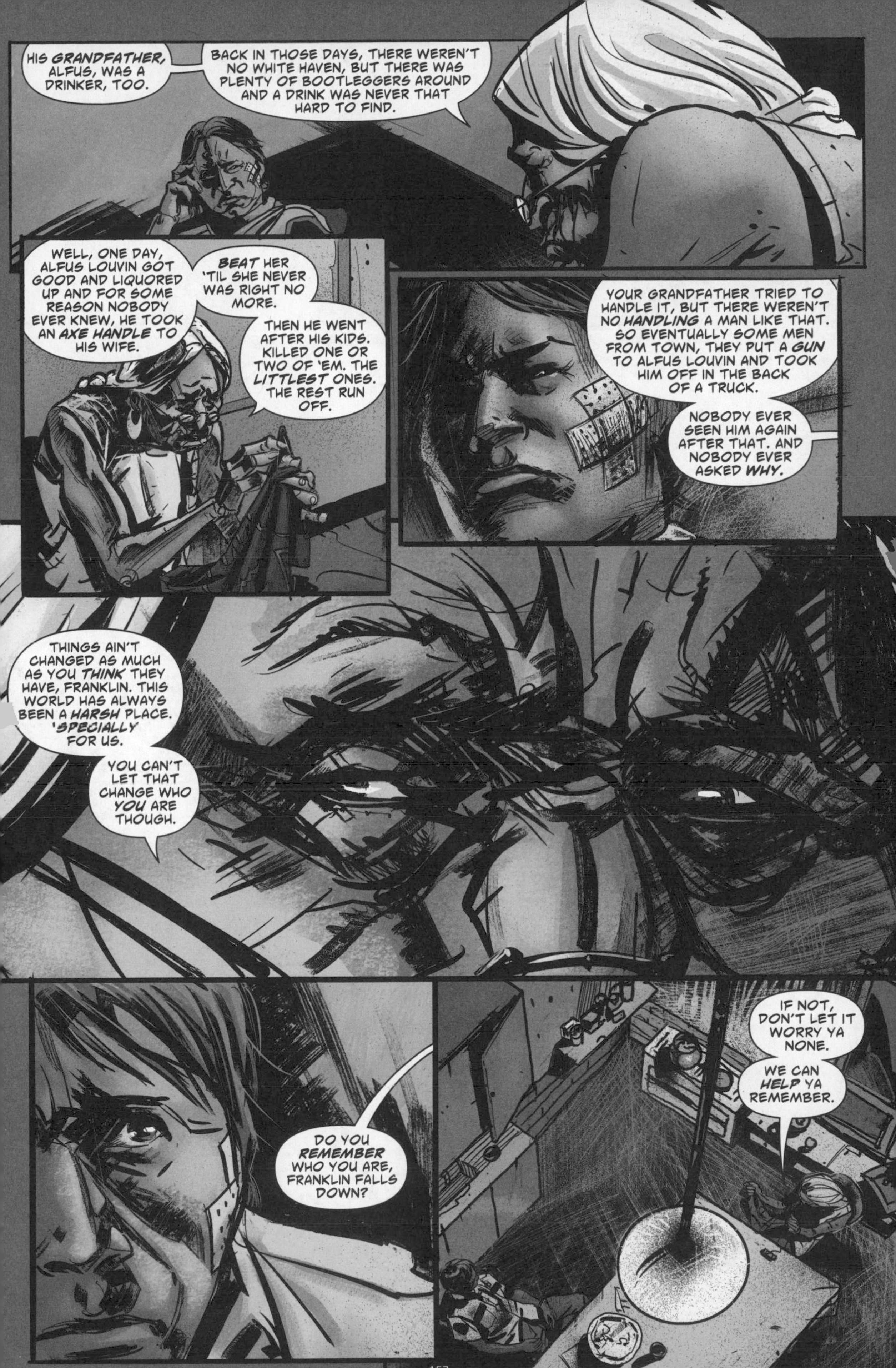
HIS GRANDFATHER, ALFUS, WAS A DRINKER, TOO.
BACK IN THOSE DAYS, THERE WEREN'T NO WHITE HAVEN, BUT THERE WAS PLENTY OF BOOTLEGGERS AROUND AND A DRINK WAS NEVER THAT HARD TO FIND.
WELL, ONE DAY, ALFUS LOUVIN GOT GOOD AND LIQUORED UP AND FOR SOME REASON NOBODY EVER KNEW, HE TOOK AN AXE HANDLE TO HIS WIFE.
BEAT HER 'TIL SHE NEVER WAS RIGHT NO MORE.
THEN HE WENT AFTER HIS KIDS. KILLED ONE OR TWO OF 'EM. THE LITTLEST ONES. THE REST RUN OFF.
YOUR GRANDFATHER TRIED TO HANDLE IT, BUT THERE WEREN'T NO HANDLING A MAN LIKE THAT. SO EVENTUALLY SOME MEN FROM TOWN, THEY PUT A GUN TO ALFUS LOUVIN AND TOOK HIM OFF IN THE BACK OF A TRUCK.
NOBODY EVER SEEN HIM AGAIN AFTER THAT. AND NOBODY EVER ASKED WHY.
THINGS AIN'T CHANGED AS MUCH AS YOU THINK THEY HAVE, FRANKLIN. THIS WORLD HAS ALWAYS BEEN A HARSH PLACE. 'SPECIALLY FOR US.
YOU CAN'T LET THAT CHANGE WHO YOU ARE THOUGH.
DO YOU REMEMBER WHO YOU ARE, FRANKLIN FALLS DOWN?
IF NOT, DON'T LET IT WORRY YA NONE.
WE CAN HELP YA REMEMBER.

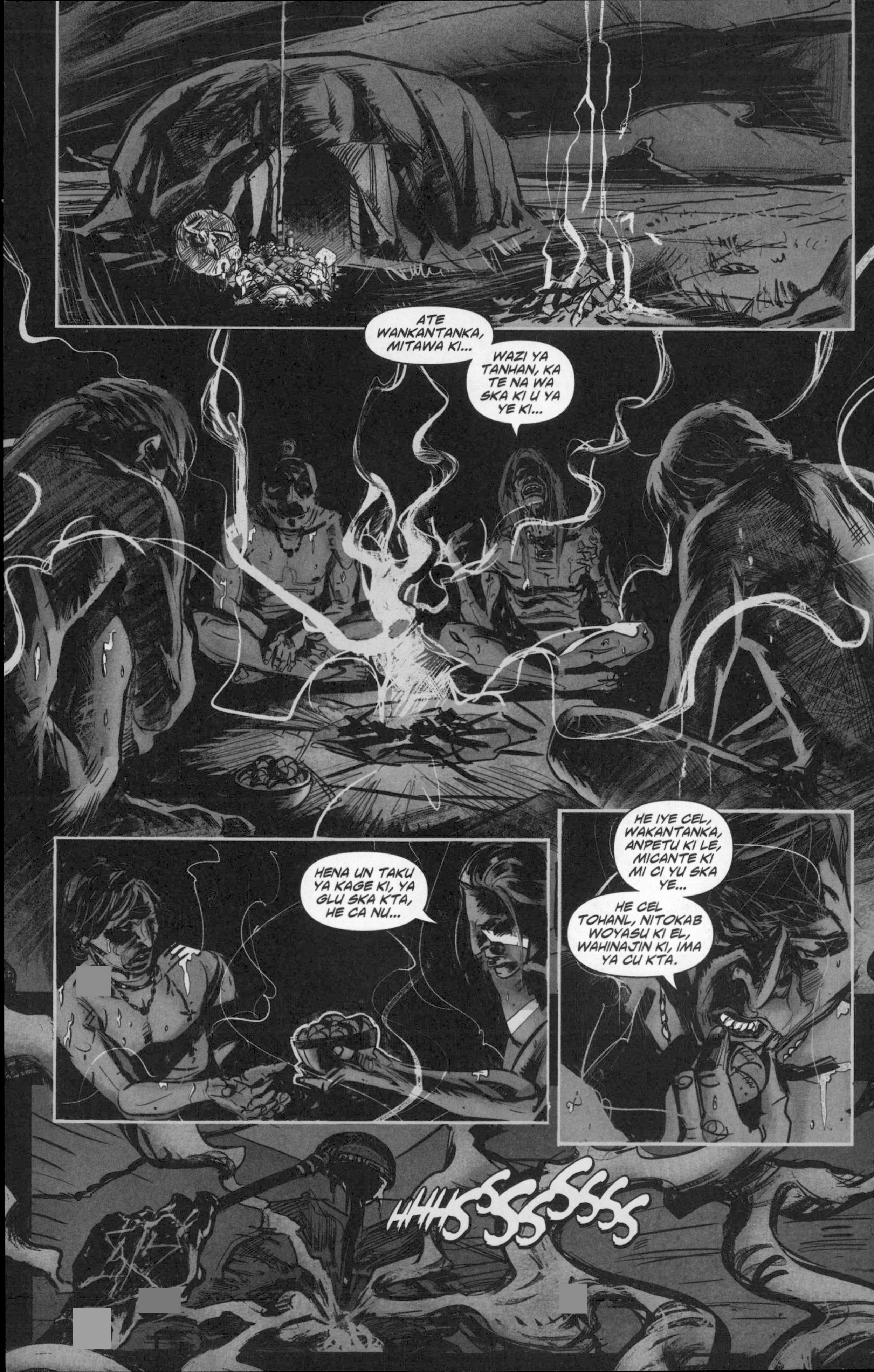
ATE WANKANTANKA, MITAWA KI...
WAZI YA TANHAN, KA TE NA WA SKA KI U YA YE KI...
HENA UN TAKU YA KAGE KI, YA GLU SKA KTA, HE CA NU...
HE IYE CEL, WAKANTANKA, ANPETU KI LE, MICANTE KI MI CI YU SKA YE...
HE CEL TOHANL, NITOKAB WOYASU KI EL, WAHINAJIN KI, IMA YA CU KTA.
HHHSSSSSSSSS

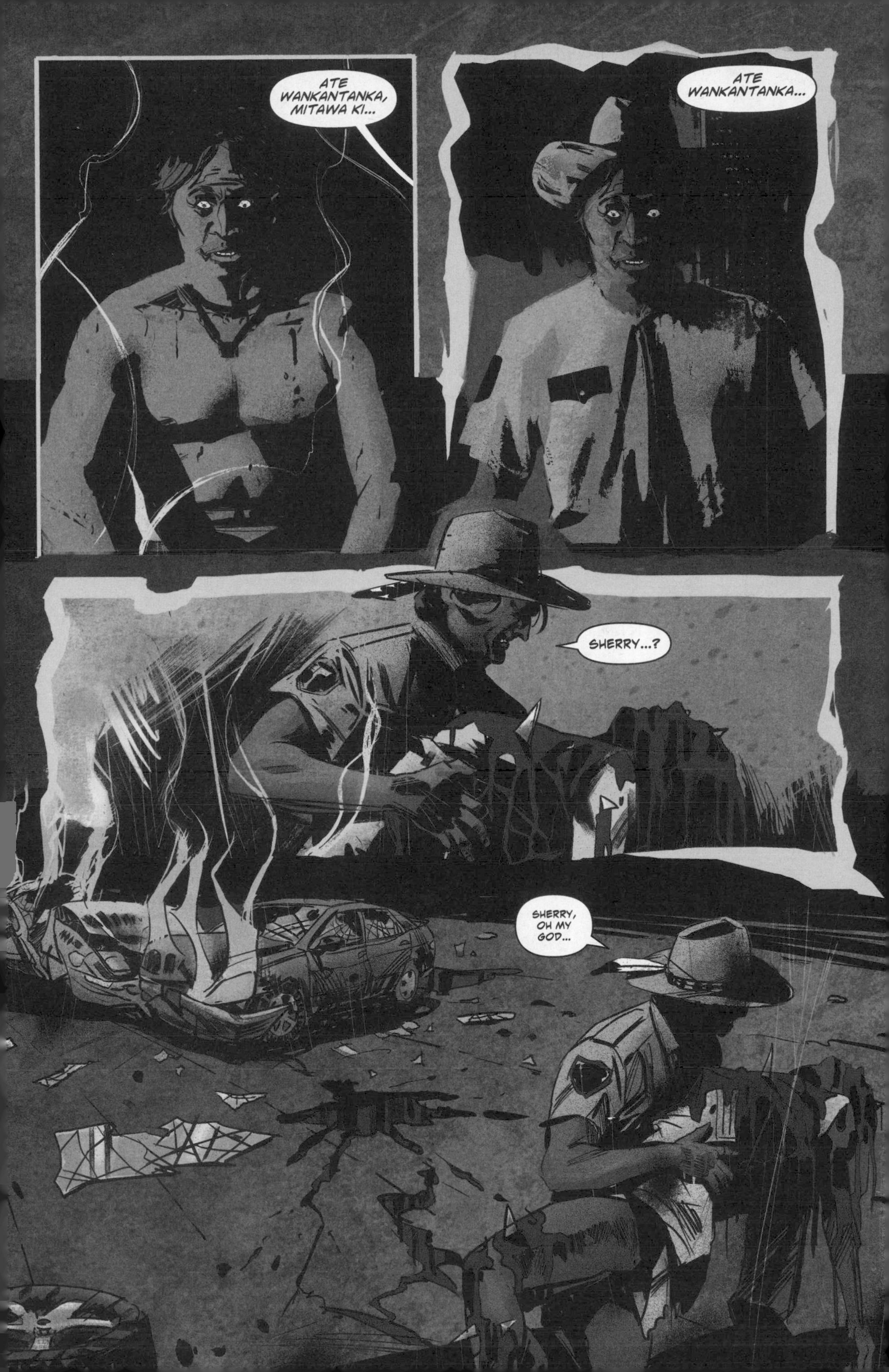
ATE WANKANTANKA, MITAWA KI...
ATE WANKANTANKA...
SHERRY...?
SHERRY, OH MY GOD...

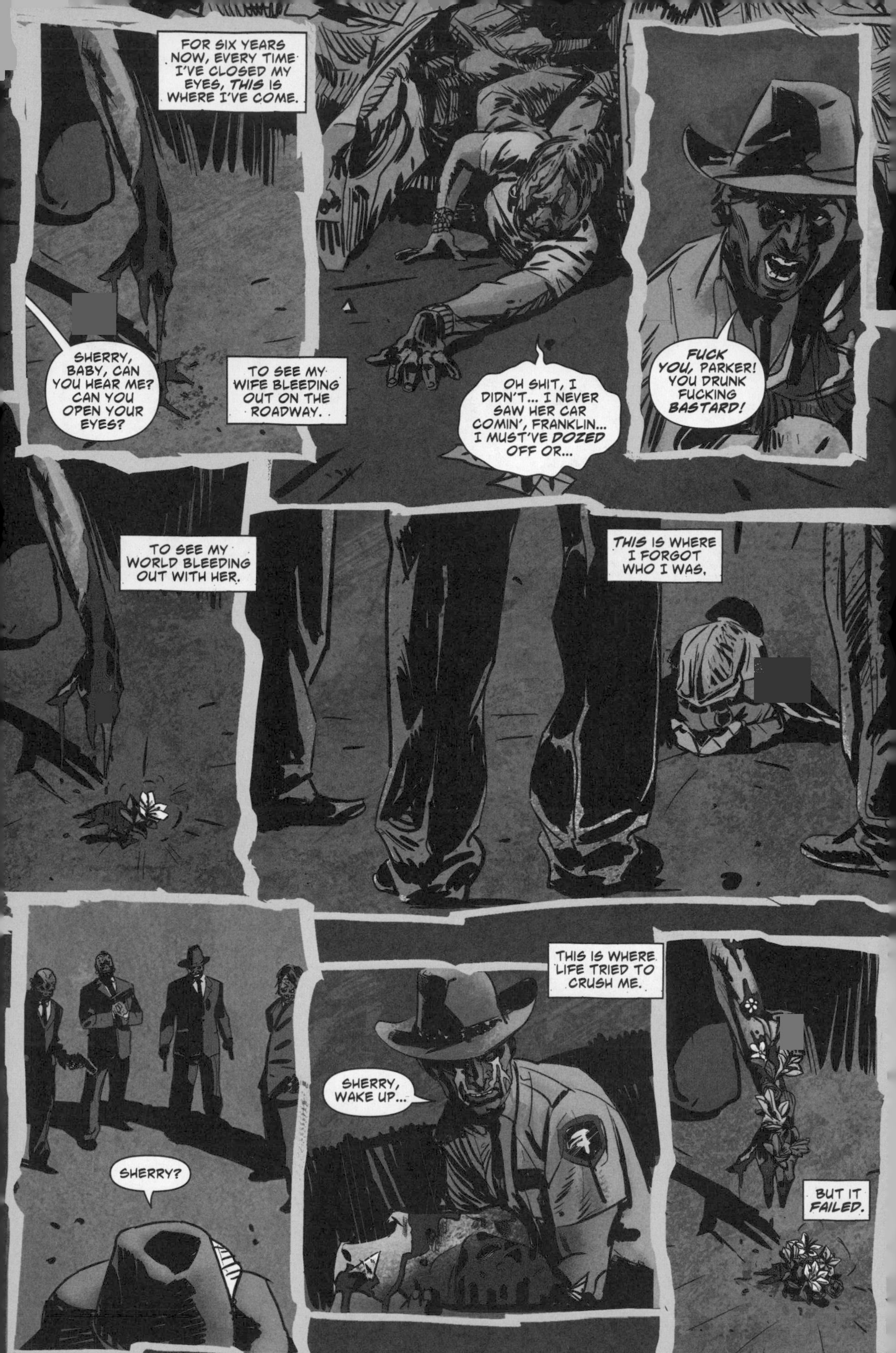
FOR SIX YEARS NOW, EVERY TIME I'VE CLOSED MY EYES, THIS IS WHERE I'VE COME.
SHERRY, BABY, CAN YOU HEAR ME? CAN YOU OPEN YOUR EYES?
TO SEE MY WIFE BLEEDING OUT ON THE ROADWAY.
OH SHIT, I DIDN'T... I NEVER SAW HER CAR COMIN', FRANKLIN... I MUST'VE DOZED OFF OR...
FUCK YOU, PARKER! YOU DRUNK FUCKING BASTARD!
TO SEE MY WORLD BLEEDING OUT WITH HER.
THIS IS WHERE I FORGOT WHO I WAS.
SHERRY?
THIS IS WHERE LIFE TRIED TO CRUSH ME.
SHERRY, WAKE UP...
BUT IT FAILED.

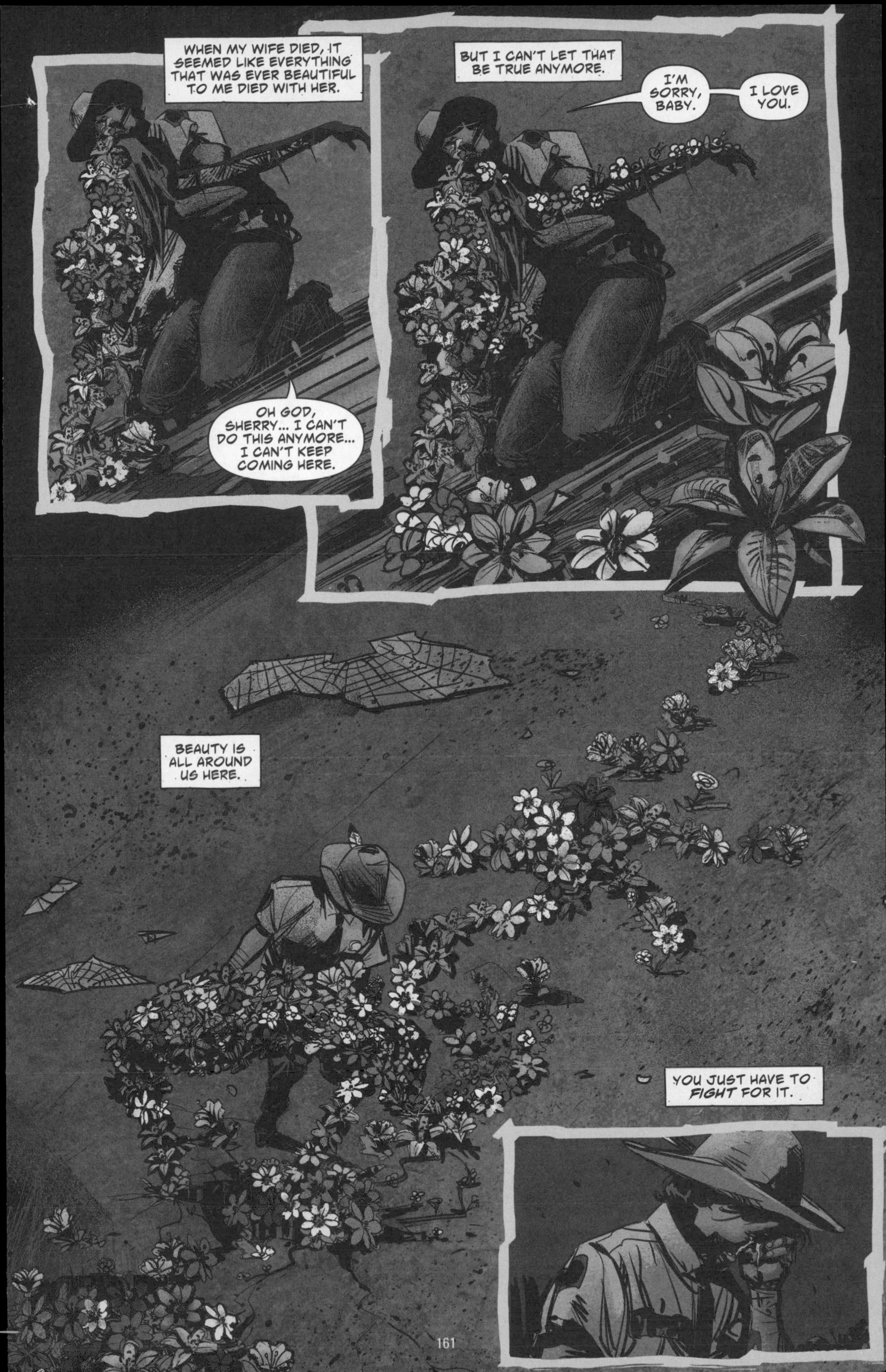
WHEN MY WIFE DIED, IT SEEMED LIKE EVERYTHING THAT WAS EVER BEAUTIFUL TO ME DIED WITH HER.
OH GOD, SHERRY... I CAN'T DO THIS ANYMORE... I CAN'T KEEP COMING HERE.
BUT I CAN'T LET THAT BE TRUE ANYMORE.
I'M SORRY, BABY.
I LOVE YOU.
BEAUTY IS ALL AROUND US HERE.
YOU JUST HAVE TO *FIGHT* FOR IT.

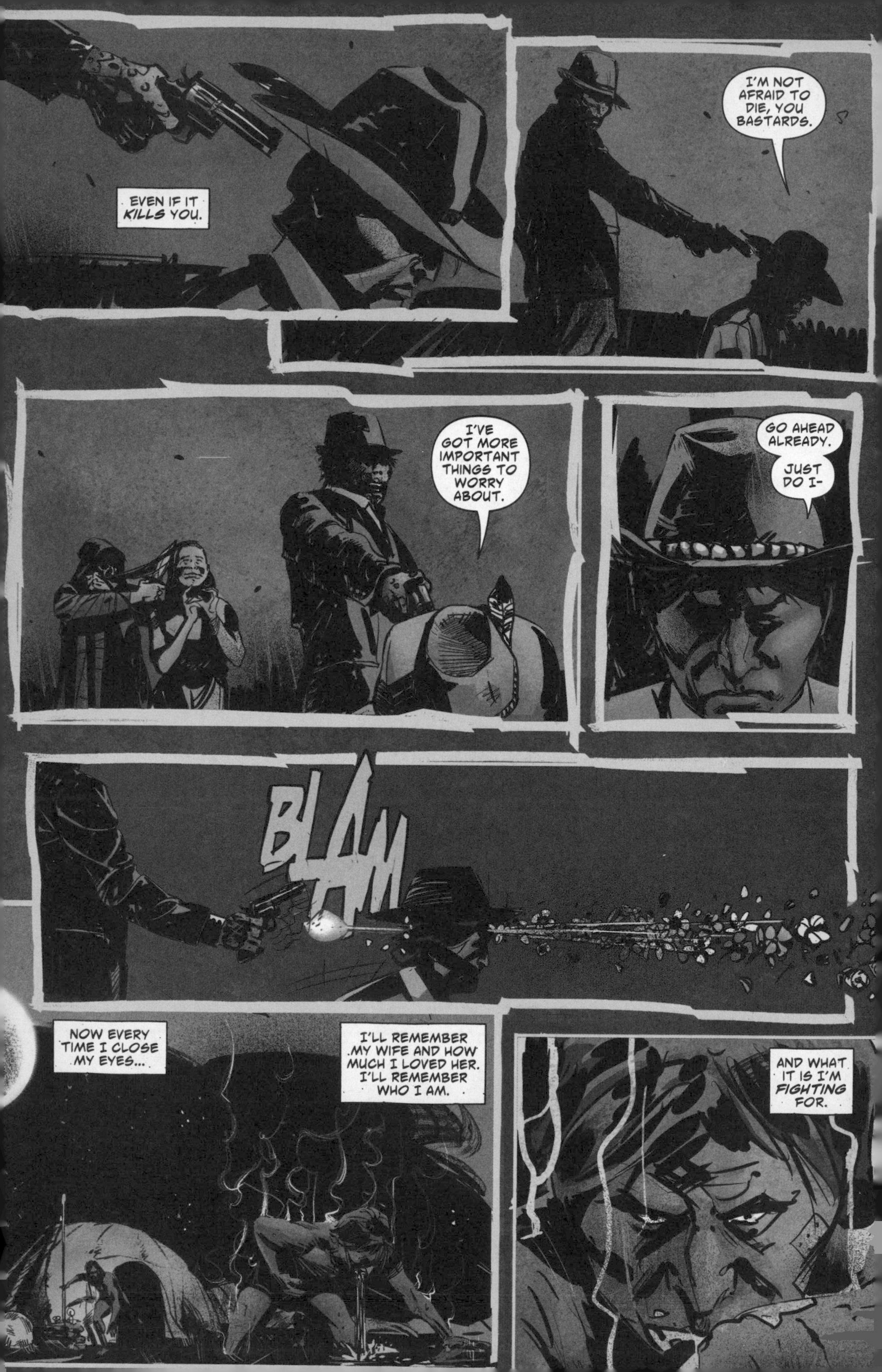
EVEN IF IT *KILLS* YOU.
I'M NOT AFRAID TO DIE, YOU BASTARDS.
I'VE GOT MORE IMPORTANT THINGS TO WORRY ABOUT.
GO AHEAD ALREADY.
JUST DO I-
BLAM
NOW EVERY TIME I CLOSE MY EYES...
I'LL REMEMBER MY WIFE AND HOW MUCH I LOVED HER. I'LL REMEMBER WHO I AM.
AND WHAT IT IS I'M *FIGHTING* FOR.

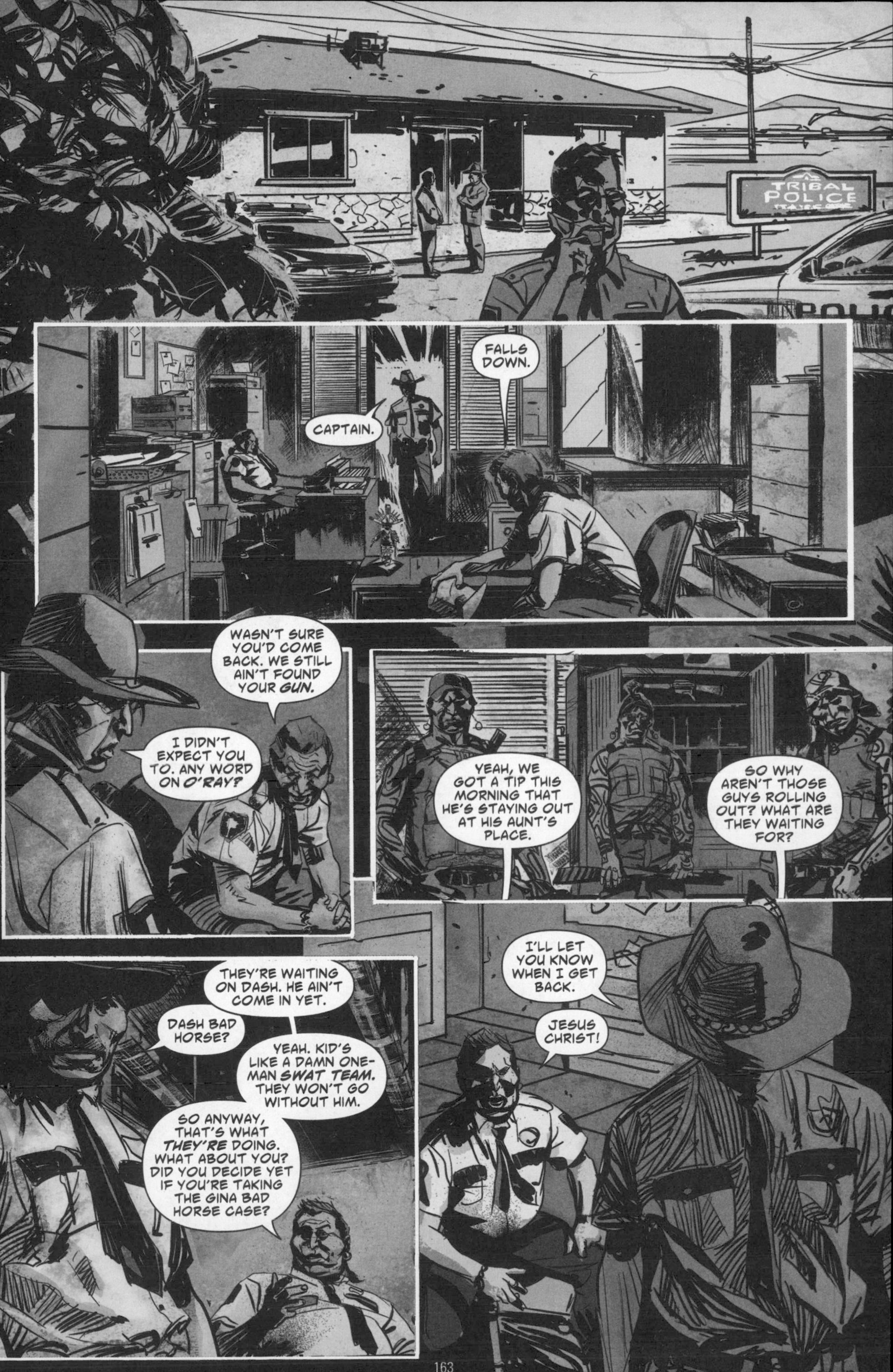
TRIBAL POLICE
POLICE
CAPTAIN.
FALLS DOWN.
WASN'T SURE YOU'D COME BACK. WE STILL AIN'T FOUND YOUR GUN.
I DIDN'T EXPECT YOU TO. ANY WORD ON O'RAY?
YEAH, WE GOT A TIP THIS MORNING THAT HE'S STAYING OUT AT HIS AUNT'S PLACE.
SO WHY AREN'T THOSE GUYS ROLLING OUT? WHAT ARE THEY WAITING FOR?
THEY'RE WAITING ON DASH. HE AIN'T COME IN YET.
DASH BAD HORSE?
YEAH. KID'S LIKE A DAMN ONE-MAN SWAT TEAM. THEY WON'T GO WITHOUT HIM.
SO ANYWAY, THAT'S WHAT THEY'RE DOING. WHAT ABOUT YOU? DID YOU DECIDE YET IF YOU'RE TAKING THE GINA BAD HORSE CASE?
I'LL LET YOU KNOW WHEN I GET BACK.
JESUS CHRIST!

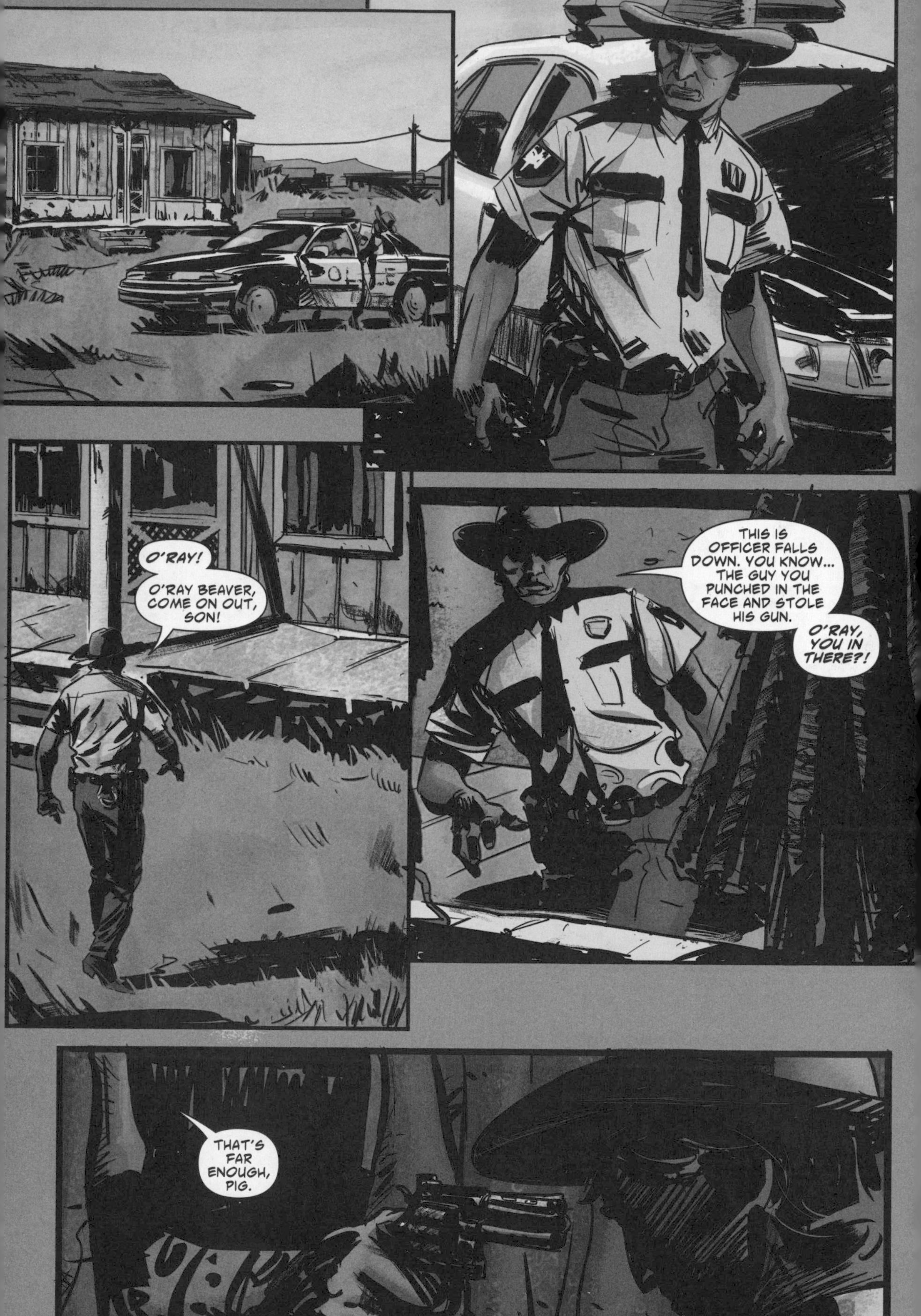
O'RAY!
O'RAY BEAVER, COME ON OUT, SON!
THIS IS OFFICER FALLS DOWN. YOU KNOW... THE GUY YOU PUNCHED IN THE FACE AND STOLE HIS GUN.
O'RAY, YOU IN THERE?!
THAT'S FAR ENOUGH, PIG.

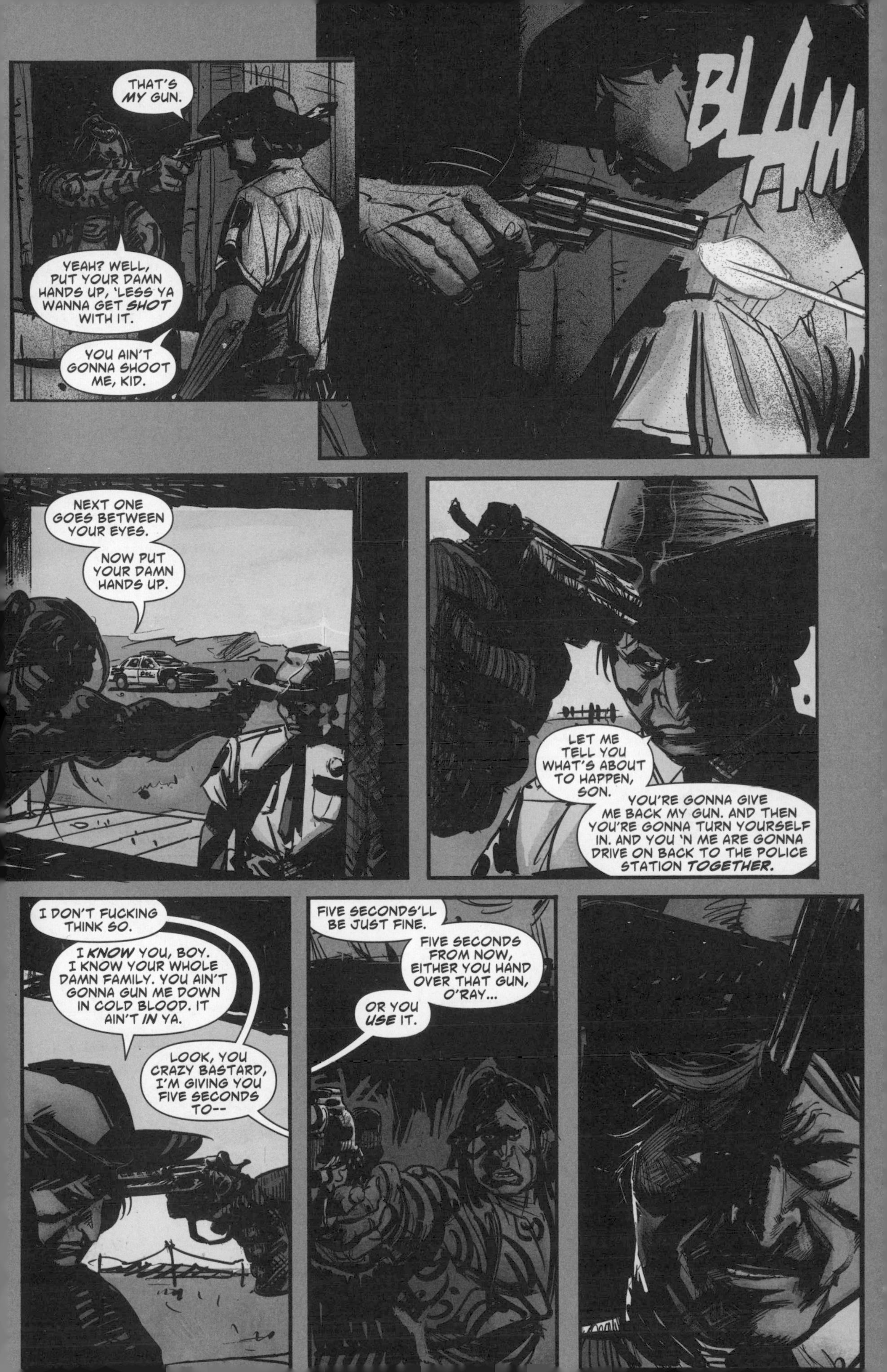
THAT'S MY GUN.
YEAH? WELL, PUT YOUR DAMN HANDS UP, 'LESS YA WANNA GET SHOT WITH IT.
YOU AIN'T GONNA SHOOT ME, KID.
BLAM
NEXT ONE GOES BETWEEN YOUR EYES.
NOW PUT YOUR DAMN HANDS UP.
LET ME TELL YOU WHAT'S ABOUT TO HAPPEN, SON.
YOU'RE GONNA GIVE ME BACK MY GUN. AND THEN YOU'RE GONNA TURN YOURSELF IN. AND YOU 'N ME ARE GONNA DRIVE ON BACK TO THE POLICE STATION TOGETHER.
I DON'T FUCKING THINK SO.
I KNOW YOU, BOY. I KNOW YOUR WHOLE DAMN FAMILY. YOU AIN'T GONNA GUN ME DOWN IN COLD BLOOD. IT AIN'T IN YA.
LOOK, YOU CRAZY BASTARD, I'M GIVING YOU FIVE SECONDS TO--
FIVE SECONDS'LL BE JUST FINE.
FIVE SECONDS FROM NOW, EITHER YOU HAND OVER THAT GUN, O'RAY...
OR YOU USE IT.

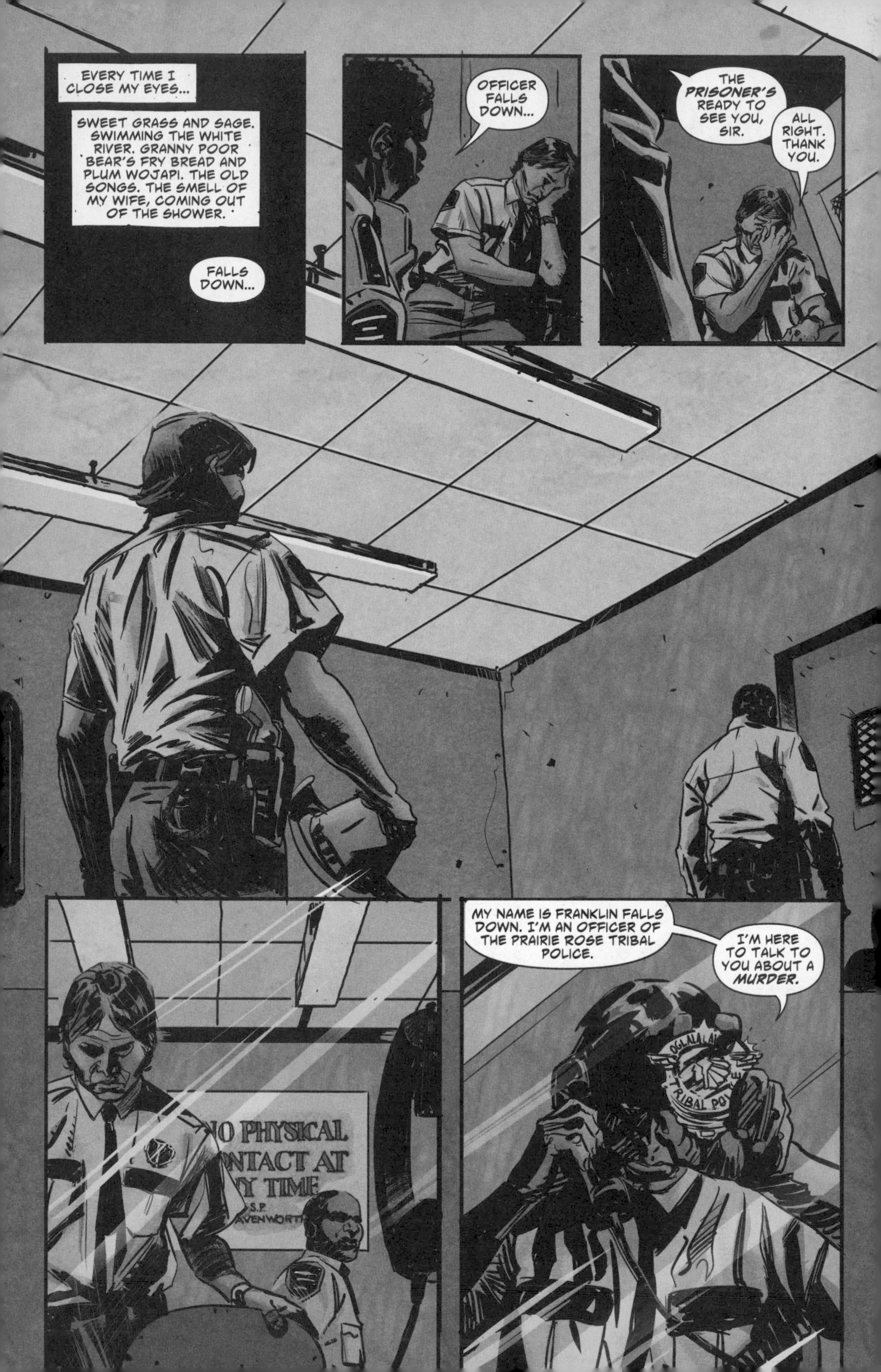
EVERY TIME I CLOSE MY EYES...
SWEET GRASS AND SAGE. SWIMMING THE WHITE RIVER. GRANNY POOR BEAR'S FRY BREAD AND PLUM WOJAPI. THE OLD SONGS. THE SMELL OF MY WIFE, COMING OUT OF THE SHOWER.
FALLS DOWN...
OFFICER FALLS DOWN...
THE PRISONER'S READY TO SEE YOU, SIR.
ALL RIGHT. THANK YOU.
NO PHYSICAL CONTACT AT ANY TIME
MY NAME IS FRANKLIN FALLS DOWN. I'M AN OFFICER OF THE PRAIRIE ROSE TRIBAL POLICE.
I'M HERE TO TALK TO YOU ABOUT A MURDER.

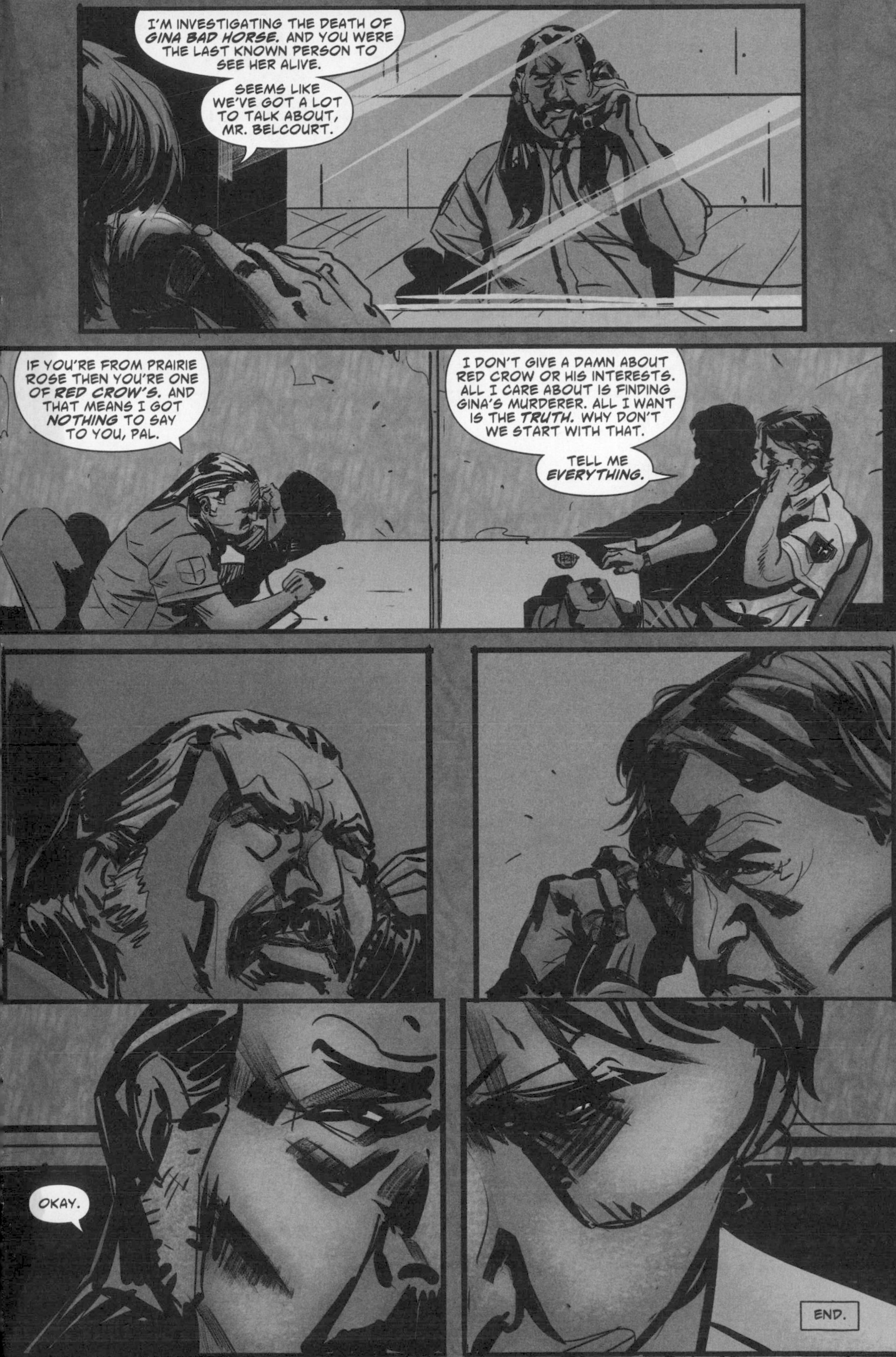
I'M INVESTIGATING THE DEATH OF GINA BAD HORSE. AND YOU WERE THE LAST KNOWN PERSON TO SEE HER ALIVE.
SEEMS LIKE WE'VE GOT A LOT TO TALK ABOUT, MR. BELCOURT.
IF YOU'RE FROM PRAIRIE ROSE THEN YOU'RE ONE OF RED CROW'S. AND THAT MEANS I GOT NOTHING TO SAY TO YOU, PAL.
I DON'T GIVE A DAMN ABOUT RED CROW OR HIS INTERESTS. ALL I CARE ABOUT IS FINDING GINA'S MURDERER. ALL I WANT IS THE TRUTH. WHY DON'T WE START WITH THAT.
TELL ME EVERYTHING.
OKAY.
END.

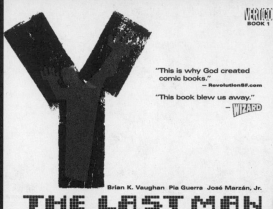

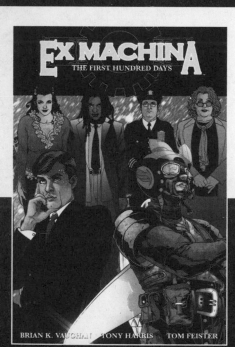